Books by Fulton Oursler

The Greatest Faith Ever Known (*With April Oursler Armstrong*)
The Greatest Book Ever Written • The Greatest Story Ever Told
Why I Know There Is a God • The Precious Secret
A Child's Life of Jesus • Modern Parables
Father Flanagan of Boys Town (*With Will Oursler*)
Three Things We Can Believe In • A Skeptic in the Holy Land
Behold This Dreamer • Sandalwood • Stepchild of the Moon
Poor Little Fool • The World's Delight • The Great Jasper
Joshua Todd • The True Story of Bernarr Macfadden
A History of Protestant Missions • The Reader's Digest Murder Case
The House at Fernwood

AS ANTHONY ABBOT:

About the Murder of Geraldine Foster
About the Murder of the Choir Singer
About the Murder of the Circus Queen
About the Murder of the Man Afraid of Women
About the Murder of the Frightened Lady
The Shudders • The Creeps • These Are Strange Tales

WITH ACHMED ABDULLAH:

The Shadow of the Master • Emerald Annie
Paradise Kate • The Flower of the Gods

PLAYS

Sandalwood (*With Owen Davis*)
The Spider (*With Lowell Brentano*)
All the Kings' Men • Behold This Dreamer
The Walking Gentleman (*With Grace Perkins Oursler*)

Books by April Oursler Armstrong

The Greatest Faith Ever Known (*With Fulton Oursler*)
When Sorrow Comes (*With Grace Perkins Oursler*)

The Greatest Faith Ever Known

THE
GREATEST FAITH
EVER KNOWN

*The Story of the Men
Who First Spread the Religion of Jesus
and of the Momentous Times
in Which They Lived*

BY

FULTON OURSLER

AND

APRIL OURSLER ARMSTRONG

AN IMAGE BOOK
DOUBLEDAY
NEW YORK   LONDON   TORONTO   SYDNEY   AUCKLAND

An Image Book
PUBLISHED BY DOUBLEDAY
a division of Bantam Doubleday Dell Publishing Group, Inc.
666 Fifth Avenue, New York, New York 10103

IMAGE, DOUBLEDAY, and the portrayal of a cross
intersecting a circle are trademarks of Doubleday, a
division of Bantam Doubleday Dell Publishing Group, Inc.

Nihil Obstat: John M. A. Fearns, S.T.D.
Censor Librorum

Imprimatur: ✠ Francis Cardinal Spellman
Archbishop of New York

The nihil obstat and imprimatur are official declarations that a book or
pamphlet is free of doctrinal or moral error. No implication is contained
therein that those who have granted the nihil obstat and imprimatur agree
with the contents, opinions, or statements expressed.

New York, July 1, 1953

Library of Congress Cataloging-in-Publication Data
Oursler, Fulton, 1893–1952.
    The greatest faith ever known: the story of the
    men who first spread the religion of Jesus and
    of the momentous times in which they lived
    by Fulton Oursler and April Oursler Armstrong.
    —1st Image Books ed.
      p.   cm.
    "An Image Book"—T.p. verso.
    1. Bible. N.T.—History of Biblical events. 2. Apostles.
I. Armstrong, April Oursler. II. Title.
BS2618.O8 1990   53-9979   89-35502
225.9′5—dc20   CIP
ISBN 0-385-41148-0

INTRODUCTION

In my opinion, *The Greatest Faith Ever Known* by Fulton Oursler and April Oursler Armstrong (who lovingly completed the book after her father's death) is one of the few most important books produced in the twentieth century. In subject matter, scope, and treatment it stands in the front rank of the select books every thoughtful person should read in his or her lifetime. And that is being made possible by the reissuing of the book at this time.

The Greatest Faith Ever Known captured my interest at once and had considerable impact on my own faith, answering puzzling questions and undergirding my structure of belief. I'd been a believer since childhood, and while later educational experiences did not shake my faith, they did raise some questions to which Fulton Oursler's book gave satisfying answers. If any reader whose sturdy faith is in any state of disrepair will read *The Greatest Faith Ever Known*, I sincerely believe that such a person will regain a faith able to sustain one in all the vicissitudes of life.

I was fortunate in having had the rare privilege of a close friendship with Fulton Oursler. Fulton had the capacity for a friendship that was not only enjoyable but creative as well. He was good company at all times and was stimulating as a thinker and keen observer of people and issues. He was one of the most spiritually minded men I ever knew. He once told me that he had "fallen away" from Christianity, but that was before I knew him. Those who come back to faith—the "reborn," as he phrased it—sometimes have an enthusiasm for religion which seems to go beyond that of those who have always been practicing Christians. In his commitment to faith he certainly made up for any "lost years." For when I knew him I considered him probably the top layman in his understanding and exposition of faith.

To me he was the perfect sort of Christian. He was a solid believer both intellectually and emotionally, he was a mind-and-heart disciple convinced in his intellect and committed in his deepest inner emotional life. He stood for what Christianity stands for, and he was certainly not given to compromise. He lived up to his faith in all circumstances.

Yet at the same time, and perhaps because of his belief, he was one of the happiest of men. And I never knew him to put on piosity. As a raconteur he could not be surpassed. On many an evening spent in his company he regaled us with hilarious stories out of his eventful life. Experiences with the great and near great of his time as told by Fulton were always invested with his narrative genius.

And if the exciting evening was spent in his apartment on West Fifty-ninth Street, we would all go away thoughtful, for in the entryway on the wall, above an old-fashioned receptacle containing umbrellas and canes, was a framed placard that read, "Lord, I may forget you today but please don't forget me."

Fulton and his wife Grace were at our house on Quaker Hill, Pawling, New York, one Friday for lunch. Ruth unthinkingly served delicious steak prepared with her usual skill. In those days Catholics were supposed to eat fish on Fridays and Fulton was a meticulous practicing Catholic. But he was so taken up with the lively and somewhat uproarious conversation around the table, to which he was the chief contributor, that he was quite unconscious of enthusiastically devouring the forbidden steak on a Friday. Becoming suddenly conscious of his "fall from Grace," he put down knife and fork, and lifting up his face, said, "Lord, I forgot. Please forgive me but this steak is so delicious. Amen."

When our magazine, *Guideposts*, was a mere fledgling publication back in 1945, Mr. DeWitt Wallace, founder and publisher of the *Reader's Digest* and my longtime friend, took great interest in helping it along. He assigned Fulton Oursler, at that time Senior Editor and one of the acclaimed writers of the era, to counsel *Guideposts* editorially. Though Fulton appointed his wife Grace as Editor, he gave the new magazine generously of his talent and experience. Indeed, Mr. Wallace and Fulton and Grace are responsible for getting it widely accepted, so that today, with 4,300,000 paid subscribers, its circulation is the thirteenth largest in the nation.

Fulton was enthusiastic about *Guideposts*, as he was about any effort, eager to present Christianity in a way that appeals to everyone. He was always ready to answer honest questioning and to enter into a discussion of religion where divergent views were expressed. But he would not tolerate hate-motivated attacks on his faith. He and Grace were at a party in Hollywood where the subject of religion was raised at the table and the ensuing discussion grew heated, even acrimonious. The venom against his particular faith was ill disguised. And a discussion that had begun intellectually degenerated, he told me, into scurrilous references to his faith. Finally Fulton arose and quite calmly said, "Come, Grace, we are leaving these people since they have no respect for our faith or for us." So Grace and Fulton walked out amidst a hush. Later some of the guests apologized with the excuse, "Some of us had been drinking too much."

This man had faith, he loved his faith. It was everything to him. Had he lived in early times, he would have had the stuff in him of the martyrs. He was never a fanatic, nor an uncompromising zealot. He was just a loyal, faithful man who loved God, who had done so much for him. Fulton Oursler was perhaps the one writer of his era who could have conceived the vision of *The Greatest Faith Ever Known* and articulated that faith so effectively for the average person as well as for the Biblical scholar.

As a writer Fulton Oursler was always interesting, mentally provocative, and stimulating. He made sense. He was a skillful writer because he had something worthwhile to say and he said it clearly. He was a genius with words. They poured out of him in orderly array like well-trained soldiers on parade. Thus these genius-touched words marched into the reader's mind, entertaining him, enlightening and inspiring him.

When I think of Fulton Oursler as a writer, I shall always remember the writing desk at which he sat while working. Always, there was a candle on that desk which Fulton lighted as he began writing. As long as the candle remained lighted, everyone was forbidden to interrupt him for anything save sickness or death. When he finished he would snuff out the candle and be ready to take "important" phone calls.

Fulton Oursler had wide-ranging interests. In fact, at one time he actually edited thirteen magazines. He wrote novels, movies, plays, radio shows, and mystery stories. But it was in writing about faith that the true genius of this man was employed. He was a believer. He believed in the faith, knowing very well that it worked as promised, in human experience. He kept the faith totally. He wrote about it graphically and thrillingly.

One time he was with me in my office in the Protestant Church on Fifth Avenue, where I was the minister. Finally I accompanied Fulton to the street door. "Let's go in the sanctuary for a minute where you preach on Sundays," he said. In the great empty church I watched as Fulton paced the aisles. Finally, in a sweeping gesture with his hand, he declared, "This holy place is packed full of faith and love."

So is this great book, *The Greatest Faith Ever Known*.

Norman Vincent Peale

NORMAN VINCENT PEALE
July 7, 1989

FOREWORD

"THE SUGGESTION that I write a book about the acts and letters of the apostles was made to me by the poet, John Masefield.

"In the spring of 1947 my wife and I paid a visit to the home of the Poet Laureate of England and sat down to tea and cakes with him at his lodge not far from Oxford.

"He asked me about the radio play of *The Greatest Story Ever Told*, and I told him of the inspiration I had received from repeated readings of his wonderful three-act play on the trial and conviction of Jesus. It was then that he urged me to go on and recount the Acts of the Apostles. I told him of the scheme I had in mind for three books, a trilogy on the Scriptures, of which this one is the last. The idea had been mentioned by others, and when people responded to the retelling of the Gospels in *The Greatest Story Ever Told* I had already been working on the retelling of the Old Testament. The most exciting book of all, of course, would be the story of Christianity as reported in the Acts and the Epistles.

" 'Then,' said Mr. Masefield, 'you must get an old book called *The Voyages and Shipwreck of St. Paul*. It was written by James Swift and published by Longmans Green in 1880, with an introduction by the Bishop of Carlysle. There, my friend, is a book about a traveler at sea, written by a man who really knew the sea. In his own sailing craft he duplicated the journeys of St. Paul. You will find it immeasurably helpful.'

"The prediction of the Poet Laureate was fulfilled. That very night I cabled from London asking New York booksellers to try to turn up a copy of the old volume. Eventually they did. Except for the Acts of the Apostles, the first book I read in research for the present volume was that recommended by Mr. Masefield—*The Voyages and Shipwreck of St. Paul.*"

My father wrote the paragraphs above, intending to include them in his foreword to this book. He never completed the foreword.

He never completed this book.

On the evening of May 23, 1952, he was stricken with a heart attack. Shortly past midnight, after he had received the last sacrament, I was alone with him at his bedside for a few moments talking. Suddenly he looked at me and smiled. He said: "April, you must finish *The Greatest Faith* for me." I promised that I would. Six hours later my father was gone.

The morning finally came when I began to try to fulfill that promise. Alone I entered his study and opened the large green steel box in which he always kept his current work. Inside lay 1027 pages of *The Greatest Faith Ever Known*, in his handwriting, interrupted in midsentence in Chapter 86.

Alongside, in another strongbox, I found the first typed version of those pages bearing his corrections, marks, and reminders to himself. On shelves overhead stood ten tall black notebooks filled with the product of years of research on the lives of Peter and Paul and the early days of Christianity.

Silently I stood by the massive table that served as his desk. It was as he left it. A row of fountain pens stood ready to his hand. A candle stood in an olivewood holder; its flame had long been a family signal that he was not to be disturbed. The elephant inkwell. The giant shears. The wooden file trays. The "magic" coins he used to practice sleight of hand. The old blue "Home, Sweet Home" paperweight, and the one with the picture of our front door at Cape Cod. And in the center, the small olivewood crucifix he had carried home from Jerusalem.

Almost all my memories of my father are bound up in that desk. And as I stood there that warm spring morning, my thoughts went back over the years to a thousand other days and nights when he had sat there working and I stood beside him, learning.

Long before I left high school I had begun to work with my father, an apprentice in the workshop of a master in the field of writing.

From him I had caught the excitement of putting words on paper. I absorbed what I could of the practical details of style and construction, of plot, and research, and character development. But I learned a rarer secret—the devotion that can transform the meanest drudgeries of writing into a joy and a delight.

My father was a relentlessly painstaking craftsman. In his first drafts he poured out his ideas, feverish to imprison them on paper because, as he always said, only after that could the real work begin. For weeks he would revise his manuscripts, paring and carving thoughts and sentences, searching for the exact words and phrases. As a result his stories lived, vibrant with power and with love. For my father loved his work.

He loved this book. He had a full schedule of work and countless other obligations. But every morning for nearly a year until his death, he rose at five to work on *The Greatest Faith Ever Known*. His whole being was fired with enthusiasm and excited plans for the completion of the last of this trilogy.

It is the book my father most wanted to write. Only God can know why he was not given time to finish it—or why it was left to my unsure hands.

I can only hope that what I have done pleases him.

APRIL OURSLER ARMSTRONG

N.B. Today, in 1990, most biblical scholars believe that Paul did not write the Letter to the Hebrews. However, in 1953 it was believed that he was the author. Chapter 94 reflects this earlier view.

—A.O.A.

Contents

BOOK III

The Man from Tarsus

BOOK IV

The Doors Open to the Gentiles

BOOK V

Paul's First Journey

BOOK VI

The Second Journey

BOOK VII

The Third Journey

BOOK VIII

Apostle in Chains

BOOK IX

Nero Ends Christianity

The Greatest Faith Ever Known

BOOK ONE

"I Am with You Always"

Chapter 1. EARTHQUAKES AND OPEN GRAVES

WHEN Jesus of Nazareth was put to death, there were strange happenings in Jerusalem.

The three crosses—on which two thieves and the Son of God were hanging together on Calvary—stood in crisp, black silhouette against the ill-omened light in the sky. But those three gaunt crosses seemed to leap out of sight in the instant that Jesus, with a loud cry, bowed His head and gave up the ghost. For the earth under the feet of weeping women and gawping men began to tremble from some vast, inner convulsion; great rocks on the side of the Hill of the Skull—or Golgotha, as this Calvary was called—boulders and granite fragments were shaken and ripped apart as if they were bread and not stone.

Messengers, fleeing from the Temple Courts, panted the frightening news that the veil of the Holy of Holies had been torn across by some invisible hand, a sign of dreadful and mysterious portent. The veil had long since replaced the solid partition that in olden times separated the Holy Place from the Holy of Holies; it stood for the mysteries of God. No mortal hand could have sliced the two thick rich curtains of the veil as they swung in the wind and the intensifying darkness. Three cubits apart were the twin curtains, the one toward the Holy Place being open at its north end and the one toward the Holy of Holies at the south end, hung so especially to avoid any risk of exposing the sacred interior to profane eyes on the Day of Atonement when the high priest entered for the most solemn rites.

Now both curtains of the veil were frazzled into rags, at the very moment when the tortured figure on the middle cross gave that fearful cry and breathed His last breath, about three o'clock in the afternoon, on that first Good Friday, which now we mark as April 7, A.D. 30.

Many strange events in Jerusalem, then, with the opening up of old graves all exposed by no visible hands, and bodies of long-perished saints came tottering out of the prison houses of death, pushing away the stones rolled against the rocky caverns, and rising through the earth like divers up from the sea. These saints marched through the dimmish streets of Solomon's capital and stared at feeble men cowering in doorways, showing their presence to old acquaintances as if preparing them for the miracle of grace that within forty-eight hours would be coming to the world.

Who could mistake such signs and omens as the quaking earth, the returning dead, the torn veil of the Temple? The Roman centurion Longinus, assigned to Golgotha to make sure that Jesus and the two thieves were well and truly despatched, looked wildly around him and, hearing the tales, seeing the falling rocks, feeling the earth sway and shudder under his mailed boots, fell on his knees, in manner unbecoming to a Roman officer. Yet his face was not fearful but convinced.

"He was a just Man! Indeed, this Man was the Son of God," he repeated, as one who has discovered the greatest of secrets. He had just seen the truth which changed his life, the life which he would one day surrender as a martyr in the service of this just Man.

And there was a light in his eyes that was not in the eyes of those who now began to back down the swaying sides of Calvary; the multitude of those who, thanks to Him, had known a larger life and who had stood there to watch Him die. They were striking their breasts as they backed away, and they looked neither to the right nor to the left. They did not see the ecstatic centurion on his knees. They did not notice the steadfast women who had followed Jesus from Galilee, and who stood watching everything: Mary Magdalene; Mary of Cleophas, and Mary Salome, the mother of the sons of Zebedee, James the Greater and John the Beloved. They did not recognize Joanna, Christian wife of one of Herod's own stewards.

At the very foot of the cross stood Mary, the mother of Jesus, the mother whom Jesus in His dying words had given to the world. And beside her, supporting her with a strong arm, stood the apostle John, called the Beloved or the Divine, to whose earthly care the Master had just confided Mary. As he stood next to her, eyes closed in prayer, John could not guess the destiny that lay ahead for him, the years of white-haired age when he would write one of the four Gospels, and the Book of Revelations, the Apocalypse. In those agonied hours of the crucifixion, John did not dream that he would live to see heaven plain, before he himself died!

Suddenly the prayers of mother and apostle were interrupted. A friend came and touched Mary gently on the arm. She turned to face that stanch defender of her Son's case in the council trial, Joseph of Arimathea.

"I come direct from Pontius Pilate," said Joseph of Arimathea softly. "I have begged him to let me have His body. For I have a plan for the burial of your Son, my lady!"

Mary looked at him, pain-darkened eyes troubled with questions.

"Pilate did not consent at first," said Joseph of Arimathea. "The Roman procurator wanted to be careful; to protect himself. You see— he wanted to make sure your Son was dead, beyond all doubt. He suspected that I might even be trying to spirit away the Body and restore Jesus to consciousness. So Pilate sent for the centurion captain that you saw fall to his knees a little while ago. 'Is He dead?' Pilate wanted to know from the centurion; 'Is it finished?' The centurion declared on his oath that it was so—and here I am, with official leave from Pilate himself to take down the body of Jesus."

There was still a question in Mary's great sorrowful eyes. She looked back thirty-three years to a winter twilight, when Joseph, her spouse, had scoured Bethlehem seeking a place for Jesus' birth, and there had been no room at the inn. And Mary, the widow, stared now at this second Joseph, who had come to tend her Son in death, and wondered.

Mary remembered that Joseph of Arimathea, this learned and wealthy Jew, an honored judge of the Temple court, the Sanhedrin, had long ago heard the call of faith. She knew that he had decided he could best serve the Master secretly, from the august heights of his own worldly power. But at the trial, he had spoken out valiantly for Jesus and voted for His acquittal, for the first time publicly admitting sympathy with the Nazarene. And now, Mary wondered, what did this elderly judge mean to do with the body of her Son?

"I shall bury Him in the tomb I long ago prepared for myself," said Joseph of Arimathea. "It is only a little way on the other side of the hill—in the garden of my house. It will be very simple."

But it was not to be quite as simple as Joseph of Arimathea expected.

Chapter 2. THE CENTURION'S SPEAR

COMPLICATIONS arose from two factors: the persistent anxiety of the Temple aristocracy to make absolutely certain that Jesus was dead; and the preparations for what was both a Sabbath and a Feast.

It was now about five o'clock in the afternoon, the time of these preparations which the Jews called the parasceve. It was an intolerable thought that the dead bodies of three malefactors—a "blasphemer" and two thieves—should be left hanging on their crosses to sully this double holiday. Hence, others besides Joseph of Arimathea were busy on Calvary Hill in that early twilight. Ritualistic Jews, who wanted to get the corpses down, had also been to Pilate; that was why the hill was crowded again with Roman soldiers bearing fresh orders. Climbing ladders and carrying the forked tongues of hammers to pull out the nails, they busied themselves at a gruesome task; not merely to release the hands and feet of the men on whom the sentence of death had been executed, but by law to break the bones, proving the victims dead beyond doubt.

Yet they made a strange decision, those Roman soldiers, in spite of their grim orders. They broke the legs of Dysmas, that poor, repentant robber who, while hanging in agony on the cross, had called out adoringly to Jesus and was forgiven and promised Paradise that same day. They broke the legs of the unrepentant thief who had died mouthing stubborn curses. But for some reason they left the legs of Jesus unbroken.

Instead, the centurion named Longinus lifted a spear, gleaming in the harshness of the weird light, and plunged the spear into the side of Jesus, opening the pale flesh in a long gash through which water and blood began to flow—the one a symbol for ages to come of baptism, the other of redemption. With such a wound in His side, Jesus was surely dead, reasoned the Roman authorities and forthwith turned the body over to Joseph of Arimathea. And in that moment Longinus had helped fulfill another Scriptural prophecy.

And John stood by and watched; beloved John who was to write of himself: "And he that saw it hath given testimony: and his testimony is true. And he knoweth that he saith true; that you also may believe. For these things were done that the Scripture might be fulfilled: 'You shall not break a bone of Him.' And again another Scripture says: 'They shall look on Him whom they pierced.'"

Chapter 3. THE BORROWED TOMB

JOSEPH of Arimathea had everything ready: the fine linen; the servants from his summer home to help in lowering the body of Jesus into His mother's arms as she sat on her heels at the foot of the cross. Then He was carried through the narrow farm field to the grave, the new monument hewn out of solid rock in the ground, the tomb that Joseph of Arimathea had meant for his own final resting place. Travelers to Jerusalem for many centuries have prayed in that cramped interior, with its slender shelf in the wall on which Joseph and his workmen now deposited the body of Jesus.

The mourning women from Galilee surrounded Mary at the door of the tomb, watching with her as Joseph, with the tenderness of a son, straightened the legs, smoothed the last wrinkle from the linen cloth that was wound all around Him, hiding the face as well as the feet.

Then, while the women covered their eyes with their hands, praying softly, Joseph of Arimathea rolled down from a maze of dark bushes a round boulder as tall as himself.

"We must go home," the women were telling Mary, as if to keep her thoughts away from the great stone rolling toward them in the gloom. "We must go home and prepare spices and ointments."

There was a silence. Mary, looking at them somberly, made no reply, but they well understood what she could not bring herself to say. A few funeral spices and embalming ointments Joseph had brought with him and used, with his linen cloths. But these would hardly be enough to preserve unliving flesh against the forces of pollution. More spices, more ointments, would be needed in a few hours.

Yet they could not be forthcoming, for the same ritualistic reason that had hurried the burial itself—the parasceve was here, and with it, rushing on the wings of night, was the Sabbath, when they must rest according to the Commandment; the Sabbath, which we call Saturday, and which would begin at sundown, any moment now.

So Mary Magdalene and Mary of Cleophas turned Mary's face away from the rolling stone closing the sepulcher of her Son.

And then another man came forward. He had been helping Joseph, but now for the first time, by the gleam of a lantern in his hand, the women could see that he was not a workman from Joseph's farm but another great judge from the Sanhedrin, Nicodemus. He was that rich man who once had come cautiously to Jesus after nightfall, so that he might not be recognized and gossiped about in his exalted position. To him Jesus had spoken what had seemed riddling words: "Except a man be born again, he cannot see the Kingdom of God."

But Nicodemus came to understand that strange, enigmatic utterance in his soul, which had, indeed, been born again of water and of the Spirit, so that Nicodemus was of a new character, with a new love for God and for all his fellowmen. Because he had been born again, he had also fought beside Joseph of Arimathea to save the life of the accused Jesus in the trial of the seventy judges of Israel.

Here he was now, at the tomb, helping Joseph with the great stone rolled against the door of the tomb. It was Nicodemus who had brought the spices and the ointments: aloes, mixed with myrrh, that sweet perfume, not the kind obtained by puncturing the bark of the acacia tree, but the self-exuding mordror that had once been brought in a vase by one of the royal Wise Men, the Magi from the East who had seen Christ's star and had come to worship.

Chapter 4. THAT UPPER ROOM

THAT night Mary, mother of Jesus, spent in the Cenacle, that upper room where Jesus and His disciples had partaken of the Last Supper, less than twenty-four hours before. That coenaculum, or dining room, was soon to become the recognized headquarters of the new faith.

From earliest times its site on a Zion hill has been reverenced by Christians. Church after church has been raised on that spot, and a building is there now, with a large and authentic-seeming Upper Room, which no pious traveler to Jerusalem would fail to visit. The present structure is largely the result of restoration work done by the Franciscans in 1342. In 1551 it came into the hands of the Moslems, who turned it into a mosque, declaring that under the Upper Room lies the veritable tomb of David, psalmist and king. Only at certain hours could Christians ascend to the Cenacle when I was there in the 1930's, and then only by grudging permission of the Moslems.

Mary, the mother of Jesus, with her friends the other women of Galilee, for most of the night remained in the hall where the Last Supper had been served. John the Beloved was beside her as she talked to them, in her sorrow, of the boyhood of Jesus back in Nazareth when His foster father had his carpenter shop.

Her calmness astonished them all, and the completeness of her faith. Mostly she prayed, and the others followed her example. Sorrow she knew because of the pain, the humiliation that had been inflicted on her Son. But she had listened to all that He had said, and she had kept these sayings in her heart.

Perhaps she also knew what meanwhile was happening between those Pharisees, who had plotted the death of Christ, and Pilate, who had let Him die.

Now Annas and his son-in-law, High Priest Caiphas, and their satraps came again to the threshold of Pilate's house, faces ominous, full of threats for the procurator, unless he did exactly as they desired. They were still afraid of Jesus, and there were new orders they wanted Pilate to give.

"This seducer!" they called the executed Jesus, as they stood in the courtyard.

"Sire," said High Priest Caiphas to Pilate, "we have remembered that that seducer said, while He was yet alive: 'After three days, I will rise again.' Command therefore His sepulcher to be guarded until the third day."

Pilate stared at them blankly. Would they never go home, go to bed, to sleep? Would their pertinacity and their fears of this crucified malefactor not be buried with Him? What were they afraid of now from a dead Man, if they had no belief in Him as one with supernatural power? What were they so excited about; what did they fear?

Or was it possible they half believed? Pilate could not guess the agony of agitation consuming Caiphas and his even more distinguished father-in-law, Annas. He did not know that in the last words of Jesus on the cross these two Jewish priests had recognized with horror the possible fulfillment of certain Scriptural prophecies, and that they were indeed terrified that by miracle or ruse the prophecy of resurrection might also be fulfilled.

That dread was cloaked in their unctuous voices as they spoke now, Annas and Caiphas to Pilate explaining that they were concerned, "lest perhaps His disciples come, and steal Him away, and say to the people, 'He is risen from the dead': and the last error shall be worse than the first."

With a shrug of weary shoulders, Pilate again gave the high priests and the Pharisees what they wanted: "You have a guard; go, guard it as you know."

A sign to a waiting lieutenant confirmed his orders. But the Pharisees, led by Caiphas, took no chances. They went with the company of Roman soldiers now assigned to the tomb. With their own hands they tried the stone, made sure that the sepulcher where Jesus lay was indeed sealed, its inert remains safe from kidnaping.

These high priests and Pharisees, the ceaseless enemies of Jesus, thereby made themselves the chief witnesses for Him in all the centuries to come. They made sure there could be no deception on that first holy Saturday, reckoned now as the eighth day of April, A.D. 30, which in the Jewish calendar would be the fifteenth Nisan. They made conspiracy and deception by friends of Jesus impossible. To guard the tomb of Christ they set up soldiers of the empire—not one of whom could be bribed, or drugged, or hoodwinked, because their lives depended on fulfilling their instructions. The priests and the scribes had sealed up the body of Jesus Christ against all possibility of being removed.

These same men had already unwittingly fulfilled the Scriptures when they engineered the crucifixion of our Lord. Now without suspecting it, they had made the perfect setting for the miracle of the Resurrection, the hope of the world.

Chapter 5. MYSTERY AT DAWN

THE first Christian to reach the tomb when the long night was over was Mary Magdalene. She came by herself in the dark just before dawn on Sunday, the ninth of April.

She had sat with the others in the stillness of the Cenacle through hour after hour of night. Mary, the mother of Jesus, had gone apart to pray in another room, without rest, hearing and seeing nothing that was of the earth. None dared intrude upon her.

Eleven men from Galilee, apostles bereft of their Master, and four faithful women, prayed and wondered and wept through the dark watches of that holy Saturday night. They could not sleep. The silence of grief lay on them like a spell.

And in the deepest shadow of a corner near the door, a woman sat huddled away from the others, and in her soul was a turmoil she could not understand.

She had planned to go with the other women in the dawn to purchase the extra spices needed to complete His burial arrangements. Now dawn was close, and she could not wait.

Unseen in the gloom, driven by seething emotion, she wrapped her veil and mantle close about her and stepped noiselessly out the door into the black-shadowed streets. The skies far overhead hinted at the first lightening of day, as Mary Magdalene sped on tiptoe through the city.

In her memory's eye she saw only a night that now seemed so long ago, the night in the house of a Pharisee when she had knelt and washed with her tears the feet of Christ. She saw again those warm deep eyes of His looking at her, and knowing her for the adulteress she was, and she heard Him say:

"Her sins, which are many, are forgiven, for she loved much."

That love drove her now through the streets, flaming in her heart in the chill before dawn. Her alabaster box was long since emptied of ointment. Her tears could not touch Him now. But she longed to be close to Him, as near His tomb as soldiers and stone would allow.

Breathless she entered Joseph of Arimathea's garden. And what she saw there in the dimmish light filled her with anguish and dread.

The stone had been rolled away!

That great boulder of gneiss and spar and quartz and granite, sealing the door of the sepulcher, had been moved. In spite of Roman guards, in spite of its weight, in spite of all probability, the stone had been taken away. The entrance of the tomb gaped at her, black and forbidding.

Mary Magdalene saw no more. She turned on her heels and ran back to the Cenacle, back to tell Peter the incredible, fantastic fact.

The other three women were already on their way to the tomb. Mary Cleophas, and Mary Salome, and Joanna, carrying their own precious store of money, had gone to bang on the doors of sleeping merchants, demanding to buy sweet spices and precious ointments for burial. Nicodemus had brought a hundredweight of spices on that sad Friday afternoon, but still more were needed to fulfill the ritual of burial.

These women had believed with sweet-faced obstinacy that they could wake a man from his bed to open shop in the half-dark, just to make a small sale to three strange women. And they were right. In less than half an hour they had the newly purchased jars of ointment, the boxes of herbs and spices triumphantly in their hands. The grumbles of the shopkeepers faded in their ears as they scurried through Jerusalem toward the garden tomb.

But what good would their ointments be, they murmured to each other, if they could not enter the tomb? What real hope had these three good wives that the Roman soldiers would let them in? The tomb was sealed, they knew. They could not have told how they expected to gain entrance. Theirs was an errand of blind faith.

In whispers they asked each other as they hastened on: "Who shall roll us back the stone from the door of the sepulcher?"

Inside the garden their whispers ceased as they stared at the tomb that seemed so mysteriously forsaken in the pink and gray light of dawn. Their problem was vanished.

They saw the stone rolled back, and the door wide open.

Who was to tell them that in the dark watches of the lonely night there had been another earthquake—and that an angel of the Lord, descended from heaven, had walked in this garden and, with the supernatural touch of one finger, rolled back the stone, and even now sat upon it?

The women stared at this strange being upon the stone. His countenance was radiant as if lightning played over it and never left it, and his raiment was shining as snow, and they wondered and were afraid.

Where were the guards? In the light of the rising sun the women saw them cowering in a paralyzed and most unwarlike posture. A cataleptic group, kneeling frozen with terror, they were as dead men at this tomb of the One who had already overcome death.

And while all this was held in uncanny tableau at the tomb, Mary Magdalene was running fast as morning sunlight down the narrow Jerusalem streets, until she reached the Cenacle.

"Peter! Peter!" cried Mary Magdalene. And she looked at the huge man from the Galilee fishing fleet and beside him, John the Beloved, and she blurted out her news:

"They have taken away the Lord out of the sepulcher and we know not where they have laid Him."

Chapter 6. "HE IS RISEN!"

AT THE DOOR of the tomb a feeling of mystery drenched the early morning air. The women could not know then the cosmic events that shaped themselves around the garden sepulcher. It was too soon for them to realize that though Jesus, Son of Mary and of God the Father Almighty, had been laid on the stone shelf within the tomb, He was not to remain there.

His soul had descended to the nether regions of the lower world, where imprisoned saints had awaited Him for thousands of years. These souls He delivered, new citizens of heaven. That was the start of the new dispensation, of the salvation of the world, begun in the mystic hours between sundown on Good Friday and the dawn of Easter.

And all around the garden tomb were angels keeping watch, and venerating what had lain lifeless behind the stone at the door. There were many angels in Joseph of Arimathea's garden on that first bright Easter morning, while Patriarchs and Prophets and Holy Fathers of past centuries communed with their Redeemer, come at last to free them from the bondage of original sin. He who was the Incarnate Word had truly taken upon Himself the sorrows and infirmities of men, as Isaiah had long ago foreseen. From Adam and Eve, whose first disobedience had brought sin into the world, down through all the saints, the curse of Eden was lifted from those waiting ones. And amid that long-promised deliverance the soul of Jesus returned from the realm of death and was reunited with His body, giving it then the glory and radiance of immortal life.

What were they to think, these three women at the tomb of Jesus? The Sabbath and its restrictions being ended, they had come with their ointment and spices to preserve the body against decay as long as possible. And they saw that the stone had been inexplicably rolled away, that the Roman guards were held in a frieze of terror against the green hillside, and that sitting on the translated boulder was a being so radiant that he seemed to be clothed with light.

Timidly, two of the women advanced. The next few minutes they were to remember only with difficulty for the rest of their lives, so mighty, so wonderful, and so confusing. They walked through the open portal into the faint light that reached inside the tomb.

The shelf was empty, except for a little heap of linen bandages. That was the first overwhelming fact that seemed to stop the breaking of their hearts, the breath in their throats, the very flaring of blood in their veins.

Then, and for the first time, they noticed two strangers in shining white robes. At first they saw but one; then they saw two figures whose apparel of light proclaimed their supernatural nature. The women dropped to their knees, covered their faces with their hands, and with quivering apprehension waited. The two supernatural voices spoke in unison:

"Be not affrighted. You seek Jesus of Nazareth Who was crucified. Why seek you the living with the dead? He is risen! He is not here! Behold the place where they laid Him: come and see the place where the Lord was laid."

The women opened their eyes and looked again at that vacant shelf. But the angels were not finished:

"Remember how He spoke unto you, when He was yet in Galilee, saying: 'The Son of Man must be delivered into the hands of sinful men, and be crucified, and the third day rise again.'"

Indeed, yes. They well remembered those strange words. Then the angels gave them a command:

"Going quickly, tell you His disciples that He is risen."

Where shall we find Him, see Him again, talk with Him, rejoice with Him? All who love Him will want to know these things! Questions in the hearts of the Galilee women answered now:

"And behold, He will go before you, into Galilee. There you shall see Him. Lo, I have foretold it to you, as He told you."

Suddenly the strangeness of the scene, of the facts, of the message were all too much for them at last! St. Mark's Gospel tells it: "But they, going out, fled from the sepulcher. For a trembling and a fear had seized them; and they said nothing to any man; for they were afraid."

Yet the angels had commanded them to tell the disciples that Jesus is risen.

Joanna and Mary Salome and Mary Cleophas paused inside the Cenacle dining hall. They were flushed and windblown from their long flight through the streets, but the paroxysm of fear was gone from them like an illness. They could speak with some calmness now.

Nine men stared at them, nine friends of the Master still sitting together in their grief: Andrew, Thomas, Nathaniel Bartholomew, Simon the Zealous, Philip, and Matthew, James, called the Less, and Jude Thaddeus, sons of Mary of Cleophas; and the other James, called the Greater, son of Mary Salome and brother of John the Beloved.

But John the Beloved was not there to hear his mother's wide-eyed tale. With Peter he had heard the news from Mary Magdalene and had gone running to search for the truth in the garden.

The men in the Cenacle listened with amazement as the three women told their story.

And none of them believed it. Not even their own sons could credit the women's words. They thought that great sorrow had so afflicted their gentle hearts that they told what must seem to all stolid, unshaken citizens to be idle tales.

Jude Thaddeus and the two men named James saw the blue circles of weariness under their eyes, and their own hearts ached with fresh pain as they led Mary Salome and Mary Cleophas to rest in chairs at the long table.

The proof, if proof there ever was to be, must come from Peter and John at the sepulcher.

And the three women obediently kept silent, for the nine apostles were afraid that the tale would be heard in the next room, and disturb Mary, the mother of Jesus, who still prayed alone.

Peter ran all the way. His great body, tired from no sleep in three full days, was dripping wet, his beard and long locks were sopping with sweat, and his breath rose in exhausted gulps as he came running through Joseph of Arimathea's gate up to the door of the tomb.

John had run slightly behind him in the beginning, but as they entered the garden, his younger strength enabled him to pass the gasping, middle-aged fisherman. It was John who first reached the door of the tomb. He stooped down, the full morning sunlight streaming over his head, and looked in at that enigma of the room from which the treasure was gone, the corpse vanished, leaving only the linen cloths in a heap on the shelf.

Dumfounded, John did not move as the shadow of Peter's tall figure fell across him and the fisherman's hand was laid on his shoulder. Together the two apostles stood at the door of the tomb, looking in upon the mystery.

Peter, bending down, crept through the open door and entered the tiny area of the tomb first. Peter, who from the moment he was commissioned to lead the Church Jesus founded had been first in everything, now made a special discovery. Within the tomb, he could see something not visible from the outside.

The napkin that had been wrapped about the head of Jesus was lying not with the other linen cloths but apart and folded, wrapped up neatly and put off to itself as if in a special and particular place. One glance over Peter's shoulder, and John, too, came inside and saw and believed.

Now it has been said that these two men, until this fantastic discovery, knew not the Scripture, that He must rise again from the dead. Those are the words of John himself, set down in his own Gospel.

If ever the light of humility has shone in this world, it glares through all the centuries in John's own words. Humbly he makes a confession: until this moment he had not understood the Old Testament prophecies of the coming of the Messiah, His death, and resurrection. Not fully understanding them, he had not, therefore, fully believed them—those ringing prophecies in the Psalms, in Isaiah, and elsewhere in the Scriptures, especially in David's song: "Thou shalt not permit Thy Holy One to see corruption."

The witness of the senses was needed, even for John, the son of Zebedee and Mary Salome, whose mother at that very moment was trying to tell the other apostles the glorious truth of that open tomb. This John, who, with his brother James the Greater, was a cousin of Jesus and to whom the Lord had entrusted the care of His own mother, this dearly beloved disciple whose head had lain on the bosom of Christ at the Last Supper; this same John had needed the evidence of his eyes to convince him.

The human nature of those apostles, over which Jesus had sorrowed more than once, was never more apparent than here on the first Easter. John had been with Jesus almost from the beginning, an eyewitness of many wonders. He was present when Jesus raised the dead child who was the daughter of Jairus, whose very name meant "he will awaken." John had seen life return to the small corpse of the daughter of that synagogue ruler. John had stood on the mountain top in the very midst of the Transfiguration. He had been with the Master during the agony in the olive garden of Gethsemane. So fervent was John, together with his brother James, that Jesus had called the two of them "Boanerges," a surname meaning "Sons of Thunder." They were positive, dynamic fellows, these brothers, as the fire of faith breathed through their nostrils and the rumbles of Sinai thundered in their voices. John had been the only one of the twelve who did not flee from the condemned Christ, the only one who stood on Calvary with Mary, the mother of Jesus, at the cross.

Yet John, for all this background, records that only after he found the tomb empty, and the linen cloth folded away, was it that "he saw and believed." Many a good man, full of faith yet finding doubts creeping through his mind in solitary moments, has taken heart from the humble confession of John, the saint, standing with Peter in the empty tomb.

The two holy apostles did not speak in the presence of this mystery. Silently praying, they walked home to tell the others the strange things they had seen. They did not know, because they went down one street and she came up another, that in the fullness of morning light Mary Magdalene was going back again to the tomb alone.

Chapter 7. "WHY DO YOU WEEP?"

SOBBING, she stood there, soon after the departure of Peter and John. Her heart failed her at joining the darkness of the tomb within. Yet her deep desire to know what had happened was ungovernable; John tells us in his Gospel that Mary Magdalene stooped down and looked into the sepulcher.

To her, then, a wonder that the others had not seen!

For sitting there, one at the head, the other at the foot of the place where the body of Jesus had been laid, were two angels in white. And as she regarded them, all atremble and afraid, she heard their gentle voices, speaking directly to her:

"Woman, why do you weep?"

And Mary Magdalene, with faltering voice, told them the simple truth:

"Because they have taken away my Lord; and I know not where they have laid Him."

Perhaps the angels smiled, wiser than she, knowing the miracle so close to her that as yet she had not seen. Their serene silence must have puzzled and yet alerted her, for she looked up and around, and at last behind her.

And then she saw the figure of one who seemed to her a stranger, and she heard a tender voice say:

"Woman, why do you weep? Whom do you seek?"

In the surging confusion of that instant, in spite of the blinding radiance behind her at the door of the tomb and the familiar echoes in the voice, still, as Mary Magdalene afterward admitted to the others, she had the sudden, mistaken idea that she was talking to the gardener.

"Sir," she said, "if you have taken Him away from here, tell me where you have laid Him and I will take Him away."

"Mary!"

That voice she could not mistake. That pronouncing of her name awoke her to the truth.

"Rabboni!" she sobbed. "Master!"

And she, out of whom He had once cast seven devils, fell to the ground, her hands reaching out to caress His feet, white and bare on the green grass before the tomb. The Son of God, who had before her eyes given up His life in the blood and sweat dropping from the cross, stood before her now, all alive, and yet with such a glory around His face and form that she knew it was as if a door had been opened into another world.

"Fear not," He said tenderly, with the same tones, speaking the same words and in the same way as she so often had heard Him comfort His followers, up and down the dusty roads of Galilee and Judaea. "Mary! Fear not!"

She knelt, as His voice deepened:

"Do not touch Me! For I am not yet ascended to My Father, and to your Father; to My God and your God."

There was no sharpness in His words and Mary Magdalene understood perfectly what He meant her to understand. It was as if He were saying: "Things are different between us now—between Me and all human beings, even those I have known and loved. The old human relations between us are at an end, and I have entered on a glorified life as a preparation for My final departure from the world." That is what He meant her to hear and that is what Mary the Magdalene understood.

In His next words to her He made His commission explicit:

"All hail!"

That was addressed to all His old friends, all who grieved for Him as though He were dead. And so:

"Go, tell My brethren that they go into Galilee. There they shall see Me."

But the brethren did not believe, not though Mary Magdalene told them over and over, with all the eloquence that comes to the mouth of a witness who has looked on infinity and heard it speak to her. They mourned and they wept, in spite of all that she said; shaking their heads and believing her delirious in her own grief, when she told them:

"I have seen the Lord, and these things He said to me."

No, they would not believe her. Not though they knew the frightful malaise from which He had once fully restored her, and the devotion that sent her trudging after Him through all His later journeys, the love that kept her by the side of Mary, His mother, throughout the long hours of His agony. Why would they distrust her? Not because they thought she lied intentionally, but because they felt sure that sorrow had turned her mind.

They could not believe her.

Chapter 8. THE LIE

BUT Annas and Caiphas and their satraps were in no doubt about what had happened. The Roman guards, assigned to Joseph of Arimathea's garden by Pilate, came running back to town, released from their first stupor of fear, to confess their failure. They told the scribes and the high priests, and especially the old Sadducean enemies of Jesus, men who did not believe in a resurrection for anybody:

"The body is gone! We watched all night. Our eyes were never closed in sleep. We were completely faithful to our assignment. But in spite of our vigilance, He is gone."

Crafty old Annas believed them. He had traded in human nature too long not to know the truth when he saw it. The blanched faces of these soldiers of the Empire bespoke no ordinary cowardice. But whatever the nature of the mystery, the fact remained—a miracle that might have a dangerous effect upon public opinion. The Sabbath and the feast were past; soon the streets would be thronged again: what if people began to say it was indeed a prophet they had nailed to the cross?

Annas could see a crisis a long way off, and his remedies in all such emergencies were simple and dependable.

"Here is money!" he cried, pouring two bagfuls ringing on the council table. Other veterans of the trial of Jesus joined him; even Caiphas, the miser, had to contribute. Soon a heap of Roman money, all coins bearing Caesar's head, lay in a glittering pile. Annas told the soldiers to stow the money unseen in their armor; to divide it evenly among all the guards who had spent the night as sentinels in the garden and:

"Say, you," entreated Annas with a wheedling smile, all the brighter for his knowledge of the danger, "say you His disciples came by night and stole Him away when you were asleep. And if Pilate hears about all this, don't you worry for a moment. You will be thoroughly protected. We will persuade him and secure you."

That assurance was most potent of all. Those soldiers were more frightened of Pilate than of any dead man rising to life. Their own lives would be forfeit, if Pilate were to believe that they slept on duty, or that they had taken bribes. But they also knew, as all Jerusalem knew, of Pilate's obsessive fear of the high priests during these last years as procurator of Judaea. If these powers of the Temple backed them up, they felt safe in lies. The tale that they slept must be for the street crowds only, and the whole mystery of the open tomb must be kept from Pilate.

Both sides carried out their plans faithfully. The soldiers talked out of the sides of their mouths, telling this man and that the lie they were paid to spread—that the disciples of Jesus had stolen His body and hidden it.

As Matthew reported in his Gospel, "So they, taking the money, did as they were taught; and this word was spread abroad among the Jews. . . ."

Chapter 9. DINNER AT EMMAUS

THE disciples of Jesus were still confused. They did not know what to believe.

Soon reports of mysterious meetings with Jesus began to reach them. Most startling of these was the visit He had with two of His followers on the way to the town of Emmaus, about seven miles from Jerusalem, probably on the site of the modern Qalunya.

On that first Easter Sunday morning two devoted followers of the Christ, Cleophas and his youngest son Simon, were walking toward Emmaus, conversing about the marvels and sorrows of the last four days, all unaware that at that very moment Jesus was drawing near to them. Cleophas certainly knew Jesus well. And he had heard from his own wife, Mary Cleophas, of the empty tomb and the angels' words.

"But their eyes were held" is St. Luke's cryptic way of explaining that "they should not know Him." The historic fact is that Cleophas and Simon, who had been so close to Jesus in His lifetime, were now, nevertheless, to walk with Him on the open road, and not recognize Him. Singular paradox!

He met them in the middle of the road, standing in their way, and saying to them:

"What are these discourses that you hold one with another as you walk and are sad?"

If there were no familiar accents in the well-beloved voice, certainly reminders in the very nature of the question should have stirred the torpid recognition of these two followers. In other days, Jesus had asked just such questions, especially when His disciples were disputing among themselves, full of error and pride. But His words failed to stir their lethargic minds.

"Are you only a stranger in Jerusalem," Cleophas replied, "and have not known the things that have been done there in these days?"

"What things?"

"Concerning Jesus of Nazareth? He was a prophet, mighty in work and word before God and all the people. And how our chief priests and princes delivered Him to be condemned to death and crucified Him?"

The unrecognized figure stared, silent and compassionate, as Cleophas floundered on:

"But we hoped that it was He that should have redeemed Israel; and now, besides, today is the third day since these things were done. Yes, and certain women, also of our company, affrighted us today. Before it was light, they were at the sepulcher. And not finding His body, came, saying that they had also seen a vision of angels who say that He is alive. And some of our people went to the sepulcher: and found it so as the women had said, but Him they found not."

Only then did the unknown figure reply to this impassioned recital of grief:

"O, foolish and slow of heart to believe in all things which the prophets have spoken! Ought not Christ to have suffered these things and to enter into His glory?"

And smiling at their puzzled air, the dazed attention they gave to Him, Jesus began to recount and expound to them the prophecies concerning the coming of the Messiah, beginning with Moses and continuing through all the prophets. But they still did not recognize Him.

They walked together toward Emmaus as Jesus gave Cleophas and his startled son this amazingly appropriate and timely scriptural lesson. The long list of forecastings which the last three days had fulfilled came to an end as they reached the first little houses of the town of Emmaus. There He was for parting from them, but they entreated Him not to leave them:

"Stay with us! Because it is toward evening, and the day is now far spent."

With them, He entered a house where they would tarry for that night. He sat at table with them, and once again, three days after the Last Supper, "He took bread, and blessed and brake and gave to them."

And at that moment their minds were flooded with wonder. Was this again a eucharistic consecration, the miracle of bread and wine becoming the blood and body of the Lord, as at that supreme time in the Upper Room of the house of the Cenacle? Who can answer? There is no proof.

Neither Cleophas nor Simon had been with the twelve at the great feast. But they had heard from James and John about the Last Supper.

And suddenly they realized the literal truth of the prophecy the Lord had made long before the crucifixion. The resurrection—not of the spirit alone—but of the body as well, a risen body that could walk and talk, and even eat!

A hoodwink seemed to fall from their eyes; they knew the stranger for whom and for what He was, the visible victor over death! They knew Him and in the instant of their knowing, He was gone, vanished from their sight.

And they whispered to one another:

"Was not our heart burning within us while He spoke in the way and opened the Scriptures to us?"

No wonder that they hurried back to Jerusalem to tell this singular adventure to the eleven apostles and the other disciples.

Chapter 10.   A SPIRIT WITH FLESH AND BONE

ALL eleven apostles were sitting disconsolately together in the upstairs room of the Cenacle when the wayfarers came puffing back from their hard, swift return from Emmaus. The Upper Room of the Last Supper was now filled with friends. The voice of Cleophas, shaking with emotion, resounded in the high joists and beams of the room, as he cried:

"The Lord is risen, indeed, and has appeared to Simon."

The echoes of his voice died away in the darkness of the rafters, but there came no answer from the crowd of grieving skeptics. They had heard the reports being circulated by rumor and gossip of what Peter and John had seen at the tomb, yet Peter and John had remained silent.

Now Cleophas wanted to tell them a direct story! So did Simon. Together they had shared a fantastic adventure on the road and at table; let everyone in the Cenacle listen to a straightforward account of what happened down in the highway and at table when the living, risen Master broke bread for them to eat.

Fear blanched the faces of the disciples, not fear of the supernatural, but concern that Temple spies might be listening. If reports of such a miracle tale reached Annas and Caiphas everyone in the room might be in danger of crucifixion. Without a word, as one of the eleven impulsively left the house on a private errand, the other apostles rose and shut fast the doors, bolting them against eavesdroppers.

Only then did they allow Cleophas to go on with his story.

He answered their questions, rehearsed in detail the meeting with the Master, and still no one believed him. Profound depression gripped the grieving group. Never had their faith fallen so low, never had they been so bereft of hope.

And in that ignoble hour a light suddenly began to shine in the room, and they all, except the one apostle who was elsewhere, saw Him for themselves. They saw Jesus standing visibly among them, in this room made sacred by the Last Supper, Jesus come back to them, and to so many others who had not sat at the final feast— Jesus, the Son of God and the Son of Man, victor over death, risen from the grave, standing in a clear light.

And they heard His voice:

"Peace be to you. It is I. Fear not."

He was speaking in His wonted idiom, in phrases He had cherished and used over and over again when they were frightened—"It is I" in the very midst of the storm. "Be not afraid."

Yet they were terrified. What men would not be?

Jesus read their hearts: "Why are you troubled? And why do thoughts arise in your hearts?"

He held out His hands.

"See My hands!"

Everyone could see the wounds where the nails had been driven through His palms. He drew back the hem of the robe that was without a seam to reveal the marks of the nails in His feet.

"See My hands and feet, that it is I, Myself. Handle and see: for a spirit has not flesh and bones, as you see Me to have."

From every mouth a gasp of awe and at every throat a feeling of insupportable relief. *It was true*—all that had been reported, all that had been promised. Here indeed was the Master, not in the spirit alone, but with a body resurrected from death. And then, as if to prove Himself to them finally and forever, He looked around Him with the friendliest of smiles and inquired:

"Have you here anything to eat?"

One disciple scrambled a little noisily to his feet. From a bundle he had laid by him on a windowsill he brought out a broiled fish and a slice of honeycomb wrapped in an oak leaf.

Jesus ate of the fish and honey Himself, offering some to the others with that ineffable smile of invitation which, ever since His birth in a stable, has been blessing the world.

And then—just before He left them in the opening and closing of an eye—he breathed upon the ten lovingly and whispered:

"Receive you—the Holy Ghost! Whose sins you shall forgive, they are forgiven them; and whose sins you shall retain, they are retained."

Then He was gone. In the space of a very few minutes, He had said and done great things, signs and pronouncements which have influenced Christians ever since that mysterious twilight in the Upper Room.

He had proved to this selected, opinion-making group that He was actually the revenant Jesus, risen from death, restored to life. He appeared before them, speaking words of reassurance, of peace. He showed them His hands, His feet, His side. He ate their food, proving beyond question that He was risen Body and Soul! And finally, He capped all His precious words and deeds by promising them one gift of the Holy Spirit for the forgiveness of sins.

What more proof could anyone demand?

Yet one did demand more—the first of the scientific-minded men to receive a spiritual experience: Thomas Didymus, a hardheaded fellow, who even in the simplest matters of life took a lot of convincing. When he returned from his errand the other apostles and the disciples told him how Jesus had appeared to them as they sat at table in the Upper Room. They said to Thomas:

"You were not with us when Jesus came. But it is true—we have seen the Lord."

With their own eyes? Yes! Dismally, Thomas Didymus shook his head. It was too much to ask of human belief, no matter how lovingly disposed one might feel; no—

"Except I see in His hands the print of the nails, and put my finger into the place of the nails, and put my hands into His side, I will not believe."

The other ten apostles dared not blame their doubting comrade, remembering their own skepticism at first sight of the risen Christ and His tacit rebuke when He had shown them His wounds to convince them. No matter what they said to Thomas, they could not persuade him. A week and a day were to pass with his skepticism unshaken, before the irrefutable evidence was given him.

Once again the apostles and disciples were shut together in prayerful companionship in the blue-walled hall of the Last Supper. The doors were locked and bolted. Suddenly and softly the figure of Jesus appeared in their midst.

Once again the well-remembered voice:

"Peace be to you!"

Jesus turned and directly faced Thomas Didymus, the most doubting of His apostles. And He said to Thomas, with a frank smile that held no slightest trace of reproach:

"Thomas, put in your finger hither and see My hands. And bring hither your hand and put it into My side. And be not without faith—but believing."

And what could Thomas say then? Only what millions of believers have repeated every day for more than two thousand years, as he fell to his knees and clasped his hands together, crying out in a husky voice:

"My Lord! And my God!"

The words that Jesus then spoke to Thomas Didymus were addressed to the endless legions of men still to be born into the history of the world—words that are a key to the wonderful, interior life of the soul:

"Because you have seen Me, Thomas, you have believed. *Blessed are they that have not seen, and have believed.*"

And then Jesus vanished from their sight as a rainbow can suddenly fade from the sky.

He was next to be seen by the Sea of Tiberias, that strange home-town lake, 600 feet below the level of the sea, and one of those to whom He showed Himself was again that doubter, Thomas Didymus.

Chapter 11. "FEED MY SHEEP!"

THE faithful had been directed to go to Galilee and they had obeyed. Peter was there, still not fully conscious of his destiny, not yet having been told the details of the part he was to play on the stage of history. He had gone back to his home, his old place on the pebbly beach, and his boat, which he reclaimed from the friend to whom he had lent it. There it lay now, tugging at the hawsers on the Sea of Tiberias (or of Galilee, or of Chinnereth, as the body of water was variously known) lying blue and peaceful under the still, starry sky.

With Simon Peter in that dark and early hour were Thomas, the doubter, and Nathanael, whose home was in Cana, where Jesus had turned the wedding water into wine; James the Greater and John, the sons of Zebedee, who had been a fishing partner of Jonas, Peter's fa-ther; and two others of Jesus' apostles, all standing on the shore.

Suddenly the silence was broken by Peter's rumbling voice, saying: "I go a-fishing."

The others looked at each other and shrugged: Why not?

"We also will come with you," they said to Peter. And for the first time since Calvary they began to feel relaxed. It was good to be again at the work they had been accustomed to since childhood. The smell of the boats and the sight of the little waves rolling in had a comfort of familiarity that soothed the pain of spirit which had pos-sessed them constantly in the weeks since Jesus was put to death. That dread event had been on April 7; now it was already May and after those first early visits, Jesus had come to them no more.

So they went forth in the boat, letting out into the deep as Jesus had once bade them do. Through the darkness they sailed with a wind racing before the dawn, carrying them far out into the middle of the lake, while behind them they dropped their nets, hoping to snare a shoal of fish.

There were times when Peter and James and John had fetched back to the beach a catch of more than five hundred pounds, but to-night they had none. The morning light came as they returned with empty nets to the shore, and presently their tired eyes saw a figure standing at the edge of the water.

They should have known and yet, again, they could not believe the evidence of their own eyes. John declares that "the disciples knew not that it was Jesus."

They heard a voice calling to them:

"Children, have you any meat?"

"No!"

Just as He had commanded them at another time, long ago, He bade them now:

"Cast the net on the right side of the ship and you shall find."

They looked at each other doubtfully, but obediently they cast out their empty nets, and now "they were not able to draw it for the multitude of fishes."

Then John, whose Gospel relates this scene, said to Peter in a strangled voice and great agitation: "It is the Lord."

Peter looked back at the shore. He was a towering figure as he stood there, naked, in the prow of the ship, shouting orders to the crew. But now—the Lord? *The Lord!* Peter threw his fisher's coat around him and leaped into the water, swimming as fast as he could for the beach, to reach Jesus.

The other apostles headed the ship back to the strand—they had been only about three hundred feet out—dragging the loaded net forward.

And Peter, dripping wet, charged up on the shore, where the tall figure, wrapped with light, awaited them. Beside Jesus Peter saw a little fire of hot coals on the ground, and beside the fire some loaves of bread.

Yet Jesus called out to the others again, saying:

"Bring hither of the fishes which you now have caught."

Peter ran to tug with John and James and Andrew, to pull the overladen net to shore.

A great catch it was, too. When they counted the fish, there were 153 powerful fellows caught in the toils, but not a string in the net was broken. And as they turned toward the Lord and made a little ring around Him, Jesus said:

"Come and dine."

They all sat with Him, and He went from one to another, distributing generous pieces of roasted fish and new baked bread to each. And not one of them needed to ask Him: "Who art thou?" They knew their host was the Lord.

When they had all dined, Jesus came directly to the point.

He turned to that turbulent man whom He had selected out of the twelve for His most special commission: impetuous Peter, who three times while Jesus was on trial for His life, had denied even knowing Him. To that eager and often undisciplined Peter He said:

"Simon, son of Jonas, do you love Me more than these?"

And His smile embraced all the others.

"Yes, Lord," came the booming reply of Peter. "You know that I love You."

There was a moment of deep, expectant silence, and then Jesus said:

"Feed My lambs!"

No one dared to speak. Jesus repeated His question to Peter:

"Simon, son of Jonas, do you love Me?"

"Yea, Lord! You know that I love You."

"Feed My sheep!"

And now, after another pause, and for a third time, Jesus asked:

"Simon, son of Jonas, do you love Me?"

At this third pressing of the question, Peter felt aggrieved that the Master was not satisfied with his first reply, nor his second. In a deepening tone he answered:

"You know all things; You know that I love You."

And Jesus said:

"Feed My sheep!"

Did Jesus mean to set a difference between sheep, which He had twice mentioned, and the lambs of which He spoke the first time? Theologians have disputed that question, but it was clear to all the apostles on that singular morning, and to none clearer than to Peter himself, that Jesus was reaffirming the commission given to the big Galilean long before. No matter that Peter might feel unworthy, might indeed argue in favor of someone else. Let no one, not even Peter, challenge the decision of the Lord. The shepherd was Peter;

to him Jesus was entrusting the pastoral office; Peter was to lead the flock.

And why the three questions? Why was one not enough? Three times Peter had denied his beloved Master, in the hour of supreme danger. Now, in the presence of the apostles whose captain he was to be, he had three times reiterated his overwhelming love of Jesus. Those protestations canceled out the memory of those three ignoble denials.

The slate was clean.

The morning light was all around them now. Jesus gathered them nearer as if His outstretched arms would embrace them all, but He spoke again only to Peter:

"Amen, amen, I say to you: when you were younger, you did gird yourself and you walked wherever you wished. But when you are old, you shall stretch forth your hands and another shall gird you—and lead you whither you would not. Follow me!"

And this Jesus said, John tells us, signifying by what death Peter should glorify God: a prophecy of how Peter was to be led in bonds to die in the gardens of Nero; crucified, but upside down at his own request, because he did not feel worthy to die in the same position as his Master.

Peter, looking about him wonderingly, saw the troubled face of John. And Peter, humbled before the great favor that was being shown him, looked apprehensively at Jesus, as if asking: "Why do You not pick John instead of me? You know the unreliable kind of fellow I am!" Now Peter brought himself to put that question another way. Nodding at John, he asked: "Lord! And what shall this man do?"

Jesus replied again enigmatically:

"If I will that he tarry till I come, what is that to thee?"

Without waiting for them to puzzle out what He meant, Jesus went on to say in final and authoritative tone to Peter:

"What is that to you? You follow Me!"

It is John who so circumstantially relates these words: "This," he tells us, "is that disciple who gives testimony of these things and has written these things: and we know that his testimony is true. But there are also many other things which Jesus did: which, if they were written every one, the world, I think, would not be able to contain the books that should be written."

And in a previous chapter of his Gospel, he had also said:

"Many other signs also did Jesus in the sight of His disciples, which are not written in this book. But these are written that you may believe that Jesus is the Christ, the Son of God: and that believing, you may have life in His name."

Scholars have ever since been grateful to John for making this fact perfectly clear: it is a further proof, in addition to the literary character of the Gospels, that they are not so much biographies of Jesus as selected incidents from His life. For a fuller story men must rely on the traditions handed down by eyewitnesses too busy to write, truths preserved by word of mouth through the centuries.

On this most special morning in Galilee Peter's heart was filled with humility and glory. He could never doubt again. He had supped with the risen Lord, who had repeated His assignment to Peter to lead the Christian flock; to feed the lambs and the sheep.

In just a little while, the work of the Church would begin.

Chapter 12. "THE PROMISE OF MY FATHER"

IN THE remaining days of the forty that followed the resurrection, there were to be still other visits of Jesus. He next appeared to His apostles on a mountain in Galilee, to tell them more of the work the Church must do. The original remaining eleven waited for Him there, on the small plateau where long ago He had preached what has ever since been called the Sermon on the Mount.

And Jesus spoke to them, saying:

"All power is given to Me in heaven and earth. Go you into the whole world and preach the Gospel to every creature."

They knew then, if they had held any doubt previously, that the divine truth entrusted to them through three years of intimacy was nothing exclusive. Here was the final confirmation of the missionary duty of the Church that was, in these last days, coming into organic life.

"Going therefore, teach all nations; baptizing them in the Name of the Father, and of the Son, and of the Holy Ghost. He that believes and is baptized shall be saved: but he that believes not shall be condemned.

"And these signs shall follow them that believe: In My Name they shall cast out devils: they shall speak with new tongues. They shall take up serpents; and if they shall drink any deadly thing, it shall not hurt them: they shall lay their hands upon the sick, and they shall recover."

Their work was blessed and sealed with a heavenly promise for all men:

"Behold I am with you all days, even to the end, the consummation of the world."

The most vital instructions He reserved for the final appearance in the Holy City, just before the ultimate parting and farewell.

As they met together again in Jerusalem, He gave them the parting counsel:

"These are the words which I spoke to you while I was yet with you, that all things must needs be fulfilled, which were written in the Law of Moses, and in the Prophets, and in the Psalms, concerning Me."

Here Jesus was being most technically precise. He referred to the threefold division of the Scriptures which we know today as the Old Testament—the Law, the Prophets, and what are called the Writings, which include the treasury of the Psalms.

For a long time He expounded to them from these threefold Scriptures, "opening their understanding" as St. Luke phrased it. And He said to them:

"Thus it is written and thus it behooved Christ to suffer, and to rise again from the dead, the third day. And that penance and remission of sins should be preached in His Name, unto all nations, beginning at Jerusalem. And you are witness of these things.

"And I send the promise of My Father upon you—"

Here, Jesus referred to the great gift which the Father had promised, the coming of the Paraclete, the Comforter, the Holy Ghost. But He warned them to wait. They must not attempt to do the work of God without the aid of the Spirit:

"But stay you in the city of Jerusalem, till you be endued with power from on high."

They would not have to wait long.

At the time of His going He led them out of the city, in the direction of Bethany, a town about a Sabbath day's journey from the house of the Cenacle; el Azariyeh the modern Arabs call the town, in honor of Lazarus, the brother of Martha and Mary, who lived there, and died, and was brought back to life as if to prepare the disciples for the shock of the Resurrection. Bethany, near the Garden of Gethsemane, was itself a part of the slope of the Mount of Olives.

This was to be the place of the Ascension.

The Ascension? Skeptics speak the word with disdain. But the Scriptures tell us just what the apostles saw on that glorious day when Jesus ascended to His Father.

The traditional site of the Ascension of Jesus into heaven is at the very peak of the Mount of Olives. As the agonied Garden of Gethsemane lies near the foot of that storied hill, so the place of triumphant farewell is at its crown.

Below that lofty summit lay a grand panorama, best of all views of the Holy City of David, on that Ascension Day, just as now. As He stood before the devoted assembly of His followers, Jesus could see the towers and domes of Jerusalem, the city that He had loved, the city of God's heroes and villains of past ages, and the seat of two Temples, the last of which, as He foretold, would soon be no more. Looking to the east, He could see the still waters of the Dead Sea and the mountains where Moses had been buried such a long time ago, as man must reckon time. And southwest, behind the Valley of Jehoshaphat, was that other valley called Gehenna, the Place of Fire.

All the past of the chosen people lay within view, as Jesus lifted up His hands and blessed the followers who ringed Him round on the sunshiny, windy height. In intense stillness He raised His hands, the cruel wounds still clearly visible, above them all. With those nail-pierced hands still spread in benediction over their heads, Jesus, the Son of Mary and the Son of God, departed from them, and being raised up a little from the earth, vanished into the silver shelter of a cloud, which received Him out of their sight.

Jesus, true man and true God, had finished His mission and left the earth.

"The Lord Jesus was taken up into heaven and sits on the right hand of God"—so St. Mark states unequivocally.

St. Luke in his Gospel is content to say that "He departed from them and was carried up to heaven." But in writing The Acts, Luke spoke of another matter.

"And while they were beholding Him going up to heaven," he declares, "behold two men stood by them in white garments.

"Who also said: 'You men of Galilee, why stand you looking up to heaven? This Jesus Who is taken up from you into heaven, shall so come as you have seen Him going into heaven.'"

All the disciples, Luke continues, were seized with awe and adoration. With great joy they trudged down into the Kidron Valley and up the wedgelike rocky promontory on which Jerusalem was built. They went directly to the Temple, where now boldly, no longer in fear of martyrdom, they proclaimed their faith under the very noses of the High Priest Annas and Caiphas, his abominable son-in-law, praising and blessing God.

And young Mark, who was later to travel and work with both Luke and Peter and with him who was to be known as Paul, finishes the story of the Ascension in these words:

"But they, going forth, preached everywhere: the Lord working withal, and confirming the word with the signs that followed."

BOOK TWO

The Signs That Followed

Chapter 13. SIMON CALLED PETER

IN THE DAYS following the Ascension, Simon called Peter walked out alone into the country, praying for guidance. This tall man appointed to destiny tramped the hills and valleys in the Palestinian springtime; a big man all over he was, with a head round as a globe and with the prognathous jaws of a fighter—but the largest thing about him was his great loving heart.

Peter was abundantly aware of his own shortcomings, his rash temper, his impulsive emotional reactions to men and events. He knew that only the power of God could sustain him in the tremendous years of decision ahead of him, and he turned increasingly to prayer and silence, beseeching the Lord's help.

"Lovest thou Me?" Jesus had asked in that final lakeside hour of commission. And Peter had answered in truth, "Lord, You know I love You."

That love he sought to perfect now in prayer, he who had been privileged to walk and talk with the living God.

There are likenesses of Peter preserved until this day, the oldest being an early third-century bronze medallion showing Peter with rounded head, uncompromising jawbones, and thick curly hair and beard. Two later portraits of Peter are to be found in the catacombs, very like the head on the bronze medallion, and out of these there steps barefoot into our hearts a living and very human man.

Simon, called Peter by the Son of God! In Aramaic it was Kipha, which meant rock; in Latin, Petrus. Cephas was, again, another way of saying that he was a rock, and Cephas Jesus had called him at their very first meeting, when Andrew, bringing Peter to Him, said, "My brother, we have found the Messiah."

And what had the Messiah said to the flat-footed fisherman? "You are Simon, the son of Jonas; you shall be called Cephas, which is interpreted Peter."

From that moment the renamed fisherman had followed the Lord.

Peter had a house, a home, a family; a mother-in-law, whom Jesus healed; he had been married (and some ancient writers believed his wife also suffered martyrdom). He was established as a fisherman, owning his own boat and prospering in his trade. Why had he given up all this to follow Jesus? Why had he turned into a vagabond, a wanderer up and down the roads, winding up at Calvary where his Master had been put to death as a common blasphemer?

That dreadful day on Calvary was not an ending; not for Peter, not for any of the disciples; nor for the beloved Master Himself. There was the Resurrection and the final parting at the top ridge of the Mount of Olives, surrounded by all of them who had been chosen as His constant companions in preaching the Kingdom of God.

They, too, Peter knew, were looking to him, although none of them had said anything as yet. Was there jealousy among them? They had argued on the night of the Last Supper about who should sit on the right and on the left of the Lord in His heaven. There might be rivalry still. Some might undoubtedly consider themselves better fitted than Peter for the task of getting the Church started on its way through history. Not that Peter need feel ashamed of his origin or his schooling. Though not highly educated, he came from a family that had taught him the Law and the Prophets and sent him to the synagogue school. Often he had traveled with his family to Jerusalem to worship in the great third Temple that Herod had erected there. He was no stranger to those courts and arcades when he went with Jesus, to stand by while the Master preached and whipped the money-changers out of His Father's house, which they had made a market place for merchandise. Peter and his brother Andrew were fellows of a certain substance and position, not too inconsequential.

Yet essentially Peter was a man of brawn and action; a fisherman, casting drift nets to snare in the coolness of night the herring, the mackerel, and the pilchard. How was such a man with a little band of obscure people, in the teeth of government hostility, to preach the new doctrine of Christ and His salvation to the world, today in Jerusalem, tomorrow everywhere "throughout the world"?

His life was pledged to the service of the Master. How he was to serve was not clear as yet. But he would cling with the greatest fidelity and inward love to the cause of the Saviour and the advancement of His Church on earth. Rash he might be in word and in act, but his zeal was never to know moderation, not even in his flaming anguish at death, upside down on a cross in Nero's gardens.

As he prayed and meditated on lonely walks and night vigils, Peter deliberately recalled the many times when the Lord had singled him out. Peter had stood at the head of the twelve when they were first solemnly called to the apostolate before the preaching of the Sermon on the Mount. Time and again Peter had spoken in the name of the other apostles, representing them; and when Jesus addressed them all, Peter answered in their name, himself their spokesman.

Once Jesus' other followers had deserted Him wholesale, unable or unwilling to accept His universal claims. Then Christ had asked His twelve would they also desert Him, and Peter had replied with that famous rhetorical question: "Lord, to whom shall we go?"

And Peter had added:

"You have the words of eternal life. And we have believed and have known that You are the Holy One of God—You are the Christ, the Son of God."

Looking back, Peter could not disguise from himself the special place Jesus had invariably given him among the apostles; always he was present at any important event. With James and John, he witnessed the raising of the daughter of Jairus from the dead; with the same two, he was present at the Transfiguration; he shared with them their ignominious sleep during Jesus' prayers in the Garden of Gethsemane. From the prow of Peter's boat the Master spoke to the multitude, and when He was miraculously walking upon the waters of Galilee, He called Peter to come to Him; it was Peter He sent back to the lake to catch the fish in whose mouth would be found the coin to pay the taxes.

But most important of all, Christ had given Peter the keys of heaven! When the Master and the twelve were walking near the town of Caesarea Philippi, Jesus had asked them who they thought He was.

Simon called Peter had returned the answer for them all:
"You are Christ, the Son of the living God."

And Jesus had answered:

"Blessed are you Simon, son of Jonas; because flesh and blood have not revealed it to you, but My Father who is in heaven. And I say to you: That you are Peter (Kipha, a rock); and upon this rock I will build My Church and the gates of hell shall not prevail against it. And I will give to you the keys of the kingdom of heaven. And whatsoever you shall bind upon earth, it shall be bound also in heaven; and whatsoever you shall loose on earth, it shall be loosed also in heaven."

The choice of those words was of precise significance. Jesus was not speaking metaphorically. "Bind" and "loose" were technical words used in the practice of the Jewish law. Any scribe or Pharisee would understand what complete authority was here being delegated to Peter.

All these things the anxious fisherman now reviewed in his mind. But remembering it all brought him still no clear knowledge of the work that Jesus meant for him to do. And how soon was he to get that promised guidance for which his whole being began to yearn? Till then to whom could he turn? To Mary, perhaps, the mother of Jesus, whose faith had never once wavered since the time they brought Him down from the cross and laid the limp body in her arms, completing the circle from Bethlehem to Calvary.

Peter could not forget the hours between Good Friday and Easter morning in the Cenacle where Mary had prayed, with calm assurance waiting for a mystery in which none of the others could believe. That was when Jesus Himself appeared to His mother, standing before her, wounded and thorn-scarred but alive and smiling. The Bible is silent about that reunion, as it is so often about Mary, respecting her humble desire for self-effacement during her lifetime. But the old reports declare, and the tradition will not be downed, that Mary had been the first to see that her Son had won His victory over death.

Meanwhile, Peter well knew that the old enemies of the Master were aware of the return of Jesus. Caiphas of the perfumed beard had called that second rump meeting of the Sanhedrin, and paid out bribes to spread the fable that the disciples came in the night and stole the body away.

How illogical the high priests were! To say that the countrymen from Galilee, who at the first show of soldiers' torches, spears, and shields had fled the Garden of Gethsemane, leaving Jesus to His fate —that these cowards at Christ's arrest would have the courage to steal the body from under the very eyes of Roman guards!

Nevertheless, the tale was being spread. Immediate and strong-handed leadership of all the bewildered believers was imperative. And Peter had been designated as the leader. Yet he could not bring himself to act.

He had been wrong so often!

Once, and he blanched now to remember it, Peter had actually rebuked Jesus to His face. The Lord had explained to the twelve apostles that He must suffer, and be killed, and after three days rise again, and Peter had been outraged at the thought. It contradicted his understanding of what the Messiah was. And he had exploded. As Mark records, "Peter took Him, and began to rebuke Him."

And the Lord had said then to Peter: "Get thee behind Me, Satan: for thou savorest not the things that be of God, but the things that be of men."

At the Last Supper, Peter had sworn to follow his Master to prison and to death. But Jesus knew better. He had predicted that before morning Peter would deny Him three times. And from the shame of that weakness Peter still trembled whenever he thought of it, which was almost constantly.

And before that same last Passover meal, when Christ had set about washing His apostles' feet, kneeling first before Peter, the fisherman had protested vigorously. Offended by the very humility of his Lord, he had exclaimed in horror: "Thou shalt never wash my feet."

Only when Jesus declared that otherwise Peter should have no part with Him did Peter submit, saying: "Lord, not only my feet, but also my hands and my head."

How many rash mistakes can one man make?

In the Garden of Gethsemane Peter slept through the hour of his Saviour's anguish of prayer. At the arrest of Jesus, Peter in an outburst of anger had drawn his sword and cut off the right ear of the high priest's servant. And again Jesus had reproved him: "Put up your sword into the sheath! The cup which My Father has given Me, shall I not drink it?"

Peter never seemed to do anything quite right. He was a big impulsive blunderer, and he was well aware of it. His own weakness appalled him. How then could he possibly be the leader of God's Church?

Would other men, in other years, find it hard to believe that such as he had actually been singled out as the leader of the Church Christ founded? Would they balk at accepting the idea that the all-powerful God would commission such a plain and human fisherman over all others? Peter smiled to himself as he wondered.

He had been chosen because he loved Jesus, heart, soul, and mind. But he knew from his mistakes that love alone was not enough to help him do and understand the divine will without error. He knew he must wait for the guidance which Jesus had promised to send him.

But in those long and urgent days, when action seemed imperative to the life of faith, Peter found it nearly impossible to wait for the coming of the Holy Ghost.

Without that, he would be as nothing!

Chapter 14.   THE DRAWING OF LOTS

THE history of the coming of the Holy Spirit is told in the New Testament in a book call The Acts of the Apostles. The book was written by St. Luke, who was not one of the apostles, but a physician from Antioch, an early convert who left his thriving practice to work for Christianity.

His is the only contemporary account of the first years of the Church. Written in Greek, about thirty years after the Resurrection, it is a sequel to his first manuscript, the Gospel which bears Luke's name.

From The Acts we learn of the first time that Peter asserted his leadership in the Church.

After Jesus rose to heaven from the top of Mount Olivet, His followers returned to Jerusalem, and to the Cenacle. Here were gathered at that time Peter and John, James the Greater and Andrew, Philip and Thomas, Bartholomew and Matthew, Simon Zelotes, James the Less and Jude Thaddeus. All these men were persevering in prayer, with one mind, with the women and with Mary, the mother of Jesus, and all His relatives and disciples.

Nightly more men and women knocked for entrance at the Cenacle door, former disciples of Jesus, men and women who had heard Him teach, had been healed by Him during His lifetime, and had believed. Soon the house was full to the lintels with a crowd that waited and prayed for the promised signs.

To them Peter made his first official speech, facing about one hundred and twenty men and women in the historic room of the Last Supper, to announce a radical decision.

He began by recalling to them a prophecy from the Psalms of David.

"Men, brethren," said Peter, "the Scripture must needs be fulfilled, which the Holy Ghost spoke before by the mouth of David concerning Judas, who was the leader of them that apprehended Jesus, who was numbered with us, and had obtained part of this ministry. And he indeed has possessed a field of the reward of iniquity, and being hanged, burst asunder in the midst; and all his bowels gushed out.

"And it became known to all the inhabitants of Jerusalem, so that the same field was called in their tongue, Haceldama, that is to say, 'the field of blood.' For it is written in the book of Psalms: 'Let their habitation become desolate, and let there be none to dwell therein. And his bishopric let another take.'

"Wherefore, of these men who have companied with us all the time that the Lord Jesus came in and went out among us, beginning from the baptism of John, until the day wherein He was taken up from us,—one of these must be made a witness with us of His Resurrection."

Someone must be chosen to take Judas' place among the twelve! To this pronouncement of Peter's the assembly agreed. But when the vote was taken two candidates were tied—one was Joseph, called Barsabas, who was surnamed Justus, and the other was Matthias.

And facing the tie, all of the company began to pray:

"You, Lord, Who know the hearts of all men, show which of these two You have chosen to take the place of this ministry and apostleship from which Judas has fallen by transgression, that he might go to his own place."

And guidance promptly answered that earnest prayer. *Let them try lots!* He who drew the larger lot would be the one God had appointed. The other would be rejected. The two men, Joseph Barsabas and Matthias, with that prayer for divine guidance still on their lips, stepped forward humbly. The lot fell upon Matthias.

Judas was gone, but the eleven apostles were twelve once more, as the months are twelve and also the tribes of Israel. No one knows anything of the history of Matthias' life or ministry. He was chosen because he had "companied" with the other disciples and was therefore competent to witness to the works and teaching of Jesus. Some of the earliest authorities believed, for one reason or another, that Matthias was a new name for Zacchaeus, that wealthy but midget tax collector who once climbed a sycamore tree, to get sight of Jesus on His approach to Jericho.

But only as Matthias we know him surely to have been chosen just in time for twelve apostles to be present at one of the greatest events in the history of the world—the descent of the Holy Ghost at the time of the Pentecost.

Chapter 15. TONGUES OF FIRE

THE day Christians call Pentecost was a great feast among the Jews. In Hebrew it was called *Shabuoth*, the second of the major annual feasts, falling fifty days after the Passover, at the end of the grain harvest. In the year of Christ's death and resurrection, as always, Jews came traveling from many parts of the world to worship in the Jerusalem Temple at that feast, to offer to God as He commanded: "the first fruits of your labors, which you saw in the field."

On that festival of the First Fruits, as all the apostles and disciples sat together in the Cenacle suddenly there came a sound from heaven, as of a mighty, rushing wind. The noise of it could be heard through all the house where they were sitting:

"*And there appeared to them parted tongues as it were of fire, and it sat upon every one of them.*

"*And they were all filled with the Holy Ghost . . .*"

The promise of the Saviour was kept. The Holy Ghost, in the form of cloven tongues of fire, descended upon them. Go spread the tiding round, wherever man is found—the Comforter is come! The Paraclete is here. The third person of the Godhead, the completion of the

Trinity, the Holy Spirit from heaven is here on earth, here to remain until Judgment Day for the consolation and guidance of men!

The miraculous power of the Holy Ghost was instantly apparent; visible in the cloven tongues of fire, and audible in their own voices, the voices of unschooled and untraveled men which suddenly burst forth in a clamor of foreign speech. They "began to speak with divers tongues according as the Holy Ghost gave them to speak."

It was as if, here in the hallowed room of the Last Supper and the first communion, the punishment of Babel was reversed. Men who had not learned foreign languages suddenly understood them. They could go anywhere now and preach the truth to all nations, as the Lord had commanded.

And in amazement, the apostles ran into the streets, to speak with their new gift of tongues.

Soon a multitude surrounded them, and in the crowds were travelers from Europe and the Far East, men of many strains, speakers of all dialects. Yet when they called out questions to the apostles, they were answered in their own tongues. For every speech that was uttered that day, there was a Pentecostal apostle, baptized in a tongue of fire, and ready to answer in the same speech.

Parthians were in that throng, from the mountainous land south of the Caspian Sea; and Medes from a neighboring region; Elamites from east of Babylonia; pilgrims from all parts of Mesopotamia and from Cappadocia in Asia Minor; Egyptians, and Jews from the isles of Greece; Romans, Cretes, and Arabians. The story had spread, and thousands came running, all shouting at the roof of the mouth, screaming questions and getting answers. The wonder over this manifestation was intense; strangers and Jerusalem citizens alike were astounded.

"What!" they cried. "Behold these fellows. Are not all of these who speak Galileans? Nothing more. What has happened to them, then? How can we hear from these fishermen, every man the tongue he was born to?"

To them Peter was to preach the first sermon of the Church, one of the greatest speeches of all time.

In a fine, discriminating, and definitive statement Peter gave them the first fruits, not only of his inner searchings of recent days, but of the inspiration that now flooded his soul.

All the great features of the Church of which he was now the earthly head were through inspiration of the Spirit taking shape in Peter's mind and heart—the Mass, Holy Communion, Confession, Ordination, the other sacraments, and their attendant ceremonies all fusing into outward signs of inner graces.

A blessed felicity and unity became apparent to Peter now—going back to the very beginnings of the Garden of Eden. In the writings of the old Prophets, with which he had been familiar since child-hood, were constant promises of this new Dispensation that was now a reality. God, the Father, whose love for His creatures is set forth in the Old Testament, would send God the Son, whose ministry is set forth in the four Gospels, to make a reconciliation with man by the atonement on Calvary, as promised to Adam and to Eve. And then God the Father and God the Son would establish in the hearts of the people God the Holy Spirit to be with them always, even unto the consummation of the world. Through the ages mankind had struggled by the sweat of the brow to reach this reconciliation, now given freely by God, the perfect Trinity.

Nor—Peter saw the point in all its majestic importance—was this to be considered a new religion. Not at all. God, the Son, had come not to change the Law, but to fulfill it. And, indeed, it was fulfilled; the Church was now and would remain until the end of the world, the completion and perfection of Israel.

As he stood before the multitude, the wind blowing through his tawny hair and beard, his hand raised to command attention, Peter was a startling, arresting sight. In his eyes burned a mystical ardor that even the dullest eye could not miss. The other apostles and dis-ciples crowded near, behind him, their eyes lifted to heaven as they whispered their prayers. This was not like the ordinary behavior of ordinary men.

"These men are full of new wine," said many in the crowd. But they were intoxicated only with the wine of the Holy Spirit that warmed and strengthened them all.

Hear Peter speak: "Ye men of Judaea, and all you that dwell in Jerusalem, be this known to you, and with your ears receive my words. For these are not drunk, as you suppose, seeing it is but the third hour of the day!

"But this is that which was spoken of by the prophet Joel: 'And it shall come to pass, in the last days (saith the Lord), I will pour out of My Spirit upon all flesh: and your sons and your daughters shall prophesy, and your young men shall see visions, and your old men shall dream dreams. And upon my servants indeed, and upon my handmaids will I pour out in those days of My Spirit, and they shall prophesy. And I will shew wonders in the heaven above, and signs on the earth beneath: blood and fire, and vapor of smoke. The sun shall be turned into darkness, and the moon into blood, before the great and manifest day of the Lord come. And it shall come to pass, that whosoever shall call upon the name of the Lord, shall be saved.'

"Ye men of Israel, hear these words: Jesus of Nazareth, a Man approved of God among you, by miracles, and wonders, and signs, which God did by Him, in the midst of you, as you also know: this same being delivered up, by the determinate counsel and foreknowledge of God, you by the hands of wicked men have crucified and slain! Whom God hath raised up, having loosed the sorrows of hell, as it was impossible that He should be holden by it!

"For David saith concerning Him: 'I foresaw the Lord before my face: because He is at my right hand, that I may not be moved. For this my heart hath been glad, and my tongue hath rejoiced: moreover my flesh also shall rest in hope. Because Thou wilt not leave my soul in hell, or suffer Thy Holy One to see corruption. Thou hast made known to me the ways of life: Thou shalt make me full of joy with Thy countenance.'

"Ye men, brethren, let me freely speak to you of the patriarch David; that he died, and was buried; and his sepulcher is with us to this present day. Whereas therefore he was a prophet, and knew that God hath sworn to him with an oath, that of the fruit of his loins one should sit upon His throne. Foreseeing this, he spoke of the resurrection of Christ.

"For neither was He left in hell, neither did His flesh see corruption. This Jesus hath God raised again, whereof all we are witnesses. Being exalted therefore by the right hand of God, and having received of the Father the promise of the Holy Ghost, He hath poured forth this which you see and hear.

"For David ascended not into heaven; but he himself said: 'The Lord said to my Lord, sit Thou on My right hand, until I make Thy enemies Thy footstool.'

"Therefore, let all the house of Israel know most certainly, that God hath made both Lord and Christ, this same Jesus, whom you have crucified."

And every man, from every country, in that crowd understood Peter's words, as if they were uttered in his own tongue.

When they heard these things, "they had compunction in their heart," and said to Peter, and to the rest of the apostles, "What shall we do, men and brethren?"

And Peter said to them: "Do penance, and be baptized every one of you in the name of Jesus Christ, for the remission of your sins: and you shall receive the gift of the Holy Ghost. For the promise is to you, and to your children, and to all that are far off, whomsoever the Lord our God shall call."

They heard Peter's discourse with amazement, on this first Whitsunday. It was an unparalleled spectacle; this huge man of Galilean accent, so unmistakably a fisherman from a long line of boatmen; a humble and even a blundering man, yet now full of fire and light, as wisdom and prophecy seemed to leap into words from his mouth.

"Save yourselves from this perverse generation," Peter pleaded with them. And in the multiplying scores of years since that day, his entreaty has resounded in the ears of generation after generation, all untoward.

Peter's words that day won converts not by dozens, scores, or hundreds, but by thousands. About three thousand souls were baptized as the result of that first sermon. Many were foreign pilgrims come to celebrate the Jewish feast of First Fruits, who would return now to their native lands with the startling and glorious truth of salvation through Christ. And many of course were local men from the city and the outlying towns of Judaea, Jews many of whom had followed Jesus during His life, who had strewn His way with palms on a day of triumph, and wept and wondered at His death.

Christianity was in the very air of Jerusalem, and High Priest Annas and Caiphas could do nothing about it. The converts continued steadfast in the apostolic doctrine and in the fellowship of the early Christians. They lived together, pooling their small possessions for the general good, "having all things in common"; selling their superfluous luxuries and giving to the poor, just as Christ had once told the rich man to do.

Day after day, the spirit of Christ seemed to take on new power in the capital, as each morning the Christians came to the Temple to preach the doctrine of a love that had proved itself stronger than death. The people soon knew how well the Christians got on together in their communal living; how they shared, one with another, what they had; how they did "eat their meat with gladness and singleness of heart; praising God and having favor with all the people."

Those who should be saved, whose hearts were ready, in numbers increasing day by day flocked around the apostles.

High Priest Caiphas was growing apoplectic. In spite of the lies he had ordered spread about, Caiphas saw that the doctrines of the Nazarene were taking hold on more people after His death than before.

Once again the high priest was moved to desperate measures, to meet the defiance of this new faith. Take, for example, the singular miracle of the lame man in the very courtyard of the Temple. How long could the priests and the scribes allow such things as that to go on?

Chapter 16. "SILVER AND GOLD I HAVE NONE"

Just about three in the afternoon, which in those days was called "the ninth hour," Peter and John went to the Temple together to pray. As they came through the Royal Porch, up from the Huldah triple gates, and crossed the Court of the Gentiles, the two apostles saw a pitiful and familiar sight. A lame man sat on his haunches in the shade of a marble pillar, stretching out his hollowed palm to beg. The cripple had been malformed in his mother's womb. For as long as they had been visiting in Jerusalem, Peter and John could remember him squatting in the shade of a marble pillar at the gate of the Temple called Beautiful, imploring alms of all the worshipers passing by.

Now he tugged at Peter's cloak.

"Mercy!" the crippled beggar moaned. "Help me, masters! Save me from starving; me and my family who depend on me."

Peter and John gazed at him gravely.

"Look upon us," said Peter softly.

The beggar was wary as a dog waiting for a bone, certain that the two men would toss some money at his feet.

Peter's next words were full of disappointment for the cripple.

Said Peter: "Silver and gold I have none; but what I have, I give you."

No silver and no gold? Then what is it you do have, you two obvious country yokels from the north country?

"In the name of Jesus Christ of Nazareth, arise and walk!"

With quiet unassailable conviction, Peter spoke those words. The callused hand of the fisherman stretched down to take the pale hand of the sitting beggar, and Peter pulled him up, so that he was standing, and "forthwith," as St. Luke later explained, "his feet and soles received strength." The beggar at the gate called Beautiful for the first time in his life could stand alone.

The man leaped in bewildered joy, prancing and skipping like a child. Then, still running and wheeling around, he made a dash for the Temple, heading for the altar, praising God all the way.

Peter and John looked solemnly at each other. Peter's first miracle! Their hearts were too full for speech. Suddenly they heard the babble and shout of many voices, and a crowd of people came running toward them from the Temple. So soon the story of the healing had spread. The people knew this beggar; they remembered his helplessness, and now they saw him healed and well and strong. How did it happen, beggar; quick, tell us! Those men! The beggar pointed at Peter and John. The tall one with the enormous shoulders; he touched me and I was no longer a cripple. So a howling, cheering mob surrounded Peter and John.

And once again, Peter spoke with breath-taking frankness to the people. With John beside him, he stood at Solomon's Porch, a section of the range of pillared arches running all around the vast perimeter of the Temple area.

Peter raised his voice to quell the tumult and then began to speak, shocking the crowd into honest thought:

"Ye men of Israel, why wonder you at this? or why look ye on us, as if by our strength or power we had made this man to walk?

"The God of Abraham, and of Isaac, and of Jacob, the God of our fathers, hath glorified His Son Jesus; whom you indeed delivered up, and denied before the face of Pilate, when he judged He should be released.

"But you denied the Holy One and the Just, and desired a murderer to be granted unto you. But the Author of life you killed, whom God hath raised from the dead, of which we are witnesses.

"And in the faith of His Name, this man whom you have seen and known, hath His Name strengthened; and the faith which is by Him hath given this perfect soundness in the sight of you all.

"And now, brethren, I know that you did it through ignorance, as did also your rulers. But those things, which God before had shewed by the mouth of all the prophets, that His Christ should suffer, He hath so fulfilled.

"Be penitent, therefore, and be converted, that your sins may be blotted out. That when the times of refreshment shall come from the presence of the Lord, and He shall send Him who hath been preached unto you, Jesus Christ, whom heaven indeed must receive until the times of restitution of all things, which God hath spoken by the mouth of all His holy prophets from the beginning of the world.

"For Moses said: 'A Prophet shall the Lord your God raise up unto you of your brethren, like unto me; Him you shall hear according to all things whatsoever He shall speak to you. And it shall be, that every soul which will not hear that Prophet shall be destroyed from among the people.'

"And all the prophets from Samuel and afterwards who have spoken, have told of these days.

"You are the children of the prophets, and of the testament which God made to our fathers, saying to Abraham: 'And in thy seed shall all the kindreds of the earth be blessed.'

"To you first, God, raising up His Son, hath sent Him to bless you; that every one may convert himself from his wickedness."

Here Peter uncompromisingly told the people to their faces and within reach of their fists the truth about themselves. Jonah long ago had been punished by God for refusing to go to Nineveh and upbraid the inhabitants for their sins. But never Peter.

His days of vacillation were over. No one knew better than he the power in Jerusalem that could be loosed against him and the other apostles. The Temple rulers would not hesitate.

Even while Peter was delivering that discourse, schemes were being hatched against the Christians. Peter knew that many of the six thousand Pharisees, those middle-grounders and compromisers between what the stoic Essenes taught and the free-will doctrine of the Sadducees, those fence straddlers, quillet quibblers, and whisperers, were conspiring for invisible control of the governors set over

Palestine. These men, who were said to "hiss like vipers," exercised the strategy and discipline of a secret military order. In carrying out their notions under the leadership of High Priest Annas, they had for long ridden high.

The time was rapidly coming when the citizens would see the outrageous truth about them, as Christ had spoken it and so brought about His trial. On a day after Peter was dead and gone, the people of Jerusalem would rise up and storm the market stalls in the Temple courts. But there were unborn years between that coming time, when the people would destroy the "Bazaar of the Sons of Annas," and this day of Peter's second public speech. The power of the Pharisees was still frightening.

Yet Peter boldly reminded the people of what had happened. How had the lame man been healed? Not by Peter's own power, nor his own holiness, but by God, and His Son Jesus, and through faith in His name. The people could not have forgotten this Jesus, whom they had seen killed. Guilt over that crucifixion still lurked in their hearts. But though they had allowed it to be done, they could still ask for forgiveness. Therefore, the Scriptures and the "determinate counsel of God" had been fulfilled.

What did Peter mean by those singular words? He meant, in simple phrase, that first God had delivered up His Son; and His Son delivered up Himself for the love and salvation of the whole human race, including this excitable throng. Christ's being delivered up was holy and was God's own determination. They who had betrayed and crucified Him had, nevertheless, acted wickedly. They had followed their own malice and the instigation of the devil. They were not to think that the cruel wickedness they had done could be excused on the ground that the crucifixion had fulfilled the will and determination of God. Far from it. God was by no means the author of their wickedness, although He did not interfere to prevent it, because He could and did draw out of it that great good, the salvation of the world.

Peter, talking to that restless mob in Solomon's Porch, spoke fearlessly, with a profound insight into mysteries that might bewilder them.

And even as Peter was finishing this task, the insatiable enemies of Jesus were marching upon him.

Chapter 17. THE FIRST IMPRISONMENT

PETER was not surprised at the measured tramp of marching feet entering the Court of the Gentiles. That fastidious and unwarlike collection of timeservers and sinecure holders, the Temple Guard, drilled by their captain, one of the dandies of Jerusalem, was urged on by a knot of fuming priests and grumbling Sadducean theologians. Not for long could such men permit a friend of Christ to stand up and tell the public about the need for penance and the promise of everlasting life. Nor could they abide to hear Peter telling the people that Jesus had been resurrected from the dead.

Gingerly the guards laid hands upon Peter and John, brandished their clubs, threatened them in shrill voices, and led them to prison. At twilight they thrust them into a stinking cell of one of the towers in the city wall: their first prison, but not their last.

Neither Peter nor John felt dismayed. Gleeful and secretly friendly guards murmured to them in the reeking darkness of the stronghold— that Peter had not healed nor spoken in vain. Many had believed his message, and were baptized, "and the number of the men was about five thousand," so St. Luke has reported.

The next day found the two apostles on trial.

Not in grand illicit midnight mystery, as when the Sanhedrin had put Jesus to trial. Peter and John were given a most impressive hearing. Everybody important was called to sit in judgment of them at this hastily assembled meeting of the Sanhedrin. Old Annas, the political boss of Jerusalem was there, washing his one remaining tooth with dry and withered tongue; Caiphas, the son-in-law of Annas; and the many kin in the far-spread family of the religious dictator: brothers and cousins and nephews and uncles of Annas.

The healing of the lame man at the Temple gate, the immensely moving speeches by Peter, the conversion of three thousand people in one day and five thousand in another had given the Sanhedrinists an aggravated case of jitters.

"By what power," Caiphas demanded, "or by what name have you done this?"

For a moment the two prisoners remained silent, as if waiting for something. Then Peter, "filled with the Holy Ghost," as St. Luke reports, said unto them:

"You princes of the people, and ancients, hear!

"If we this day are examined concerning the good deed done to the infirm man, by what means he hath been made whole: be it known to you all, and to all the people of Israel, that by the name of our Lord Jesus Christ of Nazareth, whom you crucified, whom God hath raised from the dead, even by Him this man standeth here before you whole.

"This is 'the stone which was rejected by you the builders, which is become the head of the corner.' Neither is there salvation in any other. For there is no other Name under heaven given to men, whereby we must be saved."

There was a deep quiet upon all the judges as Peter finished his most fearless and even defiant public statement, his third.

Such boldness at this grim moment appalled the judges. They perceived, as St. Luke observed, that Peter and John were not learned men, yet their eloquence had been overpowering; the brevity, the strength and beauty of Peter's talk, the aptness of his Scriptural reference, all contradicted the origin and character of these Galilean fishermen.

Would the Sanhedrin never hear the last of this Nazarene they had sent to Calvary? These two men had been the close friends of that Jesus. And, like Him, they were not only preaching but healing. The restored beggar stood there before them all, disastrously visible proof of Christian power. How could two Galilean fishermen restore straightness to crooked bones and conjure pain away? These were realities with which the Sanhedrin had to deal promptly.

So they put out Peter and John and the healed beggar, and all the other disciples and the Galilean women and everyone there who had loved and believed in Jesus; ordered them to leave the chamber of the Sanhedrin. Then the Senate and its seventy-one members, as in the ancient court of the Elders, took council among themselves.

"What shall we do to these men?" Caiphas finally demanded. The high priest, gorgeous in his Temple robes—which by Roman law he was forced in humiliation to borrow from Pontius Pilate and which must be returned—once more faced the issue that Jesus of Nazareth had brought to his doorstep.

Caiphas lowered his voice to a confidential tone, as if to say that the admission he was now forced to make must be kept within the

Temple and was not to be bandied about in the streets of the capital.

"Everybody in Jerusalem will soon know about the healing of the cripple. If nobody else tells it, he will. The fact that indeed a notable miracle has been done by these followers of their so-called Christ will be a matter of common knowledge in Jerusalem. And that miracle we cannot deny!"

His glance around them was like a signal flash of danger.

"This tale must not be allowed to spread among the people any farther," Caiphas said solemnly. "I propose that we warn them they speak no more henceforth to any man in this name—this name of Jesus," he cried.

But this device of the majestic Caiphas only showed how hard it was for him to understand. Weary Annas, watching with a wink to himself now and then as he listened to his son-in-law, knew in his heart that no threats could frighten these followers of Jesus. He was not in the least surprised, when Peter and John returned to the council chamber and were sternly admonished "not to speak at all nor teach in the name of Jesus," to hear them reply without a trace of fear:

"If it be just in the sight of God to hear you rather than God, you be the judges!"

Again the silence that seemed to bespell men whenever the Holy Ghost spoke through the mouths of apostles, and then Peter's voice rang out in sonorous tones:

"For we cannot do anything else but speak the things which we have seen and heard."

Now, Caiphas—you have given your orders to Peter and John, and you have heard their instant answer. What next, Caiphas? That question was in the eyes of every scribe and every Pharisee and every subordinate to the high priest.

For unless they wanted to make another serious mistake, such as the incurable blunder of Holy Thursday night and Friday morning's execution of an illegal sentence; unless they wanted to run counter to the excited interest of the men, women and children who hung on every word the apostles spoke; unless they wanted to ride roughshod over the people's will, there was only one thing left for the Sanhedrinists to do, and they did it.

They dismissed the two stubborn fishermen of Galilee with a warning to behave themselves or there would be serious trouble indeed.

The Christians went back to their houses and prayed.

Chapter 18.   ALL THINGS IN COMMON

THE nature of that praying in the Cenacle was unique in the beginning
church. It was a kind of communal prayer, of choral unity. Peter and
John had come through their first arrest and trial with honor, and
their fellow Christians were filled with triumphant assurance of
divine protection. Lifting up their voice to God, they spoke in unison,
"with one accord," wrote St. Luke:

"Lord, Thou art He that didst make heaven and earth, the sea, and
all things that are in them.

"Who, by the Holy Ghost, by the mouth of our father David, Thy
servant, hast said: 'Why did the Gentiles rage, and the people
meditate vain things? The kings of the earth stood up, and the
princes assembled together against the Lord and His Christ.'

"For of a truth there assembled together in this city against Thy
holy child Jesus, whom Thou hast anointed, Herod, and Pontius
Pilate, with the Gentiles and the people of Israel, to do what Thy
hand and Thy counsel decreed to be done.

"And now, Lord, behold their threatenings, and grant unto Thy
servants, that with all confidence they may speak Thy word, by
stretching forth Thy hand to cures, and signs, and wonders to be done
by the name of Thy holy Son Jesus."

And as he prayed for greater boldness to speak the truth, Peter
marveled at the courage which the Holy Spirit had already bestowed
on him, and was grateful to God for the change that had come over
him since the shameful night when he denied his Master. And he
gloried in the dauntless faith which filled all around him.

So started a blessed, unparalleled relationship among those first
Christians—a community of loving kindness; not the companionship
of hermits and eremites, abandoning man in order to live alone with
God, but an active participation of life in cities and countryside.
They were in the world but not of it, as they sought together to know
God, to love and serve Him, and to love their fellow men as they
loved themselves. Theirs was the only true or decent communalism
ever known, and because it was not mere common sharing of goods
and services but a sharing of Christian faith, in ideal and practice, it

prospered to the astonishment of unbelievers. These Christians were, as St. Luke phrased it in The Acts, of one heart and of one soul. Not one of them ever said that anything which he possessed belonged to him, or that it should be considered his own. They had "all things in common."

The blessing and the miracle of such living and sharing was that no one among them ever lacked for anything. Some of those converts of the early months of the Church were rich men. Once they knew Jesus and His teachings and had been baptized, they found the grace and resolution which one moneyed man had lacked when, some years before, Jesus had said to him: "Sell all you have and give to the poor." These eager converts sold their lands and their houses, their farms and vineyards, the fertile lowland fields and their timber forests on the hillsides, their barns stored up with grain—all their assets these successful agriculturists sold, with shrewd and thrifty bargaining like the good business men they were. And they turned the profits over to the keeper of the bag, the successor of Judas of evil memory. Every mite and pound and shekel and drachma was laid down at the apostles' feet, to be used for the well-being of all. To every man distribution was made according to his need, and all were housed and fed and clad sufficiently. The Church which was to carry the blessing of Christ to the world flourished, "and with great power the apostles gave witness of the resurrection of the Lord Jesus; and great grace was upon them all."

One of the rich men who sold his goods and deposited the profits in the common treasury was a landowner whose parents had named him Joses, or Joseph. But when Joses became a Christian the apostles gave him the new name of Barnabas with his baptism. He was to be one of the grandest figures in that astounding galaxy of early saints. The meaning of his new name was "the son of consolation"—and no one could count the millions whose heartache was to be eased by remembering Barnabas.

Barnabas, who was the uncle of Mark, the Gospel writer, was himself soon to become the discoverer and champion of Paul, that giant soul then still waiting at the stage door not yet to take on his mighty role in the Christian drama. Barnabas would be Paul's guide and faithful friend and promoter. But that story still lay in the future; now Barnabas, the broad-shouldered Levite from the island of Cyprus and one of the few millionaires to become a saint, had joined the movement with all his cultured, ardent soul.

He came at a time when the impact of the prolonged rush of grace, of the ever increasing conversions, of the manifest strength of the movement was beginning to bring the inevitable troubles that beset any attempt at helping to save man from himself. Before long, some Christians would begin to lie to each other and take false oaths at the altar, and others would be cast into prison for speaking truth. But the glory of God would shine through the Church's weakness and strength with supernatural force and fantastic miracles.

A man called Ananias and his wife Sapphira were to make the first trouble among the Christians.

Chapter 19. THE LIAR AND HIS WIFE

There are two men in the Bible called Ananias—a name that means literally that "God has been gracious." One lived in Damascus, and had the honor of baptizing one of the greatest men in history, Saul of Tarsus, whom we know as St. Paul.

The other Ananias caused the first real trouble in the Church. He lived in Jerusalem and was a man of substance. His wife had from birth been so comely that she was called Sapphira, an Aramaic name meaning "beautiful."

This happily favored couple wanted to become Christians despite the fact that open support of the new Church was still dangerous in Jerusalem. At any moment the authorities might bear down on all its adherents, and many reasonable men lived in fear of mass crucifixion. There had been one such ghastly shambles in a year when Jesus was still a small boy in Nazareth. It could happen again.

Yet in spite of danger, Ananias the landowner and his wife Sapphira said that they too wished to be baptized and wanted to put their fortune into the hands of the common treasurer. Their forthright declaration impressed the onlookers as great evidence of the change that came over people once they embraced the new teachings.

Peter told Ananias and Sapphira just the way to go about it. They should go home and sell all they owned, bring back the cash, and give it to the cause. Smiling happily, Ananias and Sapphira hurried away.

They sold their land, with no Christian witnesses to the transaction. Then Ananias alone went back to the mother Church in the Cenacle, climbed the stone steps, and entered that sacred Upper Room. In front of Peter, he stooped and laid down a bundle.

Peter's bearded face and his large flashing eyes seemed to undergo a change as he looked down at the offering, one corner of the rolled cloth touching the toe of his sandal. By the power of the Holy Ghost which dwelt in him, he looked at the gift on the stone floor, and at the smug, complacent face of Ananias, and, without asking, knew the truth.

Ananias was cheating! He had decided to give to Christianity only a part of the price he and his wife had received. The other part they had secretly agreed to keep for themselves.

No one had forced them to surrender their wealth. Freely they had offered to follow the rules of the Church that served God, then schemed to go back on their bargain and lie their way into Christianity. From God, who had lavished on them every fruit of creation, they sought to withhold not only part of their coins but part of their souls.

In sonorous anger the great voice of Peter echoed in the Upper Room:

"Ananias!"

The deceiver began to tremble.

"Yes, Peter?"

"Why has Satan filled your heart to lie to the Holy Ghost?"

A gasp came from all the watching Christians. Lie to the Holy Ghost? Shocking! Incredible act of defiance! Of all sins, Jesus had hated hypocrisy most of all. Could Peter, chosen by Christ to be the first leader of His Church, possibly be mistaken? That thought, too, was shocking and incredible.

"And to keep back part of the price of the land?" boomed Peter, inexorable in his consuming indignation. "While it remained, wasn't it your own? After it was sold, wasn't it still in your own power? Why have you conceived this thing in your heart, Ananias? You have not lied to men—you have lied to God!"

Ananias, exposed in his sordid and unnecessary lie, turned pale as morning milk. Greater trembling seized his tall frame. He swayed sideways and back and fell in a heap.

Ananias, liar and cheat, the hypocrite who tried to hold out on God, was dead at the feet of the apostle, his gaping mouth and staring eyes close to his gift.

Solemn fear fell upon all who witnessed this ghastly fatality. Had God stricken Ananias dead with his lie still in his mouth? Was no chance given him to do penance? Or in that last moment had he understood the enormity of his offense? Had he realized that no man can hold back from God who is the Author of all man owns? Had perhaps his heart swooned with remorse in the presence of the Holy Ghost, and stopped beating in sorrow?

They were still asking questions among themselves, as some of the younger men hastened forward, wound the body of Ananias in a sheet, and carried him out and buried him, having just looked for Sapphira, no doubt, and found her missing from her house. Possibly she unwittingly passed that funeral procession in the street, for now she, too, was coming to the Cenacle, leaving her house shut behind her.

Sapphira climbed the stone stairway to the Upper Room, knowing nothing of the sudden death that had struck down Ananias there, only three hours before.

Peter instantly asked her:

"Tell me, Sapphira, whether you sold the land for so much—" and he named the price Ananias had reported.

"Yes," said Sapphira, full of duplicity. "For so much, exactly."

Peter shook his head and ran a tanned hand through his beard.

"Why have you agreed together," he marveled, "to tempt the spirit of the Lord? Behold, the feet of them who have buried your husband are at the door—and they shall carry you out!"

In that same instant, Sapphira, too, was seized with a trembling. Her lovely face became wan and fearful. Without a word, she fell dead at Peter's feet.

Many who had witnessed that tragic scene began to ponder on a curious analogy. Their thoughts darted from Ananias and Sapphira to another man and wife who began life with even greater blessings, thousands of years before: To Adam, the man who owned the earth, and Eve, whose beauty God's hands had fashioned. Adam and Eve, proud and ungrateful, had also thought to trick the Creator, and they had lost paradise.

Ananias and Sapphira had lost their lives. Only Jesus Christ, the

merciful, would know if the first to defy God in the new dispensation
had lost heaven as well.

Chapter 20.   THE SECOND IMPRISONMENT

THE people of Jerusalem and nearby towns had discovered an extraordinary fact. Peter's shadow had the power to heal their diseases.

From Bethany, the town of Lazarus; from Bethlehem, where Jesus
had been born in a stable; from Ain Karim, where once had lived the
father and mother of John the Baptist, and from a hundred other
villages, men came trooping with blankets and crude, homemade
litters. Sons and husbands and brothers and neighbors carried their
ill and their dying. Stretcher-beds lined the streets as Peter trudged
down from the Cenacle. The silhouetted shadow of the great, surging
form of the fisherman had only to cross the face of the suffering ones,
like a cloud over a lake, and fine health was restored.

"And greater things than these you shall do," the Master had promised them. Every promise was being fulfilled.

These healings had a powerful effect upon public opinion in Jerusalem. When Peter and John and the ever growing crowd of their
adherents repaired to Solomon's Porch in the Temple area and
preached, the throngs listened attentively to their words. These two
men had done signs and wonders before the eyes of all. Popular
clamor magnified their fame, under the windows of the Temple
priests. Every day more and more believers flocked to hear and be
baptized. The bearers of the sick came in increasing numbers, bringing with them those oppressed in body, mind, and spirit. And day by
day, every one was healed.

This growing procession appalled High Priest Caiphas. Even Annas,
his father-in-law, fretted at the spectacle. For many days they hesitated
to act, because, being more politicians than priests, they were afraid
of the people's voice. But their own fears betrayed them.

They called another indignation meeting, with a majority of the
Sanhedrin present, including the Pharisees as well as the Sadducees,
who did not believe in life after death. And after a great deal of
fulminating about the impudent teachings of these low-class Galileans
who stood on street corners talking to their converts, and after

especially reviling Peter and John, the judges reached a decision.
The Sanhedrin resolved to annihilate Christianity, root and branch.
Destroy the leaders and you destroy the movement; that was the
Sanhedrin theory. That same afternoon, just at gloaming, all twelve
apostles were arrested. Elegant guards from the Temple militia surrounded God's men on the street corners and hustled them off to the
foul cells of the common prison. The "house of the bound" the
people called this dungeon of the guardhouse.

To men not wrapped in divine grace, such a position would have
been deadly. No one could foretell what testimony might be brought
against the prisoners. There were liars at the trial of Jesus; could His
apostles expect truer justice than He had been given?

The twelve did not doubt that some grueling sentence awaited
them at the hands of the Sanhedrin judges. Yet they did not falter.
They knew that not even the grave can hold in bondage the children
of God. In spite of chains and fetters, bolts and bars, they sang the
old psalms together and recited the Lord's Prayer.

They were glad, but not greatly astonished, at what followed.

In the deepest darkness of night, the doors of their prison silently
opened before them. Beyond they could see the blue night of Jerusalem with its silvery lining of stars. There was no clanging of the iron
bolts, nor creaking of the leather hinges, no noise of any kind as the
door swung out and the clean, free air blew in upon them from the
frosty night.

An angel stood on the threshold; a messenger from heaven, clothed
in a quivery radiance, invisible to all eyes except those of the
twelve. His fine tone was audible only to their ears:

"Go! Stand and speak in the Temple to the people all the words
of this Life!"

What a command! They had been preaching in the Temple Porch
for many days so effectively, with so many converts, that here they
were in the watchtower, prisoners of the wrath of the high Jewish
tribunal.

Yet now they were told to leave the prison, to enter the Temple
itself in fresh defiance of the elders!

To even the gentlest of those ancients of the Sanhedrin that would
seem outrageous insolence. What were the apostles to do? Later generations might ask that question, but never Peter and John, nor their
companions in jail. God's angel had spoken.

"And," says St. Luke, "they having heard this, early in the morning entered into the Temple and taught."

Not in the porch. *In the Temple!*

The recoil from the Sanhedrin was instantaneous.

Chapter 21. GOD OR MEN?

CAIPHAS rose from his bed shortly after dawn, and without making his toilet or combing his voluptuous beard strode from his house to call the judges together.

Not that Caiphas knew the real situation; not as yet. He had only heard rumors that crowds were gathering, that a jail delivery, rioting, and bloodshed were imminent. So Caiphas and his cronies summoned the whole council and sent to the prison to have those twelve Christian fools brought to the judgment bar. They must be tried before the mobs freed them.

But the Temple officer and his mincing men returned from the keep of the tower, with a woebegone expression and no prisoners.

"Where are these Christians?" cried Caiphas, in a rage.

Almost brusquely the frightened officer made his report:

"We found the prison truly shut with all safety."

"Of course you did! Well?"

"And the keepers standing before the doors: but when we had opened, we found no man within."

There the elders had a mystery before breakfast.

To put an end to Jesus, His healings, preachings and power, they had nailed Him to a cross as a blasphemer. But the death of Jesus was only a beginning, as the members of the Sanhedrin were now really coming to see.

"Behold," a messenger told them, crowning miracle with impudence, "the men whom you put in prison are standing in the Temple and teaching the people."

The Captain and his Temple Guard were sent to fetch the fugitives. But they had special orders this time to be careful: no violence, mind!

"For they feared the people," St. Luke explains, "lest they should be stoned."

Such was the pitch of popularity to which Peter and John had climbed in the few weeks since the Holy Ghost had come upon them! The whole outraged membership of the elders, who had without compunction ordered Jesus to His death, would now deal softly with the Galilean boatmen whom Jesus had left to nurture His Church.

So, without violence, Peter and John stood once again in the great Hall of Stones and faced the Sanhedrin.

Caiphas, weary and a little bewildered, rested his puffy white hands on his lap, as he glared at these recalcitrants and said:

"Commanding, we commanded you that you should not teach in this Name. Yet see what you are doing! You have filled all Jerusalem with your doctrine."

The prisoners made no answer. There was, indeed, none to make; the accusation was true.

"And you have a mind," Caiphas went on, his voice cracking with bitter resentment, "to blame us to the crowds that listen to your talk; to bring the blood of this man Jesus upon us."

Upon whom else, elders, scribes, Pharisees? Who was guilty of His death, if not yourselves? The populace loved Him. Remember their joy, and the palms they flung before Him when He last entered Jerusalem? The love those Jews bore Him terrified you—you alone are guilty of His blood! But the words remain unspoken.

Peter, replying to Caiphas that morning, had a proper answer for him, one which made clear to all the Sanhedrin the Christian position:

"We ought to obey God," said Peter, "rather than men."

That utterance of Peter is the Christian answer to all the dictatorship of history, from Nero to Hitler and Stalin, and whatever others may lie beyond the years. However men may exalt the state, the soul's duty is to obey God rather than men whenever the two obediences conflict in conscience.

The judges stared silently at Peter, pondering the profundity in that simple phrase. Presently, Peter, without waiting for a further question, continued with a thought even more damning to the dignity of the court:

"The God of our fathers hath raised up Jesus, whom you put to death, hanging Him upon a tree. Him hath God exalted with His right hand, to be Prince and Saviour, to give repentance to Israel, and remission of sins. And we are witnesses of these things and the Holy Ghost, whom God hath given to all that obey Him."

Those quiet words of Peter slashed like a sword into the hearts of all who heard him.

Once again, history was repeating itself. When Jesus Christ was tried in this same Hall of Great Stones before these same judges less than three months ago, two objectors had defended His cause. So now, with Peter and John and the other apostles, though the atmosphere of the trial room was acrid with almost tangible hatred. Those words of Peter had stung the judges to the quick. Murder was in their hearts—judicial murder.

"They were cut to the heart," said Luke. "And they thought to put them to death."

But among the Pharisees was a doctor of the Law, named Gamaliel, a just citizen of high rank in Temple aristocracy. When Rabbi Gamaliel spoke, the Sanhedrin settled back to listen, for his wisdom was renowned, enhanced by the fact that he was a grandson of the famous Hillel. Gamaliel stood foremost among the scholars of Jerusalem, an authority on great literature and the most liberal man in the ranks of the Pharisaical conservatives. One of Gamaliel's students, graduated several years before, was a young Jew called Saul of Tarsus, as yet unknown in the great world.

Rabbi Gamaliel first asked that the twelve prisoners be led from the hall. Next, at his suggestion, Caiphas ordered that the courtroom be cleared of all spectators.

Then Gamaliel addressed the Sanhedrin. He spoke as a man of common sense, full of potent memories of past movements and excitements of the people. His argument stands today, as it did that afternoon, beyond the challenge of reason:

"Ye men of Israel, take heed to yourselves what you intend to do, as touching these men.

"For before these days rose up Theodas, affirming himself to be somebody, to whom a number of men, about four hundred, joined themselves: who was slain; and all that believed him were scattered, and brought to nothing. . . .

"And now, therefore, I say to you, refrain from these men, and let them alone; *for if this council or this work be of men, it will come to nought: but if it be of God, you cannot overthrow it, lest perhaps you be found even to fight against God.*"

And the Sanhedrin consented.

They did decide to release the Christians, but they were just as unwilling as had been the Pharaoh of Egypt, two thousand years ago, to let God's people go. As balm to their egotistic pride, they ordered all twelve prisoners to be whipped with a doubled strap of cowhide, scourging their bared backs and breasts, for each thirty-nine blows in all, and thirteen of them in front.

The apostles did not flinch from their flogging. The pain and the blood did not make them cringe and plead for mercy. Each could remember that Jesus had clearly warned them all these things would surely happen. *"The servant is not greater than the Master!"* If the judges were cruel to the Master, they would be no kinder to those who loved Him and served Him.

In their mind's ear the apostles heard again the words of the Lord: *"Blessed are they which are persecuted for righteousness' sake, for theirs is the kingdom of heaven."*

All bloody and beaten, Peter and John and the others were hauled back before the Sanhedrin to hear a final admonition.

They were to stop preaching. They must never again tell the people about Jesus, the crucified, who rose from the dead to save the souls of men, even the commonest men in the filthy gutters of Jerusalem—or even the judges of the Sanhedrin.

Luke tells us the apostles' reply, nothing in words but vivid in action:

"And they indeed went from the presence of the council, rejoicing that they were accounted worthy to suffer reproach for the Name of Jesus."

And daily in the Temple—and in the houses of their friends and of all others who wished to hear—"they ceased not to teach and preach Jesus Christ."

Chapter 22. STEPHEN AND THE CHOSEN SEVEN

So SWIFTLY was the Church growing that Peter soon realized that a more definite form of organization was needed. He acted promptly to set the new machinery in order.

The leader of any movement, especially a new and growing one, is troubled with the importunities of his followers. Some are envious. Some are jealous. Some are busybodies. And some, of course, come with honest grievances.

Peter faced, for example, a difficulty with the Grecian Jews who had embraced the new teaching and had been validly baptized in the name of the Father, and of the Son, and of the Holy Ghost. That sacrament should have brought peace to their hearts for the rest of their natural lives. Yet here they were, clamoring around Peter and his work table, insisting that the Church was already discriminating against them. The widows of the Jews from Greece were not given as much help as the widows of the Jews from Judaea. The Greeks felt they were being singled out as second-class persons while the Judaean relicts received preferential treatment.

Seven deacons should hear such disputes and settle them justly! That was the apostles' remedy for the plaint of the widows of Grecian Jews and for all the other squabbles which encroached on the time of apostles dedicated to launching a universal Church. Seven deacons— and what might a deacon be, please? Tell us, Peter, and you, Beloved John. Thousands of Christians must have that question answered immediately; something new is being started in our midst and innovation is both mother and father to suspicion.

A deacon is an assistant. Surely that definition is simple enough. Well, had God told Peter how to appoint assistants and who they were to be and what they were to be called? No. Patiently, Peter explained that this new plan carried no hint of a constitution, divinely fixed beforehand and now put into effect. It was simple that a new need had arisen in the life of the young Church, and with the guidance of the Holy Spirit, Peter was taking reasonable steps to meet it.

To critics of the plan, men who objected that now the Christians were setting up classes, groups, degrees, a hierarchy, the very things that had made the Pharisees such abominations, the reply was simple. Some organization was not only desirable; it was imperative.

Only by delegating some authority could the apostles go beyond the towering walls of the old city of Jerusalem to carry the Gospel on the next lap of its millennial journey throughout the world. Not only in Jerusalem were the twelve laboring those days. They were retaining connection with seedling Christian communities all over Palestine.

But Peter, though his word was law in the Church, did not wish to ram his decisions down the throats of his critics. The twelve, together in all things, decided to call a general conference of Christians. On a hillside just outside Jerusalem the multitude gathered.

And Peter on that bright morning, with a wind from the Dead Sea ruffling his beard, explained his idea of a deacon. It came from a Greek word that meant "minister," or "servant." Servants they were to be, ministers of charity, first in the third order of the Church ministry that was beginning slowly to take shape; below bishop and priest, but sharing with them in divinely bestowed power. Before long women would serve in kindred tasks, and they would be called deaconesses.

"It is not reason," he began, blunt and to the point as always, "that we should leave the Word of God and serve tables."

There was the core of the matter. The twelve all had received the Word of God, direct from Christ Himself. Were they to take time for the everyday needs of the faithful—of which "serve tables" was a symbol—a synecdoche—when others who had not known God on earth could tend those problems?

A murmur of understanding whistled through the throng.

"Wherefore," continued Peter, "brethren look you out among yourselves seven men of honest report, full of the Holy Ghost and wisdom, whom we may appoint over this business. But we will give ourselves continually to prayer and to the ministry of the Word."

The people, grasping the import of the decision, were wholly satisfied with the plan of Peter and the other apostles. Without much difficulty, they chose "the Seven," the first deacons of the Church.

One of the Seven was Nicolas, a proselyte from Antioch in Syria. He was a Greek, well able to help in at least one of the first disputes —those complaints of the Hellenistic widows. Of Nicolas recorded history has no more to say. But of one thing we may be sure—that on the day he was chosen by the Christians massed at the bottom of the hill outside Jerusalem, Nicolas was a man "of honest report, full of the Holy Ghost."

Timon, except for the fact that he was chosen that day as a deacon, is also lost in the mists of history. So, too, Prochorus. But two others of these seven died unforgettable deaths: Nicanor, who traveled to Cyprus and was martyred by the Roman Emperor Vespasian; and

Parmenas, who preached throughout Asia Minor, and died for his faith in Macedonia.

These five—Prochorus, Nicanor, Parmenas, Timon, and Nicolas—are dimmed figures. But their two companions, Philip and Stephen, are among the most famous saints in the galaxy of the faith and truly helped to shape the history of the world.

This Philip, who is called "the Evangelist" to avoid confusing him with the apostle Philip, was a Greek. Young, impetuous, a zealot of unquenchable enthusiasm for the Church, Philip was, like some of the apostles, a married man with a family. He had four daughters who were virgins and prophetesses. For a while Philip and his farseeing daughters lived in the magnificent seaport of Caesarea, but they died many years later in Herophilus in Asia, where their tombs were regarded as shrines long after apostolic times.

But it was Stephen—"a man full of faith and of the Holy Ghost"—who stood out. Young Stephen, who was to be first in anguish and first in glory among the martyred followers of Jesus Christ.

In the eloquent Greek language, "Stephen" meant a garland. The name graces St. Stephen, whose life and death were to change the destiny of millions.

The seven deacons chosen by the Christian assembly were led up before the half-moon of twelve apostles. The twelve closed their eyes as they prayed and, raising their hands, laid them on the heads of the deacons, in the first ordination ceremony of the Christian Church.

This "laying on of hands," which persists ritualistically until this day, was then as now a symbol of consecration to the service of God. So hands had been laid on Joshua's head when he succeeded Moses, and on the Levites—and now upon the seven deacons because they were being set apart for holy service. And the apostles prayed to God to communicate to these new servants the powers Christ had given to them. With that impressive ceremony, the meeting ended and all the Christians went back to their daily labor, singing as they returned.

The wisdom of appointing the deacons was immediately seen.

"And the Word of the Lord increased," Luke reported. "And the number of the disciples was multiplied in Jerusalem exceedingly and a great multitude of the priests also obeyed the faith.

"And Stephen, full of grace and fortitude, did great wonders and signs among the people."

In this very success lay the seeds of coming trouble.

Chapter 23. THE MAN WITH THE FACE OF
AN ANGEL

TROUBLESOME enough to hear of converts by thousands being made
to the Church, but when rabbis began deserting Herod's Temple to
be baptized in the Upper Room of the Last Supper, the fury of the
Temple aristocrats flamed high. All restraints of common sense, all
fears of outraging the popular will were devoured in their rage.

That any Sadducee should be going over to join the Christians was
inconceivable. Ever since the long-ago periods of the Maccabees, the
political power of the Temple hierarchy had swollen until, by bargaining behind closed doors with the Roman conquerors, it held
Judaea in the darkness of its pocket. The priesthood had become a
Sadducean aristocracy fattening on the enormous Temple revenues—
materialistic, corrupt, and without faith; opportunists who imitated
the agnosticism of their foreign rulers, paying lip service to altars and a
God whose existence seemed most problematical to them. Because of
these men the hands and feet of Jesus had been hammered to the cross.

That any of their high-bred number should kneel with a lot of
northern fishermen, sell their goods and share all things in common,
give to the poor, and preach the dignity and the immortality of the
individual soul through the redemption of the Risen Christ—here
was an offense most odious, a fire that must be stamped out to avoid
a conflagration.

The new trouble started in the Synagogue of the Libertines.

There were two synagogues in Jerusalem, distinct from the Temple
itself, but housed in one stone building. One was the synagogue of
African Jews from Cyrene and from the great harbor city of Alexandria, the other of the men from Cilicia and Asia.

Actually, these worshipers were former prisoners of war, taken captive in the campaign of Pompey and later freed by their Roman
masters. That was how they got the title of Libertines (men who had
been freed), which gave the name to the synagogue itself. They were
proud men, who thought especially well of themselves because they
had, by the grant of their captors, the privileges of Roman citizen-

ship, something the ordinary dweller in Judaea could never hope to obtain.

Within the memory of many living today, a trace of this old double congregation was found in Jerusalem: a large limestone block from the debris of nearly two thousand years, inscribed in Greek: "Theodotus . . . built this synagogue for the reading of the Law . . . and also this hostel for the need of those coming from the outside."

In the Synagogue of the Libertines, Stephen, the deacon, began to preach.

Perhaps the sight of the handsome Stephen aroused the wrath of these foreign sons of orthodoxy. His was the eager, young eloquence that was making converts of apparently sound Sadducean ecclesiastics. They began to ask questions, innocent seeming at first, and they received innocent answers. Followed questions of more crafty design, legal quibbles, and tricks of logic. Stephen answered them all directly without hesitation, because he was afire with grace and faith. And, as Luke said afterward, those alien Jews "were not able to resist the wisdom and the spirit that spoke."

But again, what had happened at the trial of the Master, occurred at an inquisition of the disciple. False witnesses were not hard to find. Soon enough they appeared in this synagogue, suborned men, who perjured themselves:

"We have heard him speak blasphemous words against Moses and against God."

No one had heard Stephen speak a syllable of blasphemy. But at that lying accusation the elders and petty officials threw themselves about, tearing their garments in traditional fashion and raising a general uproar, stirring the people to a smaller repetition of the mockery of Jesus' trial.

Crowds rushed young Stephen through the streets, as if he had been caught in the act of stealing God from the pockets of Annas. With shouts and jeers they dragged Stephen to the Hall of Stones, to stand where Jesus had stood, while the Temple aristocracy squatted once more on the purple cushions with the golden tassels. Another trial for blasphemy was under way.

The false witnesses were glib in their testimony, as always:

"This man ceases not to speak words against the holy place and the Law; for we have heard him say that this Jesus of Nazareth shall destroy this place and shall change the traditions which Moses delivered unto us!"

And now something happened for which none of the Sanhedrin judges could account. Not one of them could deny the evidence of his eyes. The prisoner Stephen stood at the mercy of their power. Yet,

". . . all that sat in the council, looking steadfastly on him, saw his face as it had been the face of an angel."

BOOK THREE

The Man from Tarsus

Chapter 24. "STONE HIM TO DEATH!"

AND what is the charge against this prisoner with the face of an angel?

Blasphemy, sirs; my lords and elders of the Sanhedrin, this beautiful young man called Stephen is a blasphemer: you have heard the evidence. Now, Stephen, it is your turn! Caiphas, his oxlike eyes dimmed with frustration, turned toward the defendant who was following in the footsteps of the Master the court had ordered crucified. Would these Christians never stop mouthing His Name, as if daring —no, worse—entreating to die as He had died? Said Caiphas in sepulchral tones:

"Prisoner, give answer: are these things so?"

Jesus, at His trial in this Hall of Great Stones, had remained mute until His final, cataclysmic admission that He was the Christ. But Stephen, the deacon, whose zeal had worked many miracles and changed many hearts, now began impetuously to address the court. Evening shadows lengthened in the vast chamber of justice and candles were being lighted as he began to speak in overpowering defense of Christ and His infant Church, an impassioned rehearsal of the books of the Old Testament in the light of the new dispensation.

"Men, brethren and fathers," Stephen began. "Listen to me. The God of glory appeared unto our father, Abraham, when he was in Mesopotamia before he dwelt in Charan, and said to him: 'Go forth out of thy country, and from thy kindred, and come into the land which I shall shew thee.'

"Then he went out of the land of the Chaldeans, and dwelt in Charan. And from thence, after his father was dead, He removed him into this land, wherein you now dwell. And He gave him no inheritance in it; no, not the pace of a foot. But He promised to give it him in possession, and to his seed after him, when as yet he had no child. And God said to him: That his seed should sojourn in a strange country, and that they should bring them under bondage, and treat them evil four hundred years.

" 'And the nation which they shall serve will I judge,' said the Lord; 'and after these things they shall go out, and shall serve Me in this place.'

"And He gave him the covenant of circumcision, and so he begot Isaac, and circumcised him the eighth day; and Isaac begot Jacob; and Jacob the twelve patriarchs. And the patriarchs, through envy, sold Joseph into Egypt; and God was with him, and delivered him out of all his tribulations; and He gave him favour and wisdom in the sight of Pharaoh, the king of Egypt; and he appointed him governor over Egypt, and over all his house.

"Now there came a famine upon all Egypt and Canaan, and great tribulation; and our fathers found no food. But when Jacob had heard that there was corn in Egypt, he sent our fathers first: and at the second time, Joseph was known by his brethren, and his kindred was made known to Pharaoh. And Joseph sending, called thither Jacob, his father, and all his kindred, seventy-five souls. So Jacob went down into Egypt; and he died, and our fathers. And they were translated into Sichem, and were laid in the sepulchre that Abraham bought for a sum of money of the sons of Hemor, the son of Sichem.

"And when the time of the promise drew near, which God had promised to Abraham, the people increased, and were multiplied in Egypt. Till another king arose in Egypt, who knew not Joseph. This same dealing craftily with our race, afflicted our fathers, that they should expose their children, to the end they might not be kept alive.

"At the same time was Moses born, and he was acceptable to God: who was nourished three months in his father's house. And when he was exposed, Pharaoh's daughter took him up, and nourished him for her own son. And Moses was instructed in all the wisdom of the Egyptians; and he was mighty in his words and in his deeds. And when he was full forty years old, it came into his heart to visit his brethren, the children of Israel.

"And when he had seen one of them suffer wrong, he defended him; and striking the Egyptian, he avenged him who suffered the injury. And he thought that his brethren understood that God by his hand would save them; but they understood it not. And the day following, he shewed himself to them when they were at strife; and would have reconciled them in peace, saying: 'Men, ye are brethren; why hurt you one another?'

"But he that did the injury to his neighbour thrust him away, saying: 'Who hath appointed thee prince and judge over us? What, wilt thou kill me, as thou didst yesterday kill the Egyptian?' And Moses fled upon this word, and was a stranger in the land of Midian, where he begot two sons.

"And when forty years were expired, there appeared to him in the desert of Mount Sinai, an angel in a flame of fire in a bush. And Moses seeing it, wondered at the sight. And as he drew near to view it, the voice of the Lord came upon him, saying:

" 'I am the God of thy fathers; the God of Abraham, the God of Isaac, and the God of Jacob.' And Moses being terrified, durst not behold.

"And the Lord said to him: 'Loose the shoes from thy feet, for the place wherein thou standest, is holy ground. Seeing I have seen the affliction of My people which is in Egypt, and I have heard their groaning, and am come down to deliver them. And now come, and I will send thee into Egypt.'

"This Moses, whom they refused, saying: 'Who hath appointed thee prince and judge?' him God sent to be prince and redeemer by the hand of the angel who appeared to him in the bush. He brought them out, doing wonders and signs in the land of Egypt, and in the Red Sea, and in the desert forty years.

"This is that Moses who said to the children of Israel: 'A prophet shall God raise up to you of your own brethren, as myself: Him shall you hear.'

"This is he that was in the church in the wilderness, with the angel who spoke to him on Mount Sinai, and with our fathers; who received the words of life to give unto us. Whom our fathers would not obey, but thrust him away, and in their hearts turned back into Egypt, saying to Aaron: 'Make us gods to go before us. For as for this Moses, who brought us out of the land of Egypt, we know not what is become of him.'

"And they made a calf in those days, and offered sacrifices to the idol, and rejoiced in the works of their own hands. And God turned, and gave them up to serve the host of heaven, as it is written in the books of the prophets: 'Did you offer victims and sacrifices to Me for forty years, in the desert, O house of Israel? And you took unto you the tabernacle of Moloch, and the star of your god Rempham, figures which you made to adore them. And I will carry you away beyond Babylon.'

"The tabernacle of the testimony was with our fathers in the desert, as God ordained for them, speaking to Moses, that he should make it according to the form which he had seen. Which also our fathers receiving, brought in with Jesus [Josue], into the possession of the Gentiles, whom God drove out before the face of our fathers, unto the days of David, who found grace before God, and desired to find a tabernacle for the God of Jacob.

"But Solomon built Him a house.

"Yet the most High dwelleth not in houses made by hands, as the prophet saith: 'Heaven is My throne, and the earth My footstool. What house will you build Me? saith the Lord; or what is the place of My resting? Hath not My hand made all these things?' "

For an instant Stephen paused. Then looking deep into the silent faces of his judges he said:

"You stiff-necked and uncircumcised in heart and ears, you always resist the Holy Ghost: as your fathers did, so do you also!

"Which of the prophets have not your fathers persecuted? And they have slain them who foretold of the coming of the Just One; of Whom you have been now the betrayers and murderers: who have received the law by the disposition of angels, and have not kept it!"

Thus far Stephen carried them with a supernatural flow of eloquence. His judges had sat like men bespelled, paralyzed in one posture, mouths open, ears cocked, their eyes seeing some bottomless pit, unable to move to strike down this impudent speaker.

Abraham had worshiped God truly and correctly, he was reminding them; and God had chosen the fathers before Moses was born, long before the first tabernacle and the first Temple had been built. Moses himself had witnessed Christ, so Stephen told the men who had judged Christ in this very room. All of these rites and ceremonies, of which the Sanhedrin was so proud and so meticulous, had been commanded by God for a practical end and for a limited time. Now the time was up, and Stephen told them so. He denounced them in fearless terms, for having rebelled against God and destroyed His Messiah, and so being guilty of the murder of their Christ, the Just One.

Such was the climax of Stephen's defense. When he finished, and wiped his brow, it was as if some conjuration was lifted from the court. Almost with one accord, the judges screamed at him in their guilty wrath.

"They were cut to the heart," as Luke was to report; they "gnashed with their teeth at him."

But Stephen looked steadfastly up to the roof as if he could see through the beams and rafters, straight into heaven. He had no doubt what his fate was to be, and no fear.

"Behold I see the heavens opened and the Son of Man standing on the right hand of God!" he declared.

That was enough.

This ecstatic devotion to Christ turned the Sanhedrin judges into hysterical fanatics. Stopping their ears, they sprang up at the prisoner, shoved him forth from the courtroom, and screamed:

"Stone him! Stone him! Stone him to the death!"

And there was no difference between their voices and the throaty cries of the directed mobs on the crucifixion eve, when they had dutifully screeched their hatred:

"Crucify Him! Crucify Him!"

Chapter 25. THE EXECUTIONER

STONING was an elaborate and legalistic form of execution, and the rules had to be observed.

A curious-looking young man marched with the mob as they pushed Stephen across the Temple courtyard. His job, by Caiphas' command, was to see that Stephen be killed according to due process of law. The executioner captain's name was Saul of Tarsus.

He had long been Gamaliel's brightest pupil. He knew by memory the cumbersome list of religious rules and regulations which governed the Jews. Saul of Tarsus understood just how an impudent Christian should be put to death.

The stoning must take place outside the city walls. The formal witnesses were already trudging at Captain Saul's heels as he followed the rioters toward the Gate of the Sheep. In the name of the congregation of the Libertines in whose presence Stephen had committed his blasphemy and in the name of the court that had just tried and condemned him, the witnesses for the prosecution must march with the guards and ceremoniously cast the first stones.

Captain Saul was glad of the witnesses' company, glad that this insolent Stephen was to meet his doom quickly, with his offense still moist upon his lips. Saul perfectly understood the "depravity" of Stephen's crime—his was an offense against the moral order, a premeditated transgression against the majesty of God.

Saul could quote straight from Leviticus: "*Bring forth the blasphemer without the camp and let them that heard him put their hands on his head and let all the people stone him.*"

Saul was a prematurely balding man with a shiny high forehead and a manner of suppressed fury, for all his erudition in the Laws of Moses. He looked upon Stephen, running and stumbling before the crowd that harassed him, and hated the young man because he saw him as a law violator, a blasphemer. "*He that blasphemeth the name of the Lord, dying, let him die.*"

There had been a strange look on the face of Stephen when they tried him. Healings were credited to him of the ailing and crippled. Probably, thought Saul, he was in secret a diviner, a seer. "*A man or woman in whom there is a pythonical or divining spirit, dying, let him die: they shall stone them: their blood be upon them.*" Saul knew that law from Exodus; he felt perfectly justified amidst this raving mob, eager for the brutal killing of a helpless victim.

Stephen traversed a route that strengthened him, although his tormentors had no idea that it would. The Via Dolorosa had no meaning for them. But for Stephen every cobblestone in the way of sorrow that he trod was dear and precious for the sake of Him who had already walked this way, burdened with the cross. The blood of Jesus had stained the stones of these streets. Past the home of Caiphas, past the place where Veronica laid her veil against Christ's face, and where His mother met Him; through the identical gate that led to

Calvary, Stephen now was escorted. But he was not to go up the sacred hill of the three crosses. His destination was nearer!

Before him was another Golgotha, a rock that looked like a skull, and near by, in the stony hip of the hill, a pit like the entrance to a mine. Stacked all around, in readiness for just such executions, were piles of rocks of the size recommended in the Scriptures. This was the Beth ha Segila, the traditional place of stoning, hard by Jeremiah's grotto. Here the woman taken in the very act of adultery would have been slain if Jesus had not said: "*Let him who is without sin among you cast the first stone.*"

Saul of Tarsus was a man on fire to obey God's laws, and he believed this murder of Stephen was the right thing to do. He would have said that he personally was indeed without sin.

Outside the city, by a little hill which fulfilled the tradition of taking the victim's life at a mount, the crowd made a three-quarter circle, with Stephen standing facing them, his back against the rock. The witnesses came and laid their hands on his curly head.

Lesser guards began roughly to disrobe him. They tore away his faded brown cloak—a rectangular, seamless piece of coarse wool so folded and sewn that the front was left open on either side and large holes provided for the free movement of the arms. Stephen had worn it by day, slept under its warmth at night, and when he had to ride a donkey, he folded it for a saddle. Now the cloak was ripped away and thrown to the muddy ground. So with his tunic, the sleeveless gray woolen garment next to his skin and which hung down to his knees. His tattered sandals were pulled from his feet. He stood, naked and white and clean and helpless.

The witnesses took off their own cloaks, and laid them at Saul's feet.

"And they stoned Stephen," says Luke.

Methodically they stoned him, but they could not stop their ears against the loud cries of his strong voice: "Lord Jesus, receive my spirit."

Kneeling there with the stones flying at him, sharp flints slashing his eyes, thick rounded ones breaking the bones under his brown curls, he raised his voice so that all could hear him—the mob with their stones and curses and the watching Christians weeping—as he prayed:

"Lord, lay not this sin to their charge."

He was following in his own way the example of his crucified Master.

"And when he had said this," Luke was to write, "he fell asleep."

For one last moment the young eyes of the first martyr, dying, looked into the eyes of Saul, the captain of his executioners. That gaze of a man sanctified in suffering, a sight utterly, fantastically new to the intellectual overseer of these agonies, was never to lose its freshness in Saul's memory. He was consenting to and supervising the death of Stephen. That fact would be hard to live down in the blazing glory waiting, as yet unknown in the future of this immensely capable and complicated man. Nor would Saul ever recover from the shock of the elevated look on the face of this believer who had so simply fallen asleep in the Lord. Such ecstasy affronted Saul, and roused him to unreasoning wrath.

For the moment, his job was done. He waited until the witnesses reclaimed their outer garments.

Then, brooding and thoughtful, young Saul of Tarsus started on his long walk home.

Chapter 26. SAUL THE PERSECUTOR

SAUL was a powerhouse of two energies, physical and mental. He thought and studied constantly and intensely, but he was also abundantly stored with nervous force and lean muscular power—a fellow capable of prodigious journeys, of untiring labor, and feats of endurance. He was both contemplative and active, thinker and doer.

On the night of the day that Stephen died, it would have seemed impossible that this strict Jew born and bred, this zealot and scholar of the Mosaic Law, was destined for so high a place in the history of a Christian world. Incredible to expect that Saul should turn from the old Judaism he had just defended so fiercely, to spend his life proclaiming Christianity all over the civilized earth, offering it with sublime certainty as the universal religion for man.

In a letter he would one day write to the men of the city called Philippi, thirty years after Stephen's death, Saul was to describe himself as "of the stock of Israel, of the tribe of Benjamin, an Hebrew of the Hebrews; according to the law, a Pharisee."

His was a rugged birthland in the southeastern part of Asia Minor, at the foot of the blue mountains of the Amanus range. But Tarsus, his home town, was a bustling city at the junction of the trade routes with the fabulous spice countries of the Far East. In that city which was both a colorful and wealthy merchant center and a military defense point, Saul was born, the son of a Jew who enjoyed the high privilege of being a citizen of Rome.

On this the first St. Stephen's night, in A.D. 34, Saul, deeply disturbed, sat alone after the stoning and reviewed his life. Tarsus and his childhood seemed very near. There was a bitter restless pulse to his nostalgic thoughts, some unspoken indictment of himself. And that was curious, because Saul, trained logician that he was, honest thinker that he meant to be, knew no reason to reproach himself.

He forced himself to look back to his beginning in Tarsus, the city that lay on the green flow of slime and floating trash that was called the River Cydnus. The modern Tarsus is wholly on the western bank, but in Saul's youth the stinking stream ran straight through the heart of town just as two thousand years later, when I was a boy, a foul stream snaked mistily through the midst of Baltimore and slew its victims with typhoid. Tarsus had its frequent plagues and epidemics. But it was a proud place, rejoicing in the reputation of ancient learning.

The old influences that once made Tarsus an Oriental city had by no means vanished in the boyhood of Saul. The noisy mysticism and rascality born of commerce in far-eastern by-lanes and bazaars mingled with the more self-conscious gallantry of Greek settlers. Tarsus boasted of her famous scholars. The Emperor Augustus had been instructed by Athenodorus the Stoic, a teacher from Saul's birthtown. The University of Tarsus promoted the Greek Stoic philosophy, and no studious youth like Saul could escape the Hellenic culture pervading the air of his city.

Once, because the townspeople supported Julius Caesar during the civil wars, they had changed the name from Tarsus to Juliopolis, and Caesar had paid a visit to the city on that happy occasion. Saul's father had cherished that memory. The old gentleman had also loved to sit by winter fire or in summer shade telling his son of the day when he had seen the radiant queen of Egypt, voluptuous Cleopatra. Up that loathsome Cydnus River Cleopatra had sailed past Tarsus in her gilded galley in the year 38 B.C. on her way to Rome. That barge

of Cleopatra's gave rise, sixteen centuries later, to an impassioned
bravura passage of Shakespeare, filched from Plutarch's crude treasure
and transformed incomparably:

> The barge she sat in, like a burnish'd throne,
> Burn'd on the water. The poop was beaten gold;
> Purple the sails, and so perfumed that
> The winds were lovesick with them; the oars were silver,
> Which to the tune of flutes kept stroke, and made
> The water which they beat to follow faster,
> As amorous of their strokes. For her own person,
> It beggar'd all description. . . .

Saul smiled as he remembered his father's glowing tales, and the
romance of his own boyhood thoughts.

The streets where Saul played are now buried twenty feet deep
under the shabby sidewalks of the modern town, but it is still an
exciting experience to visit Tarsus. Today the town is full of houses
made of mud and stone in the very same fashion as those built in the
time of Saul. The same kind of semitropical trees quiver in the wind.
There are opulent shade-woods of myrtle and oleander, pomegranate,
fig, orange, and citron. The farmers reap good harvests still of grain
and cotton, of valonia, of sesame seed, and apples and apricots and
grapes which grow in the foothills that creep near to the town.

As Saul sat in his room in Jerusalem brooding after the unnerving
sight of Stephen's death, the memories of his first fifteen years in
Tarsus were jumbled like a ragbag in his brain. He rummaged through
them in silence, seeking a clue to the curious feeling of self-reproach
that plagued him in the twilight.

The most potent force in shaping Saul's life had been his fervor
for the Jewish faith.

Religiously, the people of Tarsus were a broad and tolerant mixture. The Gentiles there had a god of their own of whom everybody
was fond. Baaltarz, he was called, the local way of saying "Lord of
Tarsus," but he was also entangled, in a way nobody in town would
bother to make clear even to himself, with Zeus, the supreme Greek
deity. The town also had a lesser god called Sandon, who was really
Hercules hiding out in Cilicia under an assumed provincial name.

But Saul had been born into a good Jewish family. With his
mother's milk he had learned about the One True God. He gloried

in his Hebrew heritage, even though he had been born far from the
homeland of the twelve tribes. He spoke proudly of the "advantage
of the Jew" as "entrusted with the oracles of God." He did not dream
that he could ever lose that pride in the greater awareness that
all living men and women, Jew and Gentile, were potential children
of God.

That truth would have seemed ridiculous indeed to Saul as he sat
by the open window of his room in Jerusalem and pondered the days
of his youth.

He remembered himself as a boy leaving home every morning to go
to the synagogue school. Up beside the door of his house was a scroll
rolled like a tube and kept in a metal box on the lintel post—a mezu-
zah on which the Ten Commandments were tenderly inscribed on
fine parchment. That metal box and scroll were constant reminder
that he was of a tribe that obeyed the Law—the tribe of Benjamin.

Saul had fun as well as study; he knew how to race, could wrestle
and box; he understood the need of fair play in such games. But he
cherished the memory of the musty little synagogue, so plain in appearance beside the white columns of the pagan Greek temple set in
a green grove and filled with florid figures in elegant stone. There
were no statues where Saul worshiped, only an endless store of truth
and wisdom.

Like all his fellows, Saul took personal pride in his synagogue, laid
out in three divisions: one part for the congregation, an elevated
space for the rabbis, and a third part called the Ark of the Covenant,
where the Scroll of the Law lay in solemn privacy. These three divisions were an imitation of the Jerusalem Temple, which in his boyhood Saul had resolved someday to see for himself. When he went
to the synagogue he wore a fringed prayer shawl like a special badge
that set him apart from the polyglot crowds through which he
marched on his way to school.

But Saul, like every other Jewish boy, was also required to learn a
trade. Most of the boys followed in their father's work, and Saul became a tentmaker in Tarsus. Every part of that ancient business Saul
had to learn, including the trader's skill in bartering with stubborn
mountaineers over the price to be paid for the hair of their goats. He
must comb and weave the hair into cloth, cut and sew it, dip in dyes
or bleaches, stretch the fabric, twist the ropes, shape the poles, and
then display and sell tents to the customers who came to the bazaar.

In after years, Saul was manfully proud of his trade, and of supporting himself wherever he went.

Soon enough, he came to the time of his bar mitzvah. At thirteen years old, by law and custom he was no longer a child but a man. In synagogue ritual the leather phylacteries were bound upon his left arm and upon his forehead. And his lessons grew increasingly harder, for he was preparing to go to Jerusalem and study under a master.

When he was about fifteen, financed by the savings of his father, he sailed from Tarsus to the Judaean coast, and made his way to Jerusalem. There he registered at the School of Gamaliel—that distinguished rabbi who would one day sit as one of the Sanhedrin in the trial of Jesus, the Christ, and later speak vigorous and sage advice at the hearing of the twelve apostles.

Gamaliel never had a more eager or willing pupil, or one better prepared. At heart, Saul was already a Pharisee. He had grown up memorizing the innumerable Pharisaic rules and regulations. Furthermore, old Gamaliel saw that this was a young man content to be away from home. Some of Saul's family already lived in Jerusalem; he would not be lonesome in the sprawling, noisy place. He lived with a married sister, whose small son was one day to save his uncle's life.

Saul responded to Rabbi Gamaliel's great learning and his austere kindliness to a hard-studying pupil. This august teacher was a scholar of great literature; he knew the philosophers and the poets of Athens, and he wakened a fellow-taste in Saul that bound pupil and schoolmaster closer together.

Yet Saul was no slavish imitator of his instructor. Gamaliel had a streak of liberalism that sometimes shocked his fellows in the Sanhedrin and always repelled Saul. Gamaliel had no love for the undeviating jots and tittles of the Law, and he tried gently to instill some of his heart-warming freedom of spirit in his pupils.

Saul withstood him. He clung to the familiar, the burdening and boring ordinances of the Pharisees. He had never been more legalistic than when he presided at Stephen's killing. He had felt perfectly justified in countenancing that stoning in the afternoon.

But in the evening, as Saul meditated in the balmy twilight wind, the last words, the inspired voice, the dying eyes of Stephen continued to haunt him.

He knew no way to explain the restlessness of his conscience this night. He felt that legally—and therefore spiritually—he was leading a blameless life. He did not suspect that there might be an inner meaning of the Law, a truth made clear to fishermen like Peter and John the Beloved, to which he, the learned man, was still blind. Nor did he dream of the stern power within his own soul that was presently to indict him, confiscating his peace. He did not know that in his heart lay evil, unsubdued, that would take many a solitary year to overthrow.

He had for every sin a precise Pharisaic definition. But he lacked the corresponding impulse to know God, to love Him, and to serve Him as a profound, intimate, and transforming experience.

The day would come when Saul would discover in himself every man's problem of ambivalence: the two-headed wish, one turned toward light and the other yearning for the darkness; one wish in harmony with the will of God and the other in sympathy with evil.

How can a man escape that trap, and liberate himself from guilt? What can a man do to find peace of mind, Saul? Could a study of the Law, close attention to the Prophets, break the joint of the double wish—and so make the whole man "die" to the flesh and be free from it forever?

At the moment, Saul would have counseled anyone who asked such questions to be patient. Deliverance could come to the chosen people only through the promised Messiah, whom Saul believed was still to come.

All that mattered in Saul's philosophy was that the Jews should be the righteous nation they had so often failed to be in their long history from Abraham and Judas Maccabeus. If the Jews were truly righteous, not even the Roman Empire could hold them enslaved. The divine promises of a Messiah would be fulfilled.

What angered Saul to the depths of his being was the spreading belief that the Messiah had already come to earth, the unschooled child of a carpenter's wife in Nazareth; a wandering wayside exhorter, whose tracks were dogged with fantastic tales of miracles; that He was a blasphemer, tried, condemned, and crucified on Calvary Hill. Old fishermen friends of Jesus of Nazareth were raising their voices in the streets of Jerusalem, claiming to have seen Him risen from the dead, fulfilling all the prophecies, to prove that He was indeed the Messiah.

To Saul's aristocratic mind, such claims were outrageous. The tale

of Jesus as the Christ, the Messiah, the Promised One, was a blasphemous caricature of Saul's most sacredly fostered concepts. No
wonder this rabid young Pharisee fumed and squirmed, finding no
relaxation at all as he meditated at the open window. The suggestion
that the Resurrection was the supreme credential of the whole Christian mystery, Saul idly dismissed, spitting out of the window in con-
tempt. *Am-ha-aretz!* That was a word to describe Galilean common
folk, a gem from the vocabulary of a scholar like Saul.

And in that moment, Saul was seized at last with the climax to
his vast restlessness and distress.

The time called for action. Christianity would have to be wiped
out. Weak toleration must be forthwith abandoned. He would war
to the teeth against the new faith, fulfill his duty as he saw it.

He would become Saul, the persecutor.

Chapter 27. HAVOC IN THE CHURCH

THE bloodthirsty fury that now possessed Saul fed on something
deep and unsatisfied, which made his hands itch for whips and stones
and the extirpation of all of Stephen's kind.

Had Stephen's blunt interpretation of Israel's history lodged in
Saul's conscience? The elders, the scribes, the rabbis, and the fathers
of judgment had been mistaken before in history not once, but many
times. Why not again? Saul tried to bury the question Stephen had
asked. Ruthlessly he set out to exterminate the Christians.

Everywhere he saw the glory on the face of the dying Stephen,
repeatedly stamped in joy on the faces of these Christians, even in
torture and death. Nothing infuriated Saul more.

At Saul's instigation, a great new plan of persecution was organized
against the Church. In the red-walled Roman room of his house, old
Annas received Caiphas and Saul, to plot this final destruction.

Within a few dozen hours there was left in Jerusalem, of all the
thousands of converts, not one overt, openly confessing Christian.
They scattered in haste, hiding with friends and relatives in remote
little villages in Judaea or scuttling into the heretical mountain
fortresses of Samaria.

Except the apostles! The twelve remained in Jerusalem.

"As for Saul, he made havoc of the church."

So Luke reported. He said that Saul was "entering into every house and haling men and women, committing them to prison."

The first mass persecution of the Christians was on in earnest. The zealot Saul was in his thirtieth year, no imposing or romantic figure but strong as a wrestler, short with broad shoulders, a pale but rugged athlete. A terrifying image in the eyes of every Christian.

By slander as well as by edicts, warrants, and due process of law, the "revolutionaries" were attacked. Propaganda was one of Saul's most potent weapons. To the Pharisees, it was supremely important that the Christians' reputation for kindness and mercy be wiped from the tablet of public opinion. So Saul had the word passed from barracks to tavern; from synagogue to street corner:

"These Christians are wicked fellows and all of them deserve death, for they are idolators, blasphemers, apostates. Away with the Christians."

Among the volatile mobs of Jerusalem these planted scandals spread like smoke. As the chief police agent of the Sanhedrin, Saul pounced in swift raids on suspected houses. Not only in Jerusalem did he lead his squads. Spreading out into small Judaean hamlets, he reached to the farthest part of the kingdom. No place remained where a Christian could feel safe.

Yet, in spite of floggings to break down witnesses; in spite of prizes for telltales and denouncers; in spite of persecution almost unexampled in severity, most of the Christians escaped and survived.

Among them was the mother of Jesus, whose inspired example of faith and closeness to the Holy Ghost heartened all followers of her Son. Mary was helpful to them every moment of her life, doing a woman's work among them as if there were distinction upon her—cooking, washing, nursing, encouraging—toiling with those other holy women of the first days of the Church. They prepared, too, for the frequent sacrament of Holy Communion; they spent hours on their knees, in prayer and transport. And where Mary went, John the Beloved went, as the Lord had commanded him.

By Mary, the mother, by Peter and John and all the apostles, the hearts of the crowds of converts were buoyed up in the midst of night-scampering in flight, all the way to Samaria, where Saul's whips and swords and stones could not reach.

At the risk of their lives the apostles maintained their headquarters in Jerusalem. But it soon became apparent that some of the leaders were needed elsewhere. The dispersal of the Christians was scattering the faith abroad in strange old places. The refugees' converts needed spiritual leadership; they were in pitiful need of more instruction and understanding of their exalting new spiritual experience.

Among those who went fearlessly forth was, of course, Peter. He walked the roads from town to town, repeating what, with his own ears, he had heard Jesus Christ say; and what, with his own eyes, he had seen Jesus Christ do. Peter had a wide and dangerous circuit to tramp. There were Christian communities now not only in Palestine but also in the countries lying farther north.

Peter walked in the cloak of God's grace, unafraid and unharmed, in spite of Saul of Tarsus.

Chapter 28.   THE SORCERER OF SAMARIA

YET always Peter returned to Jerusalem, in spite of Saul and all his cruelties. Jerusalem with its Upper Room was the cradle of Christianity, and Peter made the holy city a Holy See—the first archbishopric. And since the twelve could not possibly reach all the new churches, and still keep their ranks firm against Saul's persecution, Peter turned to his deacons for mission duty.

First to go out was Philip the evangelist, a native of Caesarea on the Mediterranean shore, a friendly man of large and quick human sympathies.

His first journey was to Samaria, near the home of the Good Samaritan, close to the place where Christ had offered the water of life to the woman with too many husbands. To that city (called Nablus today) went Philip the evangelist and "preached Christ unto them," with great success, as Luke reported:

"For unclean spirits, crying with loud voice, came out of many that were possessed with them: and many taken with palsies, and that were lame, were healed. And there was great joy in that city."

Then the people from the Nablus hills came to him, frightened mountaineers who lowered their voices and looked over their shoulders as they told the evangelist the scandal of Samaria concerning a man named Simon. The whole countryside lived in apprehension of him. People said he was a conjurer, who in violation of the strict command of Moses practiced magical powers, communed in dark caves over burning pots, and in the midst of green and purple vapors spoke with familiar and wicked spirits. A magician, in the time of Peter and Philip, was not an entertainer, but one who used sorcery to bewitch and influence the people, as the gray-curled Simon was doing.

Oddly enough, Simon Magus was already seeking the deacon's acquaintance; knocking at his door, ready to bargain with him.

Simon Magus had seen with his own eyes the healing in Philip's prayers. He himself could not do such things, though his incantations were older than Solomon. He would pay well for the secret by which Philip made the dumb to speak, the blind to see, and the crippled to leap and dance. Hell was eager to do business with heaven.

Simon's eminence as a wonderworker, a soothsayer, a thaumaturge, as the Greeks might call him, was complete. But Simon knew that he could be dislodged by a greater magician, and so with his toothless mouth gaping through the gray-black tangles of his beard he looked sideways as he whispered to Philip. He wanted to strike a bargain with his Christian rival to save himself from being outclassed.

Philip explained gently that he was merely the instrument of holy powers and sacred truths, and sent Simon Magus on his way.

Fiercely the magician renewed his spells, bewitching the people by his humming voice, his recurring, unintelligible syllables, his swaying from side to side, his rhythmic clanging of battered old cymbals from beyond the long desert—by all the fakir tricks of the Far East he had learned in a runaway youth with a caravan master. He could plant a mango seed and make it bloom swiftly into a tree. He could make his wrists beat with pulses that contradicted each other, and he could dance on beds of heated stones. Such yogi tricks, some general hypnosis, and a dash of sleight of hand, along with his habit of fastening curses on his enemies, made Simon Magus again a man to be feared, placated, and paid.

The Samaritans saved their face by ascribing the supernatural to the trickster, saying to each other, "This man has the great power of God."

But Philip knew better. He feared no one, and was deceived by no one. He would not listen to any renewed proposal of a bargain.

Philip the evangelist followed a very simple program. Briefly but with vivid lovingness he told the Samaritans the story of Jesus from the Annunciation to the Resurrection. He explained the teachings of the Master. Finally he healed the diseases of these men and women, even as Christ had promised His followers they should be able to do.

Such miracles were beyond Simon Magus. The magician was frightened. He knew there were not drachmas and talents enough in Samaria to tempt Philip into selling the secret of his powers. So he followed Philip from street to street, town to town, watching and listening, hoping to catch on to the trick. Unwittingly and wholly without intention, he was exposing himself to Divine Truth and that is a dangerous hazard for anyone. It put Simon in the way of escaping evil and saving his soul.

Before long the sly, determined old sorcerer was kneeling before Philip, waiting to be baptized. Simon Magus joined himself with the thousands of Samaritans, men and women, who were converted by Philip!

Philip could not shake off Simon Magus. Every dumb man who was made to speak caused the magician to praise God with new found faith; every blind man whose sight was restored made Simon's eyes shine with his new illumination.

"He continued with Philip," Luke reported; "and wondered, beholding the miracles and signs which were done."

Chapter 29. "GIVE ME ALSO THIS POWER!"

WHEN news of the sorcerer's conversion, along with that of the thousands of others whom Philip had baptized, reached the Cenacle in Jerusalem, the twelve resolved that Peter and John the Beloved together must go to Samaria to solidify these gains.

Peter's and John's first act after greeting Philip was to call a general assembly of all the converted Samaritans. They came not to lecture to them, nor to improve on Philip's admirable way of teaching, but to implore of heaven the descending gift of the Holy Ghost for these newcomers. They had journeyed here to confirm what Philip had preached: to confirm and ordain.

But Peter had another unspoken purpose. He knew of the sorcerer who became a Christian and he understood well the latent danger to the faith in the presence of Simon Magus.

Who could believe sorcerers? Their talk was often as false as their sleeves, full of hidden things yet to be produced. Peter hoped that Simon Magus had indeed dropped the crimson cloak of duplicity, that his heart had actually changed. But he feared that the magician still meant to deceive the people and so become a false prophet.

Years later Peter in his Second Epistle would state the attitude of the Church toward all such men:

"But there were also false prophets among the people, even as there shall be among you lying teachers, who shall bring in sects of perdition, and deny the Lord Who bought them: bringing upon themselves swift destruction. And many shall follow their riotousnesses, through whom the way of truth shall be evil spoken of. And through covetousness shall they with feigned words make merchandise of you. Whose judgment now of a long time lingereth not, and their perdition slumbereth not. . . .

"The Lord knoweth how to deliver the godly from temptation, but to reserve the unjust unto the day of judgment to be tormented. And especially them who walk after the flesh in the lust of uncleanness, and despise government, audacious, self willed, they fear not to bring in sects, blaspheming. . . .

"These are fountains without water, and clouds tossed with whirlwinds, to whom the mist of darkness is reserved. For, speaking proud words of vanity, they allure by the desires of fleshly riotousness, those who for a little while escape, such as converse in error: promising them liberty, whereas they themselves are the slaves of corruption. For by whom a man is overcome, of the same also he is the slave. . . .

"For it had been better for them not to have known the way of justice, than after they have known it, to turn back from that holy commandment which was delivered to them. For, that of the true proverb has happened to them: 'The dog is returned to his vomit'; and, 'The sow that was washed, to her wallowing in the mire.' "

This letter had its roots in the meeting between Peter and the magician of Samaria.

For the Holy Ghost, being entreated, was descending as Peter and John laid their hands on the heads of the converts, Simon Magus among them. And the Paraclete revealed the true inwardness of the magician.

This laying of hands on heads was confirmation, imposed by prayer and action. When the faithful were baptized they had indeed received the grace of the Holy Ghost. But when Peter and John confirmed them, after final instruction and their full acceptance of faith, grace came in full plenitude, in a flow of spiritual gifts.

Here, on the chilly height above the Vale of Shechem, where Abraham and Jacob and his sons had encamped, they held the confirmation service, while Simon the man of magic watched with crafty eagerness. As they received the power of the Comforter, the experience seized the converts' souls, glowing in their eyes and resounding in their deep-toned amens and shrill halleluiahs.

The sight of that mass blessing was too much for the frustrated Simon, who was at that moment to give his name to one of the vilest of sins. Ever since, "simony" has been the label given to the foolhardy error of those who seek to purchase grace.

Trembling before Peter, Simon held out long, thin, weaving fingers and gasped:

"Give me also this power!"

From his bosom he wrenched a bag, bulging with gold and silver; he was there to traffic in sacred things; he was ready to pay. He did not see the sorrow in John's gentle face, nor the kindling ire in Peter's eye.

"Give me also this power," pleaded Simon, feverishly clinking the bag, "that on whomsoever I lay hands, he may receive the Holy Ghost."

That eruptive fisherman Peter did not attack Simon, although his enormous hands must have itched to be at the scoundrel. With restraint and dignity, Peter gave Simon his lesson before the whole ecstatic audience:

"Keep your money to yourself, to perish with you, because you have thought that the gift of God may be purchased with money! You have no part nor lot in this matter. For your heart is not right in the sight of God. Do penance therefore for this your wickedness; and pray to God, that perhaps this thought of your heart may be forgiven you. For I see you are in the gall of bitterness, and in the bonds of iniquity."

Simon cringed. He bent far over, covering his eyes and nose with the right arm, and his voice came muffled from under his mountebank's gaudy coat:

"Pray you for me to the Lord! That none of these things which you have spoken may come upon me." And he hastened down the hillside, away from the apostles.

Peter and John watched him go, with prayer in their hearts.

Before long Simon Magus would set out for Rome. Amid the dizzy whirl of imperial society, he would perform feats of divination with birds and flowers and shadows. He would essay to read the future in a crystal ball mined from a cave. He would translate the lines in the palms of foolish and fragrant court ladies, spell out the ends of their amourettes and promise them new lovers, all for fat fees. Even in the emperor's household he would perform his tricks. Like Cagliostro and his "virgin bride" Teliciana, at the dayspring of the French Revolution seventeen hundred years later, Simon Magus the Impostor would insist that he had the powers that belong to God, and that his beautiful paramour, Helena, was his "First Intelligence"—what a name for a partner in bed and black magic! All the empty-headed sycophants who toadied to the emperor and his court would declare that this Simon Magus was a messenger straight from God. All this in the face of the Christian missionary labors in Rome!

As Simon Magus trudged away from the kneeling converts and was lost in the hills, Peter had an uneasy feeling that he had not seen the last of him. And Peter did indeed pray to the Lord to save Simon's soul.

Chapter 30. PHILIP AND THE ETHIOPIAN

Fond farewells echoed from the crowds of Samaritan converts as the two apostles and Philip the evangelist descended into the Vale of Shechem and started their long walk back to Jerusalem.

At the end of that journey Philip, for the first time in his career as a Christian, had a supernatural experience. An angel spoke to him and told him what to do.

Now Philip was well schooled in the history of visitations of the past: the celestial visitors who came without wings and broke bread, or wrestled, or beckoned, and who gave divine instructions from the days of Abraham, Isaac, and Jacob down to the Annunciation when Mary learned that she was to become the mother of Christ. He knew, too, of the recent delivery of the twelve apostles from prison.

But Philip the evangelist had never expected that any such thing would happen to him, or that the voice of an angel would be a prelude to a special miracle.

Dusk had spread a veil of deepening lavender and gold over the tawny walls and gates and the fortified towers of Jerusalem when Philip heard a voice that could belong only to an angel:

"Philip, arise!"

The young missionary had been lying on his folded blanket ready for a night's sleep. He sprang to his feet, obedient and alert.

"Arise and go toward the South, into the way that goes down from Jerusalem unto Gaza, which is desert."

With the same unquestioning agreeableness of the patriarch Abraham, Philip instantly did as he was told. He was weary from the journey to Samaria and the excitements of the visit there. He had hoped to remain in Jerusalem. But in the gathering darkness, with no sleep and with very little preparation, he explained about the vision to Peter, picked up his blanket, and started off briskly, walking southward.

Why should he go to Gaza? That town, ancient even before the long-ago days of Joshua, was the southernmost of the five principal cities of the Philistines. In Gaza Samson had met Delilah and had his head shaved, and there too had brought the Temple crashing down upon his Philistine captors and himself. But now the region of that caravan city was desert.

Why should Philip go there? He walked for nearly two days, southwest on the road to Gaza, before he understood.

At a resting place near a wayside inn he saw a chariot drawn up in the shade. Two horses released from the shafts were tethered to a palm tree, and there, lurched forward in the gilded and ornamented vehicle, sat a dark-skinned man arrayed in costly garments of colored brocade. In his hand he held an open scroll, on which Philip could make out the shape of Hebrew characters.

Another traveler, leaving the inn refreshed, noticed Philip's interest in the dusky wayfarer.

"He's quite a figure," the newcomer explained. "The landlord was just telling me all about him. He is an Ethiopian!"

Philip nodded agreeably; obviously the studious man in the golden chariot hailed from the land we call Nubia, whose extreme northern boundary was then near the first cataract of the Nile. But the merchant who had just dined, and well, was eager to tell Philip more about him:

"This one is a eunuch who says he is not a eunuch."

Philip stared blankly, as the chatterer continued:

"But yes! He has the title of being eunuch, and is a personage of great authority in Ethiopia. He has charge of all the treasure of the queen mother, Candace. And, while he has the title of eunuch, as well as the title of treasurer, he says that having the title of eunuch in his country does not necessarily mean that he is actually a eunuch. Oh, no! For centuries, real eunuchs were employed in such positions of responsibility. But he says that the word eunuch in the official title had long since lost its meaning."

Philip did not pay close attention to the man's prattle. Some inner compulsion trained his interest solely on the Ethiopian.

With a polite nod of his head and a lift of the hand, the deacon sped his loquacious companion on his way. Then as he stood alone, once again Philip the evangelist heard the angelic voice:

"Go near and join yourself to this chariot."

Philip approached the dark stranger. He could hear him toilsomely, haltingly reading from his scroll. And he saw that the scroll was the Book of Isaiah.

Philip's shadow fell on the dark hands of the queen's treasurer.

"Do you understand what you are reading there?" asked Philip gently.

The eunuch held his place with a forefinger as he looked up, puzzled and humbled. With a great sigh he asked:

"How can I? How can I unless somebody explains it to me?"

And moving over, with a smile that showed great, clean pearly teeth, he made room for the white man to sit beside him.

"What part of Isaiah are you reading?" asked Philip, and the Ethiopian, voice soft and reverent, repeated these verses:

"*He was led as a sheep to the slaughter; and like a lamb without voice before his shearer, so opened He not His mouth:*

"*In His humility His judgment was taken away. His generation who shall declare, for His life shall be taken from the earth?*"

Was that beyond the Ethiopian's understanding? Yes, unless someone should guide him. Who is the Bible talking about in those two verses? Could Philip explain?

Most certainly he could and would. He had seen these prophecies made by Isaiah nearly a thousand years before come true so recently that Jerusalem was still talking about it. Jesus Christ had most certainly been led as a lamb to the slaughter. Often He had referred to Himself as the Lamb of God that takes away the sin of the world. And Jesus had not opened His mouth to defend Himself before the razor-edged attack of Annas and Caiphas. He had been humiliated and judged, and His life was taken from the earth.

The Ethiopian listened attentively. Tired of sitting in the chariot, he rolled up the scroll and slid it up his sleeve, as he walked with Philip through a patch of woods. Not far off they could hear the ripple and splash of flowing water.

The Ethiopian financier asked penetrating questions. A most unusual fellow, Philip realized; a black man from the wild-tribe regions of Cush, who, putting aside all the idolatry which surrounded him, had learned Hebrew and was reading the Law and the Prophets.

Soon they returned, hitched the horses again to the chariot, and resumed the journey with Philip riding beside the eager stranger.

"Then," St. Luke reported, "Philip, opening his mouth and beginning at this Scripture, preached unto him Jesus."

They came to the tumbling, noisy little stream that rambled through the patch of woods on its way to the sea and the inquisitive eunuch asked another question:

"Philip, see—here is water. What hinders me to be baptized?"

"What hinders you, Ethiopian? Nothing. You want to be baptized. If you believe with all your heart, you may."

And the Ethiopian answered, as he looked into Philip's eyes: "I believe that Jesus Christ is the Son of God."

The horses were reined to a halt, and the great tether stones with holes in them were thrown to the ground, their chains fastened to the necks of the steeds. Now the two men forced their way through the brambles and down to the stream edged with green and bending tamarisks. There the money master of the Queen of Ethiopia was baptized and became a Christian.

He was the first black man to have his soul cleansed with water and with grace in the name of the Father, and of the Son, and of the Holy Ghost. Alas, it has been nearly two thousand years since the baptism of the first black convert, and yet there are people today who call themselves Christians and want segregation of souls.

Through this man, standing with him in the river, Philip was starting the great branch of the Church that was to wax so strong and last so long in North Africa. He would make many more converts on his solitary life journey. But the church of the dark-skinned Christians would have the most lasting effect of all Philip's efforts. It endured for centuries, until error and bickering with the foundations of the faith brought the historic church of Africa to feebleness.

Ecstatically, the queen's financier waded out of the shallow water— and gasped. He found himself alone. Philip had vanished from his sight, and he saw him no more.

The Holy Ghost had given a signal example of grace so that all mankind might share the faith. A living man had disappeared bodily at the moment of a soul's rebirth.

The Ethiopian did not bother to dry off his head or feet. Laboriously he lifted the stones weighted for tethering and led his horses back into harness. Then off he drove, rejoicing at heaven's favor.

And Philip? Where was he? At first he was not quite clear about that himself. When he opened his eyes, he had traveled some twenty miles north. He was in Azotus, a town on the coast, almost midway between Gaza and the ancient city called Joppa, from which Jonah had sailed to meet his whale centuries before.

In Ashdod, as the Jews called Azotus, Philip shook himself out of the trance of his heavenly transport, and started again on his journey, preaching in all the cities until he came to Caesarea.

The great missionary efforts were getting under way.

For Peter there were busy trips ahead. Presently he was to start an extensive tour, through Lydda—spelled that way but pronounced "Lud" even to our own times—and the maritime cities along the Philistine coast.

In his absence he left the Church in the care of the two apostles named James. James called the Greater, the thundering brother of John the Beloved, was attracting many new converts in Jerusalem, inviting on himself the deadly fury of the Temple authority. And one ardently austere cousin of Jesus, James called the Less, brother of Jude, was already moving into a position of authority second only to Peter. With their help and the untiring efforts of the other apostles, the deacons, and the evergrowing mass of believers, the Christian Church was growing despite all obstacles.

No one was more keenly aware of the increasing power of Christianity than its worst enemy, more bitter far than even Caiphas and Annas—Saul. His first ferocious attacks had not even stunted the growth of the inspired Church. Failure rankled in him; he knew the faith must be destroyed instantly, or never. And knowing that, Saul began to persecute the Christians as they had never been smitten before.

For Saul, as Luke described him, was "breathing out threatenings and slaughter against the disciples of the Lord."

And Saul decided that by fire and sword he would carry the persecution all the way to Damascus.

Chapter 31. THE ROAD TO DAMASCUS

SAUL set out on the road to Damascus with death in his heart. He could not know that he was about to keep a rendezvous with Life itself.

To Saul's mind "Pharisaism or Jesus" was the sole issue. And Saul the Pharisee went out to battle the upstart Church with a sword in his hand, and a troop of cavalry and foot soldiers at his command to pursue the Christians who had fled Jerusalem.

The military unit was the gift of Caiphas, high priest of the Jerusalem Temple. In Saul, Caiphas had recognized the perfect instrument to wipe out Christianity: a resolute man, well-educated, seething with zeal. Caiphas had given him a packet of official letters, waxed and imprinted with the seal of the high priest, and addressed to all the synagogues to the north.

Saul meant to scour the land as far north as the great desert. He promised Caiphas he would bring back, bound and captive, every Christian that he found.

But for many days and nights he rode without finding a single follower of Jesus, without excitement of any kind until he was drawing near to Damascus. From his white horse Saul could see the well-tended green gardens lying all around the ancient city and the two rivers whose embrace made this plain a lovely place of rich harvest. Even under the heel of Rome, as Damascus now was, being governed by an ethnarch called Aretas, a local king set up by the Roman Emperor, the people looked happy.

Saul, covered with dust, his throat dry, was anticipating the good dinner and the sweet night's repose he knew he could expect at the principal inn under the roofed bazaar of the "Street That Is Called Straight."

The border of the town was not more than half a mile away when Saul suddenly swayed in his saddle.

Everything he could see and hear and feel all around him underwent a change. There was a chill wind blowing at him, a blinding light shining on him from the heavens, and the roar of great waters in his ears.

Saul clutched at the reins but his palsied hands could not hold them. He pushed with his heels against the stirrups, but his ankles quaked and all power had gone out of his legs. With a great gasp he realized he had no strength to help himself. He fell to the ground and lay there helpless.

Then the roaring sound ceased and he heard a Voice assuring but compassionate:

"Saul! Saul! Why do you persecute Me?"

Groaning, not daring to lift his face from the earth, Saul replied: "Lord, who are you?"

And the answer came in winning tones:

"I am Jesus, whom you persecute. It is hard for you to kick against the goad."

There could be no answer to that. Saul knew what the words meant, especially in relation to himself. A goad was a long stick about nine feet in length, sharpened at one end for poking at cattle. And the cattle could not kick against it, for the herdsman was nine feet away. Saul felt very much as helpless now. He sensed, dimly, that that same futile rebellion had been at the root of his emotional storms in the weeks since Stephen's death.

Trembling and astonished, Saul faltered the question that spelled his immediate, instantaneous surrender:

"Lord, what will You have me to do?"

The voice of the Lord replied to the man lying face down in the dust:

"Arise and go into the city and there it shall be told you what you must do."

And the Voice seemed to pale away in the wind.

Saul raised his head, drew himself up to a sitting position, and shook himself. His soldiers stood, amazed and troubled, in a great circle. They, too, had heard the Voice; and yet they had seen no man speak except Saul, their captain. They stood in silence that was like a spell. Then two of them took Saul by the armpits and raised him to his feet. But Saul's groping hands, as they made to let go of him, told them a shocking truth.

Saul was blind!

Saul never doubted he had actually seen Jesus. Years later, in the first letter he wrote to the Corinthians, he would rehearse the familiar history of Christ's death, burial, and Resurrection. He would remind the people of Corinth that the risen Christ had appeared to Peter and the rest of the twelve, that He had been seen by more than five hundred disciples at once, many of whom were still alive when that letter was being written. And then he added, with fervent humility and thanksgiving:

"And last of all, He was seen also by me, as by one born out of due time.

"For I am the least of the apostles, who am not worthy to be called an apostle, because I persecuted the Church of God.

"But by the grace of God, I am what I am; and His grace in me hath not been void, but I have laboured more abundantly than all they: yet not I, but the grace of God with me."

Skeptics still scoff at this encounter. Nearly two thousand years away from evidence, with no testimony for their own theories, they dismiss Saul's conversion as an epileptic fit. The line of years from then to now quakes with countless epileptics, not one of whom has written a single letter that affected the world, nor converted peoples, nor captured the imagination of posterity. Only Saul did that; Saul, of whom no fit was reported before Damascus or since. No skeptic can dispute the complete change in life of Saul, or what suffering he endured for it.

In that one blinding, falling moment Saul became another man. The hunter of Christians, the heresy detective became in one instant full of yearning to be a Christian.

He had seen God. And trembling before that glory, stripped naked of his intellectual pretenses, he had cried out in the hope and fear of all believers:

"Lord, what would You have me to do?"

Saul let his soldiers lead him slowly toward the open gate of Damascus. Strangely, he felt no humiliation in being blind, helpless in the hands of underlings.

He was going into the city, as the Lord had commanded him, to wait to be told what next he must do. To him nothing else mattered.

Chapter 32. PAUL!

FOR three days, Saul was a problem in the house of a Christian who bore the unfortunate name of Judas.

The infamous reputation of the betrayer of Jesus had been such that this second Judas, this good man, has not fared well in the memories of the faithful. Yet he deserves to be remembered with hosannas.

His act was of sublime charity. He knew that Saul was the Christians' worst enemy. He also knew that Saul had met with some sudden accident outside the city gate. Judas was not so gullible as to hope that kindness would appease Saul; mercy in the eyes of the anti-Christians was a weakness. Judas had nothing to expect and much to fear when he opened the door of his house, behind the Street That Is Called Straight, and allowed the weakened Saul to be laid in his own bed.

For three days and three nights the soldiers of Saul stood guard over Judas' house while their captain lay in bed.

"Saul talks to himself," they said to one another. "He is a very sick man."

But none of the advice or the weird prescriptions of Damascus doctors were of help. Saul was blind. He ate nothing and he drank nothing. His lips moved, and he whispered softly.

One man in Damascus knew what Saul was trying to say. His name was Ananias and he is not to be confused with the liar of the same name. Here was a new part of Christian history with a new Judas and a new Ananias, accidentally serving as symbols of a better future.

To this second and admirable Ananias the Lord spoke directly, in a vision:

"Ananias!"

And not unlike devout men of the Old Testament, Ananias replied:

"Behold, I am here, Lord!"

And the Voice continued:

"Arise! And go into the Street That Is Called Straight! And seek in the house of Judas, one named Saul of Tarsus!"

A name to ignite panic in any Christian heart, Saul of Tarsus!

"For behold—he prays!"

Ananias had been instructed in the mercy and forgiveness of God. He knew that God will forgive trespasses only as we forgive them who trespass against us. But Saul was a living terror, "breathing out threatenings and slaughter against the disciples of the Lord."

And even while Ananias was cowering in the presence of such fearful instructions, a kind of vision came at the same time, halfway across the city, to the distracted mind of blinded and helpless Saul. He saw someone entering the bedroom of Judas' house, a stranger who laid pale and trembling hands over Saul's eyes.

At the instant of that vision, Ananias was already pale and trembling.

"Lord," he protested, overwhelmed with his terror, "I have heard by many of this man, how much evil he has done to Your saints in Jerusalem. And right here in Damascus he has authority from the chief priests of the Temple to bind everybody who dares to invoke Your Name."

There was a moment's silence, and then the Lord spoke with a firmness of command not to be mistaken:

"Ananias!"

"Lord?"

"Go your way. For this man is to Me a vessel of election, to carry My Name before the Gentiles, and kings, and the children of Israel. For I will show him what great things he must suffer for My Name's sake."

There could be no reply except instant obedience.

A minute later, Ananias set off down the narrow and deserted paths of early morning, to look for Saul in the house of Judas.

The sun was not yet up, and the room was dim as the messenger of Christ stood by the bed and spoke to the tossing, blinded man of Tarsus:

"Brother Saul."

The hands of Ananias, pale and trembling, touched the eyelids of the stricken man.

"Brother Saul, the Lord Jesus has sent me."

A sound like a groan came from the lips of Saul, weighted with profound and grateful relief, as if he had waited in anguish for this call.

"The Lord Jesus has sent me," Ananias repeated; "He that appeared to you in the way as you came; that you may receive your sight and be filled with the Holy Ghost."

To see again. Oh, yes, please, merciful Lord! And to be filled with the Holy Ghost! The Holy Ghost that I had sworn to drive from the hearts of men in the name of God and the Sanhedrin.

"And immediately there fell from his eyes, as it were, scales, and he received his sight. And rising up, he was baptized."

Saul baptized! Now, there was a tale the Christians back in Judaea would find it hard to believe. By the grapevine that passed from Damascus to Joppa, from Nazareth and Capernaum even to Jericho, and through Galilee into Samaria and wherever the Christians were hiding in the underground, the word would go out that Saul, the persecutor, had been stricken blind near the western gate of Damascus; had seen the Lord Jesus and heard His Voice, had been healed of his blindness by a Syrian Christian, and that now he was himself a Christian.

Who could be expected to believe a wild story like that?

Yet it was literally true. Barely able to stand in the weakness of joints and waist and thighs that was the aftermath of his fall, Saul nevertheless held himself stubbornly erect and suffered Ananias to pour the water over him in the name of the Father, and of the Son, and of the Holy Ghost.

Saul could see the room filled with sunrise; the bed, the chairs, the table, and the sweating candle; he could see the face of his new friends, Judas and Ananias.

In that moment Saul became truly, irrevocably, a new man. He was born again.

And he chose to mark that hour of transformation by shedding the Hebrew name Saul, by which all men knew him. He chose instead to be known by the name he had seldom used, his official name as a Roman citizen.

Instead of Saul, the man of Tarsus would from that day of baptism till the end of time be known as Paul.

Chapter 33. ASSASSINS AT THE GATES

AND what did Paul do when the scales fell from his eyes, and he was filled with the Holy Ghost?

He did what the daughter of Jairus did when Jesus Christ brought her back to life from death. He went to the kitchen and got something to eat.

He paced the common room of Judas' house, scarcely able to contain the emotions soaring in his spirit. Tears and laughter struggled within him—exuberance of a man freed from a dark prison and tears of wonder at the terrible nearness of heaven.

The eyes in his head were clearer than ever, and it was a joy to see. The plain tables, the stools and benches and pillows, the jug of wine, the rust-colored drapes, the tiny motes of dust shimmering before the sun-filled window—each new sight was a delight.

Glory to God. I can see! Paul hunched his shoulders and hugged that blessing to him as he walked up and down the room.

Yet another, more wondrous marvel filled him, so that he could scarce find breath to speak.

The eyes of his body had been sightless only three days. The eyes of his soul had been blind for his whole life. Into the darkness of his spirit at the moment of his baptism had burst the light of eternity, dazzling, almost unbearable in its purity.

The instant the water fell on him from the hands of Ananias, Paul had realized that this blessing was a sacrament of intimate potency. He had not been ignorant of Christian customs. In his persecution he had learned to recognize the outward show of the new faith, and he had thought he understood them. In their baptism he had seen only a revival of the old "make-holy" cleansing ceremonies of the Jews. He had heard that Jesus had permitted Himself to be baptized by John the Baptist, and Paul had sneered at the notion of a God who would feel the need of being cleansed.

Now Paul saw that Jesus had transformed the meaning of that rite of water and words, making it the passport to a new life. At Jesus' baptism the Holy Ghost descended on Him visibly in the form of a dove, winging from the sky. When Paul was baptized, the Holy Ghost filled him, as promised by the Voice Ananias had heard.

But for this day of miracle and rebirth Paul could only be silent, listening to Ananias and Judas expound the new faith.

Freedom overwhelmed him, release from the restless, unspoken search of years, from the torments of masked sin and hidden despair, which he was later to describe so vividly in his letters. The hatred that had lashed him on his bloody road to persecution was gone, and the divine love which he was to spread down through the ages, possessed him.

Like every other sincere Pharisee, Paul had always believed the Messiah would come. He had rigorously and sincerely struggled for righteousness in himself and in the whole nation of Jews, seeking in the intricate maze of the Law for the key to the messianic age. He had attacked the Christians, convinced that he was protecting the world against a movement that might harm the process of salvation.

And in spite of his hatred, God had come to him. He had seen the Messiah.

If ever a man understood the true meaning of "conversion," it was Paul. He had been literally turned around. Where he had sought to sow death, he had found the Living Spirit. Where he thought to serve God by crushing a blasphemous sect, he had met God face to face and heard His divine reproach. Even in that moment of his vision of Christ, Paul had expected only wrath from God. Instead he had met the fullness of Christ's mercy.

In the dusk of Judas' common room, Paul stood in the traditional Jewish attitude of prayer, arms outstretched, and face lifted up to heaven. He prayed that Jesus Christ, whom he had persecuted, would make him worthy of the blessing he had been given.

And silently, humbly, he thanked the God he had so misunderstood.

For some days, Luke has reported, Paul remained with the disciples in the city of Damascus.

The new convert pleaded for more instruction and for personal reminiscences from those Damascans who had met Jesus and heard His message. But Paul did more than that. He was a fiery, headstrong man, and once he got his strength back, he could not stand idly by, while a moral revolution cleansed his soul. All in an instant he had been redeemed; he must pass on the experience to others. What convert has not known the same overmastering impulse to share joy? Paul could not wait to proclaim the Gospel up and down the streets and roads, in houses and synagogues: the good news that he had seen Jesus, who was, beyond question, the Messianic Son of God.

Paul went into the Damascus synagogue and began to preach Christianity! And his listeners, both the Jews who had become Christians and those who had not, were stunned into puzzled silence.

What were they to make of this extraordinary and magnetic figure? He was telling them that Jesus Christ, the Redeemer, replaced the old Law in the form, the medium, by which a man related himself to God. Even those Christians who had fully accepted Paul's conversion as sincere were startled by his words. He was declaring to them that Christ, the Messiah, had brought a new dispensation, fulfilling and taking precedence over the Law of Moses. What Paul was saying seemed to go far beyond the teachings of the twelve apostles, and his words had a dangerous tang. What right had any newcomer, a few weeks after baptism, to seek to improve on the teachings of the twelve? The Christians of Damascus shifted uneasily in their synagogue seats.

Nor were the rabbis and the Pharisees happy over Paul's preaching! They seethed under the burning eloquence of this turncoat, this renegade. What had happened to their young defender, the persecutor sent from Jerusalem to rid Damascus of the Christian blasphemers?

In both camps controversy raged over Paul. Pharisee and Christian alike asked the same questions:

"Is this man not known as Saul, the persecutor? He was sent out to destroy everyone who believed in the Name of Jesus, wasn't he? Didn't he come here swearing to carry off every Christian bound and captive, back to the high priests? Then what does this change mean? Is he really converted? Or does he strike a pose, setting some trap?"

He was a magnetic figure standing before them, dressed simply and yet with the certain elegance that distinguishes a man who lives in a capital city and associates with the best people.

No contemporary portrait of Paul survives, but there remain to us a fourth-century diptych and a large medallion from the Roman cemetery of Domitilla, as well as a glass dish in the British Museum depicting Paul and Peter. From these, and certain ancient writings, we can visualize Paul with fair certainty.

He was not more than three cubits tall, and since a cubit was a foot and a half of our measuring, Paul, who had breathed forth fire and slaughter, was less than five feet tall. But he was broad-shouldered. Early athletic victories had hardened his well-conditioned body. He was sinewy and graceful in spite of his prematurely balding head and the early gray that encroached on his close-knit eyebrows and thick beard in this his thirtieth year. Yet it was not his stalwart figure, nor his fair complexion, nor the decision suggested by the long, aquiline nose, nor yet his impelling manner that held the crowded synagogue silent.

What transformed Paul, bespelling his hearers, was his fire of faith, a zeal that flashed and flared in those enormous eyes that were like two draft windows in a human furnace. He who often conceded that his bearing was not impressive stood in the Damascus synagogue and impressed everyone within sound of his voice, beginning there a ministry for Christ that was to last thirty-nine years.

Day by day his eloquence grew more potent. In spite of whispers and mutters, in spite of antagonism and suspicion, Paul confounded the skeptics. He made uncounted converts.

The scribes and the Pharisees were outraged, and they consulted together on the best way to kill Paul. They were still sure murder was the most effective answer to Christianity. Kill them off—kill this turncoat persecutor—and you are done with the matter!

No one reminded them that the same thought pattern had put John the Baptist's head in a dancer's hands. Nor that Caiphas had used the identical argument with Annas when they contrived the fate of Jesus Christ. Nor that the same idea had brought young Stephen to the Hill of Stoning, where Paul, the man the Damascan Pharisees now plotted to kill, had presided over the brutal death of that first martyr. It takes centuries for the enemies of God to learn that the blood of murdered believers is the water that nurtures belief!

Day and night, the assassins were waiting a convenient chance to strike at Paul.

But, as St. Luke reports, Paul was fully warned of his enemies' ambush.

"The Pharisees have called you a traitor to your own class, Paul. They are on watch by the shore of the Abana river. They know you like to walk and meditate there—"

"These men have knives, Paul, and scarves for garroting your throat.

They lurk in the stalls and bazaars under the roof of the Street That Is Called Straight."

"They are hiding outside Ananias' house this minute—waiting for you!"

"They are at every gate—expecting you to flee!"

Today the traveler to Damascus may see the rock-walled house which tradition says is the original house of Ananias. As long as memory can go back, men have said this arched and vaulted place, with the circular opening in the roof, is the room where Saul was baptized. When I was there I found it easy to believe that this incontrovertibly ancient domicile, now turned into a shrine, is the veritable spot its priests believe it to be.

But there is another ruin in Damascus with a touching importance in the story of Paul, the crumbling remains of what was once the city wall—a heap of roughhewn rocks, arched door, and steps and tower, with a few pillars still standing like stone ghosts.

Ananias and the other Christians were resolved to save Paul's life. They dared not keep him in Damascus another day. The ordinary exits from the city, the massive gates, swarmed with Paul's murderous enemies. He could not leave by the highways, and hope to live.

Ananias had the answer. That night he and his fellow disciples left his house carrying a large basket. As they lurched down the street with their heavy load, an occasional orange or pear toppled from the basket and rolled along the cobblestones. The assassins, lurking in the shadows, spat contemptuously, and turned to keep closer guard on the stone house where Paul had been baptized.

Through the silent streets, shrouded by the moonless dark, the disciples hastened with their burden to an isolated part of the city wall. They unpacked the fruit, tied sturdy ropes to the handles of the basket, and lowered it, bumping and tipping, over the wall.

As the stanch wicker bottom touched the ground, Paul scrambled out and waved a farewell to the watching shadows of Ananias and his friends.

Along the black road Paul now made his way alone. Some of the soldiers who had originally come with him to Damascus were still in the town, conspiring with his foes to murder him there, or in Jerusalem should he escape the guards at the Damascus gate.

But Paul did not go toward the Holy City. As he himself was to tell later in a vivid piece of autobiography written to the Galatians:

"Neither went I up to Jerusalem, to them who were apostles before me; but I went into Arabia, and returned again to Damascus. Then after three years I went up to Jerusalem to see Peter and abode with him fifteen days. . . . Now the things which I write unto you, behold, before God, I lie not."

So Paul would have three years to think over the weighty matters that teemed in his brain as he hurried along in the dark after his escape. Three years of contemplation and retreat—only then did he go to see Peter, the founding rock of the Church.

By then Paul knew the full measure of his own soul and its destiny.

Chapter 34. THE DESERT

WITHOUT Paul's personal statement that he waited three years before presenting himself to Peter, it would be easy to misread the facts Luke recites in The Acts. His narrative glides over those three years as if they had no significance. Yet they were among the most important in Paul's life.

Paul went into the desert wilderness to be alone with God. He retreated from the world to the silence where he could nourish his spirit; explore his new views, weigh and test his understanding and his will.

As Jesus had often "gone apart from the crowds" to renew Himself in solitary prayer, so now Paul went, driven by a command beyond his own mind. Jesus had spent three years instructing the world; Paul took three years to satisfy his intellect and bridle his will. He went from Damascus into Arabia seeking to hear the Voice of God in his soul. But he would not have dared hope for the stunning gift of glory that he was to receive, visions and revelations that were to dazzle Paul's memory the rest of his days.

Nearly fifteen years later Paul was to write to his friends in Corinth, telling them part of the wonderment of that desert time. And even that long after those soul-shaking days in the desert, Paul's voice breaks with emotion as he speaks of himself often in the third person, an anonymity many of the first Christians sought to practice:

"If I must glory, . . . I will come to visions and revelations of the Lord.

"I know a man in Christ above fourteen years ago (whether in the body, I know not, or out of the body I know not; God knows!) such a one caught up to the third heaven. And I know such a man . . . that he was caught up into paradise, and heard secret words which it is not granted to man to utter. . . .

"And lest the greatness of the revelation should exalt me, there was given me a sting of my flesh, an angel of Satan, to buffet me . . . Thrice I besought the Lord that it might depart from me. And He said to me: 'My grace is sufficient for thee, for power is made perfect in infirmity.'

"Gladly therefore will I glory in my infirmities, that the power of Christ may dwell in me."

Out in the solitary wastes, Paul's prayers were rewarded as few have ever been, with a sight of heaven itself. And, to forestall the creeping, slithering sin of pride, God gave him the paradoxical blessing of an infirmity of the body, constant painful reminder that though Paul served God, and had peered in at paradise's gates, he was mortal, pitifully human, and that through suffering spiritual powers flower.

What the infirmity was, we do not know. But Paul was forever acutely aware of it. In one of his letters he thanked the Galatians for not despising him and rejecting him because of "his humiliation." It may have been some persistent and unsightly skin infection, or perhaps even a red soreness about the eyes, sometimes distorting his vision. Whatever the affliction, it served its divine purpose. Paul never forgot the lessons God taught him in the fastnesses of Arabia, lessons he passed on with tender eagerness to all Christians living then and since, the sacred harvest of his three years' retreat. He knew he had direct revelation, communion with God, and appointment from heaven as an apostle.

Like every divinely inspired plan, Paul's retreat proved sound, not only spiritually, but for purely practical reasons. No one would have welcomed the notorious ex-persecutor in Jerusalem during those years.

At news of Paul's conversion, uproar and confusion had filled the Judaean capital. The elders, the Pharisees, the scribes, all the members of the Sanhedrin, all the haters of Christians were in a furor when the Damascus story, attested by Saul's soldiers, became gossip in the

Jerusalem streets. The Pharisees called it a lie of Christian propaganda. The Christians called it a snare and said that Paul was only masquerading, so that he could squirm his way into the confidence of the faithful.

Those were years when an insane man named Caligula ruled the Roman Empire and raised terror among the Christians. From birth he was a misfit and an unpredictable little monster; by the time he became Emperor he was a megalomaniac, unbalanced in his lightest thoughts. Perhaps Caligula heard tales out of Palestine of God becoming man. The idea in reverse seemed splendid; he ordered his subjects to worship himself as a god and actually tried to have his own statue erected in the Temple at Jerusalem. Only his favorite legate in Syria talked him out of that folly.

In Rome, Caligula had already started the construction of a circus, an amphitheater for gladiatorial exhibitions, next to a hill between Mount Marius and the Geniculum. This hill was called Vatican. And Christians in Palestine, hearing of that new arena, wondered at the shiver of premonition that chilled them.

But before long, the name of Caligula would cease to terrify Christians. A murderer was sharpening a knife and early in A.D. 41, Caligula would be assassinated.

Meanwhile, for three years Paul lived on the gray soils between Damascus and what is now called Baghdad. Gradually, he was forgotten by the Pharisees and by some of the Christians; and they lost their first bitter fear of him.

At the end of the third year, Paul revisited Damascus, then set out southward for Jerusalem, to see Peter.

What were Paul's thoughts on that solitary journey back to Jerusalem? Already as he made his way through the orchard lands, heading for the Sea of Galilee where Jesus had spent so much of His time, he was seeing a larger meaning of the Master's teachings than many of the apostles who had still much to understand. Paul, a traveled man, a cultured citizen of the vast Roman Empire, had a far-reaching horizon. Already he knew that the Gospel was meant not for a specially chosen few but for all the people on earth. The missionary prospect was like a glorious vision in his mind as day after day, for a week, he rode nearer to Jerusalem.

He did not guess what a spiritual test awaited him.

Chapter 35.   WHEN PETER MET PAUL

In the year of our Lord 38 Paul returned to Jerusalem.

The talk of what had happened in Damascus had died down in the capital, but Peter and the other Christians who had never fled or who had crept back again to the city were aware that their old persecutor was alive, planning only God knew what.

They were all afraid of Saul, St. Luke reports, "not believing that he was a disciple."

But one man refused to give way to fear and suspicion. Barnabas of Cyprus, young, clear-headed, refusing to judge that he himself be not judged, heard the news trickling from Christians working in the Damascus camel trains; word that Paul had come out of the desert and was on his way south.

Paul, scourge of the Christians, now one himself? Barnabas stood in the Cenacle and revived the three-year-old riddle. Was that too much to believe about the power of God? If the dumb and the deaf and the blind of body could be instantly healed might not God heal deafness of the heart and the blindness of a man's soul?

One thing, Barnabas reminded them, Paul had always shown an uncompromising zeal for what he had believed to be the truth—for the Law and the Prophets. If such a firebrand were to see in Jesus Christ the universal truth, the fulfillment of the Law and the Prophets, then the Church would have a new member of incalculable value.

There were no cries of welcome when Paul rode through the Sheep's Gate into the city where, three years before, he had occupied an honored and dignified place. Now his cloak was wrapped high above his chin, so that he would not be recognized by the Temple guards before he could get to Peter and offer himself to the cause.

But it was not easy for a stranger to find Peter. Are you a Christian? Every man to whom he put that question drew back and spat in the street. To admit to being a Christian in the city of Annas and Caiphas was suicide. Do you know Peter, the fisherman from Capernaum? We know him not! These people on the Jerusalem streets dared not risk their own safety—or Peter's.

But Paul was recognized, and secret word was rushed to the Cenacle that he was looking for Christians. Then Barnabas spoke his mind. What if Paul were truly converted? Would it not be a sin to cast him out?

His listeners were saints, but they were also human beings, with a man's memory and a man's capacity to hate. Paul-Saul! The names were a stink in their nostrils. Saul, the murderer of their lovable Stephen, smiling under the long hand of stones, praying for the forgiveness of his killers even while he was dying!

But if Stephen could forgive, Barnabas insisted, could they refuse forgiveness?

Amid a startled silence, Barnabas left the Cenacle. He walked carefully through the throngs, searching every face. And presently he saw the stalwart, little figure, face shrouded, riding a dusty beast.

"Come!" he said, with scarcely a movement of the lips, and, seizing the rein, he led Paul toward the Cenacle.

The apostles assembled, sitting on their heels, looking at Paul and Barnabas, to hear the Damascus story.

They listened, because Barnabas had convinced them that they ought to reserve judgment until Paul had stated his case. Already Barnabas was a powerful figure in their councils. Though not one of the twelve, he already ranked as an apostle. His name meant not only "son of consolation" but also "son of exhortation" and it was his powers of exhortation that he needed to call on today. He was divinely sympathetic on this wintry afternoon in the candlelit room of the Last Supper. On the way there he had hastily gathered the facts from Paul; now he, and not the illustrious convert, told the events—the only time in Paul's life that someone else did the talking for him.

"In Damascus he dealt confidently in the name of Jesus," Barnabas announced.

Not much had been heard lately from the Damascus brethren. At first, there had been in the fugitive, hasty messages brought by cameleers and converted merchants, much talk of Paul. But after he escaped in the basket, there came almost nothing. Now Jerusalem Christians heard that occasionally Paul, in disguise, had returned from the desert to Damascus and worshiped with the faithful, who had found him worthy to be one with them and yet felt it wiser not to mention him in letters that might be seized by Roman or Jewish guards.

Barnabas made Paul's case so clear that everyone perceived that here indeed was a Christian of Christians, who was also proud to be a Hebrew of Hebrews.

Peter, the towering fisherman, stepped forward to welcome Paul openly and fully. Two wind-burned, callused hands settled on the convert's shoulders in benison.

Their eyes were magnetized by the recognition of the Holy Spirit in each other. Peter, the untutored, the lowborn, who had denied Christ and yet was chosen by Him to be the rock of the Church; and Paul, the rabbinist, the intellectual Roman citizen, who had persecuted Christ and yet was wrenched out of his soul's darkness to become the light of the Church; they understood each other at once. Differences might ruffle the surface between them as the winds of the years blew over them. Nothing could ever destroy the deep, sure calm of faith which they shared.

The two giants of Christianity took each other's measure, and found that they were at peace together. Fifteen days, while Paul slipped in and out of Jerusalem unobserved by the spies of Caiphas and the Temple aristocracy, Peter and Paul spent together.

Peter led the short scholar to meet James called the Less, and together they shared with Paul warm, living details of the life of the Man Who was God.

Paul walked with them through the familiar streets of Jerusalem, seeing the city with new eyes. See, Paul—there is where He saw the woman taken in adultery! And here near the Pool of Siloam, He healed a blind man on the Sabbath day. That rich man's house on the corner—there Mary Magdalene washed His feet, and earned His forgiveness.

Paul stared at the Temple, where for years he had worshiped while studying under Rabbi Gamaliel, and tried to visualize the Lord preaching there and whipping the money-changers out of His Father's house. He walked past Caiphas' home; past the Sanhedrin hall; past the governor's palace, picturing the agonies of Christ's trial and scourging. With Peter, Paul walked the Via Dolorosa, Way of the Cross, where Jesus had fallen three times on the way to Calvary. And Paul shuddered at his own soul's blindness, as he realized that he had lived in this very city while Jesus lived and died—and had never known the Truth.

He had much to learn from Peter and James the Less!

But Paul, in his turn, must tell them of his years in the desert, of his unutterable vision of paradise, of all that the Spirit had taught him in the wilderness. If ever Peter and James had doubted the word of this convert, his reports of those years of retreat were credentials from heaven itself.

Yet here was Paul, gifted with miracles and revelations, trained by God Himself for the ministry, as Ananias had prophesied in Damascus three years before—here was Paul, humble, eager to learn all he could from Peter and James. That was final proof of the new apostle's worth. For who would have dreamed that a man of culture, born to command and to teach, should ever sit at the feet of a boatman from Galilee, and ask for instruction?

All too short, the fifteen days they had together, a time of fevered talk and shared prayer, of spiritual excitement and earnest plans for the future. Then they were abruptly and sadly separated.

Reports were getting to Annas and Caiphas about this stranger who visited Peter. Moreover—and this tendency made even some of the apostles uneasy—Paul had been speaking to the Gentiles and disputing with the Greek-speaking Jews. The Temple was hatching a plot to murder him—and that would mean more persecution for the rest of the Church!

Clearly enough, Peter saw, the moment was not ripe for Paul's ministry. Paul must wait. He must command his ardent spirit to sit still in obscurity.

Nothing harder could have been asked of him. Yet, without protest, he accepted Peter's decision—though it meant exile. Up to the port of Caesarea Paul went, to the ship that would take him to the place where Peter had told him to wait.

And where was that? It was Tarsus! He must go back to his boyhood home and his trade of tentmaking, instead of launching the missionary efforts of which he had dreamed!

Paul went home, to face the cold shoulders of old friends and teachers in the plain little synagogue—an apostle without a calling, a missionary with no field. He had plumbed the depth and height of spiritual experience, he had been accepted as a brother soldier by Peter—and for what? To be hurried into oblivion, to live in the confines of a bazaar, unwelcomed either by old friends or new? The Church was moving on, and it seemed that Paul was being left far behind; too far, some undoubtedly thought, ever to catch up with it again.

Yet Paul's withdrawal helped the Church. With Paul no longer in Jerusalem, no longer an embarrassment to the Sanhedrin as an illustrious convert, there was a truce in the persecutions.

"Now the Church had peace," St. Luke reports. "Peace throughout all Judaea and Galilee and Samaria, and was edified, walking in the fear of the Lord, and was filled with the consolation of the Holy Ghost."

And Paul went about his trade in Tarsus. He was to wait humbly, in prayer, study, work—unwanted by those of the new Church or the old—for thirteen years. Considering his dramatic conversion, was there ever greater test of an articulate and ardent believer, whose fire and energy were to spread throughout the world and down through history? His one avenue of service during those years of obscurity was to aid the peace of the Church by remaining silent, praying for the success of others.

BOOK FOUR

The Doors Open to the Gentiles

Chapter 36. THE MAN WITH PALSY

IN THIS precarious springtime of the Church, Peter was a tireless visitor to all the communities of Palestine. From one end of the country to another he walked, meeting the various groups, counseling with them, and deciding their disputes. Everywhere the people waited for him and embraced him at the town gates, for he was as beloved as he was respected.

On one such journey he came to the town of Lydda, not far from Joppa and the foaming breakers of the Mediterranean Sea. The modern Jerusalem Express pauses there on the way to Egypt; from the most ancient days Lydda has always been on the highroad from the coast to the capital, and so in the path of many armies—Roman, Saracen, Crusader, and Mongol. And along this same route, in haste and obscurity, the Holy Family had fled into Egypt. Travelers today, riding the train in comfort, can look out on this fertile hollow in the Plain of Sharon and visualize the donkey and the three hurrying refugees, Jesus, Mary, and Joseph.

Peter found the noisy and prosperous merchant town already a Christian center. St. Luke reports of the "saints" who lived in Lydda at the time of Peter's visit there.

That term "saint," used often in the Old Testament Psalms, at first meant "good" and "compassionate," then, increasing in significance, it came to be used as "godly." But by the time Peter came down the hilly roads from Jerusalem to Lydda, tramping along in his worn sandals and faded robe, the saints were the "holy ones," conse-crated persons in the new Church.

The first person Peter called on in the old city was a paralytic called Eneas. For eight years this man had lain in bed palsied, helpless in his affliction. The brawny apostle stood at the bedside of Eneas, who was hunched in unchanging pain but in whose filmy eyes was gathering the light of hope.

Peter's own great lake-green eyes were hidden by closed lids. His mouth moved silently in the fall of his beard, as he prayed.

And Peter said: "Eneas, the Lord Jesus Christ makes you whole. Arise! And make your bed!"

"And immediately he arose," reports Luke, the physician, who knew a cure when he saw one.

Throughout that undulating plain that runs from Joppa and Ramle all the farmers, timbermen, and herdsmen and their wives and young ones heard of Peter's miracle. They saw the cripple, up and walking, completely healed of his infirmity, and "all that dwelt at Lydda and Sharon turned to the Lord," declares the journal of Luke.

A beautiful region in which to perform so telling a spiritual feat! Ever since the days of Isaiah and long before, that plain has been a place of abundance. The oak trees grow stronger there than anywhere else in Palestine; the grass is green and luxuriant, and the wild flowers in spring make a carpet for the fields. When I was there, the sand dunes along the coast were beginning to encroach, but modern engi-neering will save these green fields and orchards from the sea.

Peter was hastening on. He left Lydda for Joppa.

Chapter 37. THE WOMAN OF JOPPA

PETER'S VISIT to Joppa marked another recorded miracle, one with symbolic meaning for Christian ladies of all time. His actions there seemed to establish womankind's special importance to the Church.

By a woman Eden was lost, and by a woman redemption was brought into the world, by Mary, the mother of Jesus, most perfect exemplar to all mothers and daughters and sisters to follow after her. So little is recorded of her activities, yet tradition abounds in tales of her courageous piety after her Son's death. Even the most important words and deeds of Jesus and His apostles themselves are but meagerly reported for posterity. In the case of Mary, and of the other humbly self-effacing women who came into the dangerous new faith, history is almost silent. Selflessly they courted obscurity.

But because of Peter, we know a little more about one good woman of Joppa.

Luke says simply: "And in Joppa there was a certain disciple named Tabitha, which by interpretation is called Dorcas."

The news of Peter's healing of Eneas came to Joppa just about the time that Tabitha breathed her last. Her family and friends washed her body and laid her in an upper chamber.

"And forasmuch," writes Luke, "as Lydda was nigh to Joppa, the disciples hearing that Peter was there, sent unto him two men desiring him that he would not be slack to come to them."

Men of faith, those urgent friends of Tabitha!

"And Peter rising up went with them. And when he was come, they brought him into the upper chamber; and all the widows stood about him weeping, and showing him the coats and garments which Dorcas made."

And now, as if in symbolism of all womankind rising in the new dispensation, Dorcas, that lovely lady, was about to rise from the dead. Dorcas was her Greek name; her name in the language spoken by the disciples and apostles was Tabitha, a Hebrew term of endearment meaning a roe or young deer.

Dorcas was a saint. Luke distinctly says that she was a disciple, a Christian "full of good works and almsdeeds." What a pity that such a woman should fall ill just at the time when Peter came to Lydda and Joppa! She had looked forward so eagerly to seeing him; she had so many questions to ask about Jesus. But sudden fever struck her down and she died.

She was lying on her bier, the corruption of death beginning, when Peter came to her. He stood and looked at her. He saw not merely Dorcas, the corpse; he saw one of the new women who were soon to bring to the Church their feminine gifts, their devotion and motherly sympathy, their nurses' hands, their sewing and weaving and scouring and baking—Priscilla and Lydia, Julia and Susannah, Chloe and others, who would open up their homes to the group meetings of the faithful.

Dorcas of Joppa was to be the first of these.

The mourners were weeping, but "they all being put forth, Peter kneeling down, prayed: and turning to the body he said, 'Tabitha, arise.' And she opened her eyes: and seeing Peter, she sat up.

"And giving her his hand, he lifted her up, and when he had called the saints and widows, he presented her alive.

"And it was known throughout all Joppa; and many believed in the Lord."

And down to this day women meet to sew, making "coats and garments" for the poor and for orphans, gathered together in Dorcas Societies the whole world over.

Chapter 38.   THE FOOD FROM THE SKY

PETER lodged during his prolonged stay in Joppa with a tanner named Simon, who made sandals, girdles, and thongs, working with the hides which he cured in a stinking vat behind his house. The proudest fact in Simon's life was that Peter was a guest under his roof.

Peter was to have a vision on that roof that would turn the tide of world thought.

This singular story did not begin in Simon the tanner's seaside house but farther up the coast in the port city of Caesarea, which Herod the Great in the days before Jesus was born had rebuilt, naming it in honor of Emperor Augustus Caesar.

In Caesarea lived a Roman military officer named Cornelius. He was a centurion, commander of the hundred men making up the unit called a "century," sixtieth part of a legion in the Roman Army. He was "of the Italian band," men who were Italian natives. Though himself a Roman, as his name suggested, he felt very much at home in his Jewish surroundings. Tired of the poetic fantasies about the pagan gods, which neither he nor anyone he knew actually believed, he had lived in Caesarea long enough to learn of the Jews' devotion to the one, true God. He was profoundly impressed by Old Testament history, by the Law and the Prophets. He had never asked to be received as a Jew; he had not contemplated being circumcised and was therefore not a member of the congregation of Israel. He was simply one of a number of Romans who in those days were drawn to the one, true God and so became known as halfway followers. These people adopted certain Jewish practices, and were even permitted to attend some services in the synagogue.

Cornelius had a special reputation as a man of deep faith and good works. Up and down the streets of Caesarea and out into the suburbs, he was known for his charities. "Cornelius prayed always," as Luke reported; and any man who prays, although he may be in darkness, will find the light.

Indeed, Cornelius had a vision, and heard a Voice unmistakably not of this world.

In the middle of the afternoon, "about the ninth hour of the day," Cornelius saw an angel of God, coming through the gate, across the yard, past the olive bushes, through the door, and into the house. And he heard the voice of an angel call his name.

"Cornelius!"

That battle-scarred veteran of many a colonial campaign was seized with fear at the sight of the supernatural being. Scarce able to form the words, he whispered:

"What is it, Lord?"

And the angel replied: "Your prayers and your alms are ascended for a memorial in the sight of God. And now send men to Joppa and call hither one Simon, who is surnamed Peter. He lodges with one Simon, a tanner, whose house is by the seaside. He shall tell you what you must do."

Awed as he was, Cornelius nodded his head in assent. The angel, satisfied that the officer would obey instructions, instantly vanished.

Cornelius leaped to his feet, full-statured and in command of himself, plunging into action. His right hand seized a pestle and struck a hanging copper disk, and the banging of it resounded through the household. Again he struck the pendulum, and again the rafters caught the echoes of the stroke. Two of his servants came rushing to his side.

His eyes dark and unsmiling, he looked at them soberly, as if already aware of the danger of the mission for which he called them. He was sending them on a friendly errand into the Christian underground, and such an action would not sit well with the Pharisaic authorities. Even as he stood silent, a third attendant appeared, Cornelius' old orderly who had been at his side in many a rainy march and many a bloody field. Like his master, this old sergeant was devout in prayer and good works; no common trait among old soldiers.

At last, Cornelius spoke. In the crisp accents of a troop commander, he told them what had happened to him. He had been talking to an angel, he said, and though they looked surprised and greatly excited, it never occurred to them to doubt.

"Go to Joppa," he bade them. "Go to the house of Simon the tanner, by the seaside, and find Simon called Peter. He shall tell you what I ought to do."

By donkey, it took the three men nearly two days to make the journey, down the hilly rim of the sea on the Plain of Sharon all the way from Strator Tower at Caesarea to the port of Joppa.

As they trotted into the city and asked their way to the house of Simon the tanner, Peter might easily have seen them from the roof if he had not been wrapped in prayer. For it was then "the sixth hour," noontime, and the sainted fisherman of Galilee had climbed the housetop of Simon's dwelling, as was his habit every day to pray.

Peter had been fasting since midnight. The moment his devotions were finished, he would be ready for a substantial breakfast.

But with the last "Amen" of his prayers, Peter was aware of some inner, irresistible seizure. Hardly had he recognized that feeling when all consciousness left him.

Peter, the holy apostle, had fallen into a trance, a coma deeper than the overmastering sleepiness that had ground him dreamlessly in the critical moments when he should have stayed on guard in the Garden of Gethsemane.

No one was near. The family of Simon the tanner had learned, as had Peter's associates in Jerusalem, to give him the solitude he needed for the intensity of his prayers. On the third hour, on the sixth, ninth, and tenth, throughout the whole day, it was Peter's custom to go to the heights, whether in town or on the road, or in the desert, to find the highest, purest spot for his devotions. Ever since the Resurrection, the mystic power of this man of rock had intensified, so that now his whole personality had become holy, attuned to the Voice that had spoken in Eden and has never ceased to speak when the hour requires man to be instructed.

Now Peter lay with his breakfast untasted beside him—a waist-bag with a few nuts and dried peas and near it a small flagon of water. Peter, shepherd of His flock, with the keys of heaven entrusted to him, the power of binding and loosing in his gnarled hands, had become more ascetic than the poor to whom he preached.

In his trance, Peter dreamed a dream that was to sow violent dissension in the early Church and create an issue which had to be decided before true Christianity could grow to its full potency. He dreamed of the food that fell from the sky.

Luke described it:

"He saw the heaven opened, and a certain vessel descending as it were a great linen sheet let down by the four corners, from heaven to the earth. Wherein were all manner of fourfooted beasts, and creeping things of the earth, and fowls of the air.

"And there came a Voice to him, 'Rise, Peter; kill and eat.'

"But Peter said, 'Far be it from me, for I never did eat any thing that is common and unclean.'

"And the Voice spoke to him again the second time, 'That which God hath cleansed, do not thou call common.'

"This was done thrice: and presently the vessel was taken up into heaven."

Chapter 39.   "NO RESPECTER OF PERSONS"

WHEN Peter opened his eyes the memory of his vision troubled him deeply.

"He doubted in himself what this vision which he had seen should mean," says Luke.

Peter knew that the Law of Moses, the words of the Prophets, all the Scriptures of Israel, were blood and bone of Christ's message; that He Himself had said He "had come to fulfill the Law and not to change it." But in the old Law there was great religious exclusiveness that shut out others—that sought to remain pure in separation. That old segregation of the Law had carried over into the Christian Church. Many of the faithful in Jerusalem, passionately devoted to the memory of Christ and His teachings, still considered the Church He had founded something for Jews and Jews alone. Peter knew this fact well. Yet he also knew that Jesus had never excluded anyone; that in a Roman centurion, a Gentile, Christ had found greater faith than in all Israel. Peter was deeply troubled.

He heard a knocking at the gate of Simon's house. Looking over the parapet, Peter saw three strangers standing on the threshold, their donkeys tied to a nearby sycamore tree. Simon, the house owner, opened a window, and the tanner's voice was cross as he asked who was there and what was wanted.

"Is one Peter lodging there with you?" one of the servants of Cornelius called.

And Peter, listening from the roof, knew that this was a divine call, a signal beyond misunderstanding. No Galilean voice had just asked for Peter; no Judaean from the south had spoken, but a traveler, a Roman by the voice of him—an outsider, a Gentile. And in the same instant that he saw them, the everlasting Voice, the Spirit of God, the Holy Ghost, spoke again to Peter:

"Behold, three men are looking for you."

"Yes, Lord. I see them."

"Arise, therefore!"

"Yes, Lord." And Peter, hands on the railing, pulled himself up from his knees.

"Go on down to them. Go with them—doubting nothing: for I have sent them."

Peter hurried down the stone steps to the gate. His host, Simon the tanner, stood respectfully beside him.

"Behold!" said Peter, a hearty grin of welcome shining through his beard. "I am he that you are looking for. What is the cause? What have you sought me out for?"

"Cornelius the centurion sent us," said the orderly. "He is a just man. He fears God—the one, true God. He has a good reputation in all the synagogues of the Jews. And Cornelius the centurion, whose servant I am, was told by a holy angel to send for you. He wants us to bring you back with us to Caesarea. He wants you to come as a guest in his house and to hear words from you—he wants you to explain the faith of Christ to him and perhaps to his family."

Peter heaved a great sigh. These men were uncircumcised foreigners, with whom a Jew was under orders to have no traffic. Yet the Voice had said, "Go, doubting nothing."

Not speech but action proclaimed Peter's decision. His hands raised in blessing welcomed the emissaries, and Simon the tanner led them quickly indoors, showed them a room with decent beds, clean linen, accommodations for three, and bade them be lodged there for the night.

"And on the morrow, Peter went away with them, and certain brethren from Joppa accompanied him."

That was Peter's answer to the first Gentile who sought to be a Christian.

But Peter was hardly prepared for the eager reception awaiting him at the house of Cornelius.

By two days' journeying, with an overnight stop at an inn, they reached Caesarea before high noon. The harbor city in all its roaring traffic and commerce was a busy place that morning. People rushed through the narrow streets, and no one had time to stop and greet the returning ambassadors of Cornelius; none to stop and stare at Peter with his shepherd's lay staff and his tumbling beard, nor the brethren from Joppa following behind.

In its way the house of Cornelius was as crowded as the streets. Having no doubt of Peter's answer, the centurion had invited relations and friends to come and hear about the wonderful new faith of Christianity from its first purely human leader. Not one was too busy or ailing to come. There were men and women in every nook and corner of the vaulted stone house of Cornelius.

His home might have been the model for the wise man's place in Jesus' parable of the two houses; the one whose door now opened to admit Peter, like the Church itself, was built upon a rock, and the winter rain could never wash it into the sea. It had large rooms with tall ceilings and was surrounded by thick walls; the arches of the roof rested on strong, massive pillars.

At the gate stood Cornelius in his rich red robe, hands clasped eagerly together as he smiled upon his approaching guest. The moment Peter's foot appeared inside the front yard, the centurion fell to his knees before Peter, "and worshiped him," as Luke puts it.

Peter, taken by surprise, moved back a step and vigorously shook his head. Then, with those strong boatman's arms, he seized Cornelius by the shoulders and lifted him to his feet.

"Stand up!" he said, almost gruffly. "I myself also am a man."

Peter was tired and dusty from his long journey. He would have liked a bath and bed and lunch. But there was no time. The kinsmen and friends of Cornelius had kept a long vigil, waiting hopefully through a day and a night. Peter agreed to speak to them at once.

And immediately he made his social and religious position clear to them. Jews, seeing him in the house of a Gentile, would say that he had no right to be there. Now Peter announced:

"You know how abominable it is for a man that is a Jew to keep company or come unto one of another nation; but God has shown me to call no man common or unclean."

A thrill ran through all the listeners, and with good cause. They had just heard a dogma that would end the separation and exclusiveness of races under the new dispensation. Without doubt, here was the most important utterance made by any man since Jesus had ascended into heaven.

From the dietary images of his dream and the call that followed instantly after, Peter had realized that the Old Testament divisions between clean and unclean, in food and in race, no longer were valid. For two thousand years sincere followers of Christ, in the midst of general hypocrisy and ignorance, would try to remind the world that Christ wanted all men to love each other. At the beginning the Jews wanted to exclude the Gentiles; later, the Gentiles scorned and excluded Jews. All that has ever been needed is the spirit of brotherhood that Peter was now, in the house of Cornelius, trying to practice, in obedience to God's direction.

"Therefore I came unto you," Peter resumed. "I came without gainsaying, as soon as I was sent for. I ask therefore—for what intent you have sent for me?"

Cornelius rose from his gilded chair and strode toward Peter, facing his relatives and friends. Mildly, carefully, he recited the circumstances just as they had occurred:

"Four days ago, unto this hour, I was praying in my house, at the ninth hour, and behold a man stood before me in white apparel, and said: 'Cornelius, thy prayer is heard, and thy alms are had in remembrance in the sight of God. Send therefore to Joppe, and call hither Simon, who is surnamed Peter: he lodgeth in the house of Simon a tanner, by the sea side.'

"Immediately therefore I sent to thee: and thou hast done well in coming. Now therefore all we are present in thy sight, to hear all things whatsoever are commanded thee by the Lord."

Then Peter said: "In very deed I perceive, that God is not a respecter of persons. But in every nation, he that feareth Him, and worketh justice, is acceptable to him.

"God sent the word to the children of Israel, preaching peace by Jesus Christ: (He is Lord of all.) You know the word which hath been published through all Judea: for it began from Galilee, after the baptism which John preached, Jesus of Nazareth: how God anointed Him with the Holy Ghost, and with power, who went about doing good, and healing all that were oppressed by the devil, for God was with Him. And we are witnesses of all things that He did in the land of the Jews in Jerusalem, whom they killed, hanging Him upon a tree.

"Him God raised up the third day, and gave Him to be made manifest, not to all the people, but to witnesses preordained by God, even to us, who did eat and drink with Him after He arose again from the dead; and He commanded us to preach to the people, and to testify that it is He who was appointed by God, to be judge of the living and of the dead. To Him all the prophets give testimony, that by His name all receive remission of sins, who believe in Him."

As Peter's voice died away in the stillness, there came into the room, into the air they breathed, into every heart present a mysterious and beautiful elation. It was the same feeling that had fallen upon all the saints as they had waited in the Upper Room at the feast of the Pentecost.

On this day in Caesarea, there were no visible cloven tongues of fire, but the gift of tongues, of speech in foreign languages and the fervent peace known only to those in the presence of the Holy Ghost came to the men and women assembled in Cornelius' house.

The brethren who had accompanied Peter from Joppa were dumfounded. They were good Hebrews, "of the circumcision," as Luke put it afterward. Tight-lipped and full of doubt, they had journeyed with Peter; they had insisted on coming with their leader on this mad expedition, not at all approving. They had not yet grasped the revolutionary fact that Christianity was for everybody in the world.

Now they stood in profound and gasping wonder. Here before their eyes was God's own seal of approval on what Peter was doing. They were astonished "for" wrote Luke, "that the grace of the Holy Ghost was poured out upon the Gentiles also. For they heard them speaking with tongues and magnifying God."

Peter's voice roared out in the midst of the inspired group a challenge to his brethren's persistent orthodoxy:

"Can any man forbid water, that these should not be baptized who have received the Holy Ghost as well as we?"

And answering his own question, he baptized Cornelius, his kin-folk, and his friends.

Peter the Jew and his circumcised brethren remained in the house of the Gentile Cornelius for many days.

Chapter 40. TROUBLE IN JERUSALEM

When Peter dared open the doors of the new Church to Gentiles, consulting no other apostles, it was bound to create an uproar.

He had told Cornelius that God was no respecter of persons, a favorite phrase, thereafter, with him. Now the Gentiles were in the Christian movement. The Holy Spirit had reached every man, woman and child in the house of Cornelius.

"And," says Luke, "the apostles and the brethren that were in Judaea heard that the Gentiles had also received the word of God."

When Peter got to Jerusalem "they that were of the circumcision contended with him."

These other apostles—all of them, like Peter, good circumcised Jews—demanded an explanation. They went for him like a grand jury investigating a suspected public official.

"You went unto men uncircumcised and did eat with them."

Flatly and bluntly they stated the indictment. There was no contest about the facts. No one was lying about what happened in the centurion's house. The sole question before the eleven apostles and all other hard-working and pious Jerusalem brethren was how Peter could justify such a heretical gesture. Rebuke and shock chilled their earnest faces.

Carefully, Peter rehearsed the sequence of events, beginning with the vision that had come to him.

"I was in the city of Joppe praying, and I saw in an ecstasy of mind a vision, a certain vessel descending, as it were a great sheet let down from heaven by four corners, and it came even unto me. Into which looking, I considered, and saw fourfooted creatures of the earth, and beasts, and creeping things, and fowls of the air: and I heard also a voice saying to me: 'Arise, Peter; kill and eat.'

"And I said: 'Not so, Lord; for nothing common or unclean hath ever entered into my mouth.'

"And the voice answered again from heaven: 'What God hath made clean, do not thou call common.' And this was done three times: and all were taken up again into heaven.

"And behold, immediately there were three men come to the house wherein I was, sent to me from Caesarea. And the Spirit said to me, that I should go with them, nothing doubting. And these six brethren went with me also: and we entered into the man's house. And he told us how he had seen an angel in his house, standing, and saying to him: 'Send to Joppe, and call hither Simon, who is surnamed Peter, who shall speak to thee words, whereby thou shalt be saved, and all thy house.'

"And when I had begun to speak, the Holy Ghost fell upon them, as upon us also in the beginning. And I remembered the word of the Lord, how that He said: 'John indeed baptized with water, but you shall be baptized with the Holy Ghost.'

"If then God gave them, the same grace, as to us also who believed in the Lord Jesus Christ; who was I, that could withstand God?"

No one in the tense crowd would raise his voice to that unanswerable challenge.

"What was I that I could withstand God?" remains a beacon to men sorely beset, confronted with the past, with tradition, and convention, in conflict with mercy and wisdom; a question which contains its own solution.

For a time there was complete silence. Then, slowly, came a sigh out of one soul yonder, thanking God for the wideness of His mercy; a rumble in the beard of a patriarch squatting by the door, as he glorified God, saying:

"God has also to the Gentiles given repentance unto life!"

And these men now understood the meaning of their ancient word, noham, repentance, as not merely the old-time concept of changing an attitude, but a rebirth in the new dispensation of Jesus Christ. Not just a sorrow for offending God, but a new way of living with prayer for a daily, hourly overcoming of evil within, that legacy of Eden. Now the Gentiles, too, could be baptized in water and in truth; the Goyim could be born again.

Thus one of the greatest issues of man and faith and fellowship seemed to have been settled for good and all—but oh, appearances are deceiving. Ahead loomed dispute after dispute over the relation of Jew and Gentile in the new faith.

The early Church was in its beginning almost entirely Jewish. That these creatures of habit and strictly imposed customs and traditions could even momentarily accept Peter's decree without argument was a fact to be marked as a milestone. Peter had exerted his spiritual leadership, and it was received without protest. There and then the authority of the Church was made completely clear in Israel.

Yet that authority would be challenged. Such is human nature—with its reluctance to change, its die-hard love of old ideas and customs.

Chapter 41.   BARNABAS AND PAUL

In the few years since Jesus had ascended into heaven, His teachings had traveled far beyond the confines of Judaea. The first fugitives from Saul's bloodthirsty persecutions, fleeing on dark roads at night to safety, settled down to become the core of Christian branches in foreign lands. As always that first persecution sowed the seeds of richer harvest for the faith.

The secret worship of the Trinity was carried throughout the east coast of the Mediterranean, from Mount Carmel in the south up to Antioch on the Orontes River in the north; and from the foamy shoreline of Palestine all the way back to the Lebanon and Anti-Lebanon Mountains. In ancient Phoenicia, home of the proud centers of Sidon and Lycus, and the island city of Tyre, famed for her purple dyes and shipwrights, Christianity was also a hidden but powerful source.

The faith was planted on Cyprus, too, that storied island off the coast of Asia Minor. Barnabas, himself a native Cypriote, had urged a few Christians to go there and quietly teach the people who tended sheep on mountain slopes or labored in the dwindling copper mines.

The new Church advanced as if by geometrical progression. A little Christianity in a town soon leavened the whole, and hundreds flocked to join the new outpost of faith. Wherever a Christian had to go, for whatever reason, he carried the glorious message further on. Over the ever increasing fold of faith, Peter the shepherd exercised his dynamic leadership. He had, through prayer, learned patience, but he had not lost his fire, and in the grace bestowed on him, his labors were enormous, incessant, and ever more successful.

Meanwhile Matthew, the sainted tax-gatherer, was preparing to write the first Gospel. Of all the twelve, Matthew was best prepared for such a learned task, for he was born to ink and quill. So Matthew, whose birth name was Levi, son of Alphaeus; Matthew, the publican, who had been called by Jesus from his moneybags and tariff desk at the city gate, was busy in these exciting days writing down, not calculations of tax debts, but golden words recording the greatest Life ever lived.

With inspired discernment he was putting down for his fellow Jews the truth about the Master, determined to prove to skeptical minds that their expected Messiah had indeed come, and that the third person of the Trinity, the Holy Ghost, would, as promised, be forever here on earth to comfort and guide the baptized. For that reason, Matthew's opening verses would lead the Jewish minds back to their own Scriptures, to the covenant that had promised redemption to fallen men, and demonstrate the royal earthly lineage of our Lord and Saviour. Soon Matthew's scroll would be ready with its priceless biography of Jesus, the Messiah born as promised and fulfilling all the prophecies.

Matthew dipped his pen in fervent fury, knowing as Peter pointed out, how needed a record was of the Redeemer's teachings, so that believers and newcomers could learn of the Word. In Matthew's Gospel we have the Sermon on the Mount, the Lord's Prayer, the Beatitudes—the pith and kernel of the Nazarene's directions for following the spiritual laws of God the loving Father.

He wrote in Aramaic Chaldee, the language they all spoke, but the Gospel we have now was translated from a Greek version and men dispute to this day whether our version is actually a translation or possibly a second book, and also whether it was written just at this time or some years later. Yet certainly Matthew was preparing to write his Gospel in those exciting days when the Christian message was spreading with stealthy rapidity throughout the world of the Roman Empire.

To those distant outposts of the faith, no word had come as yet of the extraordinary announcement of salvation for all mankind. Christianity was being spread abroad, but only to the Jews and no one else.

Neither God nor His servants could let that state of affairs continue. The time had come for a new force to share the Christian stage—an apostolate to the Gentiles.

Some of the Christians from Cyprus and from the rich and power-ful city of Cyrenaica, which Luke called Cyrene, came to visit in Antioch. There they met a colony of educated Greeks, Gentiles with open minds, hungry as the Roman Cornelius had been for the truth. And the Christians from Cyprus preached Jesus to these Greeks in Antioch.

"And," says Luke, with a certain relish, "the hand of the Lord was with them; and a great number believed, and turned unto the Lord."

Word of these Greek Gentile conversions reached Jerusalem just after the victorious announcement of the open-door policy of the Church. The apostles welcomed the news as a chance for immediate and decisive action. They sent Barnabas to Antioch, as their personal representative, to guide the new converts and their teachers, the zealous Christians from Barnabas' homeland of Cyprus.

The far-reaching consequences of that decision of the Apostles were actually to change the history of the world. For through Barna-bas the greatest of all Christian voices was to be called back to lead the martyrs' chorus of the saints. Barnabas was to summon his friend Paul of Tarsus into the front line of battle.

Barnabas was a natural choice for the important mission in Anti-och, "for he was a good man," says Luke, "and full of the Holy Ghost and of faith."

He knew how to talk with the Greek converts. He was, himself, a "Hellenist," educated in the spirit and culture of Greek philosophers, artists, and dramatists. He could quote Aristotle and Plato and was no stranger to the mysteries of old philosophical disputations. His ideas were liberal; though he was of Jewish blood, he came from a polyglot island and he saw all men as his brothers, as the Lord had taught. But he was no intellectual debater; he felt the truth instinc-tively, rather than discovering it by thought alone. In the great con-flict that was soon nearly to wreck the Church, Barnabas would stand midway. He shrank from the dogmatic exclusiveness of the rabbini-cally trained Pharisees. Though he was a Jew, he had been born away from Judaea in the Dispersion, and had been taught in a colonial synagogue colored by the broad tolerance of the Greeks.

Barnabas fulfilled his mission in Antioch well. He was like a great bridge of mind and spirit between Jew and Greek. But facing the situation there, he knew that he needed a mind more capable of dialectic, tougher in mental combat, to bring the Gentiles in.

Then Barnabas remembered the words which in Damascus the Voice had spoken to Ananias concerning Paul before his baptism: *"He is a chosen vessel unto Me, to bear My Name before the Gentiles . . ."*

Of course! Remembering, Barnabas turned his face, as if ordered, toward Tarsus to seek Paul. That was why, after thirteen years of tentmaking and meditation, Paul was invited to join in the apostolic labors.

At last he was called into action.

At last! How his heart must have leaped. After having been called by Jesus, visited and instructed by God in the desert, thirteen years of inaction must have weighed oppressively on Paul. To a young man full of zeal and proven courage God's way must have seemed most mysterious.

As he stepped forward with Barnabas, Paul realized that the stern discipline of those years of obscurity had trained his soul to a fine pitch. His restless, eloquent mind had kept silent in his tentmaking shop; his hands, which were soon to wield a fiery pen, had kept busy with needle and thread, while his spirit grew. And now he was ready.

Paul and Barnabas went to Antioch together, as they were to go side by side, on foot and on ship over a large part of the Roman Empire. Soon Paul's words and deeds were to bring both glory and trouble to those called Christians. But in his first weeks with Barnabas in Antioch, his labors were blessed with harmony and inspired fervor.

What trouble there was then for the Church came not in Antioch, but in Jerusalem.

Chapter 42. HIS MAJESTY, HEROD AGRIPPA I

THE apostles and disciples were not worldly. Simple-spirited, enchanted with the true faith, they moved through a time of seething political unrest with little thought for anything save spreading and living the Gospel. But the world would not leave them alone.

Christians could hardly ignore the complicated and murderous succession of Roman emperors, or the intrigues and scandals of local kings. From the thrones of Rome and Judaea malignant hands reached out to strike down the faithful one by one.

Who were these rulers who could arrest, torment, and kill Christians to suit their political schemes—or even for sheer sport?

In the palace of Herod Agrippa I, puppet king of Judaea, new terror was brewing for the Church. This king, grandson of that terrible Herod the Great who murdered the boy babies of Bethlehem, was about to launch the second major persecution of Christians.

Herod Agrippa I liked to think of himself as a Roman. He was proud of having all the fine airs and vices of wealthy young men raised in the cynical city that was built on seven hills. But at forty, trouble had driven him from Rome, bankrupted by gambling debts and extravagance, and very much in disfavor with the Emperor Tiberius.

He fled to Palestine. His creditors' agents trailed him. In despair, he was on the point of committing suicide.

His sister, old Queen Herodias, saved him from taking his own life. In the incestuous mix-ups of this kingly line, Herodias had married her own uncle, another Herod, called Antipas, the same king who beheaded John the Baptist and who years later had mocked Jesus Christ by dressing Him in royal robes, sending Him to Pilate for final judgment. He still held the balance of power between Rome and Palestine.

Herod Agrippa, for all his fears, was too proud to ask Antipas for help, but his wife was not. Haggard and desperate, she went to her sister-in-law Herodias, hysterically begging for help. Blood being thicker even than thieves, Herodias wheedled her husband into speaking to the Emperor. Antipas placated Rome and got the wastrel a political job. In Tiberias, the city that still broods on the shore of Galilee, they made Herod Agrippa superintendent of markets.

If sister, brother-in-law, and wife believed that Herod Agrippa would now act like a mature person, they were mistaken. Herod Agrippa had higher ambitions. By devious schemes, he wormed his way into the confidence of Caligula, heir to the imperial throne. When the old emperor Tiberius died and Caligula took power, Agrippa the schemer was crowned a king.

So now the near-suicide, the one-time market superintendent, was seated on a little throne in Israel as His Majesty Herod Agrippa I, ruler of all territory east and north of the Sea of Galilee. But he ruled by remote control. He had no taste for the dismal colony of Palestine, or its eruptive and complaining subjects. He liked Rome, and until the year A.D. 39 spent most of his time there.

In that year Agrippa concocted a new scheme. He told his friend, the new Emperor Caligula, that Herod Antipas (that helpful brother-in-law!) was a rebel, raising an army to free his country from Rome. With these slanderous lies Agrippa betrayed the man who once had saved him. Emperor Caligula believed the tales, banished Herod Antipas, giving his throne to Agrippa. At the expense of his own sister and her husband, who both died in exile in faraway Lyons, Agrippa had doubled his own territory and power!

Now he considered himself a very great king indeed. He cultivated the high favor of cruel Emperor Caligula. They were beasts of the same tastes. Shrewdly, Agrippa learned to win concessions for Israel from the Emperor, and consequently he became quite popular with his Jewish subjects. When Caligula was assassinated, he was once more on the winning side; he helped to elevate the new emperor Claudius to the throne of Rome. In payment for that aid, Agrippa was given the Kingdom of Judaea, the third ring to his crown. He thus ruled over virtually the same territory that had been the kingdom of his grandfather, Herod the Great, who was the ruler when Jesus Christ was born.

But unlike his grandfather, Herod Agrippa continued to hold the high regard of his subjects. He showed the greatest respect to all the rules and observances of the Pharisees. He strengthened the fortifications of Jerusalem walls. He took every measure to cultivate the approval of the Jews.

And to heighten his popularity, he decided in the year 44 to persecute the Christians.

Luke sadly reports, "Herod the King stretched forth his hands to afflict some of the Church."

His first move was against James, the brother of John the Beloved.

Chapter 43. THE SECOND MARTYR

JAMES THE GREATER, as history was to name him, had not wavered in his devotion to the Christ since the day when he had stood with three other boatmen on the Galilean shore and heard Jesus call them to be fishers of men.

From the beginning he and his brother, John the Beloved, had stood in a special place among the twelve apostles. With Peter, they had been the only witnesses of the Transfiguration, of the raising of the daughter of Jairus, and of the dreadful hours of Christ's agony in the Garden of Gethsemane.

"Sons of Thunder," Jesus had called these brothers, James and John. Already James the Greater had proven it no idly chosen agnomen. Like Peter, he was a bold, aggressive man, daring anything for the cause in which he believed so devotedly. No Christians in Jerusalem were more conspicuous than Peter and James the Greater.

That was why Herod singled them out as objects of cruelty in his new persecution. He intended to make an example of both these "fanatics." By death and terror he thought to stamp out the fire of Christianity, and ingratiate himself with his own Pharisee subjects.

He pounced on the thunderous James, and put him to death by the sword.

James the Greater was buried in secret, the second martyr among the followers of Jesus.

And in the councils of the Pharisees of the Jerusalem Temple the fact of the apostle's death was received with loquacious satisfaction. Thanks to Herod Agrippa, the elders and the scribes thought they were beginning to win the battle against Christianity. Too long the power of the state had held back its hand against this heretical sect. Who, they wondered, would be next? They hoped it would be that long-bearded, staff-pointing man from Capernaum, Simon—or Cephas, or Peter, or whatever his name was.

It was Easter time again, near the fourteenth anniversary of the Resurrection, as the faithful gathered in the Cenacle to mourn James the Greater.

Peter was totally unafraid though he heard the tramp of soldiers' feet mounting the stairs. He knew that the execution of James had pleased the enemies of the Church. He felt certain that he himself must be the next to feel their wrath. But he remembered that Christ had foretold for him doom *in old age*, and wondered.

That night they cast Peter into a dungeon as if they thought him a wild beast that might escape. Around the slimy, ill-smelling pit they set a guard of four quaternions of soldiers to keep him. Only one quaternion had stood at the foot of the cross on Calvary, but the officials had learned that strange aid could come to Christians in their need. They guarded Peter, the leader, in force.

Herod Agrippa I meant to keep Peter a prisoner throughout the season of unleavened bread. When the Passover time was ended, he meant to bring Peter into the daylight again and make his trial a great public process, his death an unforgettable spectacle.

But Herod Agrippa, filled with the venom of his plans, did not begin to understand the nature of the thing he sought to extirpate. He had every seeming advantage. But the disciples had a power of which Herod had never heard.

Night and day in the Cenacle and in homes throughout Jerusalem and its far-flung suburbs, keeping twenty-four hour vigil, the whole Church was praying for their captain, Peter.

"Prayer was made," says Luke, "without ceasing, of the Church unto God for him."

And God answered.

Chapter 44. PETER AND THE ANGEL

CLOSE upon midnight of Easter Sunday, Peter was most uncomfortably resting between two soldiers, bound to them with two sets of chains. His cell in the dungeon had bolts, bars, locks, and chains, and guards outside as well.

"Now," the chief guard had said, "you who have such Christian power, let's see you get free of all that!"

Peter did get free, but the chief guard was not allowed to see how.

The soldiers beside him were wide awake and the keepers before the door of the prison tramped back and forth, up and down, on duty and alert.

Peter had been praying unceasingly. Suddenly a most shining and mysterious light, without source or center, arrived luminous and full-blown in that pit of misery, warming and illuminating its darkest corners.

In the midst of that all-suffusing light stood an angel of the Lord.

With one touch of ineffable power he smote Peter on the side. He raised Peter from the floor and the apostle heard the heavenly voice:

"Arise up quickly."

The chains fell from Peter's hands and feet as the angel counseled him with great urgency:

"Gird yourself, Peter. Bind on your sandals."

Without a word, Peter obeyed. The two guards lay, transfixed, offering no resistance to this strange scene.

"And now," the angel commanded, "cast your garment about you and follow me."

Peter's mind was in an extraordinary state as he followed instructions. It seemed that he was asleep and dreaming and yet knew that he was not asleep and not dreaming. Luke put it so:

"And going out he followed him; and he knew not that it was true which was done by the angel; but thought he saw a vision."

No experience in his life was more actual. The angel led him through one corridor, or ward, to a closed and bolted door through which they passed together, unimpeded by wood or iron, as if the penetration of matter were a commonplace. They kept on, down a second corridor and through a second door, coming finally to the iron gate that led out of that foul place of detention, into the sweet, fresh air of the night.

The iron gate swung open to them, with no porter to release its hinges, no guard to lift its mighty latch.

"And they went out, and passed on through one street; and immediately the angel departed from him."

Standing there at a crossing in the pale light of the dawn, Peter gave a great sighing prayer of thanks. He had come to himself and realized with rising astonishment that he was not dreaming; that by a miracle he stood free and unguarded on the common highway in the pink and gray mist of the Jerusalem dawn.

"Now," he said, "I know in very deed that the Lord has sent His angel and has delivered me out of the hand of Herod and from all the expectation of the people of the Jews."

In all decisions on the path of life, the follower of Jesus prays for guidance. He looks for it with the eye of the soul, and with the soul's ear he listens hopefully. So Peter, alone and freed miraculously in the empty street, "considered the thing" and presently knew exactly what he was to do. He went straight to the house of Mary, Mark's mother, one of the most ardent Christians in the whole Jerusalem band.

Young Mark and his family were people of some substance. They lived in a large, ancestral house on the eastern edge of the city, set around with a grove of fragrant trees. There is a certain mystery about how Mark came to give up his comfortable life to follow the austere Christian program. Some believe that by an indefinable attraction he had found his way into the Garden of Gethsemane on the night of the Master's betrayal, and that after the traitor's kiss, Mark lost his garment and was seen, a young man fleeing naked among the trees in the moonlight. But no one was ever sure, and though Mark tells that story in his Gospel, he never publicly admitted that it was himself who hovered so close to the Christians that night, longing to be one of them. Others believe that Mark was one of those welcomed as a boy when Christ said: "Suffer little children to come unto Me."

Fourteen years had passed since that night in Gethsemane. Now it was sunrise of a spring day in the year 44 as Peter, having "considered the thing," made his way through the quiet streets, entered Mark's front gate, and stood listening below an open window.

Elsewhere in Jerusalem people might still be sleeping, but not in this house. Through the window the apostle could hear voices, low and intense and full of entreaty. Head turned aside, bright eyes halfclosed, the greatest of fishermen could make out their words.

They were praying—and for him, as Christians were doing all over the city. All night they had been on their knees. Unwearied, they continued to lift their voices, storming heaven that Peter be spared the wrath of Herod Agrippa and be loosed from prison.

Peter could not help smiling to himself as he knocked gently on the door.

Among the hired servants of the house was a damsel called Rhoda, who answered Peter's knuckles on the shutter.

"Who is it?" she whispered, the never-absent Christian fear of the authorities in her tone.

"It is I. Peter!"

Peter, for whom they had been praying all night long; Peter on their doorstep!

Rhoda was so overcome with gladness that she witlessly left Peter outside, the door still bolted against him, while she rushed down the long corridor and pulled aside the hall curtains, crying above the eager drone of the prayers:

"Listen! Listen! Peter stands before the gate."

Several voices broke the brief and sudden spell of silence, three or four shocked and incredulous Christians, who had been praying all night for this very thing, yet could not believe their answer when it came, all exclaiming together:

"Rhoda! You are mad!"

"No, he's really at the front door."

"You are beside yourself, girl."

"Come and see for yourselves!"

The whole company rose up, some going to the windows over the dewy garden, others following the maid to the door.

Surely, there was Peter! Or was it his angel?

Peter lifted his hand and beckoned them with a cajoling gesture to believe that it was really he, the Peter they all knew, in his own proper person and clad in his right mind. In the morning stillness, before the alarm was given, he had come to tell them what had happened.

Especially, Peter told them, they must go find the other James ("James the Less"), a recognized pillar of the early Church, who was now to assume heavier and more difficult responsibilities.

"Go tell these things to James," was Peter's command. "To James and to the brethren."

And upon their promise he blessed them, turned and walked out of the garden and up the street, vanishing around a bend in the line of houses. He did not say where he was going, and if cross-examined by the police, they could honestly declare their ignorance.

No one knew then where Peter was gone.

Chapter 45. EATEN OF WORMS

CONSTERNATION buzzed through the prison from which Peter had disappeared.

The guards to whom he had been chained slept late that morning. With no restless captive between them, they lay undisturbed and snoring. On routine check, the chief jailer came with his lantern and saw that their prisoner had vanished, as if with magical power.

"Where is that Christian, Peter?" the chief jailer roared. "What has become of him?"

No one in the prison could tell him where Peter was, nor the governor of the guards, nor the army board of supervision. Christians picked up for questioning swore with truth in their faces that they knew nothing of the whereabouts of that beloved Galilean. Herod Agrippa ranted from his throne, condemning his forces and commanding that the jailers be promptly and bloodily put to death.

To save face, in his sulking fury, Herod Agrippa I then left the triumphant Christian headquarters in Judaea to visit his coastal territories and see if things were better managed in the hinterland. His gilded throne was bound to the back of a donkey and guarded on four sides by soldiers.

At Caesarea the throne was set up, and where Peter had recently demonstrated such power by receiving the first Gentile converts, now Herod paraded in his purple robes and made himself the human image of imperial might.

He let the people of the cities round about know that he found a great deal to complain of; especially the misbehavior of the citizens of Tyre and Sidon. They were disobedient to new ordinances, slow with their tax money. Everywhere, the king decided, burned a restless atmosphere generated by the Christian apostles. Men wanted to be free and they wanted to be kind, a new and unbearable heresy in the kingdom.

Fright at the king's wrath began to grow. Those near him wished to show Herod Agrippa I their loyalty. They used the royal chamberlain as their go-between; a certain Blastus, who listened affably to their protestations. Their country, the concerned citizens pointed out to Blastus, was nourished by the king's country; without yearly aid from Judaea where would Caesarea be? Would Blastus not help them make peace?

So successful was Blastus that Herod Agrippa decided to make a public ceremony of reconciliation with his people. He lolled on the throne set up amid greenery and blossoms in the public market place, while brassy trumpets and pounded drum skins called the people to assembly.

Herod Agrippa I, rejoicing at these public evidences of his authority, orated by the hour, relishing the sound of his own voice as he rolled the Aramaic syllables under his tongue. In many and various ways he explained how great a king he was. He told them that his influence and wisdom had brought them peace and prosperous harvests; he had planned their welfare, even to the rain from heaven.

"And the people gave a shout, saying: 'It is the voice of a god and not of a man,'" Luke writes sadly.

At that delirious cry, Herod Agrippa smiled at Blastus the chamberlain, who was also the king's eunuch and kept order among his wives and probably hated his potent master. Blastus smiled back. Both men knew that monarchs of Egypt and Babylon and other great places had deified themselves. In fact, for a king to become a god was an astute act of statesmanship; then there could be no appeal from his decisions, no greater power to overrule the state in earth or in heaven.

So Herod Agrippa took his bows at the shouts of the worshipful people. But his triumph did not last sixty seconds after he had accepted this promotion to godhood. Luke reports most briskly and matter-of-factly:

"And forthwith an angel of the Lord struck him, because he had not given the honor to God; and being eaten up by worms he gave up the ghost."

Eaten by worms! This descendant of Herod the Great was dying even as his grandfather had died, in an agony of pollution and corruption. People jamming the market place saw him stricken at the height of his self-imposed magnificence, saw him perish in squirming, odious horror before their eyes. Beholding that fearsome judgment on mortal arrogance, they remembered the simple humility of Peter and his fellow Christians and their fearlessness as they spread Jesus' holy words.

It was not at all surprising, then, that: ". . . the Word of God increased and multiplied."

The people saw—as men eventually must—that it is footless to put your trust in kings.

Chapter 46. PAUL TAKES THE STAGE

THE infant Church by this time had emerged from swaddling clothes and was ready to walk alone.

The ideal of Christianity, in spite of the legalism of the Pharisees and the pagan agnosticism and atheism of Romans and Greeks, was spreading in an epidemic of fervor throughout Palestine, and beyond. Already Paul and Barnabas were at work among the Gentiles in the mighty Syrian city of Antioch.

Barnabas was an able teacher, full of gentle and earnest conviction. But Paul was a human volcano, erupting with fires that rose from some inner caldron of the soul and exploded in light. Soon Peter heard of Paul's extraordinary eloquence and the converts he was winning. And for the first time, Peter, the man of rock, heard a new word on the world's tongue. In Antioch, the followers and converts were given a new name:

"And the disciples," Luke reported, "were called Christians first in Antioch."

A man named Agabus from the Jerusalem center, gifted with some degree of prophecy, had journeyed with friends down to Antioch. Moved by this spirit of prophecy, Agabus stood before Paul and Barnabas and the throng of Christians to foretell a famine in the world.

The men who heard Agabus make this prognostication knew that he "signified by the Spirit"—that through him was speaking nothing less than the Holy Ghost. Although it would be some time before the prophecy of Agabus was indeed fulfilled in the reign of Claudius, his listeners in Antioch accepted it literally. No matter how distant the tragic crisis might be, the Christians of Antioch wanted to help their less fortunate brothers.

Paul urged them on in their charity. To him, fellowship was all-embracing. Perhaps he was the first to express the truth that the Church was universal, that Christians everywhere were tied by bonds of charity and love, literally brothers the world over. For the rest of his life Paul would charge local church members with the responsibility of contributing from their own wealth and blessings to the needs of the whole Church. He would carry vast collections of money from his own missions to the headquarters in Jerusalem, earthly evidence of unity in the faith.

The first of these collections Paul raised in Antioch, after the prophecy of Agabus.

"When the famine comes," Paul's followers said to themselves, "the people of Judaea, and especially our brethren in overcrowded

Jerusalem, will suffer much more than we will out here in this fertile region. Besides, they cannot act and move as freely for fear of persecutions. We must raise a relief fund for them. Then they can lay in stores of food to weather the crisis."

Soon, with a bag jingling with copper, silver, and gold, Paul and Barnabas made their way to Jerusalem, bringing this first big collection, proof that provincialism had no place in a Church where the suffering of one part was the suffering of the whole.

In the years lying ahead of the Christians, Paul of Tarsus was to move in such spectacular journeys that wherever men talked of Jesus they also spoke of the tentmaker.

But Peter, the man of rock, remained unspectacularly the head and front of the Church.

Soon his long residence in Jerusalem would come to an end. After the execution of the thunderous James the Greater and Peter's own arrest and release, and after his farewell appearance at Mark's house, Peter was hidden in "another place." Luke is no more specific than those two words in his report. Nor does he give any account of Peter's subsequent activities; there are only brief references to certain episodes in his later life. Many think that the ever nagging fear that publicity might endanger his safety kept Christians silent on his whereabouts.

Rome and martyrdom were waiting for him. The curtain which fell upon his life has been pierced only by archaeological research, tradition and legend.

But no such obscurity hides the life of Paul. Thanks to his own masterful writings and to the brilliant news coverage of his yokefellow Luke, whom he was soon to meet, Paul's incredible adventures as a missioner are preserved in breath-taking detail.

Peter and Paul would meet again. But until that time it is the tentmaker, the ex-persecutor, the man who once hated Christians, who takes the stage for Christ.

BOOK FIVE

Paul's First Journey

Chapter 47. "SEPARATE ME!"

Paul's great call came soon after he and Barnabas returned from Jerusalem and settled again in Syrian Antioch.

That city, on the banks of the Orontes, Antioch, called "the great" and "the beautiful" was soon recognized as the mother-church of Gentile Christianity, nursery of missionary efforts that would penetrate the mainland of Europe. Today a squalid village known as Antakya is all that remains of the ancient Syrian metropolis where the name "Christian" was coined for the followers of Jesus.

Those first Christians in Syrian Antioch were a strange and multicolored crew. Jews, some of them fugitives from persecutions in Palestine, some of them born Syrians, mingled with the fair-haired Greek converts whom Barnabas had been sent to instruct. Adventurers from the island of Cyprus prayed shoulder to shoulder with dark-skinned men from the northern coast of Africa.

In the Christian assembly at Antioch, as elewhere, were men who were veritable prophets, converts of profound spiritual insight, endowed by the Holy Ghost with the power of revelation. And in these days a special message concerning Paul and Barnabas came to three of those gifted souls.

One was Simeon Niger, a member of that original band of seventy-two disciples sent by Jesus Himself in His own lifetime to preach the Gospel. Another was Lucius, an African from Cyrene who had wandered to Syria in quest of truth—and found faith as well.

The third was a man named Manaen, a nobleman with a strange

and dramatic history. Manaen was the foster-brother of the gruesome Herod Antipas. He had been raised with that ugly tyrant, pampered as he was, fawned on by slaves and courtiers, high priests and Sadducees. He had seen the head of John the Baptist carried on a silver platter before the nose of his foster-brother, and had fled in horror.

Manaen had left Herod's court to follow the Christ, a convert like so many of that royal household, including Joanna, the steward's wife who wept at Jesus' tomb with Mary the mother of Jesus. Manaen had tossed aside pomp and prestige, and stayed in Jerusalem with Peter and the apostles—until the day when the murderous Captain Saul had lunged with fire at the fledgling Church.

Then Manaen went to Antioch in Syria, fleeing from the persecution after Stephen's death.

Now, fourteen years later, after fasting and ministering to the Lord, Manaen stood with Lucius and Simeon Niger and looked at Paul, the man from whom he had once fled. And the Holy Ghost spoke through Manaen and the two other prophets this divine message:

"Separate Me Paul and Barnabas, for the work whereunto I have taken them."

Profound meaning lay wrapped in that brief supernatural instruction. Paul and Barnabas were specially chosen for a unique mission designed by the Holy Spirit! Let no one detain the vigorous little scholar from Tarsus, or the august, bearded islander from Cyprus. Let them not ask why, or how—but set them apart to follow the direction they will surely be given.

Together, in strong and manly contrast, Paul and Barnabas rose before their brethren. Simeon Niger and Lucius of Cyrene and Manaen, the ex-princeling, prayed eloquently for blessings on the travelers, and, blessing them, sent them away.

Paul and Barnabas took Barnabas' young cousin Mark with them. They needed someone as an amanuensis, a combination secretary and traveler-companion, and the missionary experience should prove invaluable to Mark as well. The young man's eyes were agleam with pride and excitement as they set out, a rugged trio.

They turned their backs on Syrian Antioch, the farewells of the brethren ringing in their ears. With prayer and silence they tramped along the traffic-laden Orontes River, going sixteen miles west to the harbor of Seleucia. That port was then five miles north of the river mouth, and the roadstead there was not yet silted up with muck from

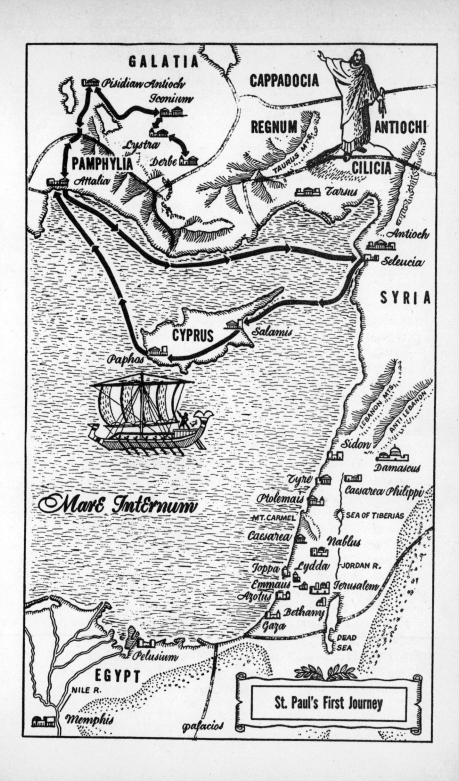

St. Paul's First Journey

upstream. The three travelers bargained with the master of a sailing ship poised for departure, and finally strode aboard. The ship's destination, and theirs, was Cyprus, the island where Barnabas was born.

Chapter 48. CHILD OF THE DEVIL

BARNABAS expanded, his eyes softening with nostalgia as, with an arm around his cousin's shoulder, he talked to his two companions about his homeland. He told them of the island's seemingly inexhaustible copper mines and boundless timber forests, of the wine and wheat and silkworms. Back into his childhood he delved for memories of Levite life on that gentle isle, peaceful at last under Roman rule in the person of a proconsul. And he reminded Paul and Mark that some Christians were living in Cyprus, worshiping secretly, too fearful of repression by the authorities to make new converts.

All through that smooth passage across the Mediterranean fair winds blew, and the three men talked and prayed. But once the mountains of Cyprus hove into view, long before they docked in the noisy port of Salamis, they pressed close to the rail, afire with eagerness to get ashore. Here in this bustling business capital of Cyprus they were to start their dangerous work.

It was Paul's usual decision to head straight for the synagogue. Paul was an ex-Pharisee, a theologian, and he thought of the holy place of God as the natural pulpit for the message of redemption. If the shy and gentle Barnabas remembered Peter's dream in Joppa and the conversion of the Gentiles in the house of Cornelius, he said nothing whatever to disturb Paul's resolution. All three of them, he knew, were under the guidance of the Holy Spirit; they would not fail.

Across all the island of Cyprus, sometimes on foot, sometimes alternating rides on a borrowed donkey, Paul, Barnabas, and Mark made their way, preaching the word of God in every community. They intended to make their headquarters in a large town, and now chose Paphos, political capital of the province and the dwelling place of the proconsul.

And there, for the first time, Paul, the convert Jew and citizen of Rome, ran headlong into black magic. He found himself confronted with Bar-Jesus, the sorcerer, also called Elymas, which meant "strong."

This spell-juggler was a fellow of obscure origin who had lifted himself by conjuring, sleight of hand, and hoodwinking to a powerful political position. By the time the three traveling Christians reached Paphos, Bar-Jesus was permanently attached to the retinue of the Roman boss of the town, the proconsul Sergius Paulus, a rich man, proprietor of great lands, appointed to represent the majesty of empire.

Sergius Paulus was more than a soldier who had well feathered his governmental nest. He had a keenly curious mind, interested in the mystery of life. Hence his attraction to this Bar-Jesus, who seemed to possess the dark secrets of nature, who even could command her forces to do his will—or so it appeared when he performed his tricks under the guise of miracles. But the ruler's restless quest for the spark of life also led Sergius Paulus to wish to meet the Christians.

Bar-Jesus grumbled when Sergius Paulus invited the strangers to instruct him in the new faith, but the Roman waved aside his sorcerer's protests. These visitors had a new doctrine, and Sergius Paulus was determined to learn about it. They carried no amulets or potions or tools of witchcraft, but only the history and promises of Christ. Let us hear these men!

Bar-Jesus claimed to be a diviner, to read the future. Perhaps if he could have read his own he would have worked harder to keep the missionaries away from the door.

Even so, when Paul and his friends arrived at the palace, Bar-Jesus stamped his foot and railed against the outlanders. He denounced them as false prophets; he hissed and spat on the floor before them.

Sergius Paulus sat back in his gilded and purple chair, watching to see how this attack would be met. He saw a man inspired. The compact figure of Paul seemed to grow visibly taller as he was filled with the Holy Ghost. Looking straight at the infuriated magician, Paul spoke with the calm, contained grace that comes only from a supernatural source:

"O full of all guile and of all deceit! Child of the devil, enemy of all justice, you cease not to pervert the right ways of the Lord!

"And now behold, the hand of the Lord is upon you, and you shall be blind, not seeing the sun for a time!"

Instantly darkness fell upon the pretender. He began to moan as he groped helplessly across the room, begging for someone to lead him by the hand.

Bar-Jesus was blind.

And the man by whose words darkness had fallen on the sorcerer was the man the Lord Himself had blinded on the road to Damascus, fourteen years before!

Sergius Paulus was too intelligent not to have had some suspicions of the thaumaturgy of Bar-Jesus. But now he knew beyond any doubt that he was in the presence of an indisputable miracle—the first ever performed by Paul.

And Sergius Paulus, the proconsul, was converted. "He believed," says Luke, "admiring at the doctrine of the Lord."

Chapter 49.   "BEHOLD, YE DESPISERS!"

WITH that flamboyant sign of the triumphant power of the Lord Jesus, Paul, Barnabas, and Mark made ready to leave Cyprus. Now that Sergius Paulus was won to eager acceptance of the faith, the Christians on the island, childhood friends and relatives of Barnabas, could worship openly. They could, with their ordained deacons and priests, teach and pray without fear of persecution.

Paul, driven on by the Holy Ghost, could not linger on Cyprus. From Paphos, the town where the sorcerer lay in the temporary prison of blindness, the travelers took ship again. Paul's heart was high at the first taste of success in a difficult task.

In the midst of this felicity came trouble. They were already at sea, sailing for Pamphylia, when Mark decided to abandon his two saintly companions and return alone to Jerusalem.

Why? What happened among them so soon after their initial victory? No one has ever fully revealed the cause of the dissension.

No one can say what made Mark quit Paul to go back to Peter, but the mind is tempted to speculate. It cannot be that a young man who had already shown such courage could have shrunk from the dangers of their new destination. When they boarded ship at Paphos, all three were well aware of the kind of place to which they were being led by the inspiration of the Holy Ghost. Pamphylia was notorious both for its crime and its equally evil climate.

Today Pamphylia is in what we call Turkey; a level coastal plain lying south of the Taurus Mountains, on the mainland of Europe. It was a down-at-the-heel place, always subject to some foreign domination, inhabited by men with no heroic history. Once upon a time the great Cicero had been its governor. But neither he nor the procurators that came after could prevent these people from being pirates. For centuries of corsair dynasties they had plundered Mediterranean ships and harbors, doing an especially profitable business in human captives at the slave market in the town of Side. A place of swamp fevers and criminal gangs, Pamphylia was the next port of call for Paul and Barnabas.

But not for Mark. He went as far with them as Attalia, the port of this small Roman province. There he refused to go ashore.

Was Mark afraid? Was he homesick for Jerusalem and Peter? Did he dislike Paul, or resent the ex-persecutor's leadership of the trio? A great career of service awaited Mark. He was to walk with Peter till the man of rock died. He was to write from Peter's own lips the history which today we call the Gospel According to St. Mark.

Eventually, Mark would win his way back into Paul's graces, and serve him again before the apostle's death. But some deep split of temperament or belief drove a wedge between them on the isle of Paphos. Years later Paul would speak ruefully of the young man's "desertion" from the mission effort; but he would never explain the cause of it.

Whatever the reason, Mark sailed away from Paul and Barnabas, and they went on sadly without him into the land of Pamphylia.

Several miles inland they trudged to Perga, near the mouth of the Cestrus River. Perga was not a big place, but it was prosperous and imposing. Surprise showed in the eyes of Paul and Barnabas at sight of a theater with seats for thirteen thousand, and a stadium holding many more.

Dominating the scene was the temple of the city's goddess, a nature deity who fostered excesses of human appetites and smiled on those who debased their lust in her honor. Here in Pamphylia the flamboyant goddess of masked evil was known as "Queen of Perga." Her graceful figure, and the temple of her cult, were even stamped on the local coins of copper and silver.

In the shadow of her temple Paul and Barnabas preached the word of God, and the message of Jesus Christ was delivered all the more eloquently because of the sordid human misbehavior for which the Pergan Queen stood.

Next, the two companions struck out north into the higher country of central Asia Minor. Miasmas of the swamps around Perga had crept over Paul, and fever had come to him with the pains of malaria. The higher altitudes now steadied his health.

But Paul was never patient with his infirmities. Regardless of his fevers and agues, he plunged into action as they reached the Roman province of Galatia, and the cities of Iconium, Lystra, Derbe, and another Antioch—called Pisidian Antioch to distinguish it from its namesake in Syria. It was a free city, a center of Hellenistic culture, straddling a major trade route between Ephesus and Cilicia. And in this Pisidian Antioch lived a sizable colony of Jews.

Paul always went, as his letters state, "to the Jews first," as Christ Himself did. Now with Barnabas he went to the synagogue during the Sabbath services and sat down. The Law was read aloud and selections from the Prophets, just as in synagogues today. The ushers came down to the back of the room, where Paul and Barnabas had taken their places, and invited them to participate.

"You men, brethren, if you have any word of exhortation to make to the people, speak."

And as Luke tells it, Paul stood up, and "with his hand bespeaking silence," said:

"You men of Israel, and you that fear God, give ear.

"The God of the people of Israel chose our fathers, and exalted the people when they were sojourners in the land of Egypt, and with a high arm brought them out from thence, and for the space of forty years endured their manners in the desert. And destroying seven nations in the land of Canaan, divided their land among them by lot, as it were, after four hundred and fifty years: and after these things, He gave unto them judges, until Samuel the prophet.

"And after that they desired a king; and God gave them Saul the son of Cis, a man of the tribe of Benjamin, forty years. And when He had removed him, He raised them up David to be king: to whom giving testimony, He said: 'I have found David, the son of Jesse, a man according to My own heart, who shall do all My wills.'

"Of this man's seed God according to His promise, hath raised up to Israel a Saviour, Jesus: John first preaching, before His coming, the baptism of penance to all the people of Israel.

"And when John was fulfilling his course, he said: 'I am not He, whom you think me to be: but behold, there cometh One after me, whose shoes of His feet I am not worthy to loose.'"

Paul paused to measure his audience in one long moment of silence. Then:

"Men, brethren, children of the stock of Abraham, and whosoever among you fear God—to you the word of this salvation is sent!

"For they that inhabited Jerusalem, and the rulers thereof, not knowing Him, nor the voices of the prophets (which are read every Sabbath) judging Him have fulfilled them. And finding no cause of death in Him, they desired of Pilate, that they might kill Him. And when they had fulfilled all things that were written of Him, taking Him down from the tree, they laid Him in a sepulchre.

"But God raised Him up from the dead the third day:

"Who was seen for many days, by them who came up with Him from Galilee to Jerusalem, who to this present are His witnesses to the people!

"And we declare unto you, that the promise which was made to our fathers, this same God hath fulfilled to our children, raising up Jesus, as in the second psalm also is written: 'Thou art My Son, this day have I begotten Thee.'

"And to show that He raised Him up from the dead, not to return now any more to corruption, He said thus: 'I will give You the holy things of David faithful.'

"And therefore, in another place also, He saith: 'Thou shalt not suffer Thy Holy One to see corruption.'

"For David, when he had served in his generation, according to the will of God, slept: and was laid unto his fathers, and saw corruption. But He whom God hath raised from the dead, saw no corruption.

"Be it known therefore to you, men, brethren, that through Him forgiveness of sins is preached to you; and from all the things, from which you could not be justified by the Law of Moses, in Him every one that believeth, is justified.

"Beware, therefore, lest that come upon you which is spoken in the Prophets: 'Behold, ye despisers, and wonder, and perish: for I work a work in your days, a work which you will not believe, if any man shall tell it to you.'"

For a while it looked as if here in Pisidian Antioch Paul and Barnabas were to have an unprecedented triumph.

The city buzzed with talk about Paul's sermons. When the service in the synagogue was over, many of the Jews, as well as others who had joined the congregation of Israel, followed Paul and Barnabas all the way to their lodgings over a shop in a busy street. They plied the two evangelists with questions; they were excited, hungering and thirsting after knowledge and eager to be filled.

"Won't you come next Sabbath and tell us more?" they begged.

And when the next Sabbath came, and Paul and Barnabas approached the synagogue they were astounded at the sight awaiting them. The open space in front of the synagogue and the branching streets were packed solid. Pirates and cobblers, men and women of all the crafts and combines, farmers from far around were standing close together, all for one purpose: to hear the remarkable message of Jesus Christ and His redemption, brought by the two visitors from across the Mediterranean.

"The whole city, almost," Luke reported, "came together to hear the word of God."

And, as might have been expected, there was trouble.

Hardly had Paul started on his oration, lifting his voice to reach them all, his head gleaming in the sunlight, when the heckling began. Up rose one elder and contradicted a statement. Evidently, he said, this Paul of Tarsus is ignorant of the Law.

Ignorant of the Law? Take care. Don't tangle with Paul the ex-Pharisee! The elder recognized a sharp opponent soon enough and changed his tactics, deciding it was not wise to debate with this scholar; better to shout him down. The resultant heckling turned the meeting into a hubbub of clamoring Pharisees.

But above the clamor Paul and Barnabas managed to be heard, and what they said was clear and positive:

"To you it behooved us first to speak the word of God; but because you reject it, and judge yourselves unworthy of eternal life, behold we turn to the Gentiles. For so the Lord hath commanded us: 'I have set thee to be the light of the Gentiles; that thou mayest be for salvation unto the utmost parts of the earth.' "

From the throats of the Gentiles in the crowd there rose a cry of joy, and many converts were made among them that day. They glorified the word of the Lord; they believed and their lives were changed.

But the Pharisees were not yet defeated. The fact that the message of Jesus Christ was being spread all through the country inflamed them. All night long they sat up, complotting the ruin of the two Christian teachers. Next day they were busy knocking on the doors of leading citizens, powerful laymen who listened believingly to the elders' outrageous tales.

The Pharisees did not even stop with the men—some of whom had been impressed by Paul and Barnabas—but stirred up religious and honorable Jewish women, spinsters, housewives, widows, and young maids looking forward to being brides. With a clattering of tongues, these women began to repeat the tales, elaborating and inflating them into vast, dismal, and foul exaggerations, beginning soon themselves to believe what they were saying.

Before long, armed men came to the house where Paul and Barnabas were staying, to accuse them of heretical doctrines and vile behavior and threaten their lives. They shoved the preachers out of the house, into the street, through the gate, and onto the open road, all the way down to the coast. They were driven out of Antioch.

The harried pair remembered instructions given long ago in Galilee, and repeated by Peter. Now they followed those words meticulously. They "shook off the dust of their feet against" their foes. Then they boarded a ship which was just getting under way.

Antioch, how goes it with you today? You are a huddle of ruins, important only to archaeologists who read what is carved on your tumbled stones. But Paul and Barnabas still live in the hearts of men across the world.

Chapter 50. TURMOIL IN ICONIUM

THEIR next goal was Iconium, also in Galatia.

In this city (known today as Konya, Turkey) things were to be different. The town was actually an oasis in the high, unwatered plateau of Lycaonia, a busy place on one of the long roads leading to Rome.

The reputation of the two missioners had reached Iconium before them. An intensely interested crowd awaited them at the local synagogue; not only the Jews of the congregation but Greeks also, who had been converted to the one, true God of the Old Testament and worshiped there.

The crowd was a heartening sight. Both Paul and Barnabas were suffused with the power of the Holy Spirit as they talked. The simple, strong delivery of Barnabas and the increasingly impassioned speech of Paul stirred the emotions of their listeners like a cleansing wind.

There is a story told of Paul's visit to Iconium that will not down through all the centuries—the romantic history of a beautiful Greek maiden of an important family, who sat secluded in her house by an open window and heard the missioners speak. Her name was Thecla, and legend tells that she thereupon dedicated herself to perpetual virginity and the service of God. Traditions abound of her faithfulness under trial. It is told that she was bound to a stake, about to be burned alive, but was miraculously set free. In another city, thrown into the cages of wild beasts, she was again miraculously saved. She finally overtook Paul at the city of Myra and was allowed by him—so the legends say—to serve as a "female apostle."

Was there ever really a Thecla? Learned writers of history in modern encyclopedias are inclined to believe the legend stems back to some authentic root. There is today a church near ancient Iconium in Sophia called *St. Philip and St. Thecla,* and her name is greatly venerated in the Greek and Oriental Christian churches. She first appeared in literature in what might be compared to a religious novel, which appeared a hundred years after Paul and Barnabas stopped in Antioch and Iconium. That fiction of 160–170 was lost for longer than a millennium, but a Coptic copy of it turned up in 1856. Whatever the actual truth, the fact that Thecla has survived the centuries invests her with a singular importance.

The strict attitude of Paul toward women, in and out of the Church and in all their relationships with men, is a topic of endless debate. But the girl at the window in Iconium found nothing forbidding in the apostle's ideas of woman's place in the world. She was only one of many who would serve in his mission fields, forerunner in truth or legend of such dedicated women as Priscilla, a tentmaker's wife, and Lydia, the seller of purple.

Thecla may be fact or fiction, but there was nothing imaginary about the crowds of people in Iconium who clamored to talk to Paul and Barnabas after their speech in the synagogue. Christian fervor seethed in the streets of Iconium. The Pharisees found the situation intolerable.

The same kind of unbending legalists who had made war upon Paul and Barnabas elsewhere sought in Iconium to stir up the Roman authorities against them, calling them subversive agents, advance men for revolution, enemies of Caesar.

At first their guileful schemes did not work. The apostles went on with their preaching, baptizing, confirming, and giving of Holy Communion, and no one interfered.

Then suddenly the smothered fires of hatred burst into flame. The town was divided against itself, "and some of them indeed held with the Jews but some with the apostles." Civil war within the city walls might break out at any moment, and then the Roman soldiers would take over, blood would flow, and the city would come under the cruel domination of the troops. Some demanded that the rulers order Paul and Barnabas to be stoned to death. Others swore they would give their own lives to protect the preachers of God's word.

But as the evil brew stirred by the Pharisees was coming to a boil, Paul and Barnabas took the situation into their own hands. While other men muttered and wrangled, the two apostles, Paul, short, stocky, and fairly hopping with energy in spite of his lingering blackwater fever, and Barnabas, bearded, kingly, and at peace with himself, slipped through the city gates.

They were far beyond the Iconium walls before their enemies knew that they had escaped.

Chapter 51. LEFT FOR DEAD

THEY toured the southeast part of the land, from Iconium to the smaller cities of Lystra and Derbe. To all the country around about they preached, in farm houses and at the crossroads of small villages, and they never left any place without seeding it with converts.

At the gate of Lystra a challenge confronted them—which they met with a miracle.

Through that gate, as they stood in its cool but bustling shadows, they could see at the green square in the midst of the town a great stone pedestal supporting a statue of the "divine" Augustus. The old pedestal is still there, its Latin inscriptions still readable and helpful to historians and archaeologists. The two apostles passed through the gate and beheld a most pathetic wreck of humanity sitting on an old rock against the wall.

He looked helplessly at the rushing crowds. No one gave him a glance. No one would fetch him a drink of water. Yet he could not go after a drink himself because his feet were paralyzed; he had never in all his life been able to move right foot or left, not from his mother's womb. Relatives carried him to his place against the wall in the morning and lugged him home at night. They left him an old skin of water and a handful of figs to munch on, together with some wheaten cakes—food enough to keep him alive.

Not even Paul and Barnabas noticed him at first. They had their own dangerous project foremost in mind; they were in Lystra to preach the word of God, having just escaped being stoned to death in Iconium.

Near to the gate they began at once: "Listen, you men of Lystra. We tell you of Jesus Christ; true God and true Man, this Jesus, whose yoke is easy and whose burden is light; come unto Him all you that labor and are heavy laden and He will give you rest."

The rushing crowds slowed down and gathered around as Paul told them of the miraculous and healing Christ.

"He heals, you say? Can He still heal, now that He has gone, leaving you with the Comforter, the Holy Ghost you tell us of? Can He heal me?" In a croaking voice, the paralyzed man made his plea, holding out entreating, clawlike hands, his soul yearning in his eyes. "Let me walk! In the name of Christ, let me walk."

Paul knew the first spring of faith when he saw it; the man's face was like a light. Without a moment's hesitation, Paul cried in a loud voice:

"Stand upright, on your feet."

And the old man leaped up, and walked.

Down many centuries we can hear the cries of the watching pagans:

"The gods are come down to us in the likeness of men!"

In their native language, they called Barnabas "Jupiter" and Paul, because he was the chief speaker, "Mercury." And they stared at the miracle workers and believed they saw living gods.

It was embarrassing to those two truth-loving apostles of Christ to be mistaken for the gods of Mount Olympus. More embarrassment was to follow.

With all his eloquence, Paul tried to convince the crowd that neither he nor his friend were deities. They were men, and nothing more; a tentmaker from Tarsus and a student from Cyprus; and they came, not preaching about themselves but of the Messiah, whose messengers they were. But the crowd ignored his protests.

Paul must have been a far handsomer man than the Corinthians were willing to admit when, later on, they spoke of him so scornfully as "a man of little stature," of insignificant personal appearance. These Galatians of Lystra mistook him for a god, a very handsome one indeed; for none less than Hermes, whose other name was Mercury, the bright first-born of Jupiter and patron of wrestling and other gymnastic exercises (in which Paul, as we know, was expert). Many marbles of every Grecian city were shaped to show Hermes as a magnificent figure, with wings on his cap and his shoes. And he was the messenger of his father, who rules the heavens! To be taken for Hermes was indeed a compliment.

While Paul was trying desperately to dispel this unfortunate impression, two men left the crowd that swayed and milled around the strangers and rushed toward the temple of Jupiter, a handsome shrine with graceful Ionic marble columns, carved pediment, and architrave gleaming in the mellowing rays of the sunset. The high priest there heard the news from the two messengers and gasped with excitement.

Jupiter and his son come to earth? To Lystra? Hermes is healing the paralyzed at the city gate? Why had the god not come immediately to his father's own temple, where he belonged?

The priest of Jupiter was beside himself with excitement and curiosity. He cupped his hands and bellowed for help. Attendants came running from every direction: acolytes and censer carriers and couriers and scullion boys. The whole population of the temple area answered the flailing commands of the high priest. "Bring the oxen from the stables! Twine blossoms from our gardens and garland the necks of the oxen and take them after me, as I start for the city gate where Hermes is preaching and healing the unhealable. Drive the flowery oxen; goad them, prick them, whip them on. We must get there before it is too late."

From far across the city square, Paul saw the procession. He had watched the rising fever of the mob, had tried to restore calm and common sense. But now the hysteria was soaring; bodies swaying, eyes glittering, lips drooling, a frenzy seizing every mind, firing the blood, raising a storm of emotion that no mere mortal could still.

Paul and Barnabas were appalled. These people were adoring them idolatrously, and coming toward them was a fresh crowd, following the priest of Jupiter and the pair of oxen wreathed in red and white roses, preparing to stand before the missioners and cut the throats of the oxen so that their blood would stain with scarlet the feet of the people.

"Sirs!" bellowed Paul, "why do you do these things?"

He tore his garments before them all, as Caiphas had done falsely at the trial of Jesus; as any faithful Jew must do truly when he is in the presence of blasphemy or idolatry.

Paul and Barnabas both rent their clothes. With tears on their cheeks, they leaped headlong into the crowd, and Paul's voice could be heard above all the uproar:

"We also are mortals, men like unto you, preaching to you that you should be converted from these vain things to the living God, who made the heaven, and the earth, and the sea, and all things that are in them, Who in times past suffered all nations to walk in their own ways. Nevertheless He left not Himself without testimony, doing good from heaven, giving rains and fruitful seasons, filling our hearts with food and gladness."

But the fact that they repudiated the sacrifice only increased the general huggermugger, turning it now into rage. The crowd that wanted to bow down and worship these two visitors, the priest that wanted to sacrifice before them—the whole hooting rabble turned against them, infuriated at denial.

At that very moment there entered town, dusty and wroth through the gates of the city, certain agents of the Pharisees, emissaries of Jewish opposition come from Pisidian Antioch and Iconium.

They screamed their denunciations, adding fuel to the mob's anger. They insisted that Paul and Barnabas were impostors and blasphemers; they demanded that the missioners be turned over to them.

And now Paul remembered Stephen, and so did Barnabas.

Out through the city gate their enemies dragged them to an execution hillside. The Pharisees made a half-moon around the prisoners, as others had done before Stephen. One functionary held the stoners' outer garments, as once Paul had held such garments.

The mob, that had wanted to worship these two as gods half an hour earlier, waited now, popeyed and gleeful at the bloody death that would be done. The Christians stood by, helpless.

"I have been stoned once!" This moment Paul would one day recall to the minds of the Corinthians, when he wrote to them all he had suffered for the faith.

The first shower of missiles came flying, sharp-edged rock fragments, and then another and more and more, all aimed at Paul. Somehow they were not stoning Barnabas. Only Paul stood, as he had seen Stephen stand, ready to die as bravely as he had died.

He fell under that hail of rocks. He lay stilled. They left him for dead. Only mourning Christians stood near, ready to carry away his body for burial.

Then Paul moved. He turned, groaned, and raised himself up, balancing his weight on one bloody hand. They helped him to stand. He leaned heavily upon Barnabas, hearing the Christians counsel him to fly into some other safer place under cover of the lowering darkness.

But Paul shook his head. He was not ready to leave Lystra. Better to show converts and enemies alike what an apostle can endure in the sacred cause.

"He rose up and came into the city," Luke tells us crisply.

Christianity had a missioner to be reckoned with, a man who could never be called a coward. He went back to the people who thought they had killed him.

The wisdom of Paul's resolution was soon proved.

He left Lystra the next day, proudly, of his own free will, under his own power. Every soul in the city knew that he had survived the stoning and had shown himself again in the midst of his destroyers. No one dared lay a hand on him.

They had thought him the son of a god named Jupiter. As they lined the streets, thousands strong, silently watching Paul's triumphant departure, they pondered on the Christ he had tried to preach to them—the One who is the Son of God!

Chapter 52.   FULL CIRCLE

THE afternoon shadows were growing out of noon's heat as Barnabas and Paul started to walk the high road that led from Lystra to the town of Derbe.

The two missioners of Christ preached with success in that small, half-Greek community on the southeastern border of the province of Galatia. The calm after such violences as they had lived through gave them time to reflect, while Paul's hideous wounds healed.

What was it God wished them to do? To go on, being hustled out of danger in town after town, stalking away once they had recited the oral gospel and done a few baptizings? Neither Paul nor Barnabas was concerned by any lost personal dignity. They had no mean pride to stand in the way of their missionary task; but, with the stoning of Paul still fresh in their minds, they felt the need of guidance.

Nothing would have pleased them more than to leave Derbe and follow a route that led far away from the enemies who hated them so belligerently.

But the guidance given to Paul and Barnabas by the Holy Ghost was altogether of a different sort. They were to retrace their steps, returning over the same route by which they had come through malignant persecutions.

They must go back to Lystra, to Iconium, to Pisidian Antioch, where they had shaken the dust from their feet!

The Holy Ghost gave them specific and unmistakable directions. They must not desert the Galatian churches they had started. The people of those towns had first heard Paul and Barnabas with delight, then seen them worsted by the Pharisaical authorities, driven out, forbidden to return. Now Paul and Barnabas must return, armed with faith, to strengthen and encourage the converts their first sermons had won.

For a little longer these two servants of God remained in Derbe, preaching the Gospel. Elsewhere, in the cities of their persecution, the authorities were writing them off as nuisances to be forgotten.

When a few weeks later they returned to Lystra, the town of the stoning, the authorities paid no heed to them. The accusing Jews from other towns who had denounced them were gone. Having shown the utmost in innocent courage, by returning to face their foes, Paul and Barnabas were to be molested no further. Often when good Christians give their all, angels hover near to guard them from harm.

As Luke declares:

"They returned again to Lystra, and to Iconium, and Antioch, confirming the souls of the disciples, and exhorting them to continue in the faith, and that through many tribulations we must enter into the kingdom of God. And when they had ordained them priests in every church, and had prayed with fasting, they commended them to the Lord, in whom they believed.

"And passing through Pisidia, they came to Pamphylia. And having spoken the word of the Lord in Perga, they went down into Attalia: and thence sailed to Antioch [in Syria] from whence they had been delivered to the grace of God unto the work which they accomplished."

The first journey was over, as Paul and Barnabas gratefully reached the haven of Syrian Antioch. There was no question in the mind of Barnabas that Paul was his definite superior. Paul's courage, his executive abilities, his converting eloquence all filled Barnabas with admiration. He could not wait to go before the Church council in Jerusalem and tell them of this hero of the faith. Plainly Paul was the one to carry the message to the Gentiles.

Mercifully, neither Paul nor Barnabas could foresee what awaited them in Jerusalem.

Chapter 53.   CAN A GENTILE BE A CHRISTIAN?

THE two travelers planned a brief respite in Syrian Antioch. The rigors of long journeying and persecutions were written in their lean faces and the deep hollows of their eyes. The people of Antioch were breathless to hear their story, and, says Luke, "they related what great things God had done with them, and how He had opened the door of faith to the Gentiles."

That report about the Gentiles stirred up the trouble.

There were still valiant and earnest men among those early Christians who believed that the Messiah had come on a special mission to Israel, bearing an exclusive message of redemption for the souls of Jews. They were willing to concede that Gentiles could become Christians, but they believed that the Gentiles must first ceremoniously become Jews.

In Jerusalem the reports about the kind of converts Paul and Barnabas had made raised severe arguments. Some of the Jerusalem

Christians actually came to Antioch to deliver an announcement to Paul and Barnabas and to every church member in Antioch. They repeated it, solemnly and in an infinite variety of phrases:

"Except you be circumcised after the manner of Moses, you cannot be saved."

Now Paul and Barnabas had never dreamed of teaching any such dogma, nor did they believe that circumcision had anything whatsoever to do with Christ's salvation of the human soul. To their enlightened minds it was perfectly clear that Christ's message was for the whole world, not limited to those who observed the Jewish rites. Christianity could never be a sect of Judaism!

The arguments in Antioch were prolonged into a wrangling disturbance that rocked the congregation. Who was right? the people asked themselves. And who could say with authority?

There was only one answer. Peter, the man of rock, was the authority; on that rock the Church had been founded. Even the circumcisionists saw that. When they felt they were losing in the public debates, they personally proposed the appeal to Peter. They suggested that Paul and Barnabas and some of the leaders of the Antioch Church who sided with the missionary pair should go with their antagonists and lay the question before the apostles in Jerusalem.

The division between the two groups was deep, and what seemed perfectly clear to one side, seemed heretical and destructive of tradition and Jewish patriotism to the other. Paul had not much stomach for the journey. He preferred to settle in Antioch with Barnabas and work among the great Gentile population. That was what he had called himself; the Apostle to the Gentiles. With utmost fervor, he had poured out his soul to them on the universality of his Master's teaching. Was he now to recant and order them to become circumcised Jews before they could be considered Christians?

With a heavy heart Paul trudged southward to Jerusalem beside Barnabas, his only friend, it seemed, except for one co-worker from Antioch, a man called Titus. Titus was already one of Paul's most competent helpers; and the apostle looked on him as his spiritual son. And Titus was a Gentile, proud of his Greek parentage, without the least desire to be circumcised.

Paul had chosen him to go to Jerusalem as a living and dramatic example of the problem: a typical Gentile convert whose point of view, he felt sure, must impress the original "Pillar Apostles," who were the ruling force in the Church council. Curiously, Titus' name, although prominent in Paul's own epistles, does not appear in Luke's book of The Acts of the Apostles. Some have speculated that Titus might be Luke's own brother, reasoning that the physician, who humbly refused ever to name himself in the book, likewise avoided mentioning Titus.

However that may have been, Titus walked toward Jerusalem with Paul and Barnabas. And while they did not talk much to their circumcisionist companions, who indeed behaved at times much like guards lugging culprits into court, the three champions of universal Christianity continued to give offense all along the journey. Through Phoenicia, down the eastern coast of the Mediterranean, all the way through Samaria, they preached conversion to the Gentiles. Their opponents bristled in silence, biding their time.

At last they came again in sight of the towers and domes of Jerusalem. Through the Sheep's Gate, through the colorful human tide of the jostling thousands from all lands who thronged the streets, they made their way to the Cenacle. A crowd of Christians, including the "Pillar Apostles" with Peter in the midst, waited for them in that Upper Room.

The great debate was about to open.

Chapter 54. THE COUNCIL'S DECISION

PAUL was given the floor, all to himself. With Barnabas to buttress his account, he told the apostles and elders the history of their first missionary journey. It was a moving story of the long weary way: Cyprus and Pisidian Antioch; Iconium and Lystra; Derbe and Perga.

"How great things God had done with us, I come to tell you," declared Paul—of the miracles, the escapes from death, and of the astounding numbers of Gentile conversions. When the story was told, Paul and Barnabas waited in an uneasy silence.

Slowly, certain frowning brethren rose to break the stillness. They considered themselves Christianized Pharisees; they were of the same legalistic training as Paul, and they resented his attitude to the Gentiles all the more because they thought he was betraying his background, forgetting his basic training. So they stood up before the apostles and elders and they said that indeed Gentiles could become converts, but "it was needful to circumcise them and to command them to keep the Law of Moses."

Before long the Cenacle was in turmoil. Men took sides, apostles and elders clashing—until Peter rose. His voice rode over their clamor, commanding silence.

"Men and brethren," he began, "you know, that in former days God made choice among us, that by my mouth the Gentiles should hear the word of the gospel, and believe. And God, who knoweth the hearts, gave testimony, giving unto them the Holy Ghost, as well as to us; and put no difference between us and them, purifying their hearts by faith. Now therefore, why tempt you God to put a yoke upon the necks of the disciples, which neither our fathers nor we have been able to bear? But by the grace of the Lord Jesus Christ, we believe to be saved, in like manner as they also."

And as the Bible tells us, then "all the multitude held their peace."

With the vision of Joppa forever stamped on his heart and his brain, Peter had reminded them that God had shown him they must "call no man common or unclean." Cornelius the Roman had been the test case, decided by the actual voice of God.

Now many of the men in the Cenacle room that morning had known Jesus Christ as Peter had known Him. They knew that Jesus had Himself been circumcised in His infancy. They knew He had never criticized the rite of circumcision, nor said that it should be abolished. But they knew, too, that Jesus had preached to the outcast Samaritans and healed the servant of a Roman officer, whose faith, so said the Master, was greater than any He had found in Israel. Nor had that Roman officer been told he must be circumcised.

Calmly, majestically, Peter had just delivered a momentous decision. The atmosphere altered. The disputants fell silent and looked apologetically around at their late antagonists.

Titus, who had sat as quietly as possible in the background, permitted himself a smile and a sigh of relief. He had not relished his role as Paul's chief exhibit in the dispute. Christianity was to him a new-found treasure, unspeakably precious, worth any sacrifice. But Titus had prayed silently with dry throat and hard-clasped hands that Peter would not make circumcision, or any other Jewish rite, the price of his salvation.

As Paul was to remember in writing his letter to his friends in Galatia later:

"Neither Titus, who was with me, being a Greek, was compelled to be circumcised. . . . And when James, Peter, and John who seemed to be the pillars perceived the grace that was given to me, they gave to me and Barnabas the right hands of fellowship, that we should go unto the heathen, and they unto the circumcision."

With those firm handclasps to seal the understanding, the discussion ended. Paul and Barnabas, heartened and uplifted by Peter's words, were again on their feet, one's words following after the other's, recounting more of their adventures and more of the miracles God had wrought among the Gentiles by them—the healing of the man with paralyzed feet, and Paul's amazing recovery after the stoning at Lystra.

When they had finished, James stood up, and speaking of Peter, calling the man of rock by his childhood name of Simon, said:

"Men, brethren, hear me.

"Simon hath related how God first visited to take of the Gentiles a people to His name.

"And to this agree the words of the prophets, as it is written: 'After these things I will return, and will rebuild the tabernacle of David, which is fallen down; and the ruins thereof I will rebuild, and I will set it up, that the residue of men may seek after the Lord, and all nations upon whom My name is invoked, saith the Lord, who doth these things.'

"To the Lord was His own work known from the beginning of the world. For which cause I judge that they, who from among the Gentiles are converted to God, are not to be disquieted. But that we write unto them, that they refrain themselves from the pollutions of idols, and from fornication, and from things strangled, and from blood. For Moses of old time hath in every city them that preach him in the synagogues, where he is read every Sabbath."

James laid his emphasis, not only on Peter's vision by the sea, but also on the words quoted from the prophet Amos. His thought was that the Gentiles be advised that—while they need not be circumcised—they should refrain themselves "from the pollution of idols and from fornication and from things strangled, and from blood."

There was wisdom in James's appeal. No follower of the true God approved of idols or fornication. As Paul wrote later in a letter, "We know there is no such thing as an idol in the world . . . but such knowledge is not in everyone. Some still idol-conscious, eat idol-offerings as such." But the dietary restriction to kosher food would mean something else—proof that Jewish tradition still ranked high in the Christian Church.

Still, even Paul could see that if the Gentiles accepted this discipline willingly they would be more quickly tolerated by the Jewish traditionalists in the Church. There was practicality in the tactics James the Less was suggesting.

Peter did not object. He had neither arrogance nor the dictatorial instinct, and seeing some virtue in James's appeal, he accepted it.

The council decided that the missionary work among the Gentiles would be continued, but some representatives from Jerusalem would go along with Paul and Barnabas to carry a message from the council. Two were chosen: Judas, surnamed Barsabas, and Silas (also called Sylvanus); both were regarded as foremost men among the brethren and entirely to be relied upon.

No one today knows anything more about Judas Barsabas than that he was assigned to go back to Antioch with Paul and Barnabas. But of Silas Sylvanus we know much. He, like Paul, was proud to be a free citizen of Rome, and he was to share in all the dangers of Paul's second missionary journey. He became Paul's intimate friend.

One final step had to be taken before the plenary session on the Gentiles could be adjourned. A decree had to be issued, stating in the firmest language the council's attitude toward the Gentiles.

It was addressed to "the brethren which are of the Gentiles in Antioch and Syria and Cilicia" from "the apostles and the ancients" and reads as follows:

"Forasmuch as we have heard, that some going out from us have troubled you with words, subverting your souls; to whom we gave no commandment, it has seemed good to us, being assembled together, to choose out men, and to send them to you, with our well beloved Barnabas and Paul: men that have given their lives for the Name of our Lord Jesus Christ. We have sent therefore Judas and Silas, who themselves also will, by word of mouth, tell you the same things. For it hath seemed good to the Holy Ghost and to us, to lay no further burden upon you than these necessary things: That you abstain from things sacrificed to idols, and from blood, and from things strangled, and from fornication; from which things keeping yourselves, you shall do well. Fare ye well."

Then the four travelers were dismissed and speeded on their way to Antioch. And with them went the still uncircumcised Titus, symbol of Paul's firm victory in Jerusalem.

The troubled Gentiles were relieved at the tone and friendliness of that decree as it was read to them in their assembly. The restrictions did not seem too difficult to follow. "They rejoiced for the consolation"; they could be welcomed as Christians.

And Judas Barsabas preached to them and so did Silas. Prophets themselves, they exhorted men and women to follow Christ's teachings, and confirmed their baptism. They blessed the Gentiles and those harassed converts went in peace, feeling very much better about everything. Peter's wisdom had triumphed.

Barsabas went back to Jerusalem and obscurity.

But Silas chose to remain. He and Paul and Barnabas had a great deal they must now consider.

Chapter 55. DINNER WITH THE GENTILES

PAUL and Barnabas were burning with eagerness to talk out their problems together with Silas. Paul, the expounder, the missionary on fire for Christ, must make his friends understand how he felt.

He wanted them to grasp how he envisioned Christianity. Was it a local cult, or was it not international, interracial, universal? Were they to adapt the faith to fit the needs of differing groups or were they not to keep it a monolithic rock of truth? If disagreements threatened schism and splinter cults, was it not still better to keep the teachings of the Holy Ghost to a hair and never compromise? Only then could there be room for all, in one undivided Church. There must be no second-class Christians.

Laws were necessary for any human organization, but they must serve the Spirit, not stifle it. Paul was ready to argue from personal experience that the negative preoccupation with rules, as insisted on by the Pharisees, was an actual roadblock to salvation, as it had proved to be in his own early life. The soul's health lay in positive faith and love, transcending and ennobling the safeguards of the Law.

Paul was as eloquent as the prophets of olden days who had denounced the formalists among the Jews, who had so concentrated on the letter of the Law that they lost sight of its Author.

In Paul's own day the Pharisees, clinging fanatically to observances controlling the least important details of life, dominated the Temple and all the synagogues. And the Jewish followers of Christ, conditioned by this influence since childhood, still could not shake off the slavery of their youth. They could not seize the freedom which was their birthright from Bethlehem.

He was aware that still in the eyes of many of the brethren he was a heretic. To their minds the thought of equality with the Gentiles was abhorrent. But to Paul it was intolerable that Christianity should be a club or secret order reserved for Jews. He wanted no superiority over his fellow man.

On the surface things seemed tranquil. Peter had spoken in agreement with Paul. And Paul was resolved to co-operate in every way possible. But he was profoundly disturbed. Wise in human nature, he fully expected trouble.

It arrived, strangely enough, with Peter himself.

In Jerusalem new persecutions were threatening the faith.

When it was no longer safe to remain in Jerusalem, the apostles left, all except James. Tradition has it that Peter moved to Antioch where he remained for years, some say three, others seven. While Luke does not mention this important fact, Paul speaks of it in his stormy letter to the Galatians.

Antioch was a fortunate substitute for Jerusalem. Queen of the East, and City of the Moon, as her admirers called her, she was the third largest metropolis of the Empire. The sight of Antioch always brought a light of wonder and amazement into the eyes of Peter, the untraveled Galilean fisherman—so different this modern capital was, with broad streets and avenues and a fresh wind blowing thirty miles from the sea; such a proud contrast to the narrow, roofed streets and fetid alleys of ancient Jerusalem.

But the people here were the same as the people in Jerusalem, yes, and in Capernaum, where Peter had lived most of his life. Among the half million population, there were the usual rich pagans, the oppressed commoners, and the immense settlement of Jews.

Those first refugees who fled from Jerusalem after the stoning of Stephen years before had for a while found welcome in the ornate Antioch synagogue. But inevitably doctrinal disputes had arisen to disrupt that felicity. By the time Peter arrived the Christians were again performing their devotions at home, often behind locked doors. Peter recognized that this city, where Paul and Barnabas had made so many Gentile converts, was the very core of the Judaistic disputes among the Christians. And this once eruptive, headstrong man, now sobered by his apostleship, meant to heal the breach and prayed for wisdom to do so.

It was not easy for Peter. Close to Christ as he had been, personally commissioned and instructed, Peter was still under the spell of his boyhood training and discipline, a traditional way of looking at life hard to get over.

Paul was to declare truly of himself that he was "all things to all men," but there was no such felicity in Peter. He had seen the vision that taught him that he must look at no one as common or unclean; he had obeyed directions and surmounted his anti-Gentile prejudice against Cornelius and his family and friends. Yet Peter still felt more comfortable among his own kind. No matter how he commanded his mind and emotions to obey him, Peter could not overcome a certain squeamishness sitting at a Gentile's table and eating bread that had been kneaded by alien hands. He had been grateful that Paul was the Apostle to the Gentiles; Paul had no such qualms.

But in Antioch Peter earnestly tried to put his Master's way of universality into practice. He not only guided and taught the Gentile converts, he also ate with them, in their houses, of their cooking. And he did so with a smile of affection that brought every other Christian Jew into its warmth, and led them with him into true fellowship with their new brothers in baptism. The head of the Church had stepped over the boundaries of some three thousand years; the barrier between Jew and Gentile seemed to have melted under the sun of full love for God and neighbor.

Then suddenly Peter ate no more at the house of Titus or of Luke the physician; he was absent from all Gentile tables.

James the Less, who had been left in charge of the Jerusalem group, had heard of Peter's new dining habits, and sent messengers

down to talk to Peter. How, asked James the Less, did Peter expect
to be an apostle of the Jews if he offended every Jew in the world by
associating with Gentiles? All very well, to permit Gentile converts
to join the Church without adopting all the Hebrew rules, said James
—but a born Jew must never desert his traditional obligations, even
after baptism!

Peter let himself be swayed by James's message. And his behavior
outraged Paul. Later Paul was to explain to the Galatians:

> When Cephas (Peter) was come to Antioch, I withstood him to his
> face, because he was to be blamed. For before that some came from
> James, he did eat with the Gentiles. But when they were come he with-
> drew and separated himself, fearing them who were of the circumcision.
> And to his dissimulation the rest of the Jews consented, so that Barnabas
> also was led by them into that dissimulation.

Paul was stunned.

He simply could not stand by and let them jeopardize the faith of
the Gentiles by refusing to eat at their tables. He knew Peter to be
supreme. He knew the Holy Spirit would preserve Peter from error in
teaching faith and morals. But he knew, too, that the Vicar of Christ
was never guaranteed to be perfect in action. One minute after appointing him, Jesus had rebuked Peter's human impulses by saying:
"Get thee behind me, Satan." Reluctantly, and with all respect, Paul
felt he must admonish him now for this appeasement to the en-
trenched traditionalists.

In the Epistle to the Galatians, Paul tells us what he did:

> When I saw that they walked not uprightly according to the truth
> of the gospel, I said unto Peter before them all: "If you, being a Jew,
> live after the manner of Gentiles, and not as do the Jews, why do you
> compel the Gentiles to live as do the Jews?
> "We who are Jews by nature, and not sinners of the Gentiles, knowing
> that a man is not justified by the works of the Law, but by the faith of
> Jesus Christ, even we have believed in Jesus Christ, that we might be
> justified by the faith of Christ, and not by the works of the Law: for by
> the works of the Law shall no flesh be justified. But if, while we seek to
> be justified by Christ, we ourselves also are found sinners, is therefore
> Christ the minister of sin? God forbid."

In that letter, Paul gave his full argument. It has lasted through
the ages, a triumphant pleading of a liberal cause as against the old

legalism: "for if justification comes through the Law, then Christ died to no purpose. . . . Is God the God of Jews only? Is He not also the God of Gentiles? Yes, of Gentiles as well, as indeed it is one God Who justifies the circumcised by faith, and the uncircumcised through the same faith. Do we then nullify the Law through the faith? By no means! On the contrary, we corroborate the Law."

Paul withstood him to his face, and Peter listened. He realized in a rush of self-reproach that the same vision which had led him to the house of the Gentile Cornelius should have guided him here in Antioch. Paul had the right on his side.

Human as they were, both these men were in saintly earnest, seeking to serve God. From the smug distance of nearly two thousand years it is easy to magnify their disagreements and their mistakes. The turmoil over the place of Gentiles in Christianity was serious. But lest we judge too harshly across the centuries, let us look around and remember that there are white men and women today who consider themselves Christian leaders and still manage to avoid eating or even praying under the same roof with Christians of different skin color from their own.

Peter realized that Paul was stating the issue squarely and accurately, and he could neither dodge nor straddle it.

Humbly, Peter made the only possible decision. He walked back to the houses of the Gentiles in Antioch and ate with them again. In spite of James's understandable fears, Peter refused even the appearance of prejudice.

And Paul turned eager attention on his own plans for a new conversion campaign, the adventure history calls his Second Missionary Journey.

BOOK SIX

The Second Journey

Chapter 56. THE END OF A FRIENDSHIP

IN THE very planning of new travels Paul was faced with fresh troubles.

"Let us go again," Paul proposed to Barnabas, "and visit our brethren in every city where we have preached the word of the Lord and see how they do."

Good! Barnabas thought it was an excellent plan. And, he added, why not take his cousin, young Mark, along with them again?

"No!" said Paul. And the argument was on. Paul could not forget his previous disappointment with young Mark. Had Mark not deserted Paul and Barnabas on the first journey, leaving them to carry on their arduous task alone? Why trust him again?

Paul's logic was sound. He intended not only to revisit his first mission outposts but to go on into unknown lands, facing incalculable perils. (Though Paul did not then know it, this second journey was to last more than three years.) For such an enterprise, they would need a helper who could be relied upon. Could Barnabas contradict that fact?

Barnabas' reply put an end to one of the most remarkable of friendships. The contention between them had become so sharp that only action could conclude it. The two men parted in silence and heartache. Barnabas and Mark boarded a ship at the Orontes dock, sailed down the river and out into the Mediterranean, their prow pointed homeward to Cyprus.

Was their parting entirely over Mark? Had Barnabas' defection in quitting the Gentiles when Peter did caused the first deep abyss between these two men?

Let Barnabas and his nephew call on the churches the two missioners had founded on the island of Cyprus. As for Paul, he would go another way. For companion he chose a man he had learned to trust completely, Silas, called Sylvanus, who had originally come down from Jerusalem as one of the agents of the grand council.

But Paul could never shut Barnabas out of his heart. The tent-making Pharisee from Tarsus could never forget that it was Barnabas who found him in the streets of Jerusalem and led him to the Cenacle. Barnabas had stood up for Paul against all those who feared his presence because of the stoning of Stephen. It was Barnabas who had started the evangelizing tour and had invited Paul to join, taking him into partnership. And when Paul's eloquence plainly exceeded his own, even on his home grounds the Cypriote had taken second place with quiet humility. He seemed never to know smallness or meanness.

Together the two missioners had converted thousands. They had run desperate dangers, had been persecuted together, and escaped together. They had known chills and fevers, all kinds of hardship. Yet because of one young and unreliable relative, Mark, whom Peter was to call his adopted son, they were partners in spreading Christ's Gospel no longer.

Perhaps Paul still had a lot to learn, and this second missionary journey would help to school him, not in the concentrated wisdom of books, but in warm flesh and blood human relations. Many of his companions would have said that Paul was hard to get along with. Surrounded by so many and varied antagonists, he may well have been too suspicious.

Whatever Paul's motives, over the question of Mark he stood out against Barnabas and lost him.

It is a severe grief to lose a friend.

Chapter 57.   "HELP US!"

As THEY departed from the city on their donkeys, Paul must have wondered how his new companion, Silas, would wear on the long trip that was now beginning. Not all good friends are good travelers.

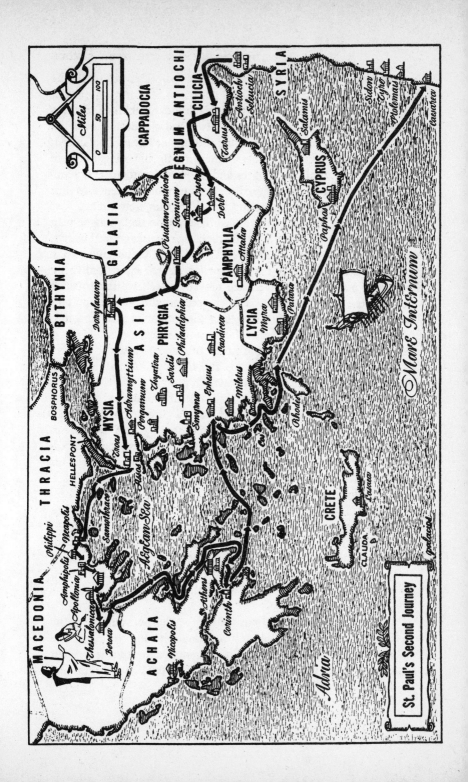

St. Paul's Second Journey

As they trotted past the tree-lined shore of the Orontes, with the farewell benediction of all the Christians in Antioch ringing in their ears, both men must have been thoughtful and silent. Behind them lay the gleaming white marble of the city called glorious. They could hear the rumble of chariot wheels and the ring of horses' hoofs down the fair broad avenues past the Corso with its imposing range of pillared arches and all the palaces and baths and gardens and fountains and teeming hordes of people. No such magnificence as this awaited them on the distant shores for which they were riding.

But Paul need have no fear about Silas. Once the younger man might have been sympathetic to the dietary-circumcision enthusiasts, but Paul knew already that phase had passed and they were in complete agreement. In all the fearful experiences that lay before them, Silas would acquit himself well. He proved himself worthy to share with Paul the glory and dangers of the second and most important journey, which brought the message of Christ out of Asia and into Europe.

The two men rode out of the northern gate of Antioch, heading for a pass in the Taurus Mountains and the high country of South Galatia, site of Paul's mission churches.

Back to Derbe they came, scene of former difficulties, and on to the scene of even worse troubles of the past, Lystra. And there Paul showed a new facet of his greatness, demonstrating that he was not the stubborn, obstinate man his antagonists believed, but one capable of mastering his own deepest resentments in the service of his Master.

In Lystra lived a lad whose name was Timothy. He had been baptized at the time of Paul's first visit, just before the stoning. Timothy's mother, Eunice, was a Jewish woman who had been converted to Christianity, but his father was a Gentile. From the very first, Paul had been warmly attracted to the young Lystrian, whose name meant "honorer of God." In time he was to become Paul's most beloved follower or "son," a devoted and sympathetic fellow worker to the death.

Now Paul, back in Lystra, was visiting at the house of Timothy and Eunice, when suddenly he felt a divine direction, through "the prophecies which pointed him out" in the soul of the apostle. He felt he had been directly commanded to take this youth as an additional companion in spreading the Gospel.

Then arose a difficulty which might well have sent a lesser man into a rage, the old question of circumcision! Because his father was pagan, Timothy had never been circumcised. But he was the son of a Jewess. To give him an important position at the right hand of the apostle, even though by an inner divine injunction, would create virulent antagonism, if anyone learned that he had not submitted to the rite.

Paul sensibly saw this point, and Silas too was sure of the strife that would be bound to follow. Timothy, recognizing the problem, was more than willing. So Paul swallowed the pride of his opinion. He himself circumcised young Timothy, following the ritual of generations of Jews. And when the soreness was healed, the party started off, three now instead of two—Paul, Silas, and circumcised Timothy.

"And as they passed through the cities, they delivered unto them the decrees for to keep, that were decreed by the apostles and ancients who were at Jerusalem. And the churches were confirmed in faith, and increased in number daily."

And now they were coming up against an imponderable Force that was to shut them out of Asia and thrust them, and Christianity with them, into another continent.

The Acts records simply: "And when they had passed through Phrygia, and the country of Galatia, they were forbidden by the Holy Ghost to preach the word in Asia. And when they were come into Mysia, they attempted to go into Bithynia, and the Spirit of Jesus suffered them not. And when they had passed through Mysia, they went down to Troas."

Paul, Silas, and Timothy had been stopped in their tracks. They had embarked on an extended tour of the Roman province called Asia—and the unmistakable inner guidance of God forbade them to carry out their own plans. They must not preach any longer in Asia.

Promptly then they had bent their steps northward through Mysia, toward the province of Bithynia, bordering on the Black Sea. Again the divine rebuff: the Spirit of Jesus would not let them enter there. And again Paul and Silas and Timothy obediently changed their course. They turned their faces to the west, retraced their way through Mysia, and followed the promptings of the Spirit. They went down to the city of Troas.

Today that once prosperous port near the Hellespont is a hapless heap of rubble; its ruins are a marble quarry for modern mosques and temples. But when Paul and Silas and Timothy entered the bastioned walls of Troas, they found a metropolis complete with temple, theater, baths, and aqueducts, all in the latest Roman fashion.

But Troas was still in the province of Asia—and that whole area had just been forbidden to Paul by the Holy Spirit. Why then had he been guided to this spot?

Paul spent a sleepless night in Troas, tossing in tormented restlessness. Suddenly his room filled with brilliance. Sitting bolt upright, the apostle stared at his open window, and saw a light-bathed apparition facing him. He saw a vision of a man "standing and beseeching" him, saying:

"Pass over into Macedonia and help us!"

Macedonia! The mainland of Europe. As the vision faded and disappeared, Paul sat gazing out of the suddenly darkened window. He breathed in deeply the salt air of the Aegean Sea.

"To Macedonia then it will be," Paul vowed. He recognized a call that was actually a command. He resolved to obey at once.

But when Paul left Troas, he would have a new companion, the man whom we know as St. Luke.

Chapter 58.   "MOST DEAR PHYSICIAN"

"AND sailing from Troas, we came with a straight course . . ."

"We came!" Without warning or fanfare, the narrative of The Acts of the Apostles switches from the third person to the first person. Quietly, unobtrusively, the author suddenly includes himself in the history of Paul's labors. St. Luke now testifies to his own part in the drama of the early Church.

With humility that frustrates the curious reader, Luke tells almost nothing of himself. He is silent about that most dramatic of meetings when he joined himself with Paul, the beginning of a working friendship. In his last fateful years, Paul was to tell Timothy that of all his co-workers only Luke remained faithfully by his side as the tragic climax of his captivity neared.

They met in Troas, these two converts, Pharisee and Greek: Paul, the tentmaker and scholar, and Luke, the physician and painter. In his letter to the Colossians, Paul was to refer to him: "Luke, the most dear physician." Most dear to Paul he was, a loyal and tireless worker. "My yokefellow," Paul called him fondly.

Actually, Luke is mentioned by name but three times in the Bible, and then only in letters written by Paul. Carefully, deliberately, Luke effaces himself from both his own Gospel and The Acts. Yet he was to leave an unmistakable imprint of his personality on every word he wrote.

Nearly one third of his Gospel is new material, not included in the other two "Synoptic" Gospels. Luke was not an eyewitness but a researcher, ferreting out facts with the scientific care of a modern historian. Yet his life of the Lord glows with his own profound love of Jesus and His tender mercy. Luke himself had a tender and compassionate heart.

The meeting of Paul and Luke on the shores of the Aegean Sea was to affect their lives to the death. Surely they must have known their ends would be tragic, realizing that evangelists in such a cause were destined to follow their divine Leader into martyrdom. Yet they decided to travel that path together. Paul and Luke, Silas and Timothy left Troas and, following the vision of the Macedonian, sailed northwest across the sea—out of Asia.

Paul and Luke, a Pharisee and a Gentile, neither of whom had ever seen Jesus during His lifetime, were charged now with the historic task of bringing Christianity into Europe.

They would be older and far wiser men before that task was done.

Chapter 59. THE WIDOW AND THE SLAVE GIRL

"AND sailing from Troas, we came with a straight course to Samothracia, and the day following to Neapolis . . ." and there Paul set foot for the first time on European ground!

Still on sea legs, the four missioners tramped the ten miles from the noisy port of Neapolis through gray swamplands to Philippi, capital of Macedonia.

Philippi was both a city and a fortress, situated on a steep hill overlooking the bland green valley of the Gangites River. Only recently, while Jesus was still on earth preaching and healing, the Emperor

Augustus Caesar had given Philippi the distinction of being a Roman colony, and her citizens the proud boon of free citizenship.

Arrogant in its imperial preference, claiming the title of "first city" outside of Rome, Philippi was a proud place in the year 50 when Paul, Luke, Silas, and Timothy entered the gates, ready to found the first Christian Church on European soil.

There was no synagogue in this Gentile metropolis, but the few Hebrews in Philippi welcomed the four wayfarers into their own homes to preach. Over the years other travelers had brought garbled tales of the heroic new faith that was spreading in Palestine and Asia since the death of Jesus. The Jews of Philippi were eager to get the truth from Paul and his cohorts.

They asked all the questions which Paul had answered thousands of times, and would answer many more thousands of times. Were there living witnesses who had seen and known Jesus Christ? Many! Who were they? Peter, the man of rock, who was still preaching and traveling and healing. Peter was just one of hundreds who had seen Him on earth. Had Paul ever seen Jesus? Oh, yes! Where? On the road to Damascus. They plied Silas and Timothy and Luke, too, with their cross-examination; there were scholars among them, but they had their match in Paul, the Pharisee who knew the Law and the Prophets and the Christian teaching as few other men.

On the Sabbath day, having no synagogue in which to worship, a little band of Philippian Jews always marched together through the city gate and out into the country. In a quiet, gladelike place on the bank of the Gangites River, a Sabbath prayer service was held by a group of women, who generally keep prayer alive in the world more than the men do.

Paul preached to those women, long and earnestly. His story of the gentle Nazarene who taught that love was all made a profound impression.

When he had finished, one of the women stepped forward and declared for all to hear that she had always worshiped God and now she knew that her heart had been opened by the Lord "to attend those things that were said by Paul."

The apostle called her to come near to him and questioned her. "Daughter, your name?"

"My name is Lydia. I am a seller of purple cloth in the city."

"And from where do you come?"

"From Thyatira."

Paul's eyes gleamed with excitement. From Thyatira—a city notorious among the good Jews of the Empire! The large Hebrew colony of that city on the River Lycus had corrupted the ancient faith of Abraham, the stern commands of Moses, with witchcraft and magical rites and foul pagan practices.

Yet here was Lydia, the career woman from Thyatira, standing unabashed in the presence of Paul's burning holiness, his first convert on European soil.

At her request he baptized her with all her household, and his face glowed with content when Lydia said:

"If you have judged me to be faithful to the Lord, come into my house, and abide there."

"And," Luke reported, "she constrained us."

The four missionaries followed Lydia from the river bank, musing on the Providence that had brought this successful business woman into the vanguard of the faith. Her household, a retinue of servants and secretaries and clerks schooled in the intricacies of trade, trudged with them back toward the gates of Philippi.

Suddenly Paul halted, staring.

A slave girl stood near the city wall, hands pressed against the grimy old stone blocks, her head thrown back, eyes fixed on Paul as if she were seeing a vision.

"Keep away from her," someone urged the apostle. "She has a pythonical spirit! People believe she divines the future, tells their fortunes."

"For money?"

"Oh, yes. Her owners send her out every day, and she comes home at night with a bag of coins."

As he studied her, Paul concluded that this slave girl was possessed of a demon. Some outside entity had burglarized her soul and seized authority over all her behavior. Here was magic, spiritualism for gain in the gutters, not at Lydia's purpled birthplace but in the midst of modern Philippi, a city as proud of its learning and sophistication as it was of its commerce and industry.

At the sight of Paul, a curious compulsion seized the slave girl. She screamed as if some unknown alien riding her soul saw and recognized this man who had the power of exorcism, and could drive it forth as once Jesus Christ drove a legion of such spirits out of a possessed man into a herd of swine. Rigid against the wall, the girl cried out:

"These men are the servants of the most high God, who preach unto you the way of salvation."

That first time, Paul walked resolutely past her in silence. But day after day, the same thing happened; the slave girl near the city gate would stare and scream—and the words were always the same: "These men are the servants of the most high God, who preach unto you the way of salvation."

Paul was moved with pity. The girl was nearly torn apart with the anguish of inner struggle. The evil spirit consuming her shrank from the sight of the messengers of Christ and thought to save itself by proclaiming the truth in howls of fear.

One morning after prayer, Paul could be silent no longer. He passed the girl by the wall, heard again that tormented voice:

". . . the way of salvation . . ."

Paul wheeled on her, his eyes burning on her pale, distracted face, and spoke to the evil spirit which inhabited her:

"I command you, in the Name of Jesus Christ, to go out of her!"

Instantly his order was obeyed.

The insane look faded from the girl's wide eyes. The pallor in her cheeks fled before the honest flush of health and youth. With maidenly concern, she fussed with the confusion of her hair. A devil had been inside her, and was gone.

She turned to Paul with thankful entreaty. Tell me of your God! Humbly at the apostle's hands, she received baptism and the salvation her evil spirit had foretold. And now there were two women leaders in the Christian nucleus at Philippi: the rich widow who sold purple and the exorcised slave girl, strange contrast in the fledgling European church.

But Paul's unmistakable triumph over the demon at the gates made trouble for him in Philippi.

At the booths in the market place the city officials were holding audience. Suddenly two sweating, heaving fellows, the owners of the slave girl, demanded to be heard. Whips in hand, they had collared Paul and Silas—fortunate Timothy and Luke were off on an errand at the time—and dragged them before the judges in the public square.

Their real complaint was that Paul had put them out of business.

He had lifted a spell from the girl. Now she could no longer tell fortunes, and they could no longer fatten on her fees.

But of that grievance, of course, they made only casual mention.
Cleverly they cloaked themselves in righteous piety.

"These strangers disturb our city, being Jews, and preach a fashion
which it is not lawful for us to receive nor observe, being Romans."

Strange reversal! Until now Paul's enemies had been the legalistic
scholars of the Jews, but in this city the small Jewish population had
been sympathetic from the beginning. Not the Pharisees' greed for
power—but the Gentiles' greed for money caused the persecution in
Philippi. Yet the basic technique was the same—the incitement of
a mob against outsiders.

The slave girl's masters stirred up a riot. The magistrates turned
baleful eyes on Paul and Silas. No foreigners should be permitted to
disturb the peace with a fanatical new religion! In the judges' eyes the
two strangers had been tried, and must now be condemned.

"Strip them! Then beat them with rods!"

As Paul had once seen Stephen stripped, so he was now denuded
of his own simple, travel-worn robes, and Silas with him. Neither of
these two soldiers of God would ever forget the torment of that grisly
scourging with the thick wooden staffs. Front and back, their bodies
were bruised and puffed and bleeding.

Almost unconscious, Paul and Silas were lugged off by the guards,
followed by a hooting throng. At the prison they were thrown down
before the jailer, as the guards delivered the judges' orders:

"Keep them prisoners diligently!"

The jailer thrust his prisoners into an inner cell. He made their
feet fast in stocks, so that they lay on the floor, their ankles encased
in a wretched hinged and locked device—apparently beyond any
imaginable rescue.

So worried was the jailer, knowing the danger of mob violence
and the highhanded nature of the town officials, that he dared not
sleep. He had heard men say that the Christians of Palestine had out-
witted Roman guards in Jerusalem and stolen the body of their so-
called Master and then pretended that He had risen from the grave.
He resolved that no such hoax could be perpetrated in Philippi.

At the midnight watch he sat brooding by the light of a rush lamp,
listening in scornful amazement to the voices of his prisoners, strong
and unafraid, praying and praising God.

For what were the fools praising God? the irate jailer asked of himself. They had been beaten, almost to death. Their bodies at that minute were caked with dried blood, bloated with painful welts. To give thanks and praise the Lord was madness.

But harken, jailer. There is now another sound, smiting your ears. Not the droning voice of the night patrol, nor the prayers of the captives, but heaven's voice itself. Thunder, jailer; thunder out of season. And something else is happening; something fearful and unprecedented in these parts; the floor is turning, the walls are shaking, the roof is dipping. The very air of the prison house quivers against the skin. Earthquake in the middle of night when Philippi is asleep!

The jailer's superior, the chief keeper of the prison, running barefoot from his room, beheld an incredible spectacle.

The entire prison was trembling as in the shake of a mighty, unseen hand. The foundations were rocking, all the doors were opening. All the iron bands, the leg irons, the handcuffs, the chains, clattered to the floor. Every prisoner was free.

With a groan, the chief keeper of the prison ran back to his room and drew his sword. Better to take his own life, better to run himself through and die in expiation, than to live to face a base and dishonorable execution. The sword glinted in his hand even as a loud firm voice cried:

"Do yourself no harm! We are all here!"

Paul's voice. The leader of the malefactors spoke with a voice so powerful that once heard it was never forgotten:

"Ho! Chief of the prison! Put up your sword. We are all here."

The head keeper called for a light, and the night jailer came stumbling along with a taper. The two men rushed to the inner cell. The missionary pair were free from the stocks. On their knees they were praying, as light of the jailer's candle flickered over them.

The chief laid his hands gently on their shoulders. And looking into their shining faces, he asked in a trembling voice:

"Masters, what must I do, that I may be saved?"

Paul and Silas answered him with the calm of perfect assurance:

"Believe in the Lord Jesus and you shall be saved; you and your house."

Was there ever a stranger setting for instruction to a convert?

All the rest of the night those tireless missioners told the jailer and the keeper the story of Christ's life and what He had taught. The

THE SECOND JOURNEY 199

keeper aroused his wife, his daughters and sons, and all who lived in
his house to hear the Gospel, the good tidings, the happy, glorious
news these two strangers had to divulge.

Then the women brought basins of warm water and the keeper
himself washed and bathed and anointed the prisoners' wounds. The
whole family was baptized at the dawn of the new day, and Paul and
Silas were guests in the keeper's house. "He laid the table for them
and rejoiced with all his house, believing God."

But a message was on the way to the prison from the judges and
the town rulers.

Word of the mysterious events in the prison was racing through
town, and the judges themselves had become alarmed at such a supernatural intervention in the lives of two strangers who had seemed to
them only vagabonds and scoundrels.

As soon as it was light, two sergeants under orders from the magistrates were hammering on the keeper's side door:

"You are to let those men go."

Returning to the breakfast table, the keeper smiled at his two
guests and repeated the latest order: "The magistrates have sent to
let you go. Now therefore, depart, and," he added with tears in his
eyes, "go in peace!"

But Paul shook his head. He would do nothing of the sort. A Christian is a meek man, but he knows the time when he should stand on
his dignity for the glory of God.

"No. They have beaten us. They have scourged us publicly—uncondemned. They have done this to us, men who are Romans!"

The keeper gasped. These prisoners were then not mere wanderers
from some foreign clime. They were Roman citizens. They had inalienable rights to a fair, judicial trial—and now they wanted redress!

"They have cast us into prison," Paul went on relentlessly. "Now
do they thrust us out privily? Not so! Let them come and let us out
themselves."

The sergeant messengers returned to the judges and, coloring
deeply, repeated Paul's defiant answer. Then the magistrates fought
a sinking fear. Who would have dreamed that these Christians were
citizens of Rome?

"And they were afraid," Luke writes of the judges, "and coming,
they besought them, and bringing them out they desired them to
depart out of the city."

Paul had given them living proof of Christian strength in pain and humiliation, shattering evidence of the power of prayer. And in the moment of freedom, when he might have escaped, he had remained in the center of danger to give the Word of God to his keeper and his jailer.

Now he stood against the quake-cracked walls of the prison, smiling cordially at the white-faced magistrates who had condemned him. He could have carried complaint against them to the Emperor for insulting his dignity as a Roman citizen. He could have cost them their jobs, even their liberty. To their astonishment he asked no redress. Calmly he heard their pleas, and agreed. He would leave Philippi—but not at once.

With Silas at his side, Paul strode down the sun-filled streets to Lydia's house. The brethren—Luke and Timothy among them—ran to the gate to meet them with shouts of joy. And Paul stayed with them and "comforted them" with his presence.

On Paul's orders, Luke stayed behind in Philippi to watch over the new flock and guard against the missteps of untutored zeal. Luke was the natural choice. He was at home among the men of Macedonia, akin to them in thought and background; his years in Syrian Antioch had equipped him to meet the problems of church government.

Paul had broken the ground, sowed the first seeds of the faith. He had made three vitally important converts—a Jewish business woman, a slave girl, and a Roman jailer; and with those three, and their households, he had opened channels into each of the major classes of society. Already the baptized brethren in Philippi were a goodly number.

Paul, Silas, and Timothy could not tarry.

But, Paul was always to remember the church in Philippi with special affection. Twice in the years to come, this church would send him gifts when he was in some distant prison. To Paul, there was a special blessing on his work at Philippi, perhaps because the Holy Ghost had sent him there and a miracle had saved him from an ignominious end. Forever after the congregation was utterly loyal to him and to the teachings he brought them. Their life as Christians he regarded as one of the richest fuels of his ministry.

He looked forward to a return to them. But before he was to visit

them again he was to meet many strange adventures. Just beyond was
Thessalonica, and only a little farther away—Athens!

Chapter 60. WHAT HAPPENED AT JASON'S HOUSE

WESTWARD across Macedonia, along the wide Egnatian Way, Paul,
Silas, and Timothy trudged some hundred miles down to the port of
Thessalonica. Ships loaded with rich harvest from the valley behind
the city wall thronged the blue harbor. Barter and cargo were in the
very veins of these Thessalonians. A practical and realistic people,
they prided themselves on being hard to convince in any but the
most ordinary transactions of life.

But the three dusty pilgrims at the gates knew of a sizable Jewish
community in the city. Eagerly they followed directions to the synagogue, where they found a truly hospitable man, named Jason, who
invited the evangelists to make his home their home and headquarters.

The other Jews were not quite so friendly. They were frankly dis-
appointed in these tattered traveling preachers. Local pride filled the
hearts of Thessalonian merchants. But Paul and Silas and Timothy
had not come as sight-seers. They cared less than nothing that this
city was named after a stepsister of Alexander the Great, or that its
fortifications were the strongest that fronted the whole Aegean Sea.
The Thessalonians were anxious to boast of their military and com-
mercial triumphs—and Paul's heart was afire with conquest for Christ.
No wonder it was hard for them to understand each other.

As always, Paul began first to teach in the synagogue. On three
Sabbath days he stood before the congregation reasoning "with them
out of the Scriptures; declaring and insinuating" that all the prophecies had prepared them for a Messiah who was to suffer and to rise
again from the dead.

"This is Jesus Christ whom I preach to you!"

Some of them believed. Luke makes that point clear. A sprinkling
of bold souls, led by Jason, braved the scorn of their fellows and
asked for baptism. Though these Jewish converts were few, their devotion and courage heartened Paul.

But what staggered the synagogue authorities were the sudden mass conversions of the Gentiles, especially among the women. Wives, dowagers, and daughters from the noble families of the city for the first time in their lives entered a Jewish house of worship—to hear Paul and his friends. His reputation for eloquence had blazed through Thessalonica, leaping the borders of race and creed. And the women, who came out of hopeful curiosity, caught fire from his fervor, and gave themselves and their future willingly to Christ.

What right had these strangers to invade the synagogue? What were the Gentiles trying to do—take over? The Pharisees, seething with indignation, had only one idea: destroy these preachers, and their faith!

In secret they whispered their orders to certain rabble rousers and troublemakers, "wicked men of the vulgar sort," who whipped up a tumult and huggermugger in the streets shrill and violent enough to frighten the Roman governor and his quaestor in their white marble palaces on the hill.

The instigated mob paraded down the streets to Jason's house, besieging every door and window, screaming for the bodies of those three impertinent men—Paul, Silas, and Timothy. Jason stood on the threshold of his home, bravely facing the howling crowd. The preachers, he said, were away. He was alone here, he and his family.

Well, then, Jason—we take you!

Jason and some other converts they seized, shoving them through the streets and up the hill to the Roman governor's home. And like the mob that once complained of Jesus to Pilate, these mouthpieces in Thessalonica raised a cry of treason:

"They that have turned the world upside down are come here also, whom Jason has received. And these all do contrary to the decrees of Caesar, saying that there is another King—Jesus!"

Jason stood condemned for harboring a revolutionist, an enemy of the Emperor and the state. They levied a bankrupting fine on him and his friends, then scourged them within a whit of their lives. In the darkness they were left to crawl back to their homes, bloodthirsty warnings still tingling in their ears.

But their hearts were singing with pride. They had saved Paul and Silas and Timothy! Long before the rioters stormed Jason's door, these Christians had heard of the synagogue plot. By the first shades of night Jason and his friends had hustled the three evangelists away to carry the Word of God in peace—turning back to face the hostile mob in their stead. Such was their gratitude for new-found faith!

Fugitives again, Paul, Silas, and Timothy stumbled along in dark-ness toward the city of Beroea, fifty miles away. Grieved though they were by the need for flight, they could afford to waste no time on discouragement. The spreading of the Gospel, for which Jason and his brethren had preserved them, must be their only urgent concern.

Putting aside all fear, they strode into the city, headed as always directly for the synagogue. Their courage was well rewarded. In those days, Beroea was the most popular city in all Macedonia, and its Jew-ish colony, St. Luke tells us, was "more noble than those in Thessa-lonica."

An intelligent and devout lot, this congregation showed immediate interest in the Gospel of Christ. As in other places, reports had flown before the travelers; all sorts of tales about them, good and evil, had reached Beroea. And these Jews were eager to make up their own minds about Christianity and the strangers who served Jesus.

The eager, youthful enthusiasm of Timothy, the earnestness of Silas, and the fervor and blinding brilliance of Paul made a profound impression on the audience in that synagogue. As Luke says, they "received the word with all eagerness, daily searching the Scriptures, whether these things were so. And many indeed of them believed, and of honorable women that were Gentiles, and of men not a few."

As always, the joining of Jew and Gentile in the new faith made the conservatives uneasy. But without warning came troublemakers once again from outside. The synagogue in Thessalonica, hearing of Paul's success, sent their own priests and elders trooping down the highway to arouse the multitude in Beroea. With hatred and wrath they spoke out against Paul. Every lie they could think of they hurled at the head of the fiery tentmaker from Tarsus.

An emergency council of newly converted Christians met that night while Beroea slept. Paul, they realized, was the chief focus of the desperate attack by the priests of Thessalonica. If Paul were to leave the city, his good work could be carried on by others. But if the apostle stayed—a whole mission church might be wiped out.

Paul listened to their logic, and sighed in consent. He would leave Silas and Timothy to guide the Christians in this city. That same night he allowed himself to be conducted secretly aboard a sailing vessel, with a few of the new converts as escorts.

Sadly he waved to Timothy and Silas, as his ship weighed anchor and vanished into the salty fog of the Aegean Sea. Two dear friends left in Beroea—and Luke, the beloved physician, hundreds of miles away, in Philippi! Paul shivered in the loneliness of the midnight mist.

He was sailing southward—to Athens alone!

Chapter 61. THE UNKNOWN GOD

IN HISTORY, the city of Athens stands as uplifted as the white purity of her Parthenon Temple on the height of the Acropolis. When Paul arrived there the summit of her glory had passed, but Athens was still the great creditor of civilization, the sanctuary of science, philosophy, and art; still intellectual master of her conqueror, Rome.

Paul knew well the works of Athens' children—Socrates, Plato, Aristotle, and the brilliant hierarchy of Greek playwrights. As he rode his donkey up from the blue Aegean harbor, accompanied by his friends from Beroea, he thrilled to the majesty of the city before him.

Soon his thoughtful eyes beheld the snowy pillars and slanted roof of the loveliest building ever fashioned by human hands, the temple of the gray-eyed Athena. Proud and bright it stood against the cerulean sky, crowning a hill of natural rock, on three sides nearly perpendicular.

Paul was a man of God and of action—but he was an artist, too; every arrangement of his prose proves his sensitive taste. He was stirred by the beauty of the Parthenon—not the glorious ruins of today, but the original thronged abode of the Greek goddess of wisdom. The Propylaea gateway to the Acropolis was not then time's junkyard of arches and fluted columns, but a work of perfection, atop a marble stairway seventy feet wide rising from the floor of the town. Along those steps stood naked marble figures by Phidias and others of the finest sculptors that ever carved.

When I was last on the Acropolis, I remember reflecting that what I saw then, Paul had looked upon in the year A.D. 50. And scanning the city, peering beyond the Theater of Bacchus, history's witness to the opening performances of Aeschylus and Sophocles, past the Arch

of Hadrian and the platform of Demosthenes, I saw with such a thrill
as seldom comes to the heart of man the ancient Hill of Mars. The
emotion in my soul did not come because I remembered that that
hill, in ancient days, had been the seat of the Supreme Court of
Athens, when Socrates was tried and condemned to death. I put
aside all other memories I had of this wonderful height from my
history books for I was looking at a flight of sixteen roughhewn
steps, which Paul had climbed in one of the grand climactic moments
of his missionary labors.

No sooner was he settled with a family to which his Beroean friends
introduced him, than Paul acted decisively on a message received by
internal guidance.

"Go back to Beroea," he said to some of those who had made the
journey with him. "I give you a commandment for Silas and Timothy.
Bid them follow me here with all speed."

For the next few days, Paul wandered alone through the city.
Everywhere in public squares and hidden niches he saw the statues
of the Greek deities; magnificent images, conceived in the spiritual
hinterlands of superstition and the mythology of many gods.

"His spirit," Luke wrote, "was stirred within him, seeing the city
wholly given to idolatry."

To Paul, who served one God and one Lord, all the majesty of
Greece was sullied by this one tragic blunder. Had ever a city more
need of the Christian message? He could not wait for the arrival of
Silas and Timothy. Alone, he set valiantly to work.

He went first to the synagogue of the Jews, only to find to his distress that even they had taken on the polished dégagé air of the other
Athenians. They disputed him with a bored lack of passion, and
turned away in overbred disdain.

Only in the agora or market place did Paul attract attention. As
was his custom in any town where he stayed long enough, he set up
his tentmaking stall, to earn his own living without burden to anyone. And in Athens, in the market where Socrates and Diogenes had
found their disciples, Paul stood by his wares, exhorting the passing
shoppers to hear the words of Christ.

Soon he noticed two groups of men, watching him and listening
and whispering excitedly to each other. Paul discovered that they
were philosophers who belonged to contradictory schools, and could
never agree with each other. One group were followers of Epicurus,

the man who three hundred years before taught that the chief good in life is freedom from pain. This school believed that if by remote chance any gods existed they certainly had not the slightest interest in men.

In the other group were the Stoics, followers of Zeno. They practiced austerity and self-denial. They were pantheists, and believed that the ideal wise man must be unmoved by joy or grief, and submit himself uncomplainingly to the divine will.

The Stoics were attracted by Paul's preaching, and wanted to know more. They were beguiled by his calmly incisive replies to their heckling. But this shrill market place was not a fitting auditorium for the stranger; they would take him elsewhere.

"What is it this word sower would say?" asked one of the pleasure-loving Epicureans, spitting contemptuously on the ground.

"This man," the Stoics argued with dignity, "seems to be a setter-forth of new gods."

So the philosophers surrounded Paul and asked for a more solemn sermon on this Jesus and His reputed Resurrection. Would the apostle come to the top of the Hill of Mars, and there expound his doctrine?

At this point in his narrative, Luke makes a wry parenthetical comment. He says: "(Now all the Athenians, and strangers that were there employed themselves in nothing else, but either in hearing or telling some new thing!)" And indeed the Hill of Mars was thronged with such intellectual idlers on the day Paul climbed those sixteen stone steps. The judges of the Areopagus, the Supreme Court of Athens, were there, with the city elders and a crowd of gossipers and pseudo philosophers, all of whom stared at this foreign preacher with frank curiosity.

Paul plunged into the pith of his message.

"Ye men of Athens," he began, "I perceive that in all things you are extremely religious. For passing by, and seeing your idols, I found an altar also, on which was written: *To the unknown God.* What therefore you worship, without knowing it, that I preach to you: God, who made the world and all things therein.

"He, being Lord of heaven and earth, dwelleth not in temples made with hands."

Across the valley stood the pale magnificence of the Parthenon, and its beauty made Paul's heart ache. No temple ever built could contain God and hold Him prisoner! Yet by His omnipresence, He is everywhere, even in that marble shrine of Athena, even on the Hill of Mars.

Paul pursued the idea:

"Neither is He served with men's hands, as though He needed any thing; seeing it is He Who giveth to all life and breath and all things; and hath made of one, all mankind, to dwell upon the whole face of the earth, determining appointed times and the limits of their habitation, that they should seek God, if happily they may feel after Him or find Him, although He be not far from every one of us: for in Him we live, and move, and are; as some also of your own poets said: 'For we are also His offspring.'

"Being therefore the offspring of God, we must not suppose the divinity to be like unto gold, or silver, or stone, the graving of art, and device of man.

"And God indeed having winked at the times of this ignorance, now declareth unto men that all should every where do penance, because He hath appointed a day wherein He will judge the world in equity, by the Man whom He hath appointed; giving faith to all, by raising Him up from the dead!"

Till that moment, Paul had held his audience. But these last words about resurrection for the dead appalled these men of Athens. They burst out jeering and mocking. Was it not perfectly plain to any man with eyes and a nose, what happens to a body once life left it? What remained to rise? The facts of decay reduced the idea of resurrection to an absurdity! These Athenians were smug, convinced that their logic was self-evident, indisputable—devastating to Christianity.

But a few men did not mock. One was a judge whose heart leapt up at the idea of the equity of a Last Judgment. His name was Dionysius, and, like a few others around him, he had no trouble believing in resurrection. They could see beyond the obvious. They followed Paul and were baptized, and we know from Luke that a woman named Damaris was in that band of converts. One day Dionysius, the Supreme Court judge, would become the first bishop of Athens—and die a martyr for the Christ.

Paul had started a colony of true faith, to spread like leaven in the city of idolatry. Soon after his sermon on the Hill of Mars, he left Athens. He departed in peace, unpersecuted, unharassed.

He headed alone for Corinth.

Chapter 62. PEACE IN CORINTH

"1 DO NOT advise every man to go to Corinth"—so ran the proverb. In the year 51, as Paul left his ship in the blatant harbor town and climbed to the rocky citadel of the city, he understood the warning.

Prosperity hung like an evil perfume over the traffic-laden streets of Corinth. Before many years this would be the richest city in Greece. Already it was the home of extravagant luxury, aping the decadent vice and licentiousness of the dowager stepmother city of Rome, and the hetaerae and religious prostitutes paraded in the gloaming under the arcades of pillared arches.

Paul recognized the strategic position of Corinth—as a frontier between Orient and Occident it had vast importance in the Christian missionary plan. He prayed for grace to convert the Corinthians.

His answer came that first night while the city slumbered. Paul, lying wakeful in the darkness, heard a voice:

"Do not fear!"

The supernal dignity and tender intimacy of that voice could not be mistaken. Paul was hearing the Lord speak to him:

"Do not fear, but speak, and hold not thy peace, because 1 am with thee, and no man shall set upon thee to hurt thee. For I have much people in this city."

Paul's ministry in Corinth began peacefully, with divine blessing. He went first, as always, to the Jews with his message. Today we can see, saved from the crumbling ruins of ancient Corinth, an actual fragment of testimony from that colony of Jews—the Greek inscription: "Synagogue of the Hebrews," from the very building where Paul preached.

In the shelter of that synagogue Paul met a middle-aged Jewish couple from Italy—Aquila and his wife Priscilla.

In a new wave of anti-Semitism, all the Jews had been banished from Rome by the Emperor Claudius Caesar. Paul found Aquila and Priscilla among a group of other fugitive Jews soon after his arrival in Corinth. An instant bond of sympathy flashed between them. Paul had already been preparing to return to his own needle and thread; and Aquila was a tentmaker too. Together refugee and apostle set up shop in an open-faced bazaar in a covered street of the Corinthian market place.

Soon Silas and Timothy arrived, tired by their long delayed travel from Beroea but delighted at reunion. Surrounded by friends, Paul settled gratefully into a peaceful routine.

"Paul was earnest," Luke reported, "in preaching, testifying to the Jews that Jesus is the Christ."

Every Sabbath he stood before the synagogue congregation, reasoning with them about Christianity. He was opening the hearts of many Jewish men and women, and Gentiles too. Newly baptized converts thronged to Silas and Timothy for full instruction in the faith, and as they, too, were eloquent speakers and made even more converts, the Christian success was rising like a tide.

The scribes and Pharisees could no longer stomach the sight and sound of these preachers. They debated with Paul; making no headway, they then began jeering shrilly at the notion of a Crucified God.

"Your blood be upon your own heads!" cried Paul, and he shook his garments, for in their mockery they had been guilty of blasphemy. "I am clean! Henceforth I will go unto the Gentiles."

Leaving those words ringing in their ears, Paul strode out of the synagogue.

He found refuge with a Gentile convert named Titus Justus, whose house was hard by. There, only a short while afterward, Paul met one of the real surprises of his busy life.

Crispus, chief ruler of the synagogue, knocked at Titus' door and announced to the tentmaker from Tarsus that he believed on the Lord Jesus. He asked for baptism, with his whole household: his wife, sons, daughters, in-laws, and servants.

His conversion stunned the Corinthians. Crispus, the ruler, the judge, had renounced his position of authority over all the other elders, scribes, and priests to become a Christian. For once, the defiance Paul had hurled against his hecklers had marked not the end of a mission, but a new beginning.

Hundreds of Jews followed Crispus in his public acceptance of faith. Paul, Silas, and Timothy worked day and night, talking to interested groups in homes, in the tentmaking shop, or in larger gatherings torchlighted at broad crossways after dark. Conversions multiplied. The Church had strong roots in Corinth.

Chapter 63.   THE FIRST EPISTLES

IN MINUTES snatched from sleep or mealtime, Paul pondered like a loving father over the young mission churches he had left behind him. His thoughts ranged constantly back over his far-flung tracks, through Beroea, Thessalonica, Philippi, back through Syria to Antioch, wrapping in the strong warmth of loving prayer the thousands he had baptized.

From Timothy and Silas, Paul had full reports on the progress of the churches in northern Greece. Now Timothy gave him a firsthand account of the Thessalonian Church, for the most part encouraging, even thrilling.

The Jews and the "great multitude of devout Greeks" and the "not a few chief women" whom Paul had won for Christ had spread the Word all over northern Greece. The Pharisees had badgered, boycotted, and bullied every Christian in town. And, as always under violence, open or hidden, the faith had grown stronger in Thessalonica.

But though the Thessalonians were full of zeal, Timothy went on, their unguided fervor was giving birth to troublesome disputes.

Unhesitatingly, Paul squandered his few hours of nightly rest to rush paternal warning and counsel to his friends in Thessalonica. By the light of a Corinthian lamp he worked in midnight silence, penning the first of those fourteen deathless letters, which with the Gospels and The Acts make up the bulk of the New Testament.

He began by pouring out his loving gratitude to Jason and the other converts for having welcomed him and the message of faith he had carried. He congratulated them on their courage under persecution, reminding them that the older churches in Judaea and Syria had suffered the same way.

He paused in the silence of Titus' sleeping house, pondering the advice which should best counteract the disputes threatening the church in Thessalonica. Timothy had reported that certain scrupulous souls there were worrying overmuch about a detailed code of conduct. Paul grunted in impatience. They had only to follow the oral Gospel as he had delivered it to them, and the condemnation of sin contained in it. And the less time spent quibbling, the more a soul could grow in love and service of God!

For the rest therefore, brethren, we pray and beseech you in the Lord Jesus that as you have received from us how you ought to walk, and to please God, so also you would walk, that you may abound the more. For you know what precepts I have given to you by the Lord Jesus.

For this is the will of God, your sanctification: that you should abstain from fornication; that every one of you should know how to possess his vessel in sanctification and honor, not in the passion of lust, like the Gentiles that know not God. And that no man overreach, nor circumvent his brother in business: because the Lord is the avenger of all these things, as we have told you before, and have testified . . . But as touching the charity of brotherhood, we have no need to write to you: for yourselves have learned of God to love one another. For indeed you do it towards all the brethren in all Macedonia.

But we entreat you, brethren, that you abound more, and that you use your endeavor to be quiet, and that you do your own business, and work with your own hands, as we commanded you: and that you walk honestly towards them that are without; and that you want nothing of any man's.

And then Paul got down to the major dispute that Timothy had reported, a big argument about the second coming of Jesus Christ. Many men in Thessalonica had deduced that this return of God was due at any minute, in their lifetime—certainly while their children still lived. And they worried about the faithful who had already died and would miss out on that tremendous event!

Paul smiled a little sadly at the naïveté of these youngsters in the faith, so sure of their own reasoning, so ready to impute their own finite thoughts to the infinite God! And yet the Thessalonians were close to despair over the problem, and Paul's heart went out to them:

And we will not have you ignorant, brethren, concerning them that are asleep, that you be not sorrowful, even as others who have no hope. For if we believe that Jesus died, and rose again; even so them who have slept through Jesus, will God bring with Him.

For this we say unto you in the word of the Lord, that we who are alive, who remain unto the coming of the Lord, shall not prevent them who have slept. For the Lord Himself shall come down from heaven with commandment, and with the voice of an archangel, and with the trumpet of God: and the dead who are in Christ shall rise first. Then we who are alive, who are left, shall be taken up together with them in the clouds to meet Christ, into the air, and so shall we be always with the Lord. Wherefore, comfort ye one another with these words.

Who dared guess the time of the Second Advent? Not Paul!

But of the times and moment, brethren, you need not that we should write to you; for yourselves know perfectly that the day of the Lord shall so come as a thief in the night.

For when they shall say, "peace and security," then shall sudden destruction come upon them, as the pains upon her that is with child, and they shall not escape. But you, brethren, are not in darkness, that that day should overtake you as a thief. For all you are the children of light, and children of the day: we are not of the night, nor of darkness. Therefore, let us not sleep, as others do; but let us watch, and be sober.

For they that sleep, sleep in the night; and they that are drunk, are drunk in the night. But let us, who are of the day, be sober, having on the breastplate of faith and charity, and for a helmet the hope of salvation. For God hath not appointed us unto wrath, but unto the purchasing of salvation by our Lord Jesus Christ, who died for us; that, whether we watch or sleep, we may live together with Him. For which cause comfort one another; and edify one another, as you also do. . . .

And we beseech you, brethren, rebuke the unquiet, comfort the feeble-minded, support the weak, be patient towards all men. See that none render evil for evil to any man; but ever follow that which is good towards each other, and towards all men.

Always rejoice. Pray without ceasing. In all things give thanks; for this is the will of God in Christ Jesus concerning you all. Extinguish not the spirit. Despise not prophecies. But prove all things; hold fast that which is good. From all appearance of evil refrain yourselves. And may the God of peace Himself sanctify you in all things; that your whole spirit, and soul, and body, may be preserved blameless in the coming of our Lord Jesus Christ. . . .

Brethren, pray for us. . . .

The grace of our Lord Jesus Christ be with you.

Amen.

But that letter did not settle the foment in Thessalonica. Inside a few weeks Timothy had delivered the epistle, and hastened back to Corinth to report to Paul an appalling state of affairs in the church that centered around Jason's house.

Jason answered Paul's letter with news of double trouble. Now more self-designated teachers were preening in Thessalonica, setting themselves up as pundits of the new doctrine of Christ. And these homemade interpreters of the oral Gospel could not even agree among themselves!

One group said that the second coming of the Lord was so close at hand that nobody should do anything but wait for it. The world was going to end, perhaps next week or next month, so why bother sowing and harvesting or trading or studying or working at all? And a great many good men and women were listening seriously to those self-styled sages. They idled from dawn to dawn, expectant of the Christ's coming in glory, and their disorderliness was becoming public scandal.

The other faction went to the opposite extreme. They considered themselves intellectuals, and they did not believe that such a thing as the second advent could be taken seriously. They did not expect it now, or soon—or ever! Christ's second coming was a personal thing that happened privately to each man at his death—but never to all men, living and dead, together!

And that idea, Paul knew, was even more dangerous than the first. No man was obliged to believe in Christ, but, if he did believe, he could not then edit the meaning of Christ's own words. Jesus had explicitly stated that at some time far distant from the Resurrection, He would return to this world: "And then shall appear the sign of the Son of Man in heaven, and then shall all tribes of the earth mourn," said Jesus, "and they shall see the Son of Man coming in the clouds of heaven and with much power and majesty."

So Paul sat more night hours, this time in the back of the tent-making booth he shared with Priscilla and Aquila in the Corinthian bazaar, to write a second letter to Thessalonica.

Skeptics scoffed then, only twenty years after the Crucifixion, at the notion of a second advent—just as they do today. But Paul, who had talked with the Lord's earthly companions, who had even had direct counsel from God, charged his converts to believe in the literal meaning of the doctrine.

In that second letter to Thessalonica Paul rehearsed the signs which Jesus had foretold would precede His final reappearance. A Man of Sin will arise, and he will come just before Christ Himself. The Man of Sin will do three things by which he identifies himself: he will oppose God, declare himself superior to God, and finally insist that he himself is God.

This Man of Sin will be the anti-Christ, and he will take over the rule of the earth, not only by physical force and violence, but "with all power and signs of lying wonders." And in the great day when Jesus confronts that impostor, the anti-Christ, who is Satan taking mortal form, will die.

And meanwhile? In his great second epistle, Paul counsels all believers to be faithful to the Lord, through complete patience in working and waiting.

For the Thessalonians to drop their tools, abandon their plows, renounce all work because they expected the immediate return of Jesus was wrong. Paul told them in phrases flashing like knives that the time of the second coming of Christ is God's secret. And work is a holy, daily duty.

Paul in his tentmaking stall, surrounded by the products of his own skilled hands, weary from a day of preaching and prayer and of selling in the market place, shook his head and smiled at the notion of Christian virtue in idleness.

He picked up his quill, to end the letter:

And we charge you, brethren, in the Name of our Lord Jesus Christ, that you withdraw yourselves from every brother walking disorderly and not according to the tradition which they have received of us.

For yourselves know how you ought to imitate us: for we were not disorderly among you; neither did we eat any man's bread for nothing, but in labor and in toil we worked night and day, lest we should be chargeable to any of you. Not as if we had not power: but that we might give ourselves a pattern unto you, to imitate us. For also, when we were with you, this we declared to you: that, if any man will not work, neither let him eat.

For we have heard there are some among you who walk disorderly, working not at all, but curiously meddling. Now we charge them that are such, and beseech them by the Lord Jesus Christ, that, working with silence, they would eat their own bread.

But you, brethren, be not weary in well doing.

And if any man obey not our word by this epistle, note that man, and do not keep company with him, that he may be ashamed; yet do not esteem him as an enemy, but admonish him as a brother.

Now the Lord of Peace Himself give you everlasting peace in every place. The Lord be with you all.

The salutation of Paul with my own hand; which is the sign in every epistle. So I write. The grace of our Lord Jesus Christ be with you all.

Amen.

And off went Timothy again to Thessalonica, with this second papyrus scroll tucked into the sleeve of his robe.

Chapter 64. THE MAN WHO WOULD NOT JUDGE

As THE VOICE of his vision had assured him on his first night in Corinth, Paul had found many new converts, souls who belonged to God. In obedience to the vision he had spoken out freely, and did not hold his peace. He preached with unalloyed success for eighteen months.

Then a new Roman proconsul took power in Corinth. And Paul's old enemies in the synagogue, encouraged by the appointment of the new imperial representative, sprang up as from a long nap and showed their fangs.

They brought Paul to the judgment seat.

Specifically, the charges against him as he stood before Gallio, proconsul of this whole province of Achaia, were the same Paul had faced so often before:

"This man persuades men to worship God contrary to the law!"

But this time Paul could not have asked to be brought before a fairer or more just magistrate. Gallio was a brother of the famous Stoic philosopher Seneca, and the uncle of the poet Lucan.

Thus Paul stood before an imperial aristocrat, sophisticated, widely traveled, discerning, and taking real pride in Roman justice. As Gallio sat there on the judgment seat above Paul, history might have caught its breath, for these two men were to fall victims to the same insensate brutishness and cruelty within a year of each other. Gallio would be put to death in 66 by the personal orders of Nero for daring to conspire against him; the same insane tyrant would order the executions of Paul and Peter!

Now Gallio sat in judgment over Paul. The room was jammed with Christians and their enemies when the apostle's name was called and he stood up for trial. He was prepared to argue his case as a lawyer, a theologian, and a prophet. But he was not permitted to speak his first word. He was just, says Luke, "beginning to open his mouth" when Gallio took over.

Turning to the accusers from the synagogue he spoke crisply and decisively:

"If it were some matter of injustice—"

The Pharisees knew their case was nothing of that kind.

"—or an heinous deed, O Jews—"

They also knew no such crime could be alleged against the prisoner.

"—I should with reason bear with you. But if they be questions of word and names, and of your law, look you to it! I will not be judge of such things."

His refusal as a Roman jurist to trifle with a religious dispute fell like a spark in the powder barrel of the onlooking throng. Hotheaded partisans of Paul, who had kept their tempers during the legal process, now lost control in their sudden elation. Gallio's unmistakable disdain for the synagogue plaintiffs encouraged the Christians. Suddenly at the outer doors came tumult and cries of wrath.

Before the authorities could know what was happening, the mob grabbed at the fringed robes of Sosthenes, who had succeeded the converted Crispus as chief of the synagogue. Before the judgment seat where he had led Paul's accusers, they beat Sosthenes in plain sight of Gallio, who sat placidly unmoved, because, Luke explained, he "cared for none of these things."

Afterward, some said Sosthenes' own friends had attacked him in revenge for a poor prosecution of the case. Others blamed the Christians.

Paul was stunned at such violence. In crowd-hysteria it is difficult to place guilt, yet rioting belonged not to Christians but to their enemies. The shocking tumult of that bright Corinthian morning seemed to Paul to carry a message—implicit marching orders.

He had stayed in this great city long enough. Perhaps this vital new citadel of the faith would fare better if Paul now removed himself as a personal issue.

He decided it was time to return to Asia, from whence he had come.

One curious preliminary marked his departure. Paul shaved his head. The fact that he did so, as explicitly related by Luke, is evidence that Paul was not, as some insist, a completely bald-headed man. His head was shorn by the barber of Cenchreae, the harbor town near Corinth, because of a vow he had made. No one has told us the secret of that sacred oath. What the apostle had in mind has remained a secret through the ages, when he thus publicly mortified himself.

So much needed to be done, so many final instructions must be given, that many days passed between the riot in the judgment hall and Paul's actual farewell to Corinth. By the time the apostle was ready to leave, Timothy had returned, footsore but triumphant, from delivering the second letter to Thessalonica.

Taking ship with Paul, besides Silas and Timothy, were the two newly dear friends he had made in Corinth, Priscilla and Aquila. Husband and wife had consecrated their lives to their Christian faith and to Paul's leadership; they accompanied him, resolving to suffer anything with him.

Across the blue Aegean the five Christians sailed eastward to the city of Ephesus at the mouth of the Cayster River, not far from Smyrna.

Leaving Priscilla and Aquila at lodgings in the town, Paul went, characteristically, direct to the synagogue. He was anxious to look over the situation and decide whether Ephesus would be fertile ground for the establishment of another Christian church. The time was to come when he would address a masterpiece of religious literature to the church he had by then founded here, the superb Epistle to the Ephesians.

But on this day in 52, Paul contented himself with a brief speech to the elders in the synagogue. By now the most exaggerated tales about this apostle were circulated among both Jews and Gentiles throughout the Roman Empire. The elders of Ephesus listened gravely to his summary of the faith he preached in God the Father, God the Son, and God the Holy Ghost.

"Tarry with us a longer time," they said to Paul. "We desire to hear more about these matters."

But today Paul shook his head. In his soul he heard a beckoning call, tugging at him urgently each moment he tarried in Ephesus.

"I will return to you again," he promised, "God willing."

And back to the ship he went with Silas and Timothy, answering that inner call.

It was a call to Jerusalem.

Chapter 65. THE CALL TO JERUSALEM

THREE years of prodigious labors had passed since Paul and Silas had set out on the Second Missionary Journey. With Timothy they had climbed the Taurus Mountains and crossed the plateau of inland Asia Minor. Paul had revisited the churches of South Galatia, had crossed into Europe, organizing congregations of the new faith in five major cities of Macedonia and Greece.

Now he was heading back at last to lands that seemed like head-quarters, if not home. How fared the church he had helped establish in Syrian Antioch? What of the central council at the Cenacle in Jerusalem? What of the pillar apostles there—Andrew and James and John? Most especially, what of Peter?

No more conflicts of view existed between Peter and Paul. By now they fully understood and loved each other. But Paul had not re-ceived a connected history, or even a bare chronology, of Peter's travels. Even the Bible is silent about them, except for a few general references sprinkled through the Epistles. The fact that Peter ad-dressed the first of his own two letters to the faithful in the provinces of Pontus, Galatia, Cappadocia and Asia—in which Paul had worked —indicates that Peter may have actually visited the same districts, intent on harmonizing the feelings of the dispersed Jews of those colonies. There is even a strong report that Peter went to Corinth for a while after Paul's departure. Some evidence for this is cited in Paul's reference to a "Cephas party," a "Peter faction," among the unsettling problems that were later to beset the church at Corinth.

The Scriptures tell nothing of this portion of Peter's glorious ca-reer, but many think that he was traveling as energetically as Paul. They hold that among Christians everywhere there stood a vast con-spiracy of silence about the doings of Peter. So precious was he to them, that they took utmost precautions to keep his whereabouts secret from any potential persecutors. It was rumored from church to church that Peter had already ventured to Rome itself, converting many slaves and freedmen and even a senator named Pudens. He had left Rome, so it was whispered, only when Emperor Claudius had banished the Jews from the city. But the man of rock was determined to return to Rome, and no Christian wished to bring danger on Peter's white head by inadvertently giving away his plans.

Silently, without fanfare or pomp, Peter would appear in a Christian community, to preach and to administer the sacraments, to check on the welfare of his far-flung flock. We do know that Peter organized and wisely governed the great Church and that, in the things that mattered, his decisions were guided by the Holy Ghost, and so, unassailable.

From the start enemies of Christ tried to destroy His doctrines by creating divisions. Today men are just as busy sowing discord among Christians. In the early Church some of the false followers of Peter tried to play him against Paul, and among Paul's company others were equally treasonable for the same destructive ends. The old contest about circumcision and dietary laws in regard to the Gentiles had supplied the issues to heat up tempers. The "Cephas party" in Corinth—the work of which would soon begin to appear—and the bitter opposition to Paul in that local church derived from these attempts to disrupt the Church.

But Peter and Paul were sons of grace, and over them lay a divine protection. They knew in their hearts that their obedience to guidance of the Holy Spirit must be their sole concern. If they suspected that Rome and cruel martyrdom for both of them was not far distant, they let God take care of the future.

Such was the situation on that day when Paul sailed from Ephesus to Caesarea.

"And going down to Caesarea, he went up to Jerusalem, and saluted the church, and so came down to Antioch."

That is all Luke tells. Paul paid his respects to the brethren. What had been his sudden "call" then? We will never know. The felicity of the brethren, the companionable sense of the Holy Spirit blessing them as they sat and talked together exchanging experiences—such matters as these were routine in the eyes of Luke, taken for granted with no need to write them down. Just as he recorded the quarrels in synagogues and judgment halls along Paul's second journey, so Luke would certainly have written of any disputes in Jerusalem. His silence speaks only of peace.

Paul saluted the church in Jerusalem. He visited with James the

Less and John the Beloved. What the occasion, what Paul's vow may have been, the whole purpose or result of the conferences is as yet undiscovered and left to our speculations. At the finish they blessed each other, and Paul made his farewells.

His Third Missionary Journey was about to begin.

BOOK SEVEN

The Third Journey

Chapter 66. THE STRANGE STORY OF APOLLOS

Paul went directly to Syrian Antioch, and there he rested.

For the past three years he had been traveling wasting distances on foot and by ship, pausing only to pour forth the sacraments of the faith, and his own eloquent skill in teaching and debate. Rest and hours of quiet prayer and meditation were needed to recharge his energies.

Yet Paul did not wait long before launching his third missionary campaign. He had promised to return to Ephesus, the port at which he had preached so briefly on his way to Jerusalem. Aquila and Priscilla were waiting for him there now. With Silas and Timothy, Paul started off again on foot, revisiting his mission churches in Galatia and Phrygia on his way westward. Within a few months the three were back in Ephesus.

The city's heritage of history charmed Paul. He recalled that in ancient days the Hittites had built the famed sanctuary of the mother-goddess of Asia on the Ephesian shore, an inviolate asylum tended by eunuch priests and virgin priestesses. Later, at the command of the Delphic oracles, a conquering Persian tyrant had built a "columnless temple" on the site of that tabernacle, an exquisite shrine of green stone.

Roman conquerors had made Ephesus the capital of the whole province of Asia. Near the time of the Crucifixion, an earthquake had shattered the venerable architectural beauties of the city. But Emperor Tiberius had rebuilt it completely. When Paul arrived,

Ephesus was a glittering new citadel of gold and shining marble.

Here was a city of Gentiles—and of dark-hearted pagans; home of the thousand Roman gods—and even worse, a hidden stronghold of black magic. Witchcrafters nested in the new buildings of Ephesus, thaumaturges, diviners of the future, and practitioners of the iniquitous secret rites known cryptically as "Ephesian letters."

Yet inside two years, Paul was to transform Ephesus into the third Christian city of the world.

Aquila and Priscilla met him breathlessly, impatient with news. Another preacher had visited Ephesus in Paul's absence—an Egyptian Jew named Apollos, carrying an odd, half-breed version of Christianity!

This Apollos was a learned and eloquent man, well acquainted with the Law and the Prophets, quoting from them so effectively that people called him "mighty in the Scriptures." Somehow he had heard about Jesus, a sketchy outline of the faith gleaned perhaps secondhand from travelers in Africa.

What he heard had so excited this fervent Egyptian scholar that he felt driven to share his discovery with the world. He dropped every other interest, abandoned his home in Alexandria, and sailed to Ephesus, thinking to be the first to carry the news of Christ through Asia and Europe.

But Apollos, for all his exuberance, did not have the full story of Christianity. He had left home too soon. Paul sighed as he recalled the rumor that Peter had commissioned young Mark to convert the city of Alexandria. Had Apollos waited, he could have heard the true Gospel from Mark's lips—and both the Egyptian and the men of Ephesus would have been better off.

For Apollos had not really grasped Christianity—and the message he preached was wrong. A strange gap marred his understanding of the new faith. He had accepted the fact that Jesus was the Messiah promised by the Scriptures. But the only baptism of which he had heard was the one given by John the Baptist. He was completely ignorant of the saving grace of baptism in the Name of Christ!

In Paul's absence Apollos had landed in Ephesus. Hustling straight to the synagogue, he began to tell the elders what he knew about Christianity.

Aquila and Priscilla had been in the congregation that day. As they

St. Paul's Third Journey

sat listening to the stranger from Alexandria their eyes had sought each other in mutual realization. This fellow spoke well—but he must not be allowed to squander his fervor in preaching anything but the full truth.

Though they squirmed to hear anyone teaching a warped version of the faith, Aquila and Priscilla did not follow the example of Christian-haters and rise to heckle the speaker. Primly they controlled themselves till his sermon was finished and the crowds dispersed; then they drew him off alone to the privacy of their own lodgings. There "they took him to them, and expounded to him the way of the Lord more diligently."

For the first time Apollos heard of the existence of the Holy Ghost —the source of divine inspiration, part of the living experience of Christians. John the Baptist, he now learned, had been only preparing the way for the glory which Christ's death and Resurrection had opened to His followers. The Egyptian's eyes widened as Aquila explained the astounding truth that the faithful had been in spiritual union with God the Father, God the Son, and God the Holy Ghost ever since the golden fires of Pentecost had fallen from heaven.

Apollos took his lessons in good grace. He had never before heard of this man and wife—and of Paul, their mentor, he had heard only rumors. But he recognized that Aquila and Priscilla had the Truth, and he received it from them eagerly.

Yet he did not remain with them. He felt an urge, perhaps a call, to move on into Achaia and other parts of southern Greece. He especially wanted to preach in Corinth—and Paul would soon hear plenty about that!

But by the time Paul and Silas and Timothy arrived in Ephesus Apollos was gone—leaving behind him an urgent problem for the missionaries. Quickly Aquila and Priscilla explained the situation. Before they had been able to intervene and instruct Apollos more fully, the Egyptian had actually baptized a few Ephesians—not in the Name of Christ but in the old ritual of John the Baptist.

Neither Aquila nor his wife had felt equipped to cope with the situation. They were not ordained; no one ever commissioned this couple to preach. So they had welcomed the converts Apollos had made and waited patiently for Paul's promised return to Ephesus, to turn the problem over to him.

Smiling, but grave in his dignity, Paul went with Silas to greet the twelve men Apollos had baptized. He plunged straight to the core of the difficulty.

"Have you received the Holy Ghost since you believed?"

The converts' eyes dimmed with bewilderment.

"We have not so much as heard whether there be a Holy Ghost."

"In what then were you baptized?" asked Paul.

"In John's baptism!"

But John the Baptist had been only a precursor of the Christ— not an end but a prelude. John the Baptist had himself said: "I indeed baptize you with water but after me cometh a Man . . . which baptizes you with the Holy Ghost!"

And another had indeed come after John, as the Baptist had fore- told; One whose sandals John was not fit to lace. Of this Paul now told them:

"John baptized the people with the baptism of penance, saying that they should believe in Him Who was to come after him, that is to say, in Jesus."

The twelve converts listened, then stood willingly before Paul, ready for a true sacrament. They were baptized then and there in the Name of the Lord Jesus. In one instant they realized what had been in Paul's heart when he asked his first question. Even while they knelt before him, with his hands resting on their heads, the Holy Ghost entered their souls. "And they spoke with tongues and prophesied."

Chapter 67. THREE MEN FROM CORINTH

FOR two years Paul preached in Ephesus.

He began in the synagogue, "disputing and exhorting concerning the Kingdom of God." But agents of the omnipresent crew of elders, scribes, and Pharisees soon fomented an opposition party. They detested Paul and all that he stood for. They interrupted him, heckled him, challenged him. Their jeers and mockery kept the meetings in an uproar.

So Paul decided to teach elsewhere. He selected the famous school of Tyrannus, which had gained for Ephesus an enviable reputation for philosophical enquiry. Tyrannus, himself an enlightened man, was quick to see the logic as well as the revelation of the new faith. Hearing Paul in the synagogue, he invited the apostle to use his lecture hall. From the fifth to the tenth hour, the fashionable period for philosophers of the time, Paul taught Christian doctrine from the platform of the school of Tyrannus.

His old followers, deserting the synagogue, trooped in to hear him, and new disciples jammed the auditorium. Silas and Timothy spent hours daily catechizing the hundreds of converts, preparing them for the sacraments.

Paul's eloquence was potent, but more startling yet were his miracles and spectacular healings. His prayers and touch opened blind eyes, restored the maimed, and exorcised those evil spirits that roam the world seeking the ruin of souls. And a new gift came to Paul—the power of remote healing.

Sufferers too ill to be brought to the courtyard of the school of Tyrannus, some of them as far away as the other end of the province of Asia, were cured when their relatives or friends journeyed to Paul and had him touch a handkerchief, an apron, any object belonging to the ailing loved ones. These "more than common miracles," as Luke, the physician, called them, were promptly performed, "and the diseases departed from them, and the wicked spirits went out of them."

Yet, amid these brilliant demonstrations of the power of Father, Son, and Holy Ghost, in the rush of his daily routine of teaching and tentmaking, Paul never abandoned his concern for his spiritual sons across the Aegean Sea in Europe. Travelers kept him constantly attuned to the progress and problems of the churches he had established in Macedonia and Achaia. Paul received each morsel of news with paternal eagerness and prayer.

But then three men with worried faces came to Ephesus seeking Paul. Their names were Stephanas and Fortunatus and Achaicus, and they came from Corinth with word of serious trouble.

That glittering city where the fervor of belief had shone like new marble under the spell of Paul's teaching, had fallen into a slough of sinful degradation and unspirituality. Every bestial sin of paganism now paraded boldly in the outward trappings of Christianity; men even dared to receive Holy Communion reeling, staggering drunk. Corinthian morals were perverted, their faith now a travesty of what Paul had preached. Each of the hairsplitters and self-styled sages taught a new theory of Christianity.

Paul's sun-lined face grew grave as he sat in the recesses of his tent-making booth and listened to the sad news trembling from the mouths of his three earnest visitors. Their tale did not come as a complete surprise. Paul was better informed than this trio imagined. A few weeks earlier he had heard secretly from another worried observer, a woman named Chloe.

Chloe had been won to Christianity by Paul's preaching in Corinth, and like many of his woman converts, she never lost the flaming vision of the apostle's zeal. She cherished her faith, lived it, guarded it zealously. Like Priscilla, like Mary, the mother of Mark, like Lydia the seller of purple and a hundred of their spiritual sisters, Chloe had thrown open her house for meetings of the faithful, letting it serve as a church center when needed.

And in her own home Chloe had heard the first rumblings of heresy, which seemed doomed to shatter the faith in Corinth. She had listened carefully and written a full report, sending it off to Paul by some of her own large domestic staff. From this gentle widow Paul had received explicit details of the politics and cliques by which the Corinthian congregation was divided, of their schemes and pride, their forgetfulness of brotherly love.

And now here were the three stanch men from Corinth, bolstering Chloe's reports, pouring out their version of the sordid tale of debauchery and heresy in the city.

Paul's sharp eyes grew black with sadness. Eighteen months he had lived in Corinth, stitching his tents while he forged the new church, with such seemingly overpowering success! He remembered the day when Crispus, chief of the synagogue, had come and begged for baptism! In memory he relived his arrest and the moment when he had stood before Gallio, the proconsul, ready for trial, only to hear himself set free. And the ugly shouts of the mob that attacked Sosthenes, the new ruler of the synagogue, echoed again in Paul's ears.

Now the faithful of Corinth were in danger, as surely as if the city lay under siege. Stephanas, Fortunatus, and Archaicus had left their homes and business and crossed the Aegean Sea, to appeal to Paul to set their brethren straight. They and Chloe, and scores of other earnest Christians, were desperate for help.

In answer, Paul wrote his First Epistle to the Corinthians.

The letter was addressed not only to them but to all Christians, not only of the year A.D. 57 but of A.D. 2,000 or 20,000. Paul knew the

Corinthians' weaknesses, their recurrent doubtings. And he knew ours.

Chapter 68. THE GREATEST LETTER EVER WRITTEN

To the church of God that is at Corinth, to them that are sanctified in Christ Jesus, called to be saints, with all that invoke the Name of our Lord Jesus Christ in every place of theirs and ours . . .

Paul began his letter with an attack on the problems reported by Chloe, the devilish disputes that tried to split them, dividing the one true Church into three or four splinter sects headed by outstanding preachers—among them Paul himself. At the thought of a "Pauline Church" the brawny little man of Tarsus shuddered. And he wrote:

Now I beseech you, brethren, by the Name of our Lord Jesus Christ, that you all speak the same thing, and that there be no schisms among you; but that you be perfect in the same mind, and in the same judgment. For it hath been signified unto me, my brethren, of you, by them that are of the house of Chloe, that there are contentions among you.

Now this I say, that every one of you saith; "I indeed am of Paul"; "And I am of Apollos"; "And I of Cephas [Peter]"; "And I of Christ!"

Is Christ divided? Was Paul then crucified for you? or were you baptized in the name of Paul? . . . Christ sent me not to baptize, but to preach the Gospel. . . .

For while one saith, "I indeed am of Paul"; and another, "I am of Apollos"; are you not men? What then is Apollos, and what is Paul? The ministers of Him whom you have believed; and to every one as the Lord hath given. I have planted, Apollos watered, but God gave the increase. . . . For we are God's coadjutors: you are God's husbandry; you are God's building.

According to the grace of God that is given to me, as a wise architect, I have laid the foundation; and another buildeth thereon. But let every man take heed how he buildeth thereupon. . . .

For I think that God hath set forth us apostles, the last, as it were men appointed to death: we are made a spectacle to the world, and to angels, and to men. We are fools for Christ's sake, but you are wise in Christ; we are weak, but you are strong; you are honorable, but we without honor.

Even unto this hour we both hunger and thirst, and are naked, and are buffeted, and have no fixed abode; and we labor, working with our own hands: we are reviled, and we bless; we are persecuted, and we suffer it. We are blasphemed, and we entreat; we are made as the refuse of this world, the offscouring of all even until now.

I write not these things to confound you; but I admonish you as my dearest children. For if you have ten thousand instructors in Christ, yet not many fathers. For in Christ Jesus, by the Gospel, I have begotten you. Wherefore I beseech you, be ye followers of me, as I also am of Christ.

For this cause have I sent to you Timothy, who is my dearest son and faithful in the Lord; who will put you in mind of my ways, which are in Christ Jesus; as I teach every where in every church.

As if I would not come to you, so some are puffed up. But I will come to you shortly, if the Lord will: and will know, not the speech of them that are puffed up, but the power. For the kingdom of God is not in speech, but in power. What will you? Shall I come to you with a rod; or in charity, and in the spirit of meekness?

It is absolutely heard that there is fornication among you, and such fornication as the like is not among the heathens; that one should have his father's wife! And you are puffed up, and have not rather mourned, that he might be taken away from among you, that hath done this deed. . . .

Purge out the old leaven, that you may be a new paste, as you are unleavened. For Christ our Pasch is sacrificed.

Outside the tentmaker's booth the hue and cry of the bazaar hung heavy in the summer air, but Paul sat at his table wrapped in an invisible cloak of silence. In his soul's eye he was seeing again the pure faces of the Corinthian men and women who had first clustered round him, eager to learn the Way of Christ. The appeals of Chloe and the reports of Stephanas and his companions sullied over those memories with the mud and filth of sin. He had already written once to the Christian Corinthians, warning them about their indifference to the degraded morals of their pagan neighbors, and had specifically told them not to keep company with fornicators. To this he had received a stinging reply: where could anyone go and not walk with fornicators? That's the kind of world we live in, Paul.

Stephanas reported those smug words had been spewed out by the biggest hypocrites in Corinth, Christians who swore they themselves were beyond the slightest reproach. For all whose own morals might be weakened by the toleration of evildoers inside the fold, Paul grimly proceeded now to pen the first foreshadowings of the system of excommunication, and to explain precisely what he meant by "not walking with sinners."

I wrote to you an epistle, not to keep company with fornicators. I mean not with the fornicators of this world, or with the covetous, or the extortioners, or the servers of idols; otherwise you must needs go out of this world. But now I have written to you, not to keep company, if any man that is named a brother, be a fornicator, or covetous, or a server of idols, or a railer, or a drunkard, or an extortioner: with such a one, not so much as to eat. . . . For them that are without, God will judge. Put away the evil one from among yourselves.

Did some men preen themselves on being without actual sin? Let Paul remind them that quarrels and disputes are an offense against the Christian ideal of brotherly love. Troublemakers risked their place in heaven as surely as more dramatic sinners!

Already indeed there is plainly a fault among you, that you have lawsuits one with another. . . . Why do you not rather suffer yourselves to be defrauded? But you do wrong and defraud, and that to your brethren! Know you not that the unjust shall not possess the kingdom of God?

Do not err: neither fornicators, nor idolators, nor adulterers, nor the effeminate, nor liers with mankind, nor thieves, nor covetous, nor drunkards, nor railers, nor extortioners, shall possess the kingdom of God. And such some of you were; but you are washed, but you are sanctified, but you are justified in the Name of our Lord Jesus Christ, and the Spirit of our God! . . .

Know you not that your bodies are the members of Christ? Shall I then take the members of Christ, and make them the members of an harlot? God forbid! Or know you not, that he who is joined to a harlot, is made one body? "For they shall be," saith He, "two in one flesh."

But he who is joined to the Lord, is one spirit.

Fly fornication. Every sin that a man doth, is without the body; but he that committeth fornication, sinneth against his own body. Or know you not, that your members are the temple of the Holy Ghost, Who is in you, Whom you have from God; and you are not your own? For you are bought with a great price. Glorify and bear God in your body."

On the cramped table before Paul lay a letter from some puzzled elders of Corinth, a papyrus roll crammed with a host of questions about the most discussed subject in the world—the relations between man and woman. Christ had revolutionized the whole concept of sex;

He had raised marriage to the dignity of a sacrament, irrevocable and full of grace. But with Christianity had come another, seemingly conflicting, concept: the idea of chastity as a desirable sacrifice to God.

The men and women of Corinth were in a turmoil trying to understand the rules Paul had taught them about continency, marriage, and divorce.

And Paul answered:

Now concerning the things whereof you wrote to me: It is good for a man not to touch a woman. But for fear of fornication, let every man have his own wife, and let every woman have her own husband. Let the husband render the debt to his wife, and the wife also in like manner to the husband. The wife hath not power of her own body, but the husband. And in like manner the husband also hath not power of his own body, but the wife.

Defraud not one another, except, perhaps, by consent, for a time, that you may give yourselves to prayer; and return together again, lest Satan tempt you for your incontinency. But I speak this by indulgence, not by commandment. For I would that all men were even as myself: but every one hath his proper gift from God; one after this manner, and another after that.

But I say to the unmarried, and to the widows: It is good for them if they so continue, even as I. But if they do not contain themselves, let them marry. For it is better to marry than to be burnt.

But to them that are married, not I but the Lord commandeth, that the wife depart not from her husband. And if she depart, that she remain unmarried, or be reconciled to her husband. And let not the husband put away his wife.

For to the rest I speak, not the Lord. If any brother hath a wife that believeth not, and she consent to dwell with him, let him not put her away. And if any woman hath a husband that believeth not, and he consent to dwell with her, let her not put away her husband. For the unbelieving husband is sanctified by the believing wife; and the unbelieving wife is sanctified by the believing husband: otherwise your children should be unclean; but now they are holy. But if the unbeliever depart, let him depart. For a brother or sister is not under servitude in such cases. But God hath called us in peace. For how knowest thou, O wife, whether thou shalt save thy husband? Or how knowest thou, O man, whether thou shalt save thy wife? . . .

Art thou bound to a wife? Seek not to be loosed. Art thou loosed from a wife? Seek not a wife.

But if thou take a wife, thou hast not sinned. And if a virgin marry, she hath not sinned: nevertheless, such shall have tribulation of the flesh. . . .

But I would have you to be without solicitude. He that is without a wife, is solicitous for the things that belong to the Lord, how he may please God. But he that is with a wife, is solicitous for the things of the world, how he may please his wife: and he is divided. . . .

Let no temptation take hold on you, but such as is human. And God is faithful, who will not suffer you to be tempted above that which you are able; but will make also with temptation issue, that you may be able to bear it.

Wherefore, my dearly beloved, fly from the service of idols. I speak as to wise men: judge ye yourselves what I say.

The chalice of benediction, which we bless, is it not the communion of the blood of Christ? And the bread, which we break, is it not the partaking of the body of the Lord? . . .

You cannot drink the chalice of the Lord, and the chalice of the devils: you cannot be partakers of the table of the Lord, and the table of devils. . . . Therefore, whether you eat or drink, or whatsoever else you do, do all to the glory of God.

Chloe had indeed reported that some members of the congregation partook of the eucharistic sacrament and then openly and contumaciously joined their old pagan friends to eat food specially consecrated to local idols.

But more scandalous still, the Corinthians were defiling the Lord's Supper in their own churches. Men even came drunk to receive this holy sacrament. Some brought their own meals with them, too proud to share in the "charity feasts" which customarily accompanied the eucharist. The spirit of reverence and love was banished from their altar.

Paul winced at the very thought of such profanation. His pen sped over the scroll, in grim warning.

When you come therefore together into one place, it is not now to eat the Lord's Supper. For everyone takes before his own supper to eat. And one indeed is hungry, and another is drunk! What, have you not houses to eat and to drink in? Or despise ye the church of God; and put them to shame that have not? What shall I say to you? Do I praise you? In this I praise you not.

For I have received of the Lord that which also I delivered unto you, that the Lord Jesus, the same night in which He was betrayed, took bread, and giving thanks, broke, and said: "Take ye, and eat: this is My Body, which shall be delivered for you: this do for the commemoration of Me."

In like manner also the chalice, after He had supped, saying: "This chalice is the new testament in My Blood: this do ye, as often as you shall drink, for the commemoration of Me."

For as often as you shall eat this bread, and drink the chalice, you shall shew the death of the Lord, until He come. Therefore whosoever shall eat this bread, or drink the chalice of the Lord unworthily, *shall be guilty of the Body and of the Blood of the Lord.* But let a man prove himself; and so let him eat of that bread, and drink of the chalice. *For he that eateth and drinketh unworthily, eateth and drinketh judgment to himself, not discerning the Body of the Lord.*

So many problems! Niggling yet vital questions, standing between earnest Christians and the true glory of love of God.

The Corinthians wanted to know what was the greatest gift of faith. Who were more important, more holy—the prophets, the healers, the men who could read souls—or those who have the gift of tongues?

Paul sighed. In their pride they were missing the point completely! Patiently he picked up his quill:

Now there are diversities of graces, but the same Spirit. And there are diversities of ministries, but the same Lord. And there are diversities of operations, but the same God, who worketh all in all. . . .

To one indeed, by the Spirit, is given the word of wisdom: and to another, the word of knowledge, according to the same Spirit; to another, faith in the same Spirit; to another, the grace of healing in one Spirit; to another, the working of miracles; to another, prophecy; to another, the discerning of spirits; to another diverse kinds of tongues; to another, interpretation of speeches.

But all these things one and the same Spirit worketh, dividing to every one according as He will. For as the body is one, and hath many members; and all the members of the body, whereas they are many, yet are one body, so also is Christ. . . .

But be zealous for the better gifts. And I show unto you yet a more excellent way!

The more excellent way!

Paul bowed his head, imploring the grace of God to help him explain the precious secret of Christianity—the Way of Love, the Way of Christian Charity.

"Thou shalt love the Lord thy God with thy whole heart, and with thy whole soul, and with thy whole mind, and with thy whole strength"—and love your fellowman for the sake of God. The divine

gift of charity, that supernal, all-embracing love which differs so tremendously from transitory, self-centered, desirous love—that one gift is the greatest virtue of them all. Without it a man is nothing!

With a prayer in his heart, Paul penned the most glorious words ever written by man, a prose hymn to the love he called charity:

If I speak with the tongues of men and of angels, and have not charity, I am become as sounding brass, or a tinkling cymbal.

And if I should have prophecy and should know all mysteries, and all knowledge, and if I should have all faith, so that I could remove mountains, and have not charity, I am nothing.

And if I should distribute all my goods to feed the poor, and if I should deliver my body to be burned, and have not charity, it profiteth me nothing.

Charity is patient, is kind: charity envieth not, dealeth not perversely; is not puffed up; is not ambitious, seeketh not her own, is not provoked to anger, thinketh no evil; rejoiceth not in iniquity, but rejoiceth with the truth; beareth all things, believeth all things, hopeth all things, endureth all things.

Charity never falleth away: whether prophecies shall be made void, or tongues shall cease, or knowledge shall be destroyed.

For we know in part, and we prophesy in part. But when that which is perfect is come, that which is in part shall be done away.

When I was a child, I spoke as a child, I understood as a child, I thought as a child. But, when I became a man, I put away the things of a child. We see now through a glass in a dark manner; but then face to face. Now I know in part; but then I shall know even as I am known.

And now there remain faith, hope, and charity, these three: but the greatest of these is charity.

Chapter 69. "HOW DO THE DEAD RISE, PAUL?"

THE next day Paul finished that letter.

With charity aflame in his soul he plunged from the summit of inspiration back to the earthly problems of his friends in Corinth— back to the jumble of questions on faith and morals which they had heaped like sweepings on his doorstep.

Chief among these were the doubts of a few so-called rationalists who had decided to believe everything about Christianity except the resurrection of the body after death. In their intellectual arrogance they were emasculating the teachings of Christ to match their own faltering and finite minds.

Less querulous minds, who did not aspire to match wits with God, heard these ideas and began to wonder if the notion of life after death was really no more than a consoling delusion.

Paul rushed to reassure them, to rehearse in firm logic as well as faith, the truth of immortality:

Now I make known unto you, brethren, the gospel which I preached to you . . . by which also you are saved if you hold fast after what manner I preached to you, unless you have believed in vain.

For I delivered unto you first of all, which I also received: how that Christ died for our sins, according to the Scriptures; and that He was buried, and that He rose again the third day, according to the Scriptures; and that He was seen by Cephas [Peter]; and after that by the eleven. Then was He seen by more than five hundred brethren at once: of whom many remain until this present, and some are fallen asleep. After that, He was seen by James, then by all the apostles. And last of all, He was seen also by me, as by one born out of due time.

(For I am the least of the apostles, who am not worthy to be called an apostle, because I persecuted the church of God. But by the grace of God, I am what I am; and His grace in me hath not been void, but I have labored more abundantly than all they: yet not I, but the grace of God with me, for whether I, or they, so we preach, and so you have believed.)

Now if Christ be preached, that He arose again from the dead, how do some among you say that there is no resurrection of the dead? But if there be no resurrection of the dead, then Christ is not risen again. And if Christ be not risen again, then is our preaching vain, and your faith is also vain! . . .

But some man will say: How do the dead rise again? or with what manner of body shall they come?

Senseless man, that which thou sowest is not quickened, except it die first! And that which thou sowest, thou sowest not the body that shall be; but bare grain, as of wheat, or of some of the rest. But God giveth it a body as He will: and to every seed its proper body. . . .

So also is the resurrection of the dead. It is sown in corruption, it shall rise in incorruption. It is sown in dishonor, it shall rise in glory. It is sown in weakness, it shall rise in power. It is sown a natural body, it shall rise a spiritual body. If there be a natural body, there is also a spiritual body, as it is written: "The first man Adam was made into a living soul"; the last Adam into a quickening spirit. . . .

The first man was of the earth, earthly: the second Man, from heaven, heavenly. . . . Therefore as we have borne the image of the earthly, let us bear also the image of the heavenly.

Now this I say, brethren, that flesh and blood cannot possess the Kingdom of God: neither shall corruption possess incorruption.

Behold, I tell you a mystery. We shall all indeed rise again: but we shall not all be changed. In a moment, in the twinkling of an eye, at the last trumpet: for the trumpet shall sound, and the dead shall rise again incorruptible: and we shall be changed. For this corruptible must put on incorruption; and this mortal must put on immortality.

And when this mortal hath put on immortality, then shall come to pass the saying that is written: "Death is swallowed up in victory. O death, where is thy victory? O death, where is thy sting?"

Only one question raised by Stephanas and his two friends remained for Paul to answer—the problem of collecting money to be sent to Jerusalem headquarters, a forerunner of the Peter's Pence Collections still held one day each year in Roman Catholic churches. Paul had from the beginning insisted that all his missions share this responsibility. He believed that the Church was one body united in Christ— and that naturally each member should contribute to the welfare of all others.

Did Paul want the Corinthians to contribute too? Most certainly!

Now concerning the collections that are made for the saints, as I have given order to the churches of Galatia, so do ye also. On the first day of the week let every one of you put apart with himself, laying up what it shall well please him; that when I come, the collections be not then to be made. And when I shall be with you, whomsoever you shall approve by letters, them will I send to carry your grace to Jerusalem. And if it be meet that I also go, they shall go with me.

Now I will come to you, when I shall have passed through Macedonia. And with you perhaps I shall abide, or even spend the winter: that you may bring me on my way whithersoever I shall go. . . . But I will tarry at Ephesus until Pentecost. For a great door and evident is opened unto me: and many adversaries.

Now if Timothy come, see that he be with you without fear, for he worketh the work of the Lord, as I also do. Let no man therefore despise him, but conduct ye him on his way in peace: that he may come to me. For I look for him with the brethren. . . .

Watch ye, stand fast in the faith, do manfully, and be strengthened. Let all your things be done in charity.

And one final admonition: Don't blame these men, who came to me for your own good, nor treat them as tattlers!

I beseech you, brethren, you know the house of Stephanas, and of Fortunatus, and of Achaicus, and they are the first fruits of Achaia, and have dedicated themselves to the ministry of the saints: that you also be subject to such, and to every one that worketh with us, and laboureth. And I rejoice in the presence of Stephanas, and Fortunatus, and Achaicus, because that which was wanting of your part, they have supplied. For they have refreshed both my spirit and yours. Know them, therefore, that are such.

The churches of Asia salute you. Aquila and Priscilla salute you much in the Lord, with the church that is in their house, with whom I also lodge. All the brethren salute you. Salute one another with a holy kiss.

The salutation of me, Paul, with my own hand.

If any man love not our Lord Jesus Christ, let him be anathema, maranatha.

The grace of our Lord Jesus Christ be with you.

My charity be with you all in Christ Jesus.

Amen.

Timothy left that very evening, with Stephanas, Fortunatus, and Achaicus, to carry the deathless letter to Corinth. He expected to return to Paul inside a few weeks, but months of anxiety were to separate the apostle from the man he cherished as a spiritual son.

Having tended to the problems of the western church in Corinth, Paul found he must immediately wheel his thoughts to meet new troubles to the east. In his precious churches of Galatia the whole cause of Christian freedom was tottering because the die-hard Judaizers were again on the warpath.

Chapter 70. WHAT PAUL TOLD THE GALATIANS

PERHAPS never before or after, in his living or his dying, did Paul serve the Lord more effectively than in his Epistle to the Galatians.

Paul had hoped that the specter of the Jewish-Gentile problem had been decently interred and forgotten. But latest reports from Galatia proved that the Judaistic enemies of the new faith were still attacking the converts beak and claw.

In order to become a good Christian, you must first become a good Jew; that was the essence of their preaching.

And the people of Galatia submitted. Grown men, raised as Gentiles, baptized as Christians, were letting themselves be circumcised and submitting to the rigorous Jewish code of diet. They were putting on the outward shackles of the Pharisees as if these were the required costume for a follower of Christ.

Paul thought back to his first visit to Galatia, remembering the swamp fever from which those men had nursed him; recalling the day in Lystra when he and Barnabas had been stoned after being mistaken for gods. Things seemed desperate to him then, and yet, when on divine command he had retraced his steps through Iconium, Lystra, and Derbe, the eager and believing sympathy of the converts he made proved their worth.

He cherished these Galatians with a father's love. The thought that anyone was perverting their hard-won faith infuriated him. No one knew better than he the danger of trying to reduce Christianity to the level of a Jewish cult.

When the crowded auditorium was empty and his daily chores with canvas and thread in the tentmaker's booth were done, Paul sat alone by rushlight in his room, pondering the best answer to the Galatians' problem. Ephesus was asleep, and the tireless apostle was alone in meditation with his God. In that silent hour was conceived the precise explanation of the difference between the ancient "works of the Law," the fulfillment of ten hundred different regulations of conduct—and the salvation that comes through faith in Christ and works born of that faith.

Paul took up his quill and began to write a circular letter addressed to all the churches of Asia—and to us.

O senseless Galatians, who hath bewitched you that you should not obey the truth, before whose eyes Jesus Christ hath been set forth, crucified among you?

This only would I learn of you: Did you receive the Spirit by the works of the law, or by the hearing of faith? . . .

Before the faith came, we were kept under the law shut up, unto that faith which was to be revealed. Wherefore the law was our pedagogue in Christ, that we might be justified by faith. But after the faith is come we are no longer under a pedagogue. For you are all the children of God by faith, in Christ Jesus . . .

There is neither Jew nor Greek: there is neither bond nor free: there is neither male nor female. For you are all one in Christ Jesus. And if you be Christ's then are you the seed of Abraham, heirs according to the promise.

Now I say, as long as the heir is a child, he differeth nothing from a servant, though he be lord of all; but is under tutors and governors until the time appointed by the father: so we also, when we were children, were serving under the elements of the world. But when the fulness of the time was come, God sent His Son, made of a woman, made under the law: that He might redeem them who were under the law: that we might receive the adoption of sons. And because you are sons, God hath sent the Spirit of His Son into your hearts, crying, Abba, Father. Therefore now He is not a servant but a son. And if a son, an heir also through God . . .

Stand fast, and be not held again under the yoke of bondage . . . for in Christ Jesus neither circumcision availeth anything, nor uncircumcision: but faith that worketh by charity.

There was the key to the freedom of Christianity, if the Christians would but seize it. "Faith that worketh by charity . . ."

For all the law is fulfilled in one word: "Thou shalt love thy neighbour as thyself." . . .

I say then, walk in the spirit, and you shall not fulfil the lusts of the flesh. For the flesh lusteth against the spirit: and the spirit against the flesh; for these are contrary one to another: so that you do not the things that you would. But if you are led by the spirit, you are not under the law.

Now the works of the flesh are manifest, which are fornication, uncleanness, immodesty, luxury, idolatry, witchcrafts, enmities, contentions, emulations, wraths, quarrels, dissentions, sects, envies, murders, drunkenness, revelings, and such like. Of the which I foretell you, as I have foretold to you, that they who do such things shall not obtain the kingdom of God.

But the fruit of the Spirit is, charity, joy, peace, patience, benignity, goodness, longanimity, mildness, faith, modesty, continency, chastity. Against such there is no law. And they that are Christ's, have crucified their flesh, with the vices and concupiscences. If we live in the Spirit, let us also walk in the Spirit . . .

Be not deceived, God is not mocked.

For what things a man shall sow, those also shall he reap. For he that soweth in his flesh, of the flesh also shall reap corruption. But he that soweth in the spirit, of the spirit shall reap life everlasting.

And in doing good, let us not fail. For in due time we shall reap, not failing.

Therefore, whilst we have time, let us work good to all men, but especially to those who are of the household of the faith.

See what a letter I have written to you with my own hand . . .

For in Christ Jesus neither circumcision availeth any thing, nor uncircumcision, but a new creature . . .

From henceforth let no man be troublesome to me; for I bear the marks of the Lord Jesus in my body.

The grace of our Lord Jesus Christ be with your spirit, brethren.

                                                              Amen

Chapter 71. THE SEVEN SONS OF SCEVA

AND no sooner did the letter go off to troubled Galatia than trouble broke around Paul right in the streets of Ephesus, where for two years he had been working marvels of healing in comparative peace.

There were never any truces in the battle between Paul and Satan; few resting periods between struggles; little time when evil went off to lick its wounds and leave the Christian to catch his breath. Now the silent struggle of saint and devil burst into open flame amid the white marble glory of Ephesus.

The bustling city was suddenly aswarm with newly developed Jewish faith healers, men who tried to heal as Paul healed, offering their services to the families of unfortunate men and women who were possessed. They boasted to relatives of demon-ridden victims that they exercised the same power as Paul. They used their usual mumbo jumbo of conjuration, and then added a new form of exorcism, plagiarized from the apostles.

"I conjure you by Jesus, who is preached about by Paul."

Seven eminently respectable brothers now came forth pretending to possess healing powers in the holy Name of Jesus. They were the seven sons of Sceva, a chief priest of the Ephesian synagogue, and having made their lying claim to Christian power, they were about to receive a stunning surprise, in a demonstration of grim satanic humor. Even Satan, it seems, has a balance of justice!

All seven sons of Sceva stood in a ring in the Ephesian market place around a poor, raddled young man writhing on the rough cobblestones of the street. A devil had entered the body of the hapless fellow, so that all his impulses were crossed and contradictory.

The curious crowd stood agog and tense waiting to see if the united power of the rabbi's sons could oust the demon from the youth. In solemn cadence the seven bearded pretenders chanted as one person:

"I conjure you by Jesus, whom Paul preacheth!"

To their shock and astonishment, a demoniac voice seemed to leap from the mouth of the writhing lad; an evil, mocking cry that threw them into confusion with its contemptuous challenge:

"Jesus I know. And Paul I know. *But who are you?*"

The watchers chortled with laughter. Here, indeed, was sport with another world.

But their laughter was clipped when they saw the young sufferer, his devil still strong within him, rise swiftly from the stones of the street, whirl wildly upon the blasphemous brothers, and attack them with maniacal fury.

In superhuman rage he seized two of them, and in spite of their desperate defense, forced them into the loggia of a school, tore the clothes from their bodies, pummeled and scratched and bit them, ripping the hair out of their heads, "so that they fell out of that house, naked and wounded."

As Luke concludes:

"And this became known to all the Jews and Gentiles that dwelt at Ephesus; and fear fell on them all, and the Name of the Lord Jesus was magnified."

The results were far-reaching, greatly increasing the tide of converts. More and more men and women, both Jews and Gentiles, gave their lives to Christ.

But it also had an immediate effect on many of those people in the province of Asia who, in secret, practiced magic and witchcraft. Out of dark cellars and from the murky reaches of caves, the sorcerers came into the light, lugging with them their books of spells and incantations, their braziers and pentagrams, their snakeskins and other odious apparatus of the practices of the damned.

To see the bonfire they built in the market place was to believe that black magic had come to an end in the world. These pryers into the future, commanders of the jinn of the dark forces in nature and their materialized spirits; those, too, with ghost controls and spirit guides, readers of dreams, astrologers, stargazers, soothsayers of every kind, now stood by their burning books for all the populace to witness that they had given up their evil secrets forever.

The books and properties were valuable; it was no idle public sacrifice. The disciples, looking on, calculated the values burned up in that crackling green-tinged blaze, and "they found the money to be fifty thousand pieces of silver."

The bonfire of the magicians was a light shining upon Paul, calling the world's attention to the power that worked in him and through him. He was at the peak of his remarkable ministry in Ephesus, where the word of God had grown mightily, and was confirmed for all men to see.

And within the mystic attunements of his soul, Paul knew it would soon be time for him to move on.

First, he promised himself, he would pass again through Macedonia and Achaia, to check up on conditions in the troubled cities of Corinth and Thessalonica and supervise the taking up of the collection for the Church universal. Then on to Jerusalem in time for Pentecost, to deliver the funds and report to James the Less, who was now in charge of the Palestine church.

Then Paul made himself a final promise that was like a death sentence:

"After I have been there, I must see Rome also."

But Paul did not leave Ephesus at once.

Chapter 72. THE TUMULT OF THE SILVERSMITHS

HE WAS waiting for Timothy, who had gone to Corinth with Stephanas, Fortunatus, and Achaicus to deliver Paul's epistle.

He had expected Timothy to return inside a month. As moons waxed and waned, the apostle grew restless with concern for his young friend's welfare. Travel, even on Roman highways, was hazardous. Beyond the ordinary perils of the road, Christian messengers had reason to fear attack from synagogue leaders and disgruntled factions inside the Church.

Paul relied heavily on Timothy. That gentle young spirit, whom Paul had adopted as a spiritual son in the town of Lystra, had proven himself the perfect foil for the older apostle. Timothy, the "lover of God," had become in effect Paul's executive secretary, relieving him of many chores. He screened the hundreds of people who clamored daily at Paul's doors for personal interviews; he addressed distant gatherings as the tentmaker's representative; he was expert at surveying new and difficult situations, briefing them for Paul's attention.

And Timothy had also become the fiery little missionary's closest friend. The love of father and son was to link these two men until Paul's death.

When Timothy did not return and no word came, Paul persuaded two of his most valued assistants to journey after him. One was Silas, ever dear friend and companion. The other was Titus, the Gentile convert whom Paul had taken to the Jerusalem council as his prize exhibit in that dispute and who had gratefully been excused from the need to be circumcised.

The two younger men were reluctant to leave Paul. But the apostle proposed that they go to Corinth, then return through Macedonia, and he would meet them in Troas. To that they agreed.

They parted. And Paul set about taking up the big collection from the churches in Asia to be brought to Jerusalem. And that was why, except for a pair of new-made Macedonian friends named Gaius and Aristarchus, Paul was alone during the tumult of the Ephesian silversmiths.

When faith interferes with the way of commerce, what clash causes more trouble?

Luke tells the story in Chapter Nineteen of The Acts:

Now at that time there arose no small disturbance about the way of the Lord. For a certain man named Demetrius, a silversmith, who made silver temples for Diana, brought no small gain to the craftsmen; whom he calling together, with the workmen of like occupation, said:

"Sirs, you know that our gain is by this trade. And you see and hear, that this Paul by persuasion hath drawn away a great multitude, not only of Ephesus, but almost of all Asia, saying: They are not gods which are made by hands! So that not only this our craft is in danger to be set at nought, but also the temple of great Diana shall be reputed for nothing; yea, and her majesty shall begin to be destroyed, whom all Asia and the world worshipeth."

Having heard these things, they were full of anger, and cried out, saying: "Great is Diana of the Ephesians!"

And the whole city was filled with confusion; and having caught Gaius and Aristarchus, men of Macedonia, Paul's companions, they rushed with

one accord into the theater. And when Paul would have entered in unto
the people, the disciples suffered him not. And some also of the rulers of
Asia, who were his friends, sent unto him, desiring that he would not
venture himself into the theater.

Now some cried one thing, some another. For the assembly was confused, and the greater part knew not for what cause they were come
together.

And they drew forth Alexander out of the multitude, the Jews thrusting
him forward. And Alexander beckoning with his hand for silence, would
have given the people satisfaction. But as soon as they perceived him to
be a Jew, all with one voice, for the space of about two hours, cried out:
"Great is Diana of the Ephesians!"

And when the town clerk had appeased the multitudes, he said: "Ye
men of Ephesus, what man is there that knoweth not that the city of
the Ephesians is a worshiper of the great Diana, and of Jupiter's offspring?
For as much therefore as these things cannot be contradicted, you ought
to be quiet, and do nothing rashly. For you have brought hither these
men, who are neither guilty of sacrilege, nor of blasphemy against your
goddess. But if Demetrius and the craftsmen that are with him, have a
matter against any man, the courts of justice are open, and there are
proconsuls; let them accuse one another. And if you inquire after any
other matter, it may be decided in a lawful assembly. For we are even
in danger to be called in question for this day's uproar, there being no man
guilty (of whom we may give account) of this concourse."

And when he had said these things, he dismissed the assembly.

That casting down of the silversmith Demetrius was like a signal
to Paul, crowning his work in the province of Asia.

Early in the morning of the following day, Paul left through the
western gate, setting forward to go to Troas and on into Macedonia.
His stay in Ephesus had been long and arduous; his two-year mission
there, a success. Successful too had been the scion churches he had
established elsewhere in the province of Asia; having sent younger
missioners out into the field, he had the satisfaction of seeing new
congregations spring up in Colossae, Pergamum, Hierapolis, and
Laodicea.

What, now, was he to find on his return to Macedonia?

Chapter 73.   REUNION AT LYDIA'S HOUSE

ANY man trying to recreate the travels of Paul, tracing his footsteps across the earth, would have to make various journeys, because in many instances no one fully knows the exact routes the apostles took. The program Paul followed on the day he left Ephesus is still a mystery; he had a choice of itineraries, and the hints we find in his pastoral letters are sometimes apparently contradictory.

On this adventure he could have gone into Macedonia either by land or sea. Paul loved the sea and sailed whenever he could do so. Yet he often put aside his own personal preferences, his delight in the wine-dark sea and its salty spray and the spindrift on his rugged face. And on this journey he sacrificed those hardy pleasures in order to revisit the town of Troas where he had made an appointment to meet Titus and Silas on their return from Corinth.

Now as Paul trudged through the gates of Troas, and gazed out over the aqueduct and temples to the incredible blue of the Aegean, he turned with a smile to his four new traveling companions. Two were men from the province of Asia, Tychicus and Trophimus, envoys chosen by Ephesus and other Asian towns to carry the special collection to Jerusalem. The other pair were Macedonians—Gaius from Derbe and Aristarchus from Thessalonica. These were the two hapless visiting disciples who had been captured by the tumultuous silversmiths and dragged off to the theater in the riot just two days previously. Battered, pale from their ordeal, Gaius and Aristarchus still contrived a slight swagger to their walk. They could hardly wait to reach their homes in Macedonia and let Paul tell of their close escape!

And now the grizzled, graying apostle turned to them in the sun-swept streets of Troas and reminisced on the vision he had been given in this city—the vision of the pleading man calling him to Macedonia and the first mission into Europe.

He hustled his friends down the streets to the house of the Christians with whom he had lodged on that earlier visit. When the first welcomes were exchanged, he asked the question uppermost in his mind:

"Is Titus here yet? And is there news of Timothy?"

But Titus had not come. No word from Corinth at all.

Paul stayed in Troas a few days, preaching and waiting. But as he was to confide later in his second letter to the Corinthians:

"I had no rest in my spirit, because I found not Titus my brother; but bidding them farewell, I went into Macedonia."

Paul's worries melted into joy when he reached the first stop in Macedonia—Philippi, where once he and Silas had been scourged for casting the pythonical spirit out of the slave girl, where the earthquake had released them from prison and the magistrates had personally begged the apostles to depart in peace. Now, on his return, he was greeted as a hero.

Lydia, the business woman, the seller of purple, his riverside convert, welcomed him again to her house, finding rooms for all of his fellow travelers. The slave girl, who could not longer read fortunes, was there, demurely proud of her new occupation in Lydia's dye works; and the converted jailer brought his family. Lydia's highbeamed reception hall was thronged with converts: Gentiles won by the jailer, Jews who had followed Lydia's lead, and slaves who gathered round the ex-seeress. Nearly a hundred men and women pressed forward to meet Paul, and more peered in through the windows and doors and clustered in the courtyard.

And into the midst of that noisy welcome stepped a figure that brought fond tears to Paul's eyes: Luke, the "most dear physician," whom the apostle had assigned to guide the Philippian church.

Nearly two years had passed since the tall Greek doctor and the brawny, bantam tentmaker had parted, and they embraced each other with eager arms.

And then, with almost unbearable joy, Paul spied a lean-jawed man standing patiently in the background.

"Titus!"

One look at those smiling eyes, and Paul's fears vanished. All was certainly well with Timothy.

Chapter 74. AN APOSTLE'S DEFENSE

But all was not well with the Corinthians.

Titus made his report to Paul over a peaceful glass of wine as twilight seeped into the courtyard after the evening meal. Timothy was still in Corinth, and Silas had remained with him, in a joint effort to stem the tide of spiritual upheaval which threatened Christian life there.

Paul's first letter to the Corinthians had done some good. They had taken sensibly to heart his most severe strictures on their fallings away from grace. They had followed his advice, even excommunicating the offenders he had denounced. But certain doubts lingered in their minds.

After his talk with Titus, Paul realized to his dismay that vehement dispute raged in Corinth between his friends and his detractors as to whether Paul was actually an apostle, in the true sense of the word.

They asked, in effect: What right have you to preach to us?

Titus blushed to repeat such insolence. But Paul smiled.

He himself would never understand why Christ had chosen him; that paradox he could not explain. But that Christ had indeed chosen him as an apostle, of that the Corinthians should have ample proof!

In his Second Epistle to the Corinthians Paul presented his credentials.

As the prime certificate of his apostolate, he cited the Christian life of the Church as he had spread it abroad, and there is in his words something of the ring of the old voice of Socrates, defending himself before the Athenian senators:

Do we begin again to commend ourselves? Or do we need (as some do) epistles of commendation to you, or from you?

You are our epistle, written in our hearts, which is known and read by all men: being manifest, that you are the epistle of Christ, ministered by us, and written not with ink, but with the Spirit of the living God; not in tables of stone, but in the fleshly tables of the heart.

And such confidence we have, through Christ, towards God. Not that we are sufficient to think any thing of ourselves, as of ourselves: but our sufficiency is from God. Who also hath made us fit ministers of the new testament, not in the letter, but in the spirit. For the letter killeth, but the spirit quickeneth.

And what should he say to prove that he is a true apostle? To protect them from false teachers, how shall he commend himself?

In mental gifts and education, Paul knew perfectly well that he surpassed all the other apostles. That was an obvious appraisal of his worth, not a vain boast; and no one knew better than he that intellect and schooling were not at all necessary for apostleship. Peter was neither brilliant nor educated, and he was *chief* of all apostles!

But neither did Paul disparage his special gifts. No other Christian of his time had such background. He read and spoke Greek, Aramaic, and Hebrew; by the great Pharisee Gamaliel he had been meticulously instructed in ancient Jewish laws; he was a citizen of Rome, and part of the culture of the whole empire. He had traveled widely, and understood the differences and similarities of men. And though such training might not be a prerequisite of apostleship, Paul meant to use it all for the glory of Christ.

He was saddened, even wounded, that his claims had been questioned. Any man's heart shrinks from the task of justifying and defending his own value.

. . . Do bear with me! For I am jealous of you with the jealousy of God. For I have espoused you to one Husband that I may present you as a chaste virgin to Christ. . . .

For I suppose that I have done nothing less than the great apostles. For although I be rude in speech, yet not in knowledge; but in all things we have been made manifest to you. Or did I commit a fault, humbling myself, that you might be exalted? Because I preached unto you the gospel of Christ freely? . . .

They are Hebrews: so am I. They are Israelites: so am I. They are the seed of Abraham: so am I. They are the ministers of Christ (I speak as one less wise): I am more; in many more labors, in prisons more frequently, in stripes above measure, in deaths often.

Of the Jews five times did I receive forty stripes, save one. Thrice was I beaten with rods, *once I was stoned*, thrice I suffered shipwreck, a night and a day I was in the depth of the sea. In journeying often, in perils of waters, in perils of robbers, in perils from my own nation, in perils from the Gentiles, in perils in the city, in perils in the wilderness, in perils in the sea, in perils from false brethren. In labor and painfulness, in much watchings, in hunger and thirst, in fastings often, in cold and nakedness.

Besides those things which are without: my daily instance, the solicitude for all the churches.

It was necessary, so some Corinthians contended, that to be an apostle, a man should have seen Jesus Christ. Paul reminds them that he *did* see the Lord after the Resurrection, and confides to them the visions God gave him in the solitude of the Arabian desert.

True, Paul did ask the Corinthians to give to his collections for Jerusalem, as he had already asked the Asians and the Macedonians to contribute. But for himself, he reminded them he had never asked a single coin.

Yet the signs of my apostleship have been wrought on you, in all patience, in signs, and wonders, and mighty deeds. For what is there that you have had less than the other churches, but that I myself was not burthensome to you? Pardon me this injury!

Behold now the third time I am ready to come to you; and I will not be burthensome unto you. For I seek not the things that are yours, but you. For neither ought the children to lay up for the parents, but the parents for the children. But I most gladly will spend and be spent myself for your souls; although loving you more, I be loved less. . . .

Do you seek a proof of Christ that speaketh in me, who towards you is not weak, but is mighty in you?

For although He was crucified through weakness, yet He liveth by the power of God. For we also are weak in Him: but we shall live with Him by the power of God towards you.

Try your own selves if you be in the faith; prove ye yourselves. Know you not your own selves, that Christ Jesus is in you, unless perhaps you be reprobates? But I trust that you shall know that we are not reprobates.

Now we pray God, that you may do no evil, not that we may appear approved, but that you may do that which is good, and that we may be as reprobates.

For we can do nothing against the truth; but for the truth. For we rejoice that we are weak, and you are strong. This also we pray for, your perfection. . . .

For the rest, brethren, rejoice, be perfect, take exhortation, be of one mind, have peace; and the God of peace and of love shall be with you. . . .

The grace of our Lord Jesus Christ, and the charity of God, and the communication of the Holy Ghost be with you all.

                                                                                    Amen.

Chapter 75. THE MAN WHO SLEPT THROUGH
A SERMON

WHILE Titus tramped the winding summer-dusted roads south to
Corinth with that second epistle, Paul lingered in Philippi for months,
making Luke's home a headquarters for short sorties throughout the
rest of Macedonia.

Paul made an excursion to Thessalonica to revisit Jason and the
other brethren; he wanted to make certain that his letters explaining
the Second Coming of Christ had been understood, and that the
idlers had again taken up the business of life instead of waiting around
for the world to end. Further west, Paul paid his second visit to
Beroea, where he and Silas had preached with such success.

Each of these churches responded to Paul's appeal for a common
relief fund to be brought to Jerusalem. The men tithed their substance, and the widows gave their mites. Representatives were chosen
from each place to travel with Paul and present the money in the
Holy City. The representatives from Macedonia were Sopater, a
Jewish Christian from Beroea, and two men from Thessalonica,
Secundus and that dear Aristarchus who had narrowly escaped death
from the mob of Ephesian silversmiths.

With these three, and the three Asian representatives, Gaius,
Tychicus, and Trophimus, the apostle now proposed to go south to
Corinth.

In his second epistle Paul had begged the Corinthians to give
bountifully to the alms collection, which he had begun in their city
a year before.

"I boast of you to them of Macedonia, that Achaia was ready a
year ago! And your zeal has provoked very many. Yet have I sent the
brethren to you . . . lest haply if they of Macedonia come with me,
and find you unprepared, we . . . should be ashamed in this same
confident boasting."

The three treasurers of Macedonia did come with Paul—but Paul
had no need to be ashamed. Erastus, a bustling young street-paver,
who was the treasurer of Corinth, proudly produced a really staggering

leather bag of coins for this first collection from all branches of Christendom for the needs of the Church universal.

The second epistle had reached its mark. Paul was received in Corinth with rejoicing and the respect due to a true apostle of the Lord. Reunited with Timothy and Silas, Paul tasted a few days of triumph and felicity.

Then suddenly the shadow of persecution fell once more on Paul's silvering head.

Those Jews of his own blood and race who still seethed at the novelty of Christianity came after him again hip and thigh. They had heard that Paul was about to set sail for Syria, and they lay in wait for him at the wharves of Cenchreae, with some unspoken fiendish plot to ruin him forever.

But Paul was warned of the ambush. He changed his plans quickly and hurried overland in the darkness, back through Macedonia, leaving Silas and Titus behind to guide the restored church of Corinth. But his faithful Timothy went with him on this fugitive flight, and on this whole last journey to Jerusalem. At Paul's request, Timothy, for safety's sake, led the six treasurers by a different route to Troas, where they would wait till Paul rejoined them.

As for the apostle himself, he scurried out of Corinth under cover of darkness, hustling alone northward to Philippi. He had long ago decided that he could no longer travel without the other of his two stanchest friends—Luke, the beloved physician.

Foot-blistered and dusty, Paul strode once more through the gates of Philippi, past the wall where the slave girl had stood, past the home of Lydia and the jailer's residence, to clasp Luke's shoulders and entreat his company.

For the next five years Luke was almost never to leave Paul's side. And Luke tells us happily: "We sailed from Philippi after the days of unleavened bread, and came unto them in Troas in five days."

Those five days at sea in springtime must have seemed like a breath of heavenly repose to Paul and Luke, who thrived on the good, heaving salt water, the spindrift, and the wide blue sky.

And after the days of rest, Paul jumped to the dock at Troas to greet Timothy with a handclasp that belied his wearying years.

He would need that strength immediately.

For seven days the party remained in Troas, and in that week Paul was to perform one of the most vivid miracles of his ministry.

He was fevered with urgency to reach Jerusalem, longing to be there for the feast of Pentecost. But throughout the journey ahead of him, he would be torn by an equally tormenting compulsion to tarry along the way, in order to rekindle in each town the fires of the faithful. Secretly, he feared that he might never again walk these roads, never again have the chance to talk with these converts he loved.

Paul tried to satisfy both of these impulses all the way to Jerusalem. Between stops he was to drive his eight companions at breakneck speed; and in each Christian community he would teach without rest, in a last, lunging attempt to answer every problem present or future.

His seven days in Troas were dedicated to preaching and to harmonizing the clash of local personalities, setting straight the misconceptions of heretics and troublemakers. So much of this had to be done that the travelers scarcely went to their beds. Time enough, Paul insisted, to sleep when they were once more sailing on the sea!

In Troas, as elsewhere across the spreading Church, Christians had followed the lead of Peter and changed the Sabbath day. They substituted Sunday, the first day of the week, for the old Jewish Sabbath on the seventh day, Saturday. Where the Jews had commemorated the creation of the world, with observances set down in the Book of Exodus, the Christians now named the Lord's Day in memory of the Resurrection and the first Easter Sunday.

On the Sunday morning, then, before his departure, Paul joined the Christians of Troas in celebrating the Holy Eucharist, the sacrament of breaking bread. And when the solemn joys of communion were complete, Paul rose to preach to the congregation. He was leaving them the next morning, and undoubtedly he felt compelled to give them the benefit of his deepest thought.

What he gave was perhaps the longest sermon in history. He talked from midmorning until midnight!

And that was why Paul was suddenly confronted with the need for a miracle. The circumstances were not only terrible and tragic but mortally embarrassing, the kind of nightmare come true that haunts any speaker who talks too long.

He spoke in an upper chamber, on the third floor of a house belonging to a man named Carpus. The barnlike attic hall was illumined by faint oil lamps, swinging on chains from rafters in the ceiling. The room was crowded with Christians so closely packed together that a man had scarcely room to sneeze. The airlessness of the place, the shining lights all around, and the long eloquence of Apostle Paul, all had a very human effect on one young man named Eutychus.

Eutychus had climbed to a seat in the enclosure of a window case-ment, and there he had fallen asleep. In the deep of his slumber he had stirred restlessly from one side to another—and then with a waking gasp he tumbled out of the window. Three stories below in the cobbled courtyard he lay, a bleeding, lifeless mass.

With lanterns and candles the congregation hastened from the upper chamber to the courtyard where Eutychus sprawled. Paul knelt white-faced beside the luckless victim of his zeal, until Luke the physician dismally pronounced the boy dead.

Then, in the confusion of darkness and shifting spots of lantern light, of weeping women and men, Paul fell on the corpse of Eu-tychus, and embraced him. And suddenly the apostle's voice sounded out above the clamor, resonant and full of unearthly challenge:

"Be not troubled! For his soul is in him!"

His soul in that bleeding, broken body? What was Paul talking about, to say such a thing? What worse was he saying now, urging them all to return to the upper chamber, to climb the stairs again, and to bring Eutychus with them?

But they did as he bade them. They carried the body up to the assembly room, and they found they had a living man instead of a dead one in their hands; a restored Eutychus, needing only the blood to be washed away to be as whole and well as any of the others!

And now the first streaks of dawn flared in the east, and Paul, his face flushed and sweating, gave thanks to God. In the chill of early morning he broke bread again, offering the Sacrament in thanksgiving for the miracle with which God had just blessed them. Eutychus, a bit shaky in the legs, battered and bruised as any ruffian, joined the faithful and the apostle at Holy Communion with his sobbing, private prayer of thanks.

Later the women of Carpus' house found food for the whole assem-bly, and they breakfasted together for the second time in twenty-four hours.

And such is human nature, even in apostles, that Paul could not be silent. As Luke records for all to read, he began to preach again, and he "talked a long while, even till break of day. So, he departed."

Chapter 76. "I GO TO JERUSALEM"

FOR reasons he did not confide, Paul suddenly decided not to sail with Luke, Timothy, and the others. On some secret mission he traveled overland alone to the port of Assos, twenty miles from the city of Troas itself. The ruins of that hilltop port, now known as Behramköy, are still of interest to archaeologists, though its finished marbles and foundation rocks were long ago carted away to build the famous docks of Istanbul. The traveler of today can see the harbor mole that Paul saw, jutting out into the waters of the port.

No one really knows what drew the apostle to Assos. We have only Luke's laconic report of the activities of the rest of the party leaving Troas.

"But we," wrote Luke, "going aboard the ship, sailed to Assos, being there to take in Paul; for so he had appointed, himself purposing to travel by land. And when he had met with us at Assos, we took him in and came to Mitylene."

With that mysterious side trip, Paul began his last voyage to Jerusalem.

The first day they reached Mitylene, looming on its bleak promontory, dominating the rocky isle of Lesbos, and Paul gazed ashore at the haunts of Sappho. On they sailed past the mountainous isle of Chios, home of blue marbles, of fruits and brandies and antimony and ocher.

Paul was an intelligent man, and therefore an inveterate sight-seer. He longed to explore the storied wonders of those islands and preach to their teeming inhabitants. But he had his eyes fixed on Jerusalem, and he refused to let his own conflicting purposes delay the schedule longer.

They must sail on, praying for favoring winds; on, past Samos, the island city of such rich and bloody history, opposite the Bay of Ephesus. But the ship sailed boldly past familiar Ephesus, south to the port of Miletus, according to Paul's own plan, his answer to his own double-wishing.

He wanted with all his heart to get back to Jerusalem in time for the Feast of the Pentecost, and did not wish to be held back either by the importunities of warring personalities in the Asian churches or by the warmth of their hospitality. Nevertheless he felt a compelling duty to give them some parting words of advice.

Paul had kept secret from his friends a new and shaking prophecy from the Holy Spirit, warning him of prison and persecution awaiting him in Jerusalem. Calmly, humbly, he accepted the warning, willing to face whatever future God planned for him.

But like a man on his deathbed, he longed to make one last testament to all the sons of his spirit, to speak a final word. That was why he arranged for a great gathering of church hierarchy at a house in Miletus. He sent to Ephesus, thirty miles away, and asked the elders of the church there to meet in the harbor town.

And these are the words he addressed to them, briskly, bluntly, beautifully, when they came:

You know from the first day that I came into Asia, in what manner I have been with you, for all the time, serving the Lord with all humility, and with tears, and temptations, which befell me by the conspiracies of the Jews; how I have kept back nothing that was profitable to you, but have preached it to you, and taught you publicly, and from house to house, testifying both to Jews and Gentiles penance towards God, and faith in our Lord Jesus Christ.

And now, behold, being bound in the spirit, I go to Jerusalem: not knowing the things which shall befall me there, save that the Holy Ghost in every city witnesseth to me, saying that bands and afflictions wait for me at Jerusalem.

But I fear none of these things, neither do I count my life more precious than myself, so that I may consummate my course and the ministry of the word which I received from the Lord Jesus, to testify the gospel of the grace of God.

And now behold, I know that all you, among whom I have gone preaching the kingdom of God, shall see my face no more.

Wherefore I take you to witness this day, that I am clear from the blood of all men; for I have not spared to declare unto you all the counsel of God.

Take heed to yourselves, and to the whole flock, wherein the Holy Ghost hath placed you bishops, to rule the Church of God, which He hath purchased with His own blood. I know that, after my departure, ravening wolves will enter in among you, not sparing the flock. And of your own selves shall arise men speaking perverse things, to draw away disciples after them.

Therefore watch, keeping in memory, that for three years I ceased not, with tears to admonish every one of you night and day.

And now I commend you to God, and to the word of His grace, Who is able to build up, and to give an inheritance among all the sanctified.

I have not coveted any man's silver, gold, or apparel, as yourselves know: for such things as were needful for me and them that are with me, these hands have furnished. I have showed you all things, how that so laboring you ought to support the weak, and to remember the word of the Lord Jesus, how He said: "It is a more blessed thing to give, rather than to receive."

And Luke records in simple beauty the rest of that final meeting in Miletus:

"And when Paul had said these things, kneeling down, he prayed with them all. And there was much weeping among them all; and falling on the neck of Paul, they kissed him, being grieved most of all for the word which he had said, that they should see his face no more.

"And they brought him on his way to the ship."

Chapter 77. A LETTER TO ROME

WITH a straight course over a sparkling sea, the ship carried Paul and his little band of Christian travelers to the island city of Cos.

Yet, in the sunlit calm of those days, Paul's thoughts were centered nearly a thousand miles away, in the city of Rome.

Just before leaving Corinth, when first the warnings of the Holy Ghost had come upon him, he had written one of the most crucial letters of his life, an epistle to the church in Rome.

Just twenty-eight years after the Ascension of Christ, Paul composed this statement of the essence of his doctrine.

As the capital of the Empire, Rome had always flashed like an inviting beacon to Paul in all his previous labors. The intuitions which informed him had made him certain that the day would come when he must enter the imperial gates, that his final fate would lie there. But now that the Spirit had foretold disaster for him in Jerusalem, he wondered if he would ever reach Rome—where Peter secretly carried the Kingdom of Christ into the city of evil emperors.

As the imperial pageant unrolled, iniquity had followed on iniquity. When, in the year 54 of the Christian era, the foul imbecile Emperor Claudius had been killed by Agrippina (who was his niece and his fourth wife)—no one mourned. She had cooked her royally incestuous husband a mess of poisonous mushrooms, and that was the end of him.

Then the murderous Agrippina had turned to the Senate, leading her young son before them. By her own wicked means she contrived to have the boy placed on the throne.

The name of her son, the current Emperor, was Claudius Nero Caesar.

Paul and his Christian fellow workers had hoped with all the Empire that Nero would make a good ruler. There were signs that this desire of all good citizens might be realized. In the beginning Nero had chosen as his adviser one of the wisest Romans, Seneca.

But by the time Paul started for Jerusalem, the truth about the new Emperor was common gossip. Nero, a would-be actor, liked to strut on balconies before mobs of cheering subjects, playing the part of a potentate, monarch of all he surveyed. He poisoned his friends. He murdered his murdering mother and his wife. He was possessed of evil as if he found it a kind of grace turned upside down, a most unholy ghost. Already the sparks that would destroy Rome in one vast bonfire were kindling in the blackness of his heart.

And while this wicked servant of the most low ruled the Empire, Paul wrote his Epistle to the Romans.

Paul's enemies inside the Church already were trying to twist the meaning of his Epistle to the Galatians, the great treatise on Christian freedom. That letter had been designed to meet the arguments of the Judaizers in the province of Galatia, to prove once and for all that one need not first submit to Jewish rites in order to become a Christian.

But the letter had been passed on to other churches, where the question of circumcision had never been raised—and in those churches Paul's breathless lunges at the old Law were being misunderstood. Men were saying Paul believed that Christianity gave them license to break the Ten Commandments and ignore the natural law. Some glib sinners were even using the words of this austere apostle from Tarsus as an excuse for drunkenness and libertine practices.

And that turned Paul's blood cold.

So in his report to Rome, Paul tried to make certain that no one could ever misinterpret him again.

He began by presenting the case against the Gentiles, who in the days before Christ had refused to obey the natural law which God had graven in their hearts, and had thereby earned the scorn of ancient Jews:

For professing themselves to be wise, they became fools.

And they changed the glory of the incorruptible God into the likeness of the image of a corruptible man, and of birds, and of fourfooted beasts, and of creeping things . . .

For this cause God delivered them up to shameful affections. For their women have changed the natural use into that use which is against nature. And, in like manner, the men also, leaving the natural use of the women, have burned in their lusts one towards another, men with men working that which is filthy, and receiving in themselves the recompense which was due to their error. . . .

And as they liked not to have God in their knowledge, God delivered them up to a reprobate sense, to do those things which are not convenient; being filled with all iniquity, malice, fornication, avarice, wickedness, full of envy, murder, contention, deceit, malignity, whisperers, detractors, hateful to God, contumelious, proud, haughty, inventors of evil things, disobedient to parents, foolish, dissolute, without affection, without fidelity, without mercy. Who, having known the justice of God, did not understand that they who do such things, are worthy of death; and not only they that do them, but they also that consent to them that do them.

But the fact that many Gentiles sinned mightily in the days before Christ, did not mean that they were a lost people—or the Hebrews a perfect one. Those Old Testament Jews who followed the written Law of Moses were indeed fine and just men—but so too were those among the uncircumcised Gentiles who had lived up to the dictates of their God-given consciences.

Conversely, many of the chosen people of Israel had failed often and miserably in keeping the Law of God. The case against them is as damning as the case against the Gentiles. The Law of the Old Testament had been designed to help them come closer to God, but they had so abused the Law that it had served only to demonstrate their own guilt.

And in proof Paul quoted the old prophetic Psalms of David:

As it is written: "There is not any man just. There is none that understandeth, there is none that seeketh after God. All have turned out of the way; they are become unprofitable together; there is none that doth good, there is not so much as one.

"Their throat is an open sepulchre; with their tongues they have dealt deceitfully. The venom of asps is under their lips. Whose mouth is full of cursing and bitterness: their feet swift to shed blood: destruction and misery in their ways: and the way of peace they have not known: there is no fear of God before their eyes." . . .

Because by the works of the law no flesh shall be justified before Him. For by the law is the knowledge of sin.

But now without the law the justice of God is made manifest, being witnessed by the law and the prophets. Even the justice of God, by faith of Jesus Christ, unto all and upon all them that believe in him: for there is no distinction . . .

Is He the God of the Jews only? Is He not also of the Gentiles? Yes, of the Gentiles also. For it is one God, that justifieth circumcision by faith, and uncircumcision through faith.

Do we, then, destroy the law through faith? God forbid: but we establish the law . . .

Being justified therefore by faith, let us have peace with God, through our Lord Jesus Christ: by whom also we have access through faith into this grace, wherein we stand, and glory in the hope of the glory of the sons of God. . . .

For as by the disobedience of one man, [in Adam] many were made sinners; so also by the obedience of one, many shall be made just . . .

Know you not that all we, who are baptized in Christ Jesus, are baptized in His death? For we are buried together with Him by baptism into death; that as Christ is risen from the dead by the glory of the Father, so we also may walk in newness of life. . . .

What then? Shall we sin, because we are not under the law, but under grace? God forbid. . . . Being then freed from sin, we have been made servants of justice. . . .

For when you were the servants of sin, you were free men to justice. What fruit therefore had you then in those things, of which you are now ashamed? For the end of them is death.

But now being made free from sin, and become servants to God, you have your fruit unto sanctification, and the end life everlasting. For the wages of sin is death. But the grace of God, life everlasting, in Christ Jesus our Lord.

The old Law, standing by itself, unredeemed by the loving grace of God, said Paul, was a dead thing. The Law itself was good, but man cannot live a good life by that Law without the spiritual aid of Christ. All too often, the man who tries to fulfill the dead letter of the Law without the living spirit of divine love, will only fall deeper into sin:

But I do not know sin, but by the law; for I had not known concupiscence, if the law did not say: "Thou shalt not covet." But sin taking occasion by the commandment, wrought in me all manner of concupiscence. For without the law sin was dead. . . . And the commandment that was ordained to life, the same was found to be unto death to me. For sin, taking occasion by the commandment, seduced me, and by it killed me.

Wherefore the law indeed is holy, and the commandment holy, and just, and good. Was that then which is good, made death unto me? God forbid. But sin, that it may appear sin, by that which is good, wrought death in me; that sin, by the commandment, might become sinful above measure.

For we know that the law is spiritual; but I am carnal, sold under sin. . . . For the good which I will, I do not; but the evil which I will not, that I do. . . .

For I am delighted with the law of God, according to the inward man: but I see another law in my members, fighting against the law of my mind, and captivating me in the law of sin, that is in my members.

Unhappy man that I am, who shall deliver me from the body of this death? . . .

For the law of the spirit of life, in Christ Jesus, hath delivered me from the law of sin and of death. . . . For they that are according to the flesh, mind the things that are of the flesh; but they that are according to the spirit, mind the things that are of the spirit. For the wisdom of the flesh is death; but the wisdom of the spirit is life and peace. . . .

For the Spirit Himself giveth testimony to our spirit, that we are the sons of God. And if sons, heirs also; heirs indeed of God, and joint heirs with Christ: yet so, if we suffer with him, that we may be also glorified with him.

For I reckon that the sufferings of this time are not worthy to be compared with the glory to come, that shall be revealed in us. For the expectation of the creature waiteth for the revelation of the sons of God. . . .

For we know that every creature groaneth and travaileth in pain, even till now. And not only it, but ourselves also, who have the firstfruits of the Spirit, even we ourselves groan within ourselves, waiting for the adoption of the sons of God, the redemption of our body. . . .

Likewise the Spirit also helpeth our infirmity. For we know not what we should pray for as we ought; but the Spirit Himself asketh for us with unspeakable groanings. And he that searcheth the hearts, knoweth what the Spirit desireth; because he asketh for the saints according to God.

And we know that to them that love God, all things work together unto good, to such as, according to His purpose, are called to be saints. . . .

For I am sure that neither death, nor life, nor angels, nor principalities, nor powers, nor things present, nor things to come, nor might, nor height, nor depth, nor any other creature, shall be able to separate us from the love of God which is in Christ Jesus our Lord. . . .

For the scripture saith: "Whosoever believeth in Him, shall not be confounded."

For there is no distinction of the Jew and the Greek: for the same is Lord over all, rich unto all that call upon Him. "For whosoever shall call upon the name of the Lord, shall be saved." . . .

I beseech you therefore, brethren, by the mercy of God, that you present your bodies a living sacrifice, holy, pleasing unto God, your reasonable service. . . .

Let love be without dissimulation. Hating that which is evil, cleaving to that which is good.

Loving one another with the charity of brotherhood, with honour preventing one another. In carefulness not slothful. In spirit fervent. Serving the Lord. Rejoicing in hope. Patient in tribulation. Instant in prayer. Communicating to the necessities of the saints. Pursuing hospitality.

Bless them that persecute you: bless, and curse not.

Rejoice with them that rejoice; weep with them that weep.

Being of one mind toward another. Not minding high things, but consenting to the humble. Be not wise in your own conceits. To no man rendering evil for evil. Providing good things, not only in the sight of God, but also in the sight of all men. If it be possible, as much as is in you, have peace with all men. . . .

Be not overcome by evil, but overcome evil by good.

Let every soul be subject to higher powers: for there is no power but from God: and those that are, are ordained of God. Therefore he that resisteth the power, resisteth the ordinance of God. And they that resist, purchase to themselves damnation. . . .

Render therefore to all men their dues. Tribute, to whom tribute is due: custom, to whom custom: fear, to whom fear: honour, to whom honour.

Owe no man any thing, but to love one another. For he that loveth his neighbour, hath fulfilled the law.

For "Thou shalt not commit adultery: Thou shalt not kill: Thou shalt not steal: Thou shalt not bear false witness: Thou shalt not covet": and if there be any other commandment, it is comprised in this word, "Thou shalt love thy neighbour as thyself."

The love of our neighbour worketh no evil. Love therefore is the fulfilling of the law. . . .

The night is passed, and the day is at hand. Let us therefore cast off the works of darkness, and put on the armour of light. Let us walk honestly, as in the day: not in rioting and drunkenness, not in chambering and impurities, not in contention and envy: but put ye on the Lord Jesus Christ, and make not provision for the flesh in its concupiscences. . . .

Now the God of hope fill you with all joy and peace in believing; that you may abound in hope, and in the power of the Holy Ghost. And I myself also, my brethren, am assured of you, that you also are full of love, replenished with all knowledge, so that you are able to admonish one another.

But I have written to you, brethren, more boldly in some sort, as it were putting you in mind: because of the grace which is given me from God. That I should be the minister of Christ Jesus among the Gentiles; sanctifying the gospel of God, that the oblation of the Gentiles may be made acceptable and sanctified in the Holy Ghost.

I have therefore glory in Christ Jesus towards God. For I dare not speak of any of those things which Christ worketh not by me, for the obedience of the Gentiles, by word and deed, by the virtue of signs and wonders, in the power of the Holy Ghost, so that from Jerusalem round about as far as unto Illyricum, I have replenished the gospel of Christ.

And I have so preached this gospel not where Christ was named, lest I should build upon another man's foundation. But as it is written: "They to whom He was not spoken of, shall see, and they that have not heard shall understand." For which cause also I was hindered very much from coming to you, and have been kept away till now.

But now having no more place in these countries, and having a great desire these many years past to come unto you, when I shall begin to take my journey into Spain, I hope that as I pass, I shall see you, and be brought on my way thither by you, if first, in part, I shall have enjoyed you:

But now I shall go to Jerusalem, to minister unto the saints. For it hath pleased them of Macedonia and Achaia to make a contribution for the poor of the saints that are in Jerusalem. For it hath pleased them: and they are their debtors. For if the Gentiles have been made partakers of their spiritual things, they ought also in carnal things to minister to them. When therefore I shall have accomplished this, and consigned to them this fruit. I will come by you into Spain. And I know, that when I come to you, I shall come in the abundance of the blessing of the gospel of Christ.

I beseech you therefore, brethren, through our Lord Jesus Christ, and by the charity of the Holy Ghost, that you help me in your prayers for me to God, that I may be delivered from the unbelievers that are in Judea, and that the oblation of my service may be acceptable in Jerusalem to the saints, that I may come to you with joy, by the will of God, and may be refreshed with you.

Now the God of peace be with you all.

Amen.

Paul sat on a coil of rope on the ship's deck, watching the ever blue Mediterranean give way before her proud prow, and thought back to the day in Corinth when he had completed that letter to the Romans, wondering if he would ever follow it in person.

The epistle had been carried by Phebe, a devout lady from Cenchreae, one of that vast unsung army of women who gave to the early Church, not only their souls, but their houses, their money, their time, and the work of their tireless hands. By now Phebe would have reached Rome.

But Paul was sailing steadily on to Jerusalem, moving daily closer to "bands and afflictions," of which the Holy Ghost had warned.

Chapter 78. THE PROPHET IN TYRE

PAST the narrow, earthquake-ridden isle of Cos, where Luke pointed eagerly for Paul to see the birthplace of the famed physician Hippocrates, and on through the shimmering blue waters the ship sailed to the bland island of Rhodes. In the shelter of that beautiful bay the timidest traveler might feel safe, for Rhodes was a potent sea power; she had scourged the pirates off the bosom of the Mediterranean. Paul stared with tourist's delight at the symbol of her worldly might, the giant figure of the sun god towering at the harbor entrance—the Colossus of Rhodes, one of the Seven Wonders of the World.

No trace remains today of Patara, the next port of call, where the apostle and his fellows transferred to another vessel.

Luke tells us:

"And when we had found a ship sailing over to Phenice [Phoenicia], we went aboard, and set forth. And when we had discovered Cyprus, leaving it on the left hand, we sailed into Syria, and came to Tyre: for there the ship was to unlade her burden."

Many Christians lived in that proud and ancient city on the giant coral reef, and they greeted Paul with such warmth that for a week he and his eight companions remained in Tyre. Even in that year A.D. 57, centuries after the death of Hiram, the king who helped Solomon build God's Temple, Tyre wore an air of superior grandeur. Once Isaiah had called Tyre "the bestower of crowns, whose merchants are princes, whose traffickers are the honorable of the earth."

And from the Christian descendants of those merchant princes Paul heard fresh prophecies of the dangers awaiting him in Jerusalem. As Luke tells us, they "said to Paul through the Spirit, that he should not go up to Jerusalem."

But Paul stood resolute. He felt he must go to Jerusalem, and he was willing to face any terror to serve his God. At the end of the week he was ready to sail again.

With tears in their eyes, the Christians of Tyre followed the travelers to the harbor. What danger lay ahead they did not know, but they were convinced that they would never see the sturdy, smoldering apostle again.

The Christians went down to the Tyrian wharves with Paul, Luke, and the others, "bringing us on our way, with their wives and children, till we were out of the city, and we kneeled down on the shore and we prayed. And when we had bid one another farewell, we took ship, and they returned home."

Another short sail down the Palestinian coast, a twenty-four-hour stop at Ptolemais with the brethren there, "and the next day, departing, we came to Caesarea"—to a surprise and a happy reunion.

As Paul strode down the gangplank he saw the familiar figure of a friend, arms open for an embrace—Deacon Philip, called the Evangelist to distinguish him from Philip the Apostle. The years had changed both Paul and Philip, engraving their ardors deep on their foreheads and cheeks in lines like those made by an iron pen. But their love had not changed, not for each other, not for their common Lord.

As they talked, Paul's mind went flashing back to the days when Philip was chosen one of the first seven deacons of the church, appointed to oversee the distribution of alms to Greek widows, and to the time when Philip had baptized the eunuch from Ethiopia. Now Philip welcomed into his home Paul, Luke, and the six treasurers from Macedonia and Asia.

Deacon Philip was a married man, and he had four daughters, all virgins and prophetesses, as active in church work as their father. Amid a cheerful domestic flurry they made the travelers comfortable.

For some days Paul lingered in the deacon's house, till suddenly a new warning fell, not from the lips of the four mystic sisters, but from the snaggle-toothed mouth of an unexpected guest.

At the door of Philip's house one night stood a grizzled old man from Judaea, a prophet called Agabus, whom Paul had reason to remember.

Eleven years before, almost to the day, Agabus had come to Antioch where Paul was beginning his mission work with Barnabas. In the midst of that congregation Agabus had risen up to foretell "a great famine over the whole world." Paul had then and there begun raising the first of his many church collections, as a relief fund to protect the Judaean Christians in their hour of hunger. And the famine had come, as foretold, during the reign of Claudius.

Now Paul was again on his way to Jerusalem with another great collection, even as the gnarled shadow of Agabus fell across the deacon's threshold.

Agabus had come to say that Paul should not go to Jerusalem.

Why not? Was not Jerusalem the cradle of Christ's Holy Church, a city of saints? True, Paul knew there was danger ahead. He had been informed by the Holy Spirit itself. But what, Agabus, is your message?

For answer, Agabus limped across the room to Paul and unfastened the long, wide leather strap that girdled the apostle's waist. The aging prophet wound the girdle round his own feet and hands, binding them securely. In a rasping whisper he confided:

"Thus saith the Holy Ghost: the man whose girdle this is, the Jews shall bind in this manner in Jerusalem, and shall deliver him into the hands of the Gentiles."

Paul! You, who made yourself the Apostle to the Gentiles, will now be made their prisoner!

Now Paul found himself beset from all sides. Luke and Timothy and all the others pleaded with him to give up his plans. Go back to Tarsus and rest. Or go on new missionary errands. Do whatever you will, but turn back from Jerusalem!

Paul shook his head and smiled: "What do you mean, weeping and afflicting my heart? For I am ready not only to be bound, but to die also in Jerusalem, for the Name of the Lord Jesus."

And as Luke reports: "When we could not persuade him, we ceased, saying: 'The will of the Lord be done.' And after those days, being prepared, we went up to Jerusalem."

On that fateful journey to Jerusalem, new friends went with them: some of the disciples from Caesarea, parishioners of Philip. At the forefront marched one of the earliest converts, Mnason, a Cyprian who owned a house in Jerusalem where they all could lodge safely.

BOOK EIGHT

Apostle in Chains

Chapter 79. WHAT HAPPENED IN JERUSALEM

Warm welcome awaited Paul on this final visit to the city. All the Christians in Jerusalem now knew of his glorious work on the three mission journeys. They marveled at his energy and fire, his willingness to live and die for the Lord. Scarcely a Christian lived who did not know and exult in the mighty labors of this tireless and consecrated man.

That night there was a loving feast of the Christians, and the next day a formal reception. Paul beamed with pleasure; he had at last kept his promise to himself. He had arrived in Jerusalem in time for the celebration of the second great feast of the Hebrews, the one Christians called Pentecost. In the early Church, the Feast of Pentecost meant both the old Jewish joyousness of harvest abundance and, supremely, the new glory of the anniversary of the descent of the Holy Ghost in tongues of flame on the heads of the followers of Christ.

On the second day Paul, Timothy, and Luke went into the historic Cenacle room for a formal meeting with James the Less and the other elders of the faith.

And where was Peter at this solemn moment of the great reception? Luke does not say. Contemporary Christians knew why James the Less was left as Bishop of Jerusalem and, to all appearances, acting head of the Church. Peter was in daily danger of arrest as leader of the new faith. For security reasons no one dared put on paper the truth that Peter was in Rome.

To James the Less, then, Paul made his report, summarizing his activities at Ephesus and Corinth and all the other places where he had planted the seeds of faith. And as Luke adds, in his customary laconic style: "He related particularly what things God had wrought among the Gentiles by his ministry."

The listening ancients of the new Church broke into prayer, glorifying God for news of the spread of the faith. But, alas, the joy of James and the elders was still mixed with misgivings. Christian Jerusalem still wrangled over the many disturbing rumors about Paul.

The elders stopped the applause and peered at Paul with speculative eyes. They had a request to make of this Gentile-lover, and they were not too sure of his answer.

One of them cleared his throat and, with a tentative grin, put the matter frankly to Paul:

"You see, brother, how many thousands there are among the Jews that have believed: and they are all zealous for the Law . . ."

Paul sighed. Still discord?

"Now they have heard of you that you teach those Jews who are among the Gentiles to depart from Moses: saying that they ought not to circumcise their children, nor walk according to the custom. What is it, therefore?"

The elders made it plain to Paul that he would again have to meet this issue. Every Jewish convert in Jerusalem had heard these stories and was immensely troubled. Now that Paul was in Jerusalem they would insist that there be a meeting with him. He must deny or affirm; they were intent on his telling them exactly what he had been teaching.

The Hebrew elders of Christianity now gathered in the Cenacle had some advice to give Paul:

"Do therefore this that we say to you. We have four men, who have a vow on them. Take these, and sanctify yourself with them: and bestow on them, that they may shave their heads: and all will know that the things which they have heard of you, are false; but that you yourself also walkest keeping the Law.

"But as touching the Gentiles that believe, we have written, decreeing that they should only refrain themselves from that which has been offered to idols, and from blood, and from things strangled, and from fornication."

To the surprise of some of these elders, Paul gave instant obedience to this request. He believed fully in both the old Scriptures and the new Gospel. He would happily make a vow with these strangers.

He took the four men and went to the Temple, the same where Jesus Christ at the age of twelve had once debated with the scholars, where He had later forgiven the woman taken in adultery, and had rebuked the hypocrites and overturned the table of the money-changers. In that temple Paul went through the Hebrew ritual of proclaiming his innocence, giving notice to all the Jews who worshiped there of the accomplishment of the seven days of purification until a prayer should be offered up for every one of them.

But that ceremonial performance did not satisfy all of Paul's enemies.

The seven days were nearly over, when some Jews from the province of Asia, who had spread the lying tales about Paul, found a scheme to set his public piety at nought.

Six treasurers had come to Jerusalem with Paul, carrying the bags of silver coins, which they delivered to James. Of these six men, only one, Sopater of Beroea, was a Jew. All of them, naturally, were curious about the sights and wonders of Jerusalem, eager to see every landmark of the earthly life of Christ.

Paul's enemies watched the five Gentile tourists padding the cobble-stoned streets in their sandals, chasing from the Garden of Gethsemane to the house of Mary, the mother of Mark, and over to the garden of Joseph of Arimathea. They watched, and they plotted.

Then, finally, these malicious men from Asia announced to everyone in tones of dramatic horror:

"Paul has defiled the Temple! He has brought one of his Gentile friends—this Trophimus of Ephesus—into the Temple with him!"

Whereupon these enemies from Asia set up a great uproar in the Temple, crying out against Paul. As curious mobs surrounded them, they grabbed Paul as if he were a felon, shrieking:

"Men of Israel, help! This is the man that teacheth all men everywhere against the people, and the Law, and this place; and moreover hath brought in Gentiles into the Temple, and hath violated this holy place."

Every moment the crowd increased. The mob leaders dragged Paul out into the street, while priests and guards hurried to shut and bar the Temple doors behind them.

In that screaming tumult on the street, hands clutched for Paul's throat, ready to choke him to death. His eyes would have been torn out, his neck broken, his body trampled—save for the arrival of Roman troops.

The tribune of the imperial troop of horse soldiers had received word of rioting in the streets. "All Jerusalem," came the message, "is in confusion."

With soldiers and centurions the tribune, whose name was Lysias, led the way, running down the hilly street from his castle. At his command the mob left off in their frenetic business of beating Paul.

Amid sullen silence Lysias stalked to where Paul stood, bruised and bloody, and gave the orders which saved the apostle.

"Put this man in chains!"

Instantly the soldiers bound Paul, with a chain on his wrists and on his ankles, as if he were a very dangerous man—which he was.

Then Lysias demanded: "Who is this fellow? And what has he done?"

Every sort of accusation broke forth in bellows of contradiction from the blood-lusting rioters. Paul was a blasphemer, many screamed, just as they had accused his Master, a quarter of a century ago. He was a traitor, an enemy of the state; he incited people to clash and tumult in the streets, he—

The Roman tribune stopped his ears with his elegantly gloved hands. Who could make head or tail in such a din? All the tribune could conclude was that he, as a representative of the Emperor, must restore order and tranquilize the populace.

"Carry this man," Lysias ordered, "to the castle."

Paul's prison that night was the Castle Antonia, the ruins of which are still to be viewed by travelers in the old city of Jerusalem. At the northwest corner of the Temple area, one can see the pile of moss-covered ashlars and crumbling paving stones that was once the Roman fortress and arsenal. That tower prison had an ancient history. Centuries before the Roman conquest, it had been the residence of the Persian governor, and later of the Masmonean, or Macedonian, priestly kings.

Herod had rebuilt the tower, refurbished it for the Roman soldiery, and dubbed it after his old friend and battle comrade, Mark Antony; to this day it is known as the Tower of Antonia.

A short distance under the portico that connected the garrison to the Temple, steep stone steps led up to the tower. Actually, Paul had to be carried like a child up that long flight of steps; had to be held high up beyond the reach of the ravening people who wanted to kill him—"he was carried by the soldiers, because of the violence of the people"—and their voices screeched like demons: "Away with him."

The Roman tribune heaved a sigh of relief as they reached the top platform of the marble stairs. He had no interest in Jerusalem riots; he cared nothing for Paul, or for the mob, and was concerned only with his job of maintaining public peace. Now the lower steps were blocked off by Roman shields, the mob kept at bay with Roman spears and broadswords. In a few minutes Paul would be lodged safely in a dungeon, and the nasty affair would be ended.

But just at the door of the upper platform, the prisoner, again on his feet, startled his captor.

"May I speak something to you?" asked Paul in a low, polite tone.

Lysias swerved and stared at the tattered, bloody wretch he had snatched from the mob.

"Can you speak Greek?" he gasped. For an instant his surprise at hearing Paul's beautiful, cultivated Greek inflection shocked the tribune into silence. Then, anger overcame him; master of Greek or not, the prisoner had caused a great deal of trouble. He hurled an accusation at Paul's bleeding head: "Aren't you that Egyptian who, before these days, led forth into the desert four thousand men that were murderers?"

Paul shook his head. The tribune must have him confused with some long-wanted fugitive from justice. No; Paul was not that Egyptian. He told the tribune exactly what he was; and this time he spoke in Latin.

"I am a Jew of Tarsus in Cilicia, a citizen of no mean city," he replied, "and I beseech you to let me speak to the people."

Lysias laid the back of his hand against his forehead. What kind of fellow was this, who speaks perfect Armaic and Greek and Latin and who, having been nearly murdered by that crowd still surging and boiling on the marble stairs, wants to make a speech to his enemies? Lysias knew a gentleman when he saw one. With a rough nod, he gave permission.

Standing on the height of the prison stairs, Paul beckoned to the crowds held back by the Roman guards below.

"And a great silence being made," Luke reported, "he spoke to them in the Hebrew tongue. . . . (And when they heard that he spoke to them in the Hebrew tongue, they kept the more silence.)"

Was there ever anywhere another such speech—or one with a more astonishing conclusion?

Paul began in the hush of that warm afternoon by declaring to the people the history of his conversion:

Men, brethren and fathers, hear ye the account which I now give unto you. . . .

I am a Jew, born at Tarsus in Cilicia, but brought up in this city, at the feet of Gamaliel, taught according to the truth of the Law of the fathers, zealous for the Law, as also all you are this day: who persecuted this way until death, binding and delivering into prisons both men and women.

As the high priest doth bear me witness, and all the ancients: from whom also receiving letters to the brethren, I went to Damascus, that I might bring them bound from thence to Jerusalem to be punished.

And it came to pass, as I was going, and drawing nigh to Damascus at midday, that suddenly from heaven there shone round about me a great light: and falling on the ground, I heard a Voice saying to me: "Saul, Saul, why persecutest thou Me?"

And I answered: "Who art Thou, Lord?" And He said to me: "I am Jesus of Nazareth, whom thou persecutest."

And they that were with me, saw indeed the light, but they heard not the Voice of Him that spoke with me.

And I said: "What shall I do, Lord?" And the Lord said to me: "Arise, and go to Damascus; and there it shall be told thee of all things that thou must do."

And whereas I did not see for the brightness of that light, being led by the hand of my companions, I came to Damascus.

And one Ananias, a man according to the Law, having testimony of all the Jews who dwelt there, coming to me, and standing by me, said to me: "Brother Saul, look up." And I the same hour looked upon him. But he said: "The God of our fathers hath preordained thee that thou shouldst know His will, and see the Just One, and shouldst hear the Voice from His mouth. For thou shalt be His witness to all men, of those things which thou hast seen and heard. And now why tarriest thou? Rise up, and be baptized, and wash away thy sins, invoking His name."

And it came to pass, when I was come again to Jerusalem, and was praying in the Temple, that I was in a trance, and saw Him saying unto me: "Make haste, and get thee quickly out of Jerusalem; because they will not receive thy testimony concerning Me."

And I said: "Lord, they know that I cast into prison, and beat in every synagogue, them that believed in Thee. And when the blood of Stephen

Thy witness was shed, I stood by and consented, and kept the garments of them that killed him."

And He said to me: "Go, for unto the Gentiles afar off, will I send thee"——

That was the unintended end of Paul's speech.

At the very mention of the Gentiles, the mob below screamed as if in pain. Gentiles! The uncircumcised, the eaters of forbidden food—say no more, Paul! As with one voice the rioters shrieked:

"Away with such an one from the earth; for it is not fit that he should live."

And they began tearing their clothes off their bodies and to throw handfuls of dust into the air, as if they had been present at a blasphemy. Lysias, who had been listening intent and fascinated by Paul's outburst, now sprang into action.

Into the castle with Paul! Scourge him! Torture him! Even his own soldiers must have been startled at the tribune's orders.

Perhaps the faith of this prisoner, all bloody and torn, rising above everything in its pure ecstacy, had troubled the Roman's soul; perhaps he rebelled at being touched to the quick of his spirit by such as Paul. To the whips and the lash, then! He had the power to make Paul suffer until he confessed what real cause the street mob had against him, a cause so outrageous that only death would satisfy them. There must be such a cause; the prisoner must certainly be guilty of some flagrantly wicked act. Then let him be striped and scourged with the whip of the three lashes, which this screaming Judaean rabble used for punishment in their own affairs.

At Lysias' command, the foot soldiers bound Paul with leather thongs, his feet and hands made immovable, just as Agabus had foretold. Paul drew a deep breath; his face, though marred and bloodstained, was at peace. With perfect calm, he looked at the centurion who had overseen the process of tying him into a helpless bundle, and asked him a question:

"Centurion! Is it lawful for you to scourge a man that is a Roman and uncondemned?"

The centurion's face went white. A Roman! This battered mess of a man? A citizen of the Empire? One who therefore could assert his right to be safe from maltreatment until he had been given a full and fair trial under the code of the Caesars? It was hard to believe, but the centurion could take no chances!

With apologies for carrying such a tale, he reported Paul's question to Lysias. Could it be true? If so, what were they to do?

Across the cobbled pavement of the inner court of the castle, Lysias stalked, angrier than ever but more cautious now, for a man in his position working in the colonies must represent and himself scrupulously obey the *Lex Romana*.

"Tell me," he adjured Paul, biting his lips meanwhile to keep back an oath, "are you a Roman?"

"Yes!"

The tribune could not doubt the sincerity of such a hearty, resounding answer. A brief and ugly smile swept across his haughty lips, and when he spoke his tone was bitter: "I obtained the being free of this city with a great sum."

"But I was born so," was Paul's reply.

After that, Lysias dared not go through with his plan of trial by torture. With his mailed fist, he waved back the guards, who had come in with their whips and their sticks and their pronged spears. Gladly, they marched back to their games of dice. And "the tribune also was afraid," Luke remarked, "after he understood that he was a Roman citizen, and because he had bound him."

Indeed, the tribune was hoping that Paul would, in Christian charity, forgive his offense. The law read that no Roman citizen could be tortured and no citizen could be bound with thongs until he had been properly tried and condemned. Lysias had already broken that law, and he well realized he could be made to smart for it. He loosed Paul's hands and feet at once.

For one night he kept Paul in the castle. And all evening long Lysias tossed in his bed, trying to decide the best course of action. By dawn, he had thought of a plan. He would keep Paul under protective custody, so that he could not be torn to death by those crazy mobs in the street. At the same time, he would return him to local Jewish authority by taking him back to the Temple, to the throne chair of the high priest; back to the very hall of hewn stones where Annas and Caiphas had put Jesus of Nazareth on trial a quarter of a century before. The tribune would see to it that the whole Sanhedrin would be called into session, as it was on the night that Jesus Christ was condemned to death.

And at the word of Roman authority, the priests did indeed come together, and all the councilors squatted cross-legged on their crimson silk cushions, holding themselves with the greater dignity because of yesterday's disgraceful tumult of their people at the Temple doors.

Chapter 80. THE VISITOR IN PAUL'S CELL

PAUL looked like an aging and defeated prize fighter with black swellings under his eyes and bloody patches on brow and cheek. Tatterdemalion rags were all that remained of his tunic and robe.

He stood before the judges, as the tribune commanded him. And he was told to speak his mind, so that these judges could make clear to him the exact nature of the offense.

Paul well knew that these listening magistrates were hostile. Only God knew what tales they had heard during the last three years. But Paul was also a master of the Law, with a Pharisee's confidence in the integrity of judges. So he began bravely, declaring:

"Men, brethren, I have conversed with all good confidence before God until the present day."

The official who sat at the bottom of the great human "U" formed by the array of judges looked up sharply. Pointing to two attendants, one at his right, the other at the left, he ordered:

"Slap that man on the mouth!"

The order was obeyed, and two brown palms struck Paul's lips.

Paul cried out: "God shall strike you, you whited wall."

That was high and gross insult. As once Jesus had called the Pharisees "whited sepulchers," fair without and within filled with rotting corruption, so Paul the apostle, in that startled moment of pain, quoted his Master. And he went on:

"Do you sit there to judge me according to the Law—and, contrary to the Law, command me to be struck?"

Then they realized how well he knew the Law. And various of the judges, knowing how truly he spoke, expostulated:

"Do you revile the high priest of God?"

Paul had not realized that the arrogant man was the successor to Caiphas—the new high priest, Ananias. He could not forget that the Law written in the Book of Exodus forbade anyone to speak evil of such a one.

"I knew not, brethren," sighed Paul humbly, "that he is the high priest."

His apology instantly eased the situation; the noise in the Hall of Stones subsided. All was quiet as Paul resumed his statement:

"I am a Pharisee, the son of Pharisees: concerning the hope and resurrection of the dead, I am called into question."

By this simple statement, Paul moved with adroitness to divide his judges into two camps, Pharisees and Sadducees. The Sadducees considered themselves intellectuals, who believed in free will but not in immortality. For a long time, through Annas and Caiphas, and now Ananias, the Sadducees had monopolized the office of high priest, principally because the cynical Roman authorities preferred to do business with men who did not believe in resurrection than with fanatics who did believe. Besides, the Sadducees refused to accept the "oral Law" of the Pharisees with its thousand regulations governing even the smallest and simplest of human acts. Strictly speaking, the Sadducees were neither a party nor a sect; they were made up of aristocratic families—such as that of Annas and his son-in-law, Caiphas—and they looked far more favorably upon the Hellenistic culture than on the ancient Jewish ways, although they carefully refrained from saying any such thing.

Indeed, the Sadducees knew very well how unpopular they were with the people. They even pretended to go along with the Pharisees, to save themselves from being wiped out in rebellions and riots, as would certainly have been their fate if the truth about them were ever known by the populace.

But Paul's remarks concerning the hope of life after death inevitably set the judges quarreling among themselves. Luke put it succinctly when he wrote of Paul's trial by the Sanhedrin:

"And when he had so said, there arose a dissension between the Pharisees and the Sadducees; and the multitude was divided. For the Sadducees say that there is no resurrection, neither angel, nor spirit; but the Pharisees confess both."

Out of this wrangle came a sudden and bewildering climax.

The Pharisees, whose insistence on ritualistic laws was at the base of all the dissension in the Christian Church, now veered violently over to the side of Paul, the Christian apostle. Turning wrathfully away from the Sadducees, the Pharisees sprang to their feet, screaming in unwitting imitation of Pontius Pilate:

"We find no evil in this man."

Into the teeth of their enemies, they hurled a challenge which intellectuals still do not know how to meet. What if this Paul is really a prophet; a man divinely inspired with a mystical vision?

"What if a spirit hath spoken to him? Or an angel?"

The answer was renewed tumult. The judges snarled at each other; the watching crowds caught the infection and, taking sides on matters far too deep for them, roared for action. In another instant there would be sticks, knives, and blood in the council chamber.

"They will pull this man Paul to pieces," groaned Lysias in disgust at this latest eruption.

"Go down," he commanded his soldiers, "and take him by force from the council chamber and those judges. Bring him into the castle."

Back in a cell, Paul was left alone and unattended, in dark silence. The Romans, to quell the mobs, would appease them by ordering his death. Paul felt very sure of that finish to his career. Where was Timothy? Silas? Luke? James? Oh, if Peter were only here! If only he had some of the brethren to talk to before the end which now seemed so certain, so near.

But Paul was not deserted. He who had no Christian brethren to share his imprisonment, suddenly, miraculously, found himself no longer alone but in the presence of the greatest of all companions.

Not alone—because his beloved Master, Jesus Christ, stood beside him in the cold, damp cell and spoke with him; reprieving him from immediate death. That gracious and benign Presence smiled on Paul, and in tones that filled a soul with courage, spoke:

"Be constant; for as you have testified of Me in Jerusalem, so must you bear witness also at Rome."

Chapter 81. THE CONSPIRATORS' OATH

NATURALLY, Paul's enemies did not know that he had been visited in his cell and reassured by his Lord, Jesus Christ. If they had been told the facts, they would not have believed them. They were occupied with their own important business—the immediate destruction of Paul.

"Let us bind ourselves under a curse," they said to each other. "We will not drink until we kill Paul," they swore to each other. "We will not eat until we have killed Paul."

Having sworn a self-inflicting curse upon themselves if they abandoned that oath, they marched straight to the high priests, the ancients, and the elders and solemnly declared:

"We have bound ourselves under a great curse that we will eat nothing until we have slain Paul. Now therefore do you with the council signify to the tribune, that he bring him forth to you, as if you meant to know something more certain touching him. And we, before he come near, are ready to kill him."

Now, Paul's sister, who lived in Jerusalem and who had lovingly housed Paul in his student days, had a son. Of this nephew history was to know little except at this desperate crisis in his uncle's life.

There was among the early Christians a great modesty about themselves as individual persons. Only by two or three "we's" did St. Luke allow himself to appear in his own history of the early Church. Similarly, one finds complete silence about Paul's sister and nephew until they enter now upon the apostolic stage to play their brief but vital part.

Mother and son heard the news of the bloodthirsty oath taken against Paul. By the underground system of communication without which the early Christians might have perished, they learned that forty zealots from the Temple had sworn to destroy Paul before they again ate or drank.

A great knocking sounded on the sentry's gate at the Castle of Antonia; a youth was pounding with knuckles against the wooden beams, Paul's young nephew, breathless with news, pleading to see his uncle.

Paul listened attentively to the warning. He could almost smell death breathing on his face; lately that odor of the grave had followed him as if it were a familiar spirit. Mingled with his pain was the sense of the intangible presence of evil; the invisible nearness of malevolence and blood-desire; a revolting, pestilential hatred in the air, reducing any good heart to sorrow that Satan still roams the world, seeking the ruin of souls.

Paul beckoned to a friendly centurion in the far corner of the room and urged him to take the panting young visitor to Lysias, the tribune, "for he has something to tell him."

The tribune was pacing his castle rooms, pondering a very serious problem. Lysias was deeply impressed, not only because his captive was a citizen of the Empire with certain inalienable rights, but because of Paul's own dauntless spirit. Never before had he had such a rare troublemaker on his hands. He must not make a mistake. What should he do with Paul?

In the midst of his reflections, the centurion and the flushed and sweating youth appeared. The centurion began:

"Paul, the prisoner, desired me to bring this young man unto you, who has something to say to you."

With eyebrows raised, Lysias took the lad by the hand and went aside with him privately. "What is it that you have to tell me?"

Breathlessly, the boy gave him the details:

"The Jews have agreed to ask you to bring Paul tomorrow into the council—as if they meant to inquire something more certain concerning him.

"But do not believe them! For there lie in wait for him more than forty men, who have bound themselves by oath neither to eat nor to drink till they have killed him. And they are now ready looking for a promise from you."

As they stood together, secluded on a balcony overlooking the courtyard, Lysias pondered this utterly disturbing information. He faced a highly dangerous and explosive problem. If Paul were killed and a report went back to Rome that Lysias had allowed a Roman citizen to be slain by a conspiratorial mob, Lysias would be removed as tribune. He might even wind up a slave in the galleys.

He laid a heavy hand on the boy's shoulder: "Tell no one about this. I shall hold you accountable if anything goes wrong. No one must know that I know. But you can reassure your mother that all will be well with your uncle."

He sent the young man down a back staircase and home by a roundabout way so that he might not be observed by any Jewish spies who might be keeping watch on the castle. Then Lysias struck a gong and called for two centurions. As they stood rigidly at attention, he barked his orders:

"Make ready at once! Two hundred foot soldiers, with rations to see them as far as Caesarea. Seventy horsemen, the same. Two hundred spearmen, the same. And make certain they are ready to depart on the third hour of the night."

The centurions saluted, but Lysias had more to say:

"Also provide beasts so that they may set Paul on them, and bring him safe to Felix, the governor."

Not by the twitch of an eyelid did the centurions dare show their amazement at these commands. Such an array of guards—two hundred foot soldiers, seventy horsemen, and two hundred spearmen to defend that battered Christian in yonder cell! What had come over Lysias that he surrounded Paul with such princely protection? And why was he afraid to deal with the fellow himself; why was he sending him to Felix?

In the barracks that sundown there was a lot of gossip and scuttlebutt. Certainly, they gabbled, Lysias was afraid of something. No sensible officer troubled Felix if he could avoid it, for the governor was one of the most dissolute and power-drugged men in public office. The less a man had to do with him, the safer he could feel.

Antonius Felix was his name, and he had been born a slave. He was a freedman of the imperial family, and his brother Pallas had become the boon rakehell companion of young Emperor Nero. Thanks to that connection, Felix had risen with dizzying speed from slavery to the post once held by Pontius Pilate. For the past five years Felix had been procurator of Judaea, and he ruled with an aggressive hand.

From his immediate predecessor, Cumanus, he inherited a chaotic colonial office, which by his own mismanagement he would leave in even worse shape. Tacitus, in his history of Rome and her provinces, was to write of Felix that "with all manner of cruelty and lust he exercised royal functions in the spirit of a slave."

Three times Felix had been married, and each time he had chosen a bride of royal lineage. His latest marital adventure had caused a great deal of ferment, when he took for his wife the daughter of Agrippa I, a beautiful Jewess called Drusilla. Drusilla was already married, but Felix had no compunctions about the prior claims of a husband. Let her leave him! Drusilla willingly abandoned her lawful spouse, and went through a ceremony with Felix, thus doubly defying Jewish law by uniting herself to an uncircumcised man.

To Felix, this power-drunk brother of Nero's favorite, Lysias was sending Paul. The soldiers in the barrack rooms might well be puzzled by these orders, but the tribune was acting with great cunning. If Paul remained in Jerusalem, the Jews would surely kill him. Then Felix, the governor, would have to give Nero an explanation of such a failure of Roman might in maintaining security for its citizens everywhere in the Empire. Lysias could guess what explanation would pop into the mind of the ex-slave: Felix would conclude that the Temple aristocrats had bribed Lysias to let them do away with that pestiferous Christian once and for all. And Felix would send Lysias back to Rome as a scapegoat!

Lysias shuddered at the thought. "For," Luke reported, "he feared lest perhaps the Jews might take Paul away by force to kill him, and he should afterwards be slandered, as if he was to take money."

So Lysias wrote a clever letter to Governor Felix, and passed the thorny problem of Paul and the Jews over to him:

Claudius Lysias to the Most Excellent Governor Felix: Greeting:
This man being taken by the Jews, and ready to be killed by them, I rescued coming in with an army, understanding that he is a Roman. And meaning to know the cause which they objected unto him, I brought him forth into their council.

Whom I found to be accused concerning questions of their law; but having nothing laid to his charge worthy of death or of bands. And when I was told of ambushes that they had prepared for him, I sent him to you, signifying also to his accusers to plead before you.

Farewell.

The procession of nearly five hundred armed guards headed by Lysias left Jerusalem at the third hour of the night when most of the town was silent and asleep. Out through a northern gate they passed, moving along the coast road, to spend the rest of the night at Antipatris, a city that marked the northwestern frontier of Judaea, on the main road from Caesarea to Lydda. Its accommodations were limited; the soldiers and spearsmen and mounted troops had to build fires in the fields and bivouac for the night.

The next morning Lysias made a change in his plans. Since the people of Antipatris were making no outcry against Paul, there seemed no more need for the hundreds of strong guards that had surrounded the prisoner when they left Jerusalem. So Lysias sent his letter and Paul on toward the governor's home in Caesarea, accompanied only by the seventy horsemen, while he and the others returned to Jerusalem.

In late afternoon Paul found himself standing before Felix in the Herodian palace at Caesarea.

Chapter 82. TRIAL BY FELIX

FELIX, the bearded ex-slave ruler, sat on a gilded throne chair, high above the floor on which Paul stood and waited. The procurator read Lysias' letter, stared at Paul as if he were some kind of circus freak, then read the letter through twice again.

"Of what province are you?" the governor asked in a high, thin, almost feminine voice.

"I am from Tarsus, sire."

"Cilicia?"

"Yes, sire."

The governor shook his head thoughtfully. There were many Jews who were born free Roman citizens in that part of the world.

"I will hear you, when your accusers come," Felix decided. "Meanwhile, you will be kept behind bars—in the judgment Hall of Herod."

It was quite a hall that Herod had built for himself in Caesarea.

During the five days before his trial was called, Paul talked with his jailers and fellow prisoners to learn more about this place where Herod had made so much out of nothing. Following the example of the Emperor Augustus, whom he served, Herod had rebuilt a number of cities, but Caesarea was the most important and notable. It had been known once as Strato's Tower, but Herod renamed it for the Emperor, erecting here a temple to Augustus, a theater, and many public buildings, making it, fleetingly, even more important than Jerusalem. Throughout the Roman period, Caesarea remained the seat of the Roman governor of Judaea.

On the fifth day after Paul's preliminary hearing before Felix, the guards told him his accusers from Jerusalem had arrived. The trial would shortly begin.

Paul had no time to prepare what he was going to say. He relied on the "charismata," the gifts of grace, to see him through. Had not Christ Himself said to His disciples:

"*And when they bring you into the synagogues, and unto magis-*

trates and powers, take you no thought how or what thing ye shall
answer, or what you shall say. For the Holy Ghost shall teach you in
the same hour what you ought to say."

When he faced his accusers, Paul felt perfectly confident that God
would indeed be in his mind and heart to prompt him.

The spectacle of the throne room, Felix in purple and gold, and
all the bearded attendants grouped around him—these trappings and
suits of power did not intimidate the adventurer of the three missionary voyages. Nor did the sight of the crowds, straining against the
ropes that ran on three sides of Herod's great hall, the quidnuncs, the
curiosity seekers. Those gaping loafers, he knew, could turn into a
mob of destroying accusers, as a few days before he had seen worshipers transformed into lynchers in the Temple of Jerusalem. Still, Paul
was not disturbed.

They led him forward to stand at the left hand of Felix. Paul's
eyes searched his accusers, now bathed and refreshed after their swift
journey from Jerusalem.

Chief among them in his white robe with its fringes and phylacteries, was the new high priest, Ananias, present as chief prosecutor
of Paul, a kind of ecclesiastical district attorney. With him loomed
several bearded and grim-mouthed advisers, "ancients" full of ma-
turity and wisdom. But there was one younger man, who stood with
Ananias and his cronies. A vigorous fellow, very busy with scrolls and
screeds, he was forever clearing his throat, rolling his eyes, and sizing
up the crowd, as if serving notice that he was the star of the cast and
when the action began they would see a very remarkable performance
indeed.

Who was this theatrical young man with the scrolls and the vol-
umes of reference? Paul whispered the question to one of his guards,
and his eyes were startled at the answer.

The strutting swain was Tertullus, known all over Judaea, yes, into
Galilee and Samaria and some said as far away as Rome, as the outstanding orator of Jerusalem. The Temple powers had hired Tertullus and brought him to Caesarea for the sole purpose of winning this
case before Governor Felix. Here was their trial attorney, skilled in
persuasion, in the instantaneous evocation of irony or passion; a man
of fortunate gestures and pliant, responsive voice.

As anyone could see, Tertullus had no doubt whatever that his
speech in the Herodian Hall this morning would cost Paul's life. The

orator had been briefed on the facts, but most of all he would rely on flattery to win Felix to a verdict in favor of the Sanhedrin. No bow could be too low for Felix; no lie too high to please his vanity; and for Tertullus lies and bows meant an easy morning's work.

The pounding of the bailiff's staff upon the marble floor called the court to order. Felix's chamberlain stated the brief outline of the case.

Then Paul was led forward so that he stood directly before Tertullus. The apostle looked better than when he had faced the full Sanhedrin in the Hall of Hewn Stones. The blue-blackness under his eyes was fading; the bruises were healing, and the vast and plaguing weariness of his convalescence had passed, too. Paul had eaten some decent meals in the prison of Felix; he had slept soundly for five nights, and he faced the lawyer with serenity.

Tertullus launched his attack with almost demoniac impetuosity. For hours he piled infamy and blasphemy up against the name of Paul. His wringing hands, his upturned eyes, the horrified sighs that rolled between his lips, all expressed the loathing of a well-ordered and tranquil society for such as this Christian tentmaker.

Luke, standing with Timothy near the stone walls of the hall, wrote down the gist of that prolonged denunciation. He reported how Tertullus began by praising Felix as the restorer of peace to the province; a bold, unblushing falsehood. Said the lawyer to the governor:

"Whereas through you we live in much peace, and many things are rectified by your providence, we accept it always and in all places, most excellent Felix, with all thanksgiving. But that I be no further tedious to you, I desire you of your clemency to hear us in a few words.

"We have found this to be a pestilent man, and raising seditions among all the Jews throughout the world, and author of sedition of the sect of the Nazarenes. Who also has gone about to profane the Temple: whom, we having apprehended, would also have judged according to our Law. But Lysias, the tribune, coming upon us, with great violence took him away out of our hands; commanding his accusers to come to you: of whom you mayest yourself, by examination, have knowledge of all these things, whereof we accuse him."

When he had finished, Tertullus stepped aside, breathing heavily, like a man who has exhausted himself. And on this cue the others rose to give their testimony; Ananias and the rest of the ancients, at-

testing to the truth of the charges made by Tertullus in his opening
statement. They rehearsed Paul's history in carrying treason throughout the imperial territories. A dangerous fellow, indeed, and never
happy unless he was spreading sedition.

The morning was far advanced when they were finished. Felix's
debauched face showed darkening lines of weariness. Already he was
bored. With a jerky gesture, he bent his thumb at Paul, whose turn
it was now to speak.

In that moment Felix ceased to be bored.

Paul's ringing voice, although subdued, was clear and distinct to
the farthest corner of the Herodian Hall. He stood quietly, hands at
his sides, and let the truth pour forth from him. He had taken no
thought what he should say, and now the Holy Ghost was in him as
he addressed the governor:

"Knowing that for many years you have been judge over this nation, I will with good courage answer for myself.

"For you may understand that there are yet but twelve days since
I went up to adore in Jerusalem; and neither in the Temple did they
find me disputing with any man, or causing any concourse with the
people, neither in the synagogues, nor in the city. Neither can they
prove unto you the things whereof they now accuse me.

"But this I confess to you, that according to the way, which they
call a heresy, so do I serve the Father and my God, believing all
things which are written in the Law and the Prophets: having hope
in God, which these also themselves look for, that there shall be a
resurrection of the just and unjust. And herein do I endeavor to have
always a conscience without offence towards God, and towards men.

"Now after many years, I came to bring alms to my nation, and
offerings, and vows. In which I was found purified in the Temple:
neither with multitude, nor with tumult. But certain Jews of Asia,
who ought to be present before you, and to accuse, if they had any
thing against me—or let these men themselves say, if they found
in me any iniquity, when standing before the council—except it be
for this one voice only, that I cried, standing among them, 'Concerning the resurrection of the dead am I judged this day by you.'"

Paul would have gone on but Felix stopped him with his upraised
hand, every fat finger of which glittered with diamonds and rubies
and pearls. He called a halt to the flow of apostolic eloquence and
announced that for the time, he would hear no more.

Here was victory for Paul: Felix had believed him when he said he was not being faced by his real enemies, that the case against him was a sham. Quite evidently the governor determined to dig deeper. For his own purposes, Felix had learned a great deal about such delicate theological disputes as this one about the resurrection of the just and the unjust, and he also knew that the real issues of this man's guilt or innocence had not been put to trial.

To the astonishment of the deputies from the Sanhedrin and to the mortification of that star performer Tertullus, the governor let it be known that he was not satisfied with the prosecution's case. To get at the truth he was sending to Jerusalem.

And with these words Felix adjourned the trial: "When Lysias, the tribune, shall come down, I will hear you."

Felix placed Paul in the personal custody of a centurion. To that captain's complete astonishment, Felix gave him these further orders:

"Be easy with this man, Paul of Tarsus. You are not to prohibit any of his friends to come to see him or minister to him."

What was happening? The face of the well-disciplined centurion remained expressionless, as always. But what was in the mind of Felix, that he would defy the high priest and show favors to a Christian?

That question remains a riddle of two slow-paced, idle years, while Paul lived as a prisoner under Felix, guarded by the centurion in the keep of the Hall of Herod.

Two full years Paul waited for trial. The governor refused to take action against the prisoner; nothing could force him to bring the case to a conclusion. Yet he also refused to set Paul free, although at times he seemed on the verge of doing so.

As Claudia, the wife of Pilate, had tried to help Jesus, so Drusilla, the Jewish wife of Felix, now took an interest in Paul. At her behest, the governor sent for the Apostle to the Gentiles "and heard of him the faith that is in Christ Jesus."

And Felix was terrified—for a while at least—at what he heard; terrified of the judgment day that Paul assured him would finally come to every soul. But then, Paul talked to this much mismarried king about the matter of chastity. And that piece of audacity was too much for Felix. Nervously he waved the apostle out of his sight:

"For this time, go your way. Some more convenient time, I will call for you."

Weary and downcast, Paul trudged back to his cell. His steps were quieter now, his movements slower; age was creeping on him in the prolonged, frustrating suspense.

"Don't put any hopes on Felix," a guard muttered to him out of the side of his mouth. "You know what he is after, don't you?"

Paul's face was blank as he turned empty palms toward the ceiling.

"He wants money," snarled the guard.

Money? From a prisoner?

"Certainly. Felix is the kind of man who tries to get money without working from everybody he has anything to do with. There have always been politicians like that. One way or another they always seem to get into power!"

Paul shook his head in utter incredulity.

But before another day passed, messages began to come from Felix, suggesting that Paul might have his freedom for a price. Felix had convinced himself that Christianity was an intercontinental conspiracy of revolution and must, therefore, be well financed. Had not Paul admitted that he came to Jerusalem with bags of money collected in many parts of the world? Surely, then, his friends could raise funds to get him out of prison. What a miserable little man, Felix, to have set yourself in such a light before history! And what did it get you? Sermons—but not a penny of tribute from Paul!

And "when two years were ended," Luke wrote, "Felix had for successor, Portius Festus. And Felix, being willing to show the Jews a pleasure, left Paul bound."

So now Paul was in chains while a strange new governor stepped in as master of his fate.

Chapter 83. "I APPEAL TO CAESAR!"

The guards whispered to Paul that Festus, the new governor, was in their belief a good man. Paul remained dubious. How could such a ruler as Nero find any good man to serve him? Do men gather figs from thistles? No, nor good public officials from tyrants. Yet history bore out the estimates of Paul's guards; Festus proved to be of such excellent character that he was ousted as procurator of Judaea after only a few months of service!

The clash between Paul and Festus came during the first month of that governor's short reign.

When Festus had rested from his sea voyage for three days in Caesarea, he went straight to the great capital of Jerusalem of which he had heard so much. Riding in panoplied splendor on the shoulders of his slaves, he started south to the music of dulcimer and lutes. Girls sat beside him, singing and admiring him, and crowds along the highway made obeisance, welcoming their new official oppressor, hoping to soften his mood and the severity of his rule.

But no pageant of splendor awaited Festus at the Castle of Antonia. The moment he arrived, word came that a large delegation of local Jewish dignitaries awaited immediate audience with him—Ananias, the high priest, with scribes and Pharisees, elders and ancients, all highly agitated graybeards.

What did they want of Festus? They wanted the life of a good man and true, just as the delegation that had called on Pontius Pilate had wanted the life of Him who was true God and true man.

But Ananias and his cohorts did not tell Festus that they wanted to kill Paul. They hid their purpose within the coils of high-sounding legal argument. They simply asked Festus for permission to reopen the issue before him, as Supreme Judge of the land, which Festus was in his role of imperial governor. The delegates from the Temple said that they wanted only the return of Paul to Jerusalem for further questioning. They brushed aside as laughable the idea that his life would be in danger there. They pooh-poohed all tales of violence Festus might have heard, as irresponsible exaggerations.

Festus, however, was not deceived by these unctuous, oleaginous visitors. Before he came to Jerusalem, Festus had sent his own investigators throughout Judaea. Before he ever set sail to this colony, he had received accurate summaries of local politics from his spies.

Behind the blandiloquence of these graybeards from the Temple he read their murderous intentions. If he yielded to the pleas, if Paul and a few guards did set forth to travel to the capital, they would likely be waylaid in some ravine; the Apostle to the Gentiles would have his throat cut from ear to ear, and the best investigators in the troops of the tribune Lysias would probably never find out who did

it. That chance for murder was the priests' real request. Their teeth
gleamed in the depths of their beards, as they smiled cajolingly upon
their new overseer.

Festus' answer to them was fair and judicious, but a complete de-
feat to their schemes.

"Paul," he told them, "is kept under guard in Caesarea, safe from
uprisings and rebellions of mobs in the streets. Such demonstrations
cannot be tolerated ever again. Paul, let me emphasize, remains in
Caesarea. I myself shall very shortly depart from Jerusalem and also
stay in Caesarea. Now I want to be scrupulously fair to you and to
the man you accuse. You may send any that are able among you, to
go down with me. You can start all over, and accuse Paul before me.
And then I can judge from your evidence whether this tentmaker has
committed any crime."

In the eight or ten days while Festus remained in Jerusalem, he was
regally entertained by the best Sadducean families, fawned on by all
the Jewish elders. No one mentioned Paul during these gaieties. But
Festus was not surprised, when he was ready to start back to Caesarea,
to find an imposing group from the Temple, seated on donkeys,
awaiting him outside the golden gate. They were cordial but impatient to get started; they could hardly wait to get at Paul again.

In Caesarea there was no further delay. The day after the governor's
return Paul was led again into Herod's ornate courtroom to stand
before the judgment seat of Festus.

Swiftly the Jews recited their indictment. All the old accusations
of troublemaking, blasphemy, and treason were recounted. Paul stood
accused of being a subversive, an enemy of the government who
meant to overthrow the throne by violence. The state, so argued the
chief priests, had not only a right but a duty to protect itself against
any enemy within.

Festus listened to the grievous recital against the prisoner, then
curtly ordered Paul to answer.

Paul's reply was stingingly brief:

"Neither against the Law of the Jews, nor against the Temple, nor
against Caesar have I offended in anything."

The past ten days had softened Festus' resistance to the blandish-
ments practiced upon him by Ananias and his retinue of Temple
aristocrats, especially by the wealthy Sadducean families who had received the governor with lavish and flattering hospitality. He wanted,

as Luke reported, "to show them a pleasure." So bending forward and smiling a little, the new governor asked:

"Paul, will you go up to Jerusalem and there be judged of these things before me?"

There was an upside-down plea for a change of venue! Even the high priests blinked at the bluntness of the proposal. But Paul's answer was instantaneous and majestic. Once more he spoke as a citizen of the Roman Empire, one who knew his inalienable rights:

"I stand at Caesar's judgment seat, where I ought to be judged. To the Jews I have done no injury, as you very well know. For if I have injured them or have committed anything worthy of death, I do not refuse to die. But if there be none of these things whereof they accuse me, no man may deliver me to them.

"I appeal to Caesar!"

Festus sat back in his chair as if he had been pushed. His mouth fell open helplessly. Slowly he turned a melancholy gaze upon the Jerusalem priests. Then he fixed his sobered eyes for a moment on Paul.

"Have you appealed to Caesar? Then to Caesar shall you go!"

And that settled the new governor's problem nicely. He was rid of the whole difficult business of Paul!

That decision was a terrific blow to the chief priests; they saw their prey slipping from their hands. Stubbornly they remained in town, resolved to overturn that verdict of Festus, one way or another. But there was little they could do at the moment, because Festus' mind was on other things.

Down to Caesarea, with great pomp and ceremony, came King Herod Agrippa II and his sister, Bernice, to salute the new governor, and visit with him.

This king was the son of Herod Agrippa I, who had died so spectacularly in the amphitheater right here in Caesarea, eaten up by worms after letting himself be publicly worshiped as a god. The present king had been still a small boy then, and was not allowed to reign. But as he matured, he had exhibited a remarkable sagacity, and Nero had showered him with favors; by this year 59 Agrippa II ruled as Rome's puppet over most of Palestine.

He sedulously wooed the conquered people over whom he reigned; even more than his worm-devoured father, he pretended to be an admiring friend of the Jewish nation. At word of his coming, the defeated Temple deputies took hope. If Agrippa is our friend, said the Temple deputies to each other, let him overrule the fiat of Festus; let him repudiate that positive and authoritative command to send Paul out of our jurisdiction to the Emperor at Rome; let him, instead, turn Paul over to us.

As for Paul, he hoped for nothing from King Agrippa II, or from any human ruler.

Festus put the problem to King Agrippa II in these words:

"A certain man was left prisoner by Felix, about whom, when I was at Jerusalem, the chief priests and the ancients of the Jews came unto me, desiring condemnation against him.

"To whom I answered: 'It is not the custom of the Romans to condemn any man, before that he who is accused have his accusers present, and have liberty to make his answer, to clear himself of the things laid to his charge.'

"When therefore they were come hither without any delay, on the day following, sitting in the judgment seat, I commanded the man to be brought. Against whom, when the accusers stood up, they brought no accusation of things which I thought ill of, but had certain questions of their own superstition against him, and of one Jesus deceased, whom Paul affirmed to be alive.

"I therefore being in doubt of this manner of question, asked him whether he would go to Jerusalem, and there be judged of these things. But Paul appealing to be reserved unto the hearing of Augustus, I commanded him to be kept, till I might send him to Caesar."

Agrippa's curiosity was stirred by this recital, for he had heard many conflicting stories about Paul. Without a moment's hesitation he said:

"I would also hear the man myself."

"Tomorrow you shall hear him," said Festus heartily.

With great pomp of courtly attire and slaves with rainbow plumes on long staves, with stateliness and dignity and a proper crowd to stand open-mouthed before the greatness of the royal rulers, the trial began in the Hall of Audience. All the Roman tribunes were assembled around the seats of judgment—with King Agrippa, a foppish fellow, continually putting a perfume bottle to his nose against the smell of the crowd. Alongside the tribunes stood the white beards of the town's wisdom, the principal men of the city of Caesarea.

At Festus' command, in came the lonely and shabby figure of the long-imprisoned Paul. Never before had the apostle been confronted, in any of his various trials, with such spectacular magnificence. It was enough to awe a lesser man, but only God can awe a faithful Christian.

In the midst of a general silence, Festus formally addressed the king:

"King Agrippa, and all ye men who are here present with us, you see this man, about whom all the multitude of the Jews dealt with me at Jerusalem, requesting and crying out that he ought not to live any longer. Yet have I found nothing that he hath committed worthy of death. But forasmuch as he himself hath appealed to Augustus, I have determined to send him. Of whom I have nothing certain to write to my lord. For which cause I have brought him forth before you, and especially before thee, O King Agrippa, that examination being made, I may have what to write. For it seemeth to me unreasonable to send a prisoner, and not to signify the things laid to his charge."

As the voice of the procurator died away, King Agrippa turned a steady gaze on Paul. Something about this earnest man, with thongs bound around his wrists, the unbarbered gray hair falling from his temples, the inspiring confidence in his eyes, bothered the king. The very posture of this calm prisoner seemed to say:

"I have not memorized what I shall say to you. I shall be told what to say by Jesus Christ, our Blessed Lord. Amen!"

King Agrippa had lived in the world long enough to fear, above all men, those who put their trust in unseen powers outside themselves.

"Paul," he said. He leaned forward with royal unction, but a superstitious twinge edged his voice: he did not want to earn this fellow's ill will, for there were reports that he was a powerful magician. "Paul, you are permitted to speak for yourself."

And Luke, ever faithfully present in the background of the crowd with Timothy, recorded the defense of Paul before King Agrippa.

"I think myself happy, King Agrippa, because I shall answer for myself this day before thee touching all the things whereof I am accused of the Jews: especially because I know thee to be expert in all customs and questions which are among the Jews: wherefore I beseech thee to hear me patiently.

"My manner of life from my youth, which was at the first among

mine own nation at Jerusalem, know all the Jews; which knew me
from the beginning, if they would testify, that after the most straitest
sect of our religion I lived a Pharisee. And now I stand and am judged
for the hope of the promise made of God unto our fathers: unto
which promise our twelve tribes, instantly serving God day and night,
hope to come. For which hope's sake, King Agrippa, I am accused of
the Jews.

"Why should it be thought a thing incredible with you, that God
should raise the dead?

"I verily thought with myself, that I ought to do many things
contrary to the Name of Jesus of Nazareth. Which thing I also did in
Jerusalem: and many of the saints did I shut up in prison, having
received authority from the chief priests; and when they were put to
death, I gave my voice against them. And I punished them oft in
every synagogue, and compelled them to blaspheme; and being exceedingly mad against them, I persecuted them even unto strange
cities.

"Whereupon as I went to Damascus with authority and commission from the chief priests, at midday, O king, I saw in the way a
light from heaven, above the brightness of the sun, shining round
about me and them which journeyed with me. And when we were all
fallen to the earth, I heard a Voice speaking unto me, and saying in
the Hebrew tongue: 'Saul, Saul, why persecutest thou Me? It is hard
for thee to kick against the pricks.'

"And I said: 'Who art thou, Lord?' And He said: 'I am Jesus whom
thou persecutest. But rise, and stand upon thy feet: for I have appeared unto thee for this purpose, to make thee a minister and a
witness both of these things which thou hast seen, and of those things
in the which I will appear unto thee; delivering thee from the people,
and from the Gentiles, unto whom now I send thee, to open their
eyes, and to turn them from darkness to light, and from the power of
Satan unto God, that they may receive forgiveness of sins, and inheritance among them which are sanctified by faith that is in Me.'

"Whereupon, O King Agrippa, I was not disobedient unto the
heavenly vision: but showed first unto them of Damascus, and at
Jerusalem, and throughout all the coasts of Judaea, and then to the
Gentiles, that they should repent and turn to God, and do works
meet for repentance. For these causes the Jews caught me in the
Temple, and went about to kill me.

"Having therefore obtained the help of God, I continue unto this day, witnessing both to small and great, saying none other things than those which the prophets and Moses did say should come: that Christ should suffer, and that He should be the first that should rise from the dead, and should show light unto the people, and to the Gentiles."

Again that maddening phrase "to the Gentiles," filling Paul's soul with love, drove his enemies wild with hatred. Until that instant, Paul's knowledge and eloquence had held the Hall of Audience under a spell. Now bedlam broke loose before the judgment seat. Festus himself stood up and cried out in a loud voice:

"Paul! Paul! You are beside yourself. Much learning has made you mad!"

"I am not mad, most excellent Festus!"

Paul moved forward as he spoke. His words were addressed to the procurator but his gaze was fixed compellingly on King Agrippa.

"I am not mad," he repeated. "But I speak words of truth and soberness."

Still with his eyes, that glowed like coals, straight on the paling face of the king, Paul continued:

"For the king knows of these things of which I speak, to whom also I speak with confidence. For I am persuaded that none of these things is hidden from him. For neither was any of these things done in a corner."

Still nearer the throne Paul came, and his voice now echoed high overhead:

"Do you believe the prophets, O King Agrippa? I know that you believe!"

The freezing fingers of the king touched the sweating wrist of Festus, bidding him sit down. In a whisper that echoes down the ages, the king confessed:

"Almost you have persuaded me to be a Christian. In a little, you persuade me to be a Christian."

Chapter 84. TEMPEST AT SEA

But Paul had appealed to Claudius Nero Caesar. No one could change that fact. He must go to Rome:

"Have you appealed to Caesar? To Caesar you shall go!"

Paul was sent to Rome in A.D. 60, for trial before the judges of Nero. He was given into custody of one harassed centurion, named Julius. Julius was no ordinary officer. A member of the Augustan band, he was a trusted leader of the provincial troops stationed in Caesarea, a man proven in battle and to be relied upon when stationed in faraway places. While at first Julius refused to heed the warnings Paul tried to give him, the day was to come when he would take the apostle's counsel—and even save his life.

Although Paul could not guess what was to happen, he was to owe much to this tough but fair-minded Roman officer, who showed him genuine kindness.

Paul at last was going to Rome. In the prison cell of the Castle Antonia, Christ had foretold this day, and Paul remembered the Lord's words, and prayed silently that he would be worthy of them.

Two of his friends were given permission to travel with Paul—Luke the physician, and Aristarchus, who had once been nearly lynched in Paul's stead by the tumultuous silversmiths of Ephesus, and had clung faithfully to the apostle ever since. Though a free man, Aristarchus, still proud of having been chosen to carry the collection from his province to Jerusalem, was posing as Paul's slave. Only in that guise could the centurion Julius in propriety allow him passage. Paul's other friends, even Timothy, must find their own way to Rome.

Paul, and Luke, and Aristarchus—they did not make an imposing group as they marched quietly along between the rows of soldiers. They looked like ordinary prisoners; but in their hearts they marched as conquerors against the citadel of Rome.

At Caesarea the centurion Julius led them aboard a ship bound for Asia Minor. The sailing orders for this vessel laid out a course up the western coast of the province of Asia to her home harbor of Adramyttium, at the foot of Mt. Ida. But once in the open sea, the captain had to compromise with unfavorable winds, steering not west but northward toward Sidon, a day's journey by sea.

As they sat together on the sloppy, lurching afterdeck, released from chains at last, Paul and Luke and Aristarchus had much to think about; no wonder if they talked but little. Aristarchus, who had carried himself so bravely in his brush with death in Ephesus, was wondering whether he would ever see his native Macedonia or his friends again. Rome seemed so far to reach, so remote from anything

he had known in his life. Not that Aristarchus regretted his decision
to follow Paul; but any uprooting, such as this departure was, would
be bound to make a man think, and to remember pleasant days.

Paul also had much to remember—resolves and strategy, trial and
suffering and narrow escapes—while the sea surged and billowed
around the overloaded ship. The vessel pranced and pitched, swinging her hips like a hussy in the restlessness of a sea, ready to be provoked by the roaming winds. Yet the night passed without incident,
and as Paul opened his eyes and rose at sunrise from the deck, he
saw they were tied up at the dock in Sidon.

The sight of the familiar wharf stirred a sadness in Paul's heart. He
knew well the ancient Phoenician city, and many of his Christian
friends living there. If they guessed that he was aboard this ship,
they would come hastening to the piers to wave and shout. In all the
past two prison years, Paul had never felt so deprived of freedom as
in the midst of the sunrise at Sidon. Today, if you stand on a deck
and look at the historic site, you can see only a dusty village of about
eleven thousand inhabitants, its very name changed to Saida. But on
that morning when Paul sighted it, Sidon was about to become, with
its ancient rival Tyre, a free city of the Empire. Upon its grandeur,
Paul brooded with melancholy eyes. He was startled when a hand was
laid brusquely on his shoulder. Turning, he found himself confront-
ing his jailer, Julius.

"You are sad, Paul?"

The apostle nodded.

"You would like to go ashore?"

Again the nod of a most sober man.

"You may go ashore, then. I know your quality, Paul, and because
I believe I can trust you, because I have faith in you, I want to treat
you courteously. I will permit you to go to your friends and to take
care of yourself."

That night there was reunion in the Christian haunts of Sidon.
Paul and Luke and Aristarchus met with the brethren. Luke does not
linger on the details of this meeting. Instead he plunges right on in
his log of this voyage.

"And when we had launched from thence, we sailed under Cyprus,
because the winds were contrary." East of Cyprus they sailed, and
west along the southern shore of Asia Minor, tying up at last at the
docks of Myra, in Lycia.

A general air of relief pervaded crew and passengers—all except the usually amiable Julius—when the ship was finally berthed at this busy and wealthy port. It had been a dogged voyage all the way, as always at such time of the year when strong westerly winds prevail. To voyage to the west, a master must steer his bark cautiously, working north and east, hugging the coast to woo the land breezes, light and delicate as they often are, past Myra and on to Cnidus.

The modern explorer, should he chance on this stopping place on Paul's most historic voyage, will not find Myra but the town called Denbre. Still, in the midst of Denbre he can behold the ruins of the same magnificent Roman theater which Paul and Luke and Aristarchus saw that day from their ship.

Suddenly Julius loomed before his three prisoners.

"Make ready to go ashore," he told them crisply. "Bring your belongings with you; everything."

The centurion stalked off, leaving his captives baffled and perturbed. They had supposed they would load and unload cargo here, then sail on. What would happen now? They were ready in a few minutes. So barely these Christians traveled, taking neither script nor staff, that it was the work of a moment to bundle their things together. On the dock they were told to wait for further orders and, looking around them, saw the waterfront shrine of the sailor's god, a heathen deity famous on all ships everywhere.

Soon the mystery of their going ashore became clear. Another ship was tied up near by; a large merchant vessel, laden with wheat, built for the open sea, double planked, and high sparred with masts of the cedar of Lebanon. Her sails were of costly Egyptian stuff, adorned with embroidery. The awning of purple tent cloth covering her afterdeck brought a glimmer to Paul's thoughtful eyes. Surely, he thought, such a great vessel as this, a giant beside their previous one, could outrun the dread Euroaquilo, the east-northeast gale that prowled the Mediterranean in these months and made the sea lanes dangerous. He noted, too, that strong cables were placed around the sides of the ship lengthwise, from stem to stern above the waterline, for use in time of gales.

Julius had just struck a bargain with the shipmaster. He seemed certain that he was achieving a brilliant stroke of management by which they would reach Rome in quicker time; they and all the 276 souls on board.

But Paul, a knowing traveler in all kinds of weather, had his doubts. With a mind like that of Aristotle, interested in anything that came to his attention, he had not sat idly through the quiet hours in his years of goings forth and comings home but had pried into ship and caravan and into the minds of navigators and astronomers and men who calculate winds and currents.

Winter was coming on; rarely would the skies be clear enough for men to chart courses by the stars. Paul would have counseled waiting ashore, if a journey overland should prove impossible. But, kindly as Julius was, he would welcome no advice from his prisoners; and so, for as long as he could, the Apostle to the Gentiles kept his peace, while this second ship, making only a little slow progress each day, pushed westward to a point just south of the island of Cnidus, close by the larger island of Rhodes.

With every knot they made, the going became more difficult. Unable to progress against the powerful head winds, they had to alter their course again. The captain ordered the helmsman to turn the wheel a sharp left, striking south to head the ship under the lee of the long island of Crete, passing by Cape Salmone, south of Cape Sidero.

"And with much ado sailing by it," Luke wrote, "we came into a certain place, which is called the Fair Havens, nigh whereunto was the city of Lasea."

A fine-sounding name, Fair Havens, but ironic in the blow that was now gathering force and racing up and down the Mediterranean Sea. Every sailor on the inland sea knew this anchorage, a roadstead on the south coast of Crete. In summer, vessels found safe refuge there, in the bay open to the east, sheltered by two small islands to the southwest. But to be open to the east in winter when the terrible winds were blowing was to be no fair haven at all. Paul knew that, and all the sailors knew it. The captain must be desperate.

Winter had come down with wicked suddenness, and the optimistic plans of Julius and the shipmaster were blown away. They faced the immediate problem of getting the ship safely into some harbor where they could lie up, protected, until the worst of the season was over. With not an hour to waste, the captain decided to take a hazardous chance. They would face up to the winds again and try to sail west along the coast of Crete to another of its harbors, the port of Phoenix, where they felt sure of being safe.

The decision was the folly of panic. As by the grace of the Holy Spirit, Paul, having just observed the autumnal fast of the Day of Atonement, suddenly braced himself, his arms around a stanchion, as he dared to shout to officers and crew, his voice clear above the noisy winds:

"Ye men! I see that the voyage will be with injury and much damage, not only of the lading and ship, but also of our lives."

What further advice Paul had to offer was never to be made known. The shipmaster declined to hear any more from a prisoner—and a tentmaker—on how to run his ship. He felt that the ship should hug the shore of Crete and not try to battle its way forward in the jaws of such a storm as was blowing. Even Julius, the centurion, brushed aside Paul's dire prediction.

But presently they were in real trouble. No more concise description of a tortured sea and a helpless ship was ever written than Luke's:

And because the haven was not commodious to winter in, the more part advised to depart thence also, if by any means they might attain to Phenice, and there to winter; which is an haven of Crete, and lieth toward the southwest and northwest.

And when the south wind blew softly, supposing that they had obtained their purpose, loosing thence, they sailed close by Crete.

But not long after there arose against it a tempestuous wind called Euroaquilo. And when the ship was caught, and could not bear up into the wind, we let her drive. And running under a certain island which is called Cauda, we had much work to come by the boat, which when they had taken up, they used helps, undergirding the ship; and, fearing lest they should fall into the quicksands, strake sail, and so were driven.

And we being exceedingly tossed with a tempest, the next day they lightened the ship; and the third day we cast out with our own hands the tackling of the ship. And when neither sun nor stars in many days appeared, and no small tempest lay on us, all hope that we should be saved was then taken away.

But after long abstinence Paul stood forth in the midst of them, and said:

"Sirs, ye should have hearkened unto me, and not have loosed from Crete, and to have gained this harm and loss. And now I exhort you to be of good cheer: for there shall be no loss of any man's life among you, but of the ship. For there stood by me this night the angel of God, whose I am, and whom I serve, saying: Fear not, Paul; thou must be brought before Caesar: and, lo, God hath given thee all them that sail with thee.

"Wherefore, sirs, be of good cheer: for I believe God, that it shall be even as it was told me."

Chapter 85. THE SHIPWRECK

THE quiet force and strong conviction with which Paul spoke in that seemingly hopeless hour eased men's terrors in the clamor of the unceasing storm.

For fourteen days and nights the storm continued, without sight of stars or sun; half a month of unabated tempest, in which men had no time to eat, no inclination to sleep, fearing that they might never wake in this life; of almost hourly expectation of foundering or breaking apart. All aboard were hungry, drenched, aching with fatigue.

By the fourteenth night they had been driven almost in a straight line westward into the waters of the region called Adria, which included not only the Adriatic Sea between the Italian coast and Illyricum, or Dalmatia, but also the open sea between Crete and Sicily, where they had their most arduous struggle with the storm.

Then suddenly: "We have come close to land!" The word sped through the crew to the passengers.

"The shipmen are discovering some country!" the worn passengers told the prisoners.

Hoarse shouts of sailors leaning over the rails at midnight informed the deck officer by the wheel house.

"Twenty fathoms!" they shouted.

"Twenty fathoms it is."

And again a little later:

"Fifteen fathoms!"

"Fifteen fathoms."

The shipmaster was alarmed, and with good cause, at these reports. The bottom was sloping sharply the wrong way. Most likely the old sailors were right; they were close to some unknown shore, full of danger from rough places, rocks, or sudden shallows in the floor of the sea. They must not drift any further in any direction. They must try to stand still and wait for the daylight. Then if the fogs were gone, they could see where they would be lying.

The captain bellowed his orders:

"Anchor number one astern . . .

"Anchor number two astern . . .

"Anchor number three astern . . .

"Anchor number four astern!"

Four anchors to hold the battered ship against the violent yanking of the winds. And every soul on board, as Luke wrote in his book, "wished for the day."

For some, the wishing brought only panic; the waiting time through darkness to daylight seemed too long to be endured. These hotheads were not the passengers but the sailors. They decided to deceive the captain, who stood on deck bellowing new orders to them.

"Anchor number one forward . . .

"Anchor number two forward . . .

"Anchor number three forward . . .

"Anchor number four forward . . ."

The answering yells of the forward hands encouraged the master of the vessel to believe that his orders were being obeyed. Under color of the confusion, however, they had actually rushed the lifeboats, resolved to take them for themselves alone, lowering them before anyone realized what was happening, in order to abandon ship and take their chances of getting ashore.

In the midst of all the hurly-burly of raging elements and human treachery, one mind alone of all the ship's company realized what was happening in the dark. Suddenly his sonorous voice loomed above the rattle of the lines, the whistling of the winds, and the thunder of the waves against the ship's sides, the ringing voice of Paul:

"Except these men stay in the ship we cannot be saved."

The prisoner's guards did not hesitate a moment to act upon his warning. Such was the profound trust Paul had roused in them that they did not wait to find out what Julius, the centurion, wanted them to do. They asked no permission of the ship's commander. Lunging forward they fell upon the deserting seamen. With their short-swords they cut the ropes, severing the empty lifeboat from the mother ship. Almost instantly it was lost in the night sea.

"We cut off the ropes of the boat and let her fall off!" they reported to Paul. Then they put guards around the other lifeboats. If those frightened sailors were necessary to man the ship, they must have no further chance to escape.

As streaks of feeble daylight crept over the sky, Paul had further advice.

"Meat," he began telling them all. "That is what you need now. Meat! I beseech you all to take some. This day is the fourteenth day that you have waited and continued fasting, taking nothing. Therefore, I pray you to take some meat for your health's sake; for there shall not an hair of the head of any of you perish."

He spoke with the authority of a prophet. He was a holy man, a saintly man. His own captors and guards praised him for his goodness. They knew no mere belly-hunger would ever make such a leader betray his principles.

The pagans on the ship had been fasting as an appeasing gesture to the gods who ruled the winds and the waves, yet Paul, who well knew the spiritual value of fasting, was eloquently trying to persuade them to eat a meal.

Specifically, and with authority that reflected an assurance utterly from another world, Paul promised them that not a hair of their heads would be harmed. Meat, he had told them, was what they needed, using the word in its contemporary broader sense of victuals. So it was food—whatever storm-soaked morsels each man might have kept by him—that Paul was urging should be eaten, and he set the example.

As Luke wrote it down:

"And when he had said these things, taking bread, he gave thanks to God in the sight of them all; and when he had broken it, he began to eat. Then were they all of better cheer, and they also took some meat."

When all the 276 people on the vessel had eaten a meal, they looked around them with new serenity. They could consider the situation more quietly, great as their peril continued to be—unabated winds and sea, sleet pelting upon them, imminent danger of foundering.

"We must lighten our load," the captain decided flatly.

He should have sacrificed his cargo long before, but that hold full of Anatolian wheat, was his profit, his future, and he hated to jettison it. Now every tawny corded bale of it went overboard, a small fortune dropping piece by piece into the water.

Hope was stirring in every heart as day arrived. The fog did begin to lift and they could make out the dim shore line. But "they knew not the land." By this time the captain was freely taking counsel with his oldest and most experienced mariners.

"I'm afraid to go in much nearer," he said. "I cannot recognize this place on my charts."

One old sailor pointed a knotted finger at a rising blind of mist a little to the north.

"See there," he said hoarsely. "There is a stream—a creek, a river, something flowing into the sea between two capes."

"I see it," agreed the master eagerly. "If we could only steer our way between those two points of land——"

"Let's try it!" came a shout.

It was a long chance, and everyone knew it; nevertheless the master went to the wheel and through his cupped, half-frozen hands began to issue his commands. He was going to try to thrust his ship into the haven of that outflowing stream.

"Up anchor number one!

"Number two!

"Number three!

"Number four!"

Now they had loosed the chains that had held them fast to the mud of the sea's bottom.

"Let go the bands on the rudder!"

"Hoist up the mainsail to the wind!"

The choice was made; "they committed themselves to the sea . . . they made towards the shore."

With frightful speed they were driven forward by the tireless gale, scudding on to a middle point between the two small headlands of black rock. It looked at first as if they would get through, but just as they reached the place where the river emptied into the sea, a terrific jolt hurled every man to the deck; a shriek of splitting timbers, a chaos of falling spars and crosstrees, and a violent shuddering of the stricken ship. They were aground.

The bow of the ship was unshakably imbedded in the sands and mud of the shallows; aft all was wreckage and collapsing lumber. The ship was broken in two by the violence of the waves.

Shrieks of fright and despair presaged dangerous hysteria. But the discipline of the Roman guards remained perfect. Two of them made their way instantly to Julius.

"Sir," they reported, "all hope is gone. We must abandon ship, and it will be every man for himself. Is it not our duty to kill our prisoners at once, so they may not escape?"

"*Kill Paul?*" There was sheer horror in the centurion's voice.

"Paul—Luke—Aristarchus—all the prisoners; yes, sir. Do I have your order?"

"No!"

"But if they swim out, they may escape."

"Hold your peace!" Julius must have astonished himself at the vehemence of his decision. The apostle had worked powerfully on the officer's inner spirit. He not only admired Paul deeply; he had, in some oblique fashion, come to believe and trust in his prophecies. Hadn't Paul promised that everyone would be saved?

"I forbid you to destroy the prisoners," said Julius firmly. "Let those who can swim cast themselves first into the sea, and save themselves and get to land."

This order was instantly obeyed. As for the others who could not swim, Luke reported:

"Some they carried on boards, and some on those things that belonged to the ship. And so it came to pass that every soul got safe to land."

Chapter 86. ITALY AT LAST!

THEY stumbled out of the water, and found themselves on an island called Melita, which all the shipwrecked mariners believed was inhabited by barbarians who might fall upon them and hack them to pieces.

They were to be surprised by these barbarians, as, indeed, by every aspect of their place of refuge. As the morning sun appeared, comforting their bodies, life resumed its sweetness. After those enormous waves that had seemed at one moment ready to swallow them, and the next, to pitch them against the rocks, after the cold of wind and sea, the darkness and the terror of the unknown, they saw the day like a curtain rising on reality. They saw the mist dissolving under the sun's radiance; they smelled the odors of earth and fields and heard the songs of birds.

Centuries afterward, men would call this beautiful island Malta and bestow its name on a heroic order of knighthood. Eight miles northwest of its capital, Valletta, is the cloistered water that till this day is called St. Paul's Bay, where the apostle's ship under that bitter east-northeast gale struck a shoal formed between the small island of Salmenatta and the shore on the west side of the bay.

That was where they were, on the beach, when the sun blessed their sore bodies that first morning after the wreck.

Wretched as they were, they began to hope as they felt warmer and drier. They were not disheartened even when the sun disappeared in a mist, and a drizzle of rain began, but they were wondering how they would be treated by the barbarians. Yet what, after all, was a "barbarian"? Someone reminded them it was a word for "stranger," anyone who was not a Greek—an historic idiom of days before the Caesars—not necessarily meaning a wild man.

A band of men approached the beach. Instinctively the survivors of the wreck stood closer together, bracing themselves. But these barbarians came bearing gifts. Some carried logs and kindling on their shoulders, and presently welcome bonfires flamed and smoked on the sand.

Paul was greatly moved by this demonstration of human brotherhood and consideration. As a good Christian, he believed he should not stand there shivering and receive the help of the strangers; he should co-operate with them to lighten their labor. So he left his guards and busied himself, picking up sticks and drift-pieces, to be tossed on the bonfire.

But trouble reached out and laid hold upon him, through a vicious small green and yellow viper. No such poisonous serpent is to be found today on the island of Malta, but one was lurking in the rotting wood Paul had picked up. It darted forward in a slithering onslaught and bit his right hand, fastening itself in his flesh and hanging there; venom flowed into the veins of God's Apostle to the Gentiles.

His plight evoked no pity whatever in the eyes of the hospitable barbarians. Faithful to their own ideas, they reasoned that such a catastrophe must mean that Paul was a criminal and a sinner on whom eternal justice was now taking summary vengeance. Among themselves, they muttered in their native Punic tongue:

"This man must be a murderer, no doubt about it. Even though he has escaped the sea, justice overtakes him, just the same."

They waited expectantly. At any moment, they felt sure, he would fall dead.

But Paul slowly extended his hand, the green and yellow viper dangling for all to see, and shook it off into the fire. Then he turned and smiled respectfully at the men of Melita.

These natives knew that the adder-like snake's sting meant almost instantaneous death. They rushed forward and seized Paul's hand. It should have been puffed and swollen and sore to the touch, but all they could see were the two small marks of fangs. They made a ring around Paul, waiting to see the hand begin to swell, and the man himself collapse. But at last they had to face the wonderful fact that no harm had come to him at all.

"Then," said Luke, the physician, "they changed their minds and said that he was a god."

Paul had been mistaken for a god before. Once in Lystra they had called him and Barnabas Greek gods—Jupiter and Apollo. This time he prudently ignored the matter.

Luke also reports the continuing kindness of the chief man of the island of Melita. His name was Publius, and his title, as Luke reported it, of "chief man" has been found in Maltan inscriptions. He was the highest Roman official on the island and made instant friends with Paul's guardian, Julius, bringing him and the Christian prisoners directly to his own house, where they were lodged with great courtesy for three days.

At the end of those three days a miracle became necessary.

The father of Publius was suddenly taken ill, almost, it seemed, ready to die.

On all the island there was no physician so highly skilled as Luke. Luke reports the ailment of the father of Publius with meticulous precision. The man was stricken with a fever, and a bloody flux; a most dangerous form of dysentery. If Luke attended him, he failed to mention the fact, as he failed to mention almost every fact about himself. Remaining silent as to any medication he may have prescribed, he recorded only the miracle performed on Publius' father:

". . . to whom Paul entered in and prayed, and laid his hands on him and healed him."

The report of the healing spread rapidly. The house of Publius was besieged with the ailing and the dying; the crippled, the blind, the deaf, the dumb, and the paralyzed "came and were healed."

No wonder, then, as Luke disclosed, there were many "who also

honored us with many honors; and when we departed, they laded us
with such things as were necessary."

For three months the refugees wintered on the island. But, as
blossom by blossom spring arrived, it was time for them to leave
this place of kindliness and peace and resume the solemn journey
onward to Italy, to the city of Paul's final tragedy and victory, Rome.

With the coming of softer winds, the harbors of Melita were filled
with ships. Julius selected a vessel bound from Alexandria, the
Dioscuri, named for Castor and Pollux, twin deities who were supposed to teach wisdom to sailors.

With a fair breeze and a bright sky they embarked, and the eyes
of the Christians were dimmed with tears as the great sails bellied
out and the ship drew away from the shore. They had found a blessed
interlude on that enchanted isle. Paul, standing near the rail and
shading his eyes with his hand, knew he would never see its green
trees and yellow shore again.

The gray and green outline of Sicily rose from the sea. On the
third day they tied up at the wharf on the waterfront of Syracuse, an
excellent harbor where the captain decided to remain for three days.

Mare Hadriaticum, the waters were called, where they were sailing
now; Adria, too, the sailors called it; the territory it embraces was
much larger than that of the sea we know as the Adriatic, * * * (This
is the place at which Mr. Oursler's manuscript ended at the time of
his death on May 24, 1952.) * * * and included what modern maps
call the Ionian Sea, on the east coast of Sicily.

To reach her final destination the *Dioscuri* must pass from the
Ionian to the Tyrrhenian Sea through the Strait of Messina. This
channel, separating Italy and Sicily, is a twenty-mile detroit, a narrow
corridor of whirlpools, crosscurrents, and sudden winds striking
caution to the heart of the sturdiest sailor.

The ship headed out of the harbor of Syracuse into the path of the
strong northwest wind, bending her course in a circle to come up to
windward, slowly winning her way up to Rhegium, the south entrance
of the Strait, and the first sight of Italy.

Paul gripped the railing and strained forward, eyes fixed on the
landfall ahead, and was silent.

At Rhegium the ship put in to harbor, waiting for the right
moment to attempt the Strait. Fetching a compass, she had circled
from Sicily seventy-five miles to the Italian port. But the northwest

gale still funneled through the Strait and defied all comers. For a day the ship tugged anxiously at the moorings, and all aboard paced the crowded decks with sudden spurts of impatience. Next dawn the south wind blew strong and fair. The *Dioscuri* faced into the channel.

Years before, Paul had read Homer's tale of the two demons of the Strait of Messina. Now, as the ship sailed cautiously through the deceitful waters, he peered out into the foam to catch sight of a giant rock. Suddenly he grabbed Luke's shoulder and pointed to an island boulder, then scurried across the port side of the deck to watch the deadly whirlpool of Homer's story.

Scylla and Charybdis, twin threats to sailors in the Strait of Messina! Odysseus passed between them centuries ago, and Jason with the Argonauts, and now Paul, hero of the most wondrous epic of all, stared at the rock and the whirlpool, and pondered their symbolism. The Greeks, fearing these dangers, had claimed they were inhabited by monsters, who set out with the winds as their cruel conspirators to murder sailors and wreck their craft. But Paul was thinking of the strait and narrow way of Christ, and of the evil forces within a man's own soul that can drive him to eternal death while he is busy blaming an enchanted being or an unkind wind.

With precision and practice, the captain of the *Dioscuri* threaded the vessel's way smoothly through rock and whirlpool, out into the gentle waters of the Tyrrhenian Sea.

For a day and a half they sailed up the west coast of Italy, bound for a harbor not far from modern Naples—Puteoli, biggest port in south Italy. Water traffic thickened around them. Trading ships from all the Empire were heading for the bustling docks of Puteoli, bearing goods from their home provinces to exchange for perfumes and pottery and the exquisite mosaics of the port's craftsmen.

The crew of the *Dioscuri* had no time to stare at other ships. Once out of the Strait they worked with a fever of excitement, smartening up the decks, checking the rigging, readying bunting, patching worn spots in the paint. The ship was a prima donna, primping for her grand entrance. Her arrival was a major event in the life of Puteoli, not because she bore an apostle to judgment before Caesar, but because her hold bulged with wheat from Egypt, vital to Italian economy.

Suddenly a covey of *tabularia*, tiny racing vessels, darted from the shelter of the harbor to surround the onrushing *Dioscuri*, with shouts of welcome. Armed with news of the size of her cargo, they scurried home like eager children to tell of her near arrival.

Ahead of the *Dioscuri* merchant ships paused at the mouth of the harbor one by one to strike their topsails, lower and fold them in obedience to maritime law. The crewmen of Paul's ship, shouldering past the prisoner to the railing, watched this ritual with smug smiles. That law did not apply to them! Like others of the vast Alexandrian grain fleet, this ship's sails stayed up in proud announcement of her safe arrival.

Men alerted by the *tabularia* crowded onto the waterfront, jostling on the wharves, cheering and hallooing and offering loud advice on the best way to ease the ship up to her berth.

Paul and Luke and Aristarchus, their belongings in skin bundles under their arm, stood squinting into the sun that was setting now over the terraced hills of Puteoli. This was the end of the voyage.

Only a few days' land journey separated Paul from Caesar.

Chapter 87. NEWS OF PETER

Across the jumble of docks and storehouses and naval outfitters Paul saw more than the port of Puteoli. He saw the road to Rome, and in Rome stood the two strongest forces in his life—the Empire that governed his worldly affairs, and the Church that directed his soul. One empire led by Nero; one by the Christ through the person of the man He had named Peter.

Inevitably the two must clash, in spirit and in blood. That Paul knew. But for months he had been suspended from news of the world, isolated in his own pressing drama of wind and wave. He yearned for news of the Church and of Peter. Someday, he knew, Nero would recognize the kingdom of heaven as his rival, and the fury of his legions would be loosed on Christian heads. Had the time of persecution come?

Were there Christians in Puteoli, among the perfumers, the potters, the mosaic-makers, the merchants? Paul had heard that a port church had been founded here years before. If it still flourished, would there be a chance to contact the elders before Julius moved his prisoner on to Rome?

At that moment Julius himself came up beside them. His campaign-wrinkled face glowed with homeland fever. With one hand on Paul's shoulder, the officer pointed the other up to the hills above the business section of the town, singling out the homes of famous people as proud citizens do for tourists all over the world.

"See, on that hill, that large white villa? That's the home of Seneca—when he's not in Rome, of course."

Seneca! Poet, dramatist, philosopher, scholar—and virtual co-ruler of the Empire. Paul stared thoughtfully at the poplar-hedged mansion. Six years before, when young Nero had been made Emperor, Seneca had been his tutor. He and a soldier named Burrus, head of the Praetorian Guard, had run the government for the lackadaisical lad, and done a fine job. The Empire was grateful to them. Nero, so rumor said, was not.

Paul's gaze dropped from the white villa on the heights to the teeming streets below. If Christians still worshiped here, under the windows of Seneca, there would be little to fear for the Church—or for himself when he came to trial before Caesar!

Bales of grain swung down from the hold to the backs of slaves. Men swarmed around hawsers and gangplank, running and shouting and singing, in the purposeful jumble of the waterfront. Paul and his friends and Julius stood together, an island of silence in the confusion.

"As soon as they unload, we leave the ship," said Julius suddenly. "I have relatives here, and business. We will stay in Puteoli a few days, a week maybe. Then on to Rome."

He turned and looked down into his prisoner's eyes.

"Be your own guard, Paul, while we are here. I will send you word when it is time to go."

As if ashamed of his lenience, Julius strode away down the deck and stood with his back to the apostle.

So Paul and Luke and Aristarchus went ashore, paroled in their own custody. Penniless, they faced the immediate problem of finding the local church. No steeples, no crosses stood over Christian temples in these early days. The custom of marking the cryptic sign of the fish on those homes in which worship was secretly held was not yet in vogue. And, if the threat of persecution were imminent, as Paul feared, he could not risk asking a possible enemy.

Paul knew whom to ask. He stood on the dock, by the ship's side, and as the slaves ran by, half-blinded with sweat, he murmured the words of Christ in Greek, the universal tongue of slaves:

"Our Father, Who art in heaven . . ."

The slaves dropped the bales of wheat at the storehouse door and trotted back to the ship. And as they passed Paul they smiled and whispered the way to the church, the home of the only One in the Empire to care about slaves.

Paul hungered for news. He could hardly still the questions buzzing on his tongue till he found the church and introduced himself. He gave his name to the elders of Puteoli humbly, sure that if anyone in the town had ever heard of him, they would have forgotten by now.

A priest ordained by Peter himself clutched Paul's arm.

"Paul? The Apostle? God be praised! But where have you been?"

A young deacon chimed in. "For weeks Epaphroditus has been waiting for you in Rome. What happened to you?"

"Waiting for me?" Paul ran his hand over his brow, and looked at Luke in smiling wonder.

"He was sent from the church in Philippi. As soon as they heard you were to be taken to Rome for trial, they raised a purse to pay your expenses and sent it on by Epaphroditus. He's been all over Italy looking for you. We thought you were dead."

Paul sank down on a chair by the plain wooden table. He shook his head with a slow, pleased smile, savoring the half-forgotten flavor of loving thoughtfulness.

The church at Philippi! Where Paul's first convert was Lydia, the seller of purple; where he had cast the pythonical spirit out of the girl fortuneteller, and been scourged for his trouble. He had been back there only once, a brief visit some three years ago. Yet the Christians of that Macedonian city had pooled their own funds and sent one of their best men to help him.

Paul bowed his head in gratitude to God for friends.

The first favor he asked of the elders of Puteoli was to send word to Rome, to tell Epaphroditus of the shipwreck and the safe arrival, and give him Paul's blessing and thanks.

His second request was for news of Peter and the health of the Church.

Time then for seven days of rest and talk and rejoicing, for shriving and prayer. For the first time in months Paul knew the blessed pleasure of assisting another priest in the celebration of the Last Supper on Sunday, sharing the Body and Blood of Christ on land, in peace. These Italians sang hymns to God the Father, Son, and Holy Ghost, new songs of love and faith that sounded sweetly strange to Paul's ears. But the prayers were the same that Paul and Luke had known in the province of Asia and in Judaea, whether spoken in Greek and Latin, as here, or in the Aramaic of Jerusalem.

For no matter where a man went on the face of the earth, Christians worshiped God in the same way.

Before he left Puteoli, Paul had heard the full story of Peter's quiet conquest of Rome, beginning with the poor, then extending Christ's baptism even to men in Nero's own court.

With Mark at his side, Peter had walked wide-eyed in Rome, down to the Trastevere, center of Jewish life. Worldly-wise as he had become, Peter had been taken unaware by the city's blatant sin, about which even Romans were becoming self-conscious. Seneca himself was fond of saying that among the noble women of the imperial city "chastity is a synonym for ugliness."

There were so few marriages in Rome that one emperor enacted laws about legacies, in a vain attempt to encourage family life. Sodomy and homosexuality were subjects of common talk and humorous verses; the bodies of abandoned babies littered the side alleys or floated in death on the River Tiber.

Peter had refused to believe such tales, until with his own aging eyes he saw them, and wept.

How could Christ gain a hearthold in such a city? Who wanted Him?

Peter had begun with the lowest class of Rome, the slaves, who had almost forgotten they were men. They had no rights, no name, no possessions. By law, nothing done to a slave, even murder, could be called a crime. They were allowed no religion.

But Peter said that anyone could become a Christian, and follow the God who though innocent was reviled, whipped, and spat upon— the God who made Himself a slave for all man's sins. And Peter said that Christians, slave and free, were:

"A chosen generation, a royal priesthood. . . . that you should show forth the praises of Him who had called you out of darkness into His marvelous light."

That to slaves!

And they that heard him, as he came in the twilight where they sat eating scraps in the backyards of the rich, learned to love the Christ, who said: "*Come unto Me all ye who are heavy laden, and I shall give you rest.*"

Peter turned next to the middle class, the freedmen who could seldom get jobs as long as slave labor cost nothing; and to the free-born poor—shopkeepers and small businessmen, who were forbidden by law to organize for protection against either the powerful guilds of craftsmen who worked for them, or the conscienceless courtiers who refused to pay bills. The penalty for forming a union of small businessmen was death in the arena.

No one wanted freedmen or common folk in Rome, except Christ. Peter preached in cobbler shops and bazaars, in the abattoirs of dealers in stolen meat, and in the shops where men sold whips specially designed for the scourging of slaves. To these men, who though free in name were caught in the vise of a society that wanted only two classes, who struggled against the daily threat of poverty and violence, Peter said:

"Who is he that will harm you if you be followers of that which is good? And if you suffer for righteousness' sake, be happy, and be not afraid of their terror, nor be troubled. But sanctify the Lord God in your hearts, and be ready always to give an answer to every man that asks you a reason of the hope that is in you with meekness and fear, having a good conscience. . . .

"For it is better, if the will of God be so, that you suffer for well doing, than for evil doing. For Christ also has once suffered for sins, the just for the unjust, that He might bring us to God."

The freedmen heard Peter's words, and took him into their homes, and were baptized.

If the Son therefore shall make you free, you shall be free indeed.

Through a shopkeeper convert, Peter drove his first wedge into high society. He met a senator named Pudens, a member of the rich and powerful house of Cornelian. Pudens stayed to listen to the Galilean's preaching in the back room of a dry goods store. Peter was speaking that afternoon of a far-off day in Caesarea Philippi, when Jesus had said to His disciples:

"What shall it profit a man, if he shall gain the whole world, and suffer the loss of his soul? Or what shall a man give in exchange for his soul?"

And Senator Pudens, who had gained the world's treasures, had pressed forward among the freedmen and the shopkeepers till he was close to the tall, strong-shouldered man and his lithe young helper Mark. In front of everyone Pudens had bowed before Peter and asked him to come to live in his house on the haughty Aventine Way and teach his family about this One God.

Pudens and his family were baptized. Soon, high servants of Nero, other senators, a few earnest matrons of society, and even members of the Praetorian Guard came at night to the house of the converted lawmaker. Slaves, already Christian, came proudly to the marble gates of Pudens' house, to introduce the masters they had converted.

The throng of converts grew so large that Peter could no longer baptize in the River Tiber without putting on a major spectacle. One of his new catechumens, who owned a family cemetery on the Ostrian Way, several acres of gardens and landscaped tombs, offered it for Peter's use. Roman cemeteries were always crowded with visitors; every man in his will named five or six days during each year when his friends and relatives must gather at his grave to show him respect and keep his earthbound soul company, to banquet in elaborate open-air dining halls, and wander among the flowers and trees. No one would be suspicious of regular meetings in a cemetery, even one built right outside the gates of the Praetorian Camp, as this one was.

No more suitable spot could have been chosen for the first big Christian meeting place in the city. The cemetery was built over an old swamp, once known as Goat's Marsh. And in that swamp, so legend said, died Romulus, the founding god of Rome. The gardens sloped gently to a shallow basin of water, last trace of Goat's Marsh. With the water that had brought death to a pagan god, Peter baptized the men of Rome into eternal life.

He had come to Rome a stranger, forced to learn to think in two languages new to him—the Latin of official society, and the Greek of the slaves and the poor. Yet in a few tireless years he had taken the city by silent storm. In the midst of an empire of hate and misery and sin, he had set up the kingdom of heaven on earth, a kingdom of love for God.

So far, Nero had ignored Christianity, dismissing it as a Jewish sect or as a "foreign superstition," one of the many florid Eastern religions that flourished in Rome. Nero had snickered as he watched devotees of the Egyptian goddess Isis, with shaven heads and robes of linen, lead their followers in solemn parades, and in winter driving them into the ice floes of the Tiber to wash away their sins. Servants of a Syrian goddess named Ida ran through the streets whipping themselves and slashing their own bodies, catching their own blood and drinking it to wipe out sin. Nero saw little difference between such sadistic orgy and the communion feasts of Christians.

Besides, religion bored him.

The last of the haughty line of Julius Caesar, he was a meager-brained, overweening fool, a fop and a tyrant. Son of Agrippina, the queen who murdered Emperor Claudius with the poisoned mushrooms, the boy Nero had been crowned as soon as his father was buried.

At the age of twenty, Emperor Nero, who was already married, had decided he was in love with his best friend's wife, a doxy named Poppaea Sabina. Beautiful, ambitious, and crafty, Poppaea became Nero's mistress. She understood her ego-ridden Nero, and knew how to bend him to her will. She did not intend to suffer the scorn of his poisonous mother or his pie-faced wife. She had no patience with Seneca's philosophical mouthings, no use for the idealistic Burrus.

With wily pouts and crafty whispers, she convinced Nero that these people were actually overshadowing his own true brilliance, smothering him with mediocrity. Nero listened darkly and nodded. In A.D. 59, the year before Paul reached Italy, Nero quietly murdered his mother. His wife, and the imperial advisers Seneca and Burrus, slowly slid into oblivion.

In the palace in Rome, in villas and shops, backyards and taverns all over Italy, men muttered about what happens to an empire when a madman and a harlot share the crown of Caesar.

And in Puteoli, from the home of the Christian elder, Paul stared northward to Rome. The seven days were gone. Julius sent word he was ready to leave.

Paul had appealed to Caesar. To Caesar—and Poppaea—he must go.

Chapter 88. ROME!

JULIUS met Paul with a smile and a friendly clasp on the shoulders, in his private room. Then he led Paul to the courtyard of the local garrison, put chains on his hands, and started for Rome.

Now that they were so near the capital, Julius could no longer afford to be lenient to his prisoner. Paul understood. He stood patiently as the official guard of ten soldiers fell into place around him. Luke and Aristarchus took their places at the very end of the procession, as Julius sounded the order to march.

All along the streets of Puteoli, Christians looked up from their labors to wave and smile at Paul, hiding from him their concern for his safety. Paul smiled back, but he did not wave. To spare their last memories of him, he kept his manacled hands hidden from them under his cloak.

At Capua the two-lane road from Puteoli joined the most famous road ever built, the Appian Way. Paul grinned with a traveler's delight as he stepped onto one of the giant concrete blocks that made up the famed "queen of roads," main route between Rome and the eastern provinces. Over it moved the lifestream of an empire in continuous pageantry. Romans were justly proud of this marvel of their engineering. Today the modern traveler in Italy can step on some of the same concrete blocks that Paul trod, though the Appian Way is a full two thousand years old.

Julius put on an air of new dignity and reserve as he swung his cortege into step on the Appian Way. They marched proudly in the busy traffic, keeping formation as horse-drawn chariots rushed past on the broad highway. Centurions of the army, en route to Asia and Palestine, saluted each other as they passed. Caravans from the Orient and the litters of rich ladies mingled with tatterdemalion ranks of traveling peddlers and slaves in harness and wagons of produce.

On Paul marched. Past Formia, and the villa where Cicero had been murdered by Mark Antony's order a century before. Through highlands and along the seashore, past far-flung farms worked by prisoners of war, down to the Pontine Marshes.

The air was dank. The hum of mosquitoes rang in their ears, and soldiers and prisoners alike muffled hoods and necks in their cloaks. Luke, the doctor, remembering past attacks of malarial fever, kept a sharp watch on Paul. But Paul was busy peering out from his make-shift hood to see the canal that now paralleled the road, and to observe the donkeys on shore tugging flat-bottomed cargo boats slowly through the infested waters.

Then a sigh of relief came from the soldiers. Ahead, in the swamp mist they saw the outlines of the town of Appii Forum. For the four nights since leaving Puteoli their only lodging had been the grass and shade trees along the road. But at Appii Forum, only forty miles from Rome, was an inn where one could rent a bed and a mattress of reeds. Evening settled quickly over the marsh, and Julius hurried the men on to the welcome shelter.

In the courtyard of the inn Paul stood in patient silence with the soldiers. In dark corners dice cups rattled. Slave girls with too-ready eyes found errands to lead them past the soldiers. From the taproom voices roared the words of a lewd song. Somewhere a young girl screamed.

"Paul?" From the shadows by the stables came a hoarse whisper. "Paul of Tarsus?"

Paul squinted into the darkness, then stretched out his chained hands in welcome.

"Epaphroditus!"

"The same, at your service. And here are Priscilla and Aquila. And this is Linus, a priest and a close friend of Peter. Peter sent him with us to greet you."

Paul was choked with emotion. When he could speak, he gave thanks to God, for his friends and the new courage that flooded his heart.

Aquila and his wife Priscilla! Those dearly intimate old friends, who had shared his labors in the tentmaking booth in Corinth, the long hours of preaching, and the voyage to Ephesus. At sight of that faithful couple, memories surged through Paul's heart and mind like a full tide to steady the uncertain currents of the future.

He stood in grateful silence, staring at this band of old friends and new, for there were others in the shadows whom he had not yet formally met. These Christians had walked the forty miles from Rome and waited here, too poor to rent beds with or without mattresses, for two days and a night, just to welcome him.

On the pretext of saving the state the price of a bed, Julius gave Paul permission to spend the night outside with the delegation. Mosquitoes and raucous swamp frogs, the curses and bawdy songs of the inn were forgotten as the Christians talked and prayed.

Linus, a slim young man only recently freed from slavery, bore messages from Peter. First, the patriarch's grateful blessing and his constant affection. Second, an expression of great approval for the Epistle to the Romans, which had arrived while Paul was at sea, and which Peter had ordered read before Communion in churches everywhere.

But, explained Linus, Peter would not be in Rome to greet Paul personally. He was taking this rare opportunity to leave his local church in Paul's wise care, while he at last could be free to travel and tend the universal Church. Paul's trial would not be immediate, that was certain, and while he waited in Rome he could handle the constant flow of personal and doctrinal problems. Peter had recommended Paul highly to all the elders.

Paul fully understood. The other apostles were scattered now over the whole known world, carrying the Gospel far beyond the borders of the Empire. He himself was a prisoner, unable to visit the churches he had founded. Clearly Peter must make the most of this chance to travel. Paul nodded, but his heart was lonely. He had longed to see Peter in person.

In the morning the Christian delegation swelled the ranks of the soldiers, tramping down the highway behind Julius to the next town, a post station known as Tres Tabernae, or Three Taverns. Julius selected the most expensive inn.

At the fountain in the town square a man in a dusty cloak kept alert watch on three hostels. At sight of Paul he leaped to his feet and waved a brawny arm over his head. From all corners of the square, from hitching posts and blacksmith shops, courtyards and shade trees, came some thirty men of all ages. They strode together toward the new arrivals.

"Paul! Paul of Tarsus!"

Paul whirled in amazement, as Linus came to his side, proud of a well-kept secret.

The first night had brought him the warm salute of old friends. Now came the elders of the church of Rome in official welcome, formal recognition from the main Church. One by one they gave him the kiss of peace and asked his blessing.

The next morning Julius had trouble repressing a smile. Except for his chains, Paul looked more like a king than a prisoner, a ruler in a royal progress. Some fifty Christians of all ages now trooped along beside the soldiers, singing and laughing and praying.

They camped that night in the Alban Hills, overlooking the site of the ancient town that mothered Rome, Alba Longa, birthplace of Romulus and Remus. Morning led them down again to more malarial swamps, the Roman Campagna.

Aquila came up beside Paul and gripped his elbow. Paul brushed away a mosquito from his nose and stared north along his friend's pointing finger. There! That rust and gold city on the horizon with ice-white temples and palaces shimmering in the sun—Rome!

Paul's steps quickened like a boy's. Almost he was leading the strange procession. The soldiers swung along faster to keep pace.

The Appian Way broadened proudly before them. On either side the arches of three majestic aqueducts spanned the marshy Campagna, carrying fresh, pure water from the mountains to the city. One of these had been built three hundred years before Christ was born. Yet modern visitors to Rome can stand as Paul did, marveling at the strength and sweep of these same arches.

Down through a valley plunged the Appian Way, into the very shadow of Rome.

"There!" said Linus. "That is the graveyard or catacomb of Callistus. And on this side are Jewish catacombs. All these ahead of us are tombs of the very richest people in Rome."

Paul stared in amazement. The road was lined on either side with cypress trees, and with graves and monuments of every size and shape, side by side, in endless rows. On each tomb an inscription in large letters pleaded in verse or epigram for the passer-by to remember its occupant.

Linus explained that Romans were proud of the Appian Way and were eager to share personally in its glory by building their tombs alongside the road, so making sure their ghosts would never be lonely, or forgotten. Each noble family owned a cemetery, and went to extreme lengths to outdo each other in decorating their public graves.

Julius hardly glanced at the catacombs. The Christians stared at them with silent premonition.

Around them now the air was shrill with the shouts of peddlers and the bargaining of the bazaars, as they entered the main Jewish quarter of Rome.

The Jews had come to Rome as prisoners of war. But they did not make profitable slaves. No punishment, no threat, could force them to abandon the practice of their religion. On Sabbath days they would not work. They would not cook pork, even for an emperor. They would not bow to the gods of Rome, and they insisted on worshiping regularly in their own synagogues.

Romans soon learned that such slaves were more trouble than they were worth, so they made the best of a bad deal and let the Jews buy their freedom. In a few years these "Liberti" had built their own city within a city, in the section called Trastevere, across the river from Rome, and spread into many districts of the city proper. They were self-sufficient taxpayers, justly proud of their seven synagogues and their freedom.

Paul studied the faces of his fellow Jews carefully, as he strode in chains through the Trastevere. Were they enemies of Christians or friends? Did they side with their brothers in Jerusalem? The sight of their bearded faces, the sound of his native tongue stirred Paul's heart with nostalgia. He yearned toward these men. But not one turned a head to look at him.

Julius led Paul through the Trastevere to the Capena Gate between the Aventine and Caelian Hills, into the heart of Rome. Down the city streets they marched, bearing left to the Forum and the barracks of the Praetorian Guard.

How different everything, now! The stamp of a capital city was on the pressured haste of the crowds, so set apart in clothes and posture, so alert and studied in every gesture. The men about this prison bespoke *Caesar!*

The stratopedarch, the prison-camp attendant commander, met them with a sharp salute. The soldiers broke ranks, pressing Luke and Aristarchus and the other Christians back against the wall, making way for a fresh contingent of the imperial guards.

"Bring the prisoner in!" shouted the stratopedarch.

Six men, taller than any Paul had seen, surrounded him. Two grabbed his shoulders and hustled him into the barracks.

The supreme commander here was Burrus, who with Seneca had long served as Nero's adviser. Burrus must hear all cases before sending them on to Caesar for judgment, and it was before him that Paul found himself.

Julius presented the letter from Governor Festus, rumpled and water-stained after the months of voyage and shipwreck. Burrus read it without comment.

He listened gravely as Julius recited the adventures of their trip and praised the prisoner's goodness, integrity, and honor. Then Burrus cleared his throat, and smiled.

"Paul, your accusers from the Temple have not yet come to Rome. No trial can be held till they appear. Governor Festus speaks well of you, and you seem to have made a good friend out of Julius, your jailer."

In Burrus' splendid office, and outside the windows where the crowd of Christians listened, every breath was stilled to catch the next words.

"I remand you to *custodia militaris,* until such time as your trial may by held."

Custodia militaris! The same lenient treatment given to high-ranking soldiers awaiting a civil suit. The prisoner could live where he pleased, as he pleased, with a Praetorian Guard at his side. True, he must still wear chains, but Paul was free, free to teach and preach, and to serve God and the church in Rome.

Clearly Burrus did not consider Paul a dangerous man. What Nero would think was something else again!

Chapter 89. SERMON IN CHAINS

BEFORE Burrus had even dismissed Paul, three of the eavesdropping Christians scuttled away—Epaphroditus, with his purse of alms from Philippi ajingle, Priscilla and Aquila. They were off to prepare lodgings for Paul.

Rome was a city of apartment houses, called *insulae,* or islands of one to twelve rooms. Those were the first flats of modern times, housing all except the very richest, who lived in palaces and villas on the Seven Hills. The luxury of the insulae varied with a man's purse, from gardened elegance to row on row of identical wooden structures, jammed together tenement fashion on narrow, noisy, stinking streets.

The only place Epaphroditus could afford on the Philippian relief fund, even with help from the Roman church, was a room five flights up. The rumble of heavy produce wagons and the brazen cries of beggars reached the room, but little air or sun.

The two men paid Paul's advance rent for several months, haggling vainly over the price. Priscilla stood and studied the room, then went to call the active widows of the church to bring curtain stuff, needle and thread, mop, broom, and sponge.

The housing shortage might be acute, the purse thin, but no apostle would live in drab filth so long as Christian women had hands and strong backs!

The next morning Paul moved in with Luke and Aristarchus and the first shift of his constantly changing guards. He hung his cloak on a peg, and it disappeared into a woman's thimbled hand. On a table stood a steaming bowl of lamb broth, fresh rye bread, and a dish of plums. Paul looked at the shining walls, the spotless floors, the heavy sacking drapes over the long window, the borrowed cots, desks, and chairs—the first home he had known in the twenty-three years that he had served Christ!

Priscilla and her helpers disappeared before he could stop looking and marveling long enough to thank them.

Aristarchus would have enjoyed a rest. To have a clean blanket, a clean floor, an end to rocking ships on the verge of wreck, an end to marches along historic roads was luxury he had nearly forgotten. He rolled a purple-misted plum in his hands, sprawled down on a cot, and sighed with human content.

Luke busied himself settling his medicines on a set of wooden shelves in the corner. For the first time since he had left Jerusalem he could arrange his vials and ointments in plain view without expecting them to clatter to the floor with the roll of a ship, or having to repack them the next day. His soul's love of order drew comfort from the feeling of fussing with the arrangements of his remedies and his precious rolls of papyrus, his pens, and pumice.

The guard slumped in the one comfortable chair, took off his boots, and stretched.

Paul stood by the window and stared at his bound hands. For the

first time in his life he must live off charity; no tentmaking. In chains!
He could feel his pride struggling against suffocation. He smiled
wryly, and bowed his head in humility. One labor he could still perform! He would be a fool to waste time regretting that God had given
him no chance to do anything else!

Aristarchus did not rest long. Within the hour Paul had sent him
on an errand to the Jewish quarter of the city to seek out the presidents of the seven main synagogues and invite them to Paul's room
for a meeting the next day.

Paul had two reasons for calling this conference. First and foremost
was the duty that burned in him to teach the Gospel to his own kind.
He was the Apostle to the Gentiles only by default, when Israel would
not hear him. Everywhere, without fail, he had by action, speech, and
written word told of Jesus Christ "to the Jews first."

He yearned for the men of Jesus' own blood to recognize his message as truth. Always and everywhere, save for individual converts,
they had rejected and persecuted him. Yet in Rome, waiting final trial
on the accusations of fellow Jews and in chains because of them, he
spoke first to them.

"Beg them come and hear me, Aristarchus!"

On a more immediately practical level, Paul needed to sound out
the Jewish leaders on the chances for the outcome of his own trial.
In Rome the freed Jews had become not only numerous but in-
fluential. Though they lived huddled on the outskirts of the city, set
apart by religious and national ties, they controlled much of the
trade in Rome and walked confidently in Nero's court. The Emperor's
personal dramatics teacher was a Jewish playwright, and Poppaea
herself was said to be studying to become a Jewish convert. The
leaders of the synagogues could swing Paul's trial to fit their purposes.
If they believed the charges of the priests of Jerusalem, Paul was
doomed.

They came to see him the third morning he was in Rome. The
presidents of the seven synagogues brought with them the leading
merchants and the elders, the teachers and the moneylenders, all
curious to see this famous renegade.

In the streets a band of Syrian musicians chanted and blew their
horns, children shrieked in play, and wagon drivers cursed. The sultry
Roman summer brought sweat to the bored face of the Roman guard

standing in Paul's doorway. The delegation from the Trastevere puffed their way up the two hundred steps to the apartment and filed past the guard as if he were invisible.

Paul rose and stretched his manacled hands in grateful welcome. Luke produced the few chairs and the cots for seats.

In the sudden silence Paul spoke.

"Men—brethren—I, having done nothing against the people or the custom of our fathers, was delivered prisoner from Jerusalem into the hands of the Romans. When they had examined me, they would have released me because they could find no cause for death in me. But the Jews spoke against that decision, and I was forced to appeal to Caesar—not that I had anything to accuse my nation of!

"For this reason therefore I desired to see you, and to speak to you. Because it is for the hope of Israel that I am bound with this chain."

His listeners stared blandly at the chain. Not a face betrayed either friendliness or enmity. The president of the largest synagogue spoke:

"We received no letters about you from Judaea. And none of the brethren that came here has told us anything evil about you." He paused to study Paul's face, then with a faint smile of courtesy said: "But we would like to hear from your own lips what you think and believe. Because about this—uh, sect—we know that everyone everywhere speaks against it."

Paul nodded. The synagogue president thought to spring a trap on him, lure him into open blasphemy—and that was what Paul wanted: an invitation to speak about Christ. With a smile he let the Jews set their own date for the lecture on the "sect" of Christianity.

Fifteen men had come to see Paul on that first visit. More than ninety came on the second, milling and muttering and laughing in the street outside.

The guard saw them and grunted. He ordered Paul to go down to them, and arranged with the landlord for the use of the inner courtyard of the building, to avoid disturbing the peace.

Luke whispered to Paul as they walked down the narrow stairs: "They rejected Peter and blamed Christians for their troubles under Emperor Claudius. They say they hate us. But they're still curious about us. It's a healthy sign!"

In the shade of the courtyard trees Paul stood and talked to the Jews, explaining the kingdom of God, and persuading them about Jesus, quoting the Old Testament writers to them to prove what he said. And as Luke himself recorded, Paul talked to them "from morning until evening."

From morning until evening! In Rome men rose at dawn, rich and poor alike. All business stopped at noon. The rest of the day was given to siesta, followed by the long family meal which began before twilight in summer.

Three shifts of Paul's guards yawned and scratched their heads at the sight of seemingly sane men forgetting not only work, but lunch and the nap in the heat of afternoon. And for what? To talk about Yahweh, and Jesus Christ!

Finally Paul was done.

Immediately, such a squabbling filled the yard that the wealthier tenants, who paid high prices for apartments on the court away from street noises, leaned out their windows and yelled for silence. A few of the Jews believed Paul's message. Many turned it down. As always, the men who did not know what to believe talked the loudest.

Those who scoffed at Christ rose to leave, spitting on the ground in disgust. The middle men weighed their chances, and decided to go too.

Once more Paul stood and faced them. Rejected again, he flung his last challenge to the wise-beards who were leaving. With agony in his voice, he reminded them of the words of their own prophet Isaiah:

"Well did the Holy Ghost speak to our fathers by Isaiah the prophet saying: 'Go to this people and say to them: "With the ear you shall hear and shall not understand; and seeing you shall see, and shall not perceive." For the heart of this people is grown gross. And with their ears have they heard heavily, and their eyes they have shut, lest perhaps they should see with their eyes, and hear with their ears, and understand with their heart and should be converted, and I should heal them.' "

Paul looked straight at the unbelievers, and said with a catch in his throat:

"Be it known therefore to you, that this salvation of God is sent to the Gentiles—and they will hear it!"

The unbelievers walked out of the courtyard, nudging the undecided before them. Those who had believed scurried along arguing with the others all the way down the street.

Paul watched them go; a prisoner, rejected by his own people, unable to share with his blood brothers the treasure that was his.

He squared his shoulders, raised his head, and marched back up-stairs.

Chapter 90.   THE PHYSICIAN WRITES A BOOK

THE landlord scratched his head and spat. He felt he should have asked more rent. All day long, and all night too, this man Paul had visitors, tramping up and down the narrow stairs as if they owned the place. And no one, not even the Praetorian Guards, seemed to object.

True, the tiny walk-up had never been kept so clean, or so busy. In the sweltering heat of summer it had become a workshop, a power-house of mission activity the Empire over, a combination of executive offices, information bureau, and monastery.

Every morning except Sunday women in the somber stolae of widows bustled about scrubbing, cooking, washing, mending. Mes-sengers, travelers, men of all races and cities perched on the window sills or huddled in the corners of the cramped room. Nobles from the Palatine came unattended like Nicodemus at night, to ask about the new God. Slaves crept in the door, hope in their eyes, fear of capture on their sweating brows. And every eight hours there was the chang-ing of the guards, some of whom wore a bored, bloated look, some the smile of secret converts.

In the midst of this hubble-bubble, Luke sat at a desk by the window, oblivious equally to dispute, sermon, or an eager widow's feather duster. From dawn to late afternoon he sat with pen and papyrus, pumice and sand, writing a new Gospel.

While they lived, the apostles would tell the story of Jesus, with their every breath. Two versions had already been written down. Very early after the Ascension, Matthew had written his life in Christ, but the ex-tax collector wrote in Aramaic, and since his work had not yet been translated, no one outside Palestine had read it. Then, at the urgent request of text-hungry Romans, Mark had taken down Peter's most familiar sermons, a word-for-word account of the fisherman's oral memoirs. But that Gospel was not really complete. Peter never told the whole story of Jesus at once. He skipped and rambled, choos-ing the miracles and parables that bore most meaning for his Roman audience. He harped constantly on his own weaknesses, repeating in clear-eyed humility the rebukes that Jesus had given him.

No one yet had written a definitive life of Christ, and that troubled Luke's orderly mind. The rest of the twelve were scattered all over the world, from Africa to Russia, far too busy preaching to bother with writing books. And those accounts by Matthew and by Peter through Mark were the testimony of men personally involved with their Master. Enemies of God might some day try to challenge their testimony, as a pack of slanted lies, or twisted nostalgia.

Luke had set out from the beginning to do an objective, factual history of Jesus. He was a born reporter, a scientific research man, who responded to case histories and orderly facts. Faith, gift of God, had come to him in Antioch. But facts, incontrovertible, shining with truth, he had gathered everywhere he went, his gift to a dubious world. He had interviewed everyone who ever knew Him, beginning with His mother.

Years ago, Luke had gone to see Mary in Jerusalem, in the house where she lived in the care of John the Beloved. He had found her in an apron, sweeping the rough kitchen floor and singing. For weeks he had stayed in Jerusalem, seeing her daily during the few hours when she was not in ecstatic prayer or working with the other Christian women, tending the domestic chores of the apostles and the hundreds of converts and suffering needy.

At the request of Peter and John, she had answered all of Luke's questions. Her modesty, her humility astounded the young physician. Joy flared in her face when she spoke of her Son, but she felt real pain at talking of her own role in the divine mystery. She spoke of herself haltingly, begging his promise not to reveal a word while she lived. Luke, with all his professional knowledge of human weakness, had never known such a woman, so alive, so serenely happy in spite of death and persecution around her, so wise, so humble. He could not shake off her spell. For years he had waited impatiently for the day when he could tell of her. Two things had stood in his way: the lack of time while he traipsed the roads of Asia with Paul, and the long life of the most modest woman he had ever met, Mary, the mother of Jesus.

But now Mary was dead. Word had just come by messenger that Peter had reached Jerusalem only in time to bid her good-by. And with tears in his eyes, Luke at last began to write.

From the pen of a medical man to whom deceit was a stranger, the world would hear the truth about Mary and her Son. From Luke, the first scientific Christian, the first Christian reporter, came the fullest story of the woman who spoke to an angel, and conceived a Child by the Holy Ghost, the story of the virgin birth.

By his side on the desk lay his notes, carefully salvaged from shipwreck and storm, records of interviews, copies of Temple documents, genealogies, signed testimony of soldiers and maidservants, disciples and enemies, all lined up in chronological order.

As he read the scraps of papyrus, he could hear in his mind the graceful tones of the woman who had cradled Jesus in her arms; the little motherly things she told Luke, of shepherds abiding in the fields, and the heavenly host praising God over Bethlehem, of the Christ as a Baby, of a runaway Boy at Passover. And, respecting even after her death her urgent desire for self-effacement, Luke reported only those facts that were absolutely necessary for his tale of the Redeemer.

Tall and gaunt, obsessed by his task, Luke sat in the corner by the window and wrote the opening words of his Gospel:

"Forasmuch as many have taken in hand to set forth a narration of the things that have been accomplished amongst us, according as they have delivered them to us who from the beginning were eyewitnesses and ministers of the word: it seemed good to me also, having diligently attained to all things from the beginning, to write to you in order, most excellent lover of God, that you may know the truth of those words in which you have been instructed. . . ."

Directly across from Luke sat Paul, the prisoner.

Quite aside from his tears for the passing of Mary, he had every reason to be unhappy. A kind of claustrophobia filled him, a horror of confinement, a wild longing for freedom and aloneness.

The adventurer for Christ, world traveler with restless feet and tireless heart, could not help fretting at a desk job. And like all men in love with Christ, he yearned to be alone with Him, and with his own soul. In his hired room Paul could never be alone, even in the quiet of night, nor ever escape the demands men made on his wisdom and counsel.

But he had no intention of letting himself be unhappy. Age rode heavily on him, pressing wrinkles into his fever-marked face. The long voyage, the shipwreck had sapped his strength. But they had fed his faith.

When a man is forced to rest from his chosen work, his eyes rise to explore the horizon beyond his daily problems. With new perspective Paul looked around him, past the niggling jealousies of certain groups of Christians, past the doctrinal difficulties of others, past prison, hatred, and sin, to the Church of all time.

And what he saw he called *the body of Christ*.

There was a phrase that men would stumble over for centuries.

But for Paul it was a picture-thought, a deep truth encompassing the grandeur of life with Christ. And for many who came to him with their problems, it meant a practical rule of thumb to guide the mind and heart.

For a slave it was to mean freedom. And for a priest named Epaphras, it became a weapon against the devil.

Chapter 91.   THRONES AND POWERS

EPAPHRAS had been so fired by Christianity that he had, with Paul's permission, singlehandedly established a church in his home town of Colossae, in Phrygia.

Phrygia was a land breeding trouble. In that part of what we call Turkey, the earth rumbled and quaked and ravines and canyons ripped through barren hills. Men in Phrygia, peering down the sulphurous craters in the earth, spoke of demons and lower spirits. They stared at the yellow skies, and peopled the heaven with higher spirits, strange beings called Thrones and Powers, Dominions and Principalities. Now, in that strange Phrygia, where men's minds played with fantastic thoughts and strange religions, a new heresy had been born—an incredible roundabout way of denying God and excusing evil!

Men of Colossae, indeed those all over Phrygia, were quite proud of their new theory.

They had decided that this was such a messy world that it was an insult to accuse God of having created it. They called it true humility to say that God had nothing to do with us at all.

The world, they were saying, was made by various kinds of angels—thrones, powers, dominions, and principalities—who were nowhere near as perfect as God. We should worship these angels because they are powerful and we must appease them.

But because the angels who made us were not perfect, they went on, we cannot possibly ever be perfect. And if we cannot ever expect to achieve perfection, why try? We should humbly admit that we are so terrible that God does not care about us, and then proceed to live happy, and imperfect, lives.

As for Jesus Christ, said the men of Phrygia, He ranks with the angels, not with whatever far-off highbrow God there may be.

Epaphras shrugged.

"Nothing I can say can answer this. My word is not strong enough. Even so-called Christians are going around bowing down to these angels and then running off to do whatever they like. They say that they are made with base instincts and should not fight them.

"Paul, I know you never like to interfere in a church which you did not establish. But if I ask you, could you write them a letter, and tell them the truth?"

For Epaphras, Paul did write that letter, dictating it to Timothy, that gentle friend, who had hurried on the arduous overland route from Judaea to join him. And in that letter, Paul set down for the first time the doctrine of the mystical body of Christ.

For in Him were all things created in heaven and on earth, visible and invisible—whether thrones, or dominions, or principalities, or powers— all things were created by Him, and in Him. And He is before all, and by Him all things consist. And He is the head of the body, the Church . . . because in Him it has well pleased the Father that all fullness should dwell. . . .

Beware lest any man cheat you by philosophy and vain deceit—according to the tradition of men, according to the elements of the world, and not according to Christ! For in Him dwells all the fullness of the Godhead corporeally.

And you are filled with Him, who is the head of all principality and power. In Him you also are circumcised with circumcision not made by hand in dispoiling of the body of the flesh, but in the circumcision of Christ. Buried with Him in baptism, in Him also you are risen again by the faith of the operation of God who has raised Him up from the dead. . . .

Let no man seduce you, willing in humility, and the religion of angels, walking in the things which he has not seen, in vain puffed up by the sense of his flesh—and not holding the Head, from which the whole

body, by joints and bands, being supplied with nourishment and com-
pacted, groweth into the increase of God! . . .

But above all these things have charity, which is the bond of perfection,
and let the peace of Christ rejoice in your hearts, wherein also you are
called in one body—and be thankful.

For more than an hour Paul dictated. The room was absolutely still.
Even Luke, who could close his ears at will to the loudest argument,
had put down his pen to listen to that calm, sure voice.

The three men, Luke, Timothy, and Epaphras, who first heard
these words, felt the shiver of fresh truth up their spines. This was
not a new doctrine. It had all been said before, by the Lord Himself,
in different words. There can be no new doctrine in Christianity, only
a new way of showing forth the Truth. God is not altered by what
men say about Him, any more than water was changed when man
finally learned to call it a mixture of hydrogen and oxygen.

But a world can be changed when God shows man a new way to
see Him.

Paul was writing to the people of a small town called Colossae, but
his words would be read by uncounted generations, and slowly their
world would be changed.

Even as at that very moment the world began to change for a slave
from that same town. A slave who was called Onesimus, a name which
meant "profitable."

Chapter 92. THE RUNAWAY

ONESIMUS had been leading a most unprofitable life. Like all other
slaves, he was a man without a single legal right. He could own nothing. Nothing anyone did to him was against the law. He was not even
allowed to have a religion of his own; on special occasions his masters
might permit him to offer sacrifice to the lesser gods of farming and
of animals.

The Empire was overrun with slaves; wealthy men commonly
owned as many as a thousand, and even the poorest freeman had at
least one. Rome was built on the tops of seven hills, and on the backs
of seven million slaves. Christians naturally abhorred the idea of
slavery, but the apostles knew better than to try to overturn a social

system by force. The slaves themselves needed preparation for freedom, needed education and a new face to turn to the world. The Jews in Rome, who had once been slaves, knew well the prejudice against freedmen, and the wretched poverty that awaited them. And who cared to court violence from Nero and the senate by campaigning for abolition before either slaves or masters were ready?

Most converts kept their slaves, at least in name. Outwardly the household was as before. But on Sundays the master and his wife and children knelt side by side with their servants, in the equality of Holy Communion. And a slave who accepted Christ belonged to Him, not to any man; he could set out on his own whenever he wished.

Onesimus, the Profitable, had been lucky. His master was Philemon, a Christian in the town of Colossae, a convert and friend of Paul. He treated his slaves as human beings with rights and souls. His own son, Archippus, was a priest.

But Onesimus was not a Christian. He was wary of a religion that crossed social boundaries. Somewhere in the pious words of young Archippus he smelled a trap; talk about love and kindness to your fellow man made him nervous. He did not dare believe it, and so he let anger and hatred seethe inside him. He told the other slaves that baptism was a humiliation even he could not stand.

Onesimus waited his chance, broke into his master's coffers, robbed him, and ran away to Rome.

He was in real danger. Even if Philemon made no move to set the law on him, anyone at all had the right to accost him, demand his credentials, and arrest him as a runaway slave. By law he would then be branded on the forehead, and perhaps flogged to death.

Desperately Onesimus tried to lose himself in the Roman underworld, rough terrain for a naïve country lad. Women with mascaraed eyes and silken tunics, the smooth jugs of wine his stolen coins could buy, the brass bands of the priests of Isis, the trances of Syrian prophets, sent his head spinning. And all the while his heart chanted an exultant refrain of freedom!

He lived nowhere, slept in taverns and in the rooms of strange women from every land or in the fountained courtyards of some disreputable inn. He lived for the ripe, sultry Roman night, tagging along with the crowds on their way to Nero's public entertainments. He had never known there were so many kinds of sin, and he tried them all.

He woke one morning near noon with a headache. His mouth tasted like the stench of the streets. His purse sagged nearly empty beside him. And the song of his heart was still.

He wanted to wash his face in clear water, to wrap himself in a clean tunic, and run till he forgot the greedy eyes and pale face and wine-soured breath of Rome.

How does a man escape from stolen freedom? There is no place else to run away. Where can he go, who is neither slave nor free?

He lay among the swept-up refuse in a corner of the street. Two men stepped into the shadow of the corner and spoke in undertones. Onesimus squinted from under his lashes, and covered his face quickly. One of the men looked like a Roman, the other had the dark hair and accent of Judaea. They had not noticed him in his camouflage of dirt and orange peels and broken jugs.

"Which way to Paul's lodging?" asked one.

The stranger whispered the address.

"Peace be with you!"

"And with you."

The Christian salutation! Could the Paul they spoke of be the apostle?

Onesimus winced as the two men left. For long minutes he lay in the fly-buzzing heat, his eyes still closed.

Slowly he climbed to his feet and shook off the clinging rubbish. He washed his face in the lukewarm fountain pool in the square. He slapped at his tunic and smoothed his hair with wet hands.

Then slowly, painfully, he picked his way through the streets to the address the stranger had given, the lodging of his master's closest friend.

He walked into the silence that had fallen when Paul paused in his Epistle to the Colossians.

The slave stood uncertainly in the entrance. Then he blinked, and stared in terrified recognition at Epaphras. How often he had seen that man at Philemon's house!

Onesimus turned on his bare heel to flee down the stairs. With a lunge, Epaphras was out of his seat and after him.

"Onesimus! Come here! What has happened to you?"

The young man tried to pull away, but he was weak with hunger and the headache of bad wine. He stumbled back under Epaphras' grasp, sobbing. Epaphras spoke to him gently.

"My friend, I know that you have run away. But that is not why I called you back. You are sick, too sick to walk the streets. Besides, you came here for a purpose. Do not leave till you have accomplished it."

Onesimus stood uncertainly in the center of the room, swaying a bit from the unexpected blow of kindness.

"I came to see Paul. To tell him about me. And ask him what to do."

Paul knew him at once. Often Onesimus had delivered letters from Philemon, and run errands for Paul as well. Paul held out his hands in silent greeting. Only his eyes asked: "What has happened to you, Onesimus?"

Luke had been studying the visitor closely. He pushed back his curling papyrus and went to his neat shelves to mix up a dose of medicine for him and make a cold pack for his head. But the lad refused them, shamefaced. He was a prodigal son seeking a father, and he dared not delay.

On his knees he told Paul his story, stumbling at first, slowly finding the words he needed, buoyed by the kindness of his listener. And then and there, kneeling, he received the greatest gift of all, the treasure that cannot be stolen, the treasure of faith.

Paul began that afternoon to teach Onesimus the faith of Christians. For three days Onesimus ate and slept in that room, while the apostle told him of the Two Ways—the way of life, through Christ, and the way of death, through sin. And the slave listened with intelligent eyes and a smile of wondering excitement.

On the fourth day Onesimus said:

"May I be baptized?"

Paul looked deep into the young man's eyes. "And what of Philemon? You have stolen from him two things—your service, and his money. You can never return the gold you have squandered. But you must return yourself. As a slave."

Onesimus' face flushed. He turned from Paul.

"No!"

He strode back and forth in the tiny room like a lion in an arena cage, silent with anger. He whirled, and flung himself at Paul's feet.

"If what you say is true, why should I? I'll go back, but not as a slave! I'll work the rest of my life and give the money all to Philemon. I'll do anything, but how can there be slaves in a world where men have One Father? How can there be slave and free in a Christian world?"

The Roman guard had been whittling a tragedy mask out of citron wood, disdaining to seem to eavesdrop on the conversation. He was not one of Paul's many jailer converts. Now he looked up sideways at Paul, waiting for the answer. People were beginning to call Christians anarchists, dangerous to the old forms of government. A false answer from his prisoner, properly reported, might mean a promotion, and a bit of gold too.

Paul rested his hands on Onesimus' blond head and sighed.

"There is neither bond nor free. For we are all one in Christ Jesus. In Him is the only freedom."

Paul drew back his hands.

"See, I am in chains. I cannot leave this room. I cannot earn my own living. At any time, Caesar may be ready to hear me, may decide against me, and order me to death. But in chains or out, I am still free.

"The Lord Himself was put to death by men who assumed power over Him. But He was free. He suffered them gladly, and forgave them. Freedom has nothing to do with this world. Freedom lies in your heart.

"Luke has told you how Christ Jesus said: 'If any man ask of you your cloak, give him your coat also.' In giving, in loving only can you be free; and when you love Jesus, you are free no matter where you are, or what men call you."

The young rebel stared up at Paul. He saw a bold man in chains, a free man, who chose to become a slave to the Master.

But Onesimus looked away. Unconsciously his callused hands went to his forehead, fingering the spot where runaways were branded. He turned away from Paul.

"I should like to take a walk. My head aches."

"Go in peace."

The footsteps of Onesimus died away down the stairs to the street. The guard stared boldly at his prisoner, as Luke snorted, "Farewell, Onesimus!"

Paul glanced over at Timothy, who sat brooding over the motley street scene from the window.

"Timothy—we must write a letter to Philemon, and have it ready for Onesimus to take with him."

"Ha! You'll never see that mongrel again." The guard spat luxuriously on the freshly scrubbed floor.

Paul puckered his pale lips, and nodded to Timothy who had already taken up his pen.

Paul, a prisoner of Christ Jesus—and Timothy, a brother—to Philemon, our beloved and fellow laborer.

He tipped back his chair, and ran his fingers on either side of his long nose. He looked up at the simple wooden cross Priscilla had hung on the wall, symbol of the Master whose love made Him a slave, the Prisoner who was King. Paul's thoughts winged back through the years to the day he had baptized Philemon, as he had now baptized Onesimus. Slaveowner and robber-rebel, both had so much to learn from that cross! Toward both men, Paul yearned like a father loath to command his grown sons, yet impatient lest they choose wrongly.

He cleared his throat, and scratched his ear. His only chance with Philemon lay in dovelike words and serpentine wisdom—and love. With a smile he began to dictate the friendliest blackmail letter in history:

Though I have much confidence in Christ Jesus to command thee that which is to the purpose; for charity's sake I rather beseech . . . as Paul, an old man, and now a prisoner also of Jesus Christ.

I beseech thee for my son, whom I have begotten in my bands—Onesimus!

Paul chuckled to himself. How bitter Philemon must find that name Onesimus—the profitable! With a twinkle in his eye, he bent over Timothy's shoulder and launched one of the few puns in the Bible.

Onesimus—who had been heretofore unprofitable to thee, but now is *profitable* both to me and thee, whom I have sent back to thee . . . whom I would have retained with me, that in thy stead he might have ministered to me in the bands of the Gospel. But without thy counsel I would do nothing, that thy good deed might not be as it were of necessity, but voluntary.

For perhaps he therefore departed for a season from thee that thou might receive him again for ever, not now as a servant, but instead of a servant a most dear brother. . . . If therefore thou count me as a partner, receive him as myself. And if he has wronged thee in anything, or is in thy debt, put that to my account.

Paul stooped and took the quill from Timothy. Carefully, squinting at his own large letters, he wrote:

I, Paul, have written it with my own hand: I will repay it! (Not to say to thee that thou owe me thy own self, also.) Yea, brother. May I enjoy thee in the Lord. Trusting in thy obedience, I have written to thee, knowing that thou wilt also do more than I say.

Timothy looked up at Paul and winked.

"Your 'beseeching' is a lot stronger than your 'command,' Paul!"

"A fine letter," said Epaphras, "but you can never send it. Onesimus is gone for good."

The echo of footsteps on the stairs silenced him. Everyone turned to stare at the door, except Paul, whose eyes were on the cross.

"Paul?"

"Welcome back, Onesimus. Timothy has a letter for you to take to Philemon, if you are going in that direction."

"I am going, Paul."

Chapter 93. OF WOMEN AND ARMOR

THREE women slipped silently into the room, bearing a steaming kettle of stew and two small wicker baskets of fruit for the evening meal. As usual, in the lead was Priscilla, one of the hardest-working women of all time. She ran her own household. She organized the young maidens and the widows of Rome into units for nursing the sick and tending the domestic wants of the several hundred priests in the city. She helped teach catechism to the children and to women, and assisted at their baptism.

Priscilla did more than the housewifely duties of the young church. She used her mind, and spoke it discreetly. She acted as a liaison between Paul and the vigorously active feminine element of the new Church.

At the moment she was having her problems. Christians everywhere were beginning to call Paul a woman-hater. They said he despised females, and was forever telling them to keep silence and cover their heads, wear drab clothes, and obey their husbands. In vain Priscilla reminded them that Peter said the same thing, and said it first. Paul's voice was louder at the moment, and as tactless as a donkey's bray. He was making himself very unpopular with the women.

Finally, Priscilla told him how things stood. Paul smiled and buried his chin on his chest. Tact was an art he would spend his life trying to learn! Apparently the ladies did not understand what he took for granted, their tremendous role in the new order. He had promised Priscilla to explain publicly in an epistle once and for all what he thought of womankind.

As he glanced up now to welcome Priscilla and her aides, Paul remembered that promise, and it seemed that the time was at hand. That morning he had finished off the letter to the Colossians, about the invisible body of Christ and the problem of the thrones and powers. But he was already troubled about that letter.

His fingers toyed with the curling edges of the papyrus and his thoughts wandered back to another letter, the one to the Galatians. Then, too, he had been writing to an individual church about its own special problem. But the letter had been read by hundreds of other churches with slightly different problems, and it had been terribly misunderstood. With a grimace Paul recalled the resulting bitter controversy over it, which ended only when he wrote a fuller statement of his teachings in the Epistle to the Romans.

Would there be such misunderstanding now? Would his letter to the Colossians twist another storm to shake the young church? He shook his head and knew he could not run the risk. He would send the letter to Colossae, and another at the same time to all the churches of Asia Minor, with a complete explanation of this idea of the body of Christ.

He sighed without hearing himself, this old man whose wrists burned from the chafing bands and whose soul hungered for rest and quiet.

And who should carry this one? Not Epaphras, for he had business to transact in Rome and could not leave for another week. Onesimus could go no further than his master's house in Colossae. Who was in town from the churches of Asia?

Paul's eyes flicked over to his guests. "Do you remember when I came to visit Philemon long ago there was with me a man from Ephesus named Tychicus? Philemon knows him, and will trust him. He shall go to Colossae with you, Onesimus, and then—I must write a letter for him to bring to Ephesus, and all the other churches of Asia!"

Paul ate hastily and sparingly. For the first time he urged Priscilla and the other two women to remain after the evening meal.

Timothy sat with an oil lamp on the desk, ready to write. Luke, his day's stint done, relaxed across from him. Onesimus sat tailor-fashion on the floor with Epaphras, and the women seemed hidden in the flickering shadows of a corner. The Praetorian Guard in full regalia lounged on Paul's cot. His eyelids drooped over drink-reddened cheeks.

Before that strange audience Paul began to speak, as Timothy's pen scratched quickly on the fresh sheet of papyrus. The old voice was low-pitched in the September heat, cutting under street noises and the hum of green-winged insects in the room. In his soft, clear tones sounded a hymn of praise to God the Father, and to the Lord Jesus Christ whom the Father placed:

above all principality, and power, and virtue, and dominion, and every name that is named, not only in this world but also in that which is to come. And He has subjected all things under His feet, and has made Him head over all the Church, which is His body, and the fullness of Him who is filled all in all. . . .

God, (who is rich in mercy) for His exceeding charity wherewith He loved us even when we were dead in sins, hath quickened us together in Christ, (by whose grace you are saved) and hath raised us up together, and hath made us sit together in the heavenly places through Christ Jesus. For by grace you are saved through faith, and that not of yourselves, for it is the gift of God.

No longer were the Jews the only chosen people. No longer did the Gentiles stand apart as aliens—

. . . strangers to the testament, having no hope of the promise, and without God in this world. For He is our peace, who hath made both one, and breaking down the middle wall of partition, the enmities in His flesh . . . that He might make the two in Himself into one new man.

The weary voice rolled on as simply as the sea, pleading with men to remember that all good comes from Christ, beseeching them to walk worthily in their new honor as members of His body—

. . . careful to keep the unity of the Spirit in the bond of peace, one body and one spirit, one Lord, one faith, one baptism, one God and Father of all, who is above all, and through all, and in us all. . . .

Be ye therefore followers of God, as most dear children, and walk in love. . . . But fornication and all uncleanness—

Paul's eyes sped in mute apology to the cross on the wall, as he named the sins that dog Christians then and now—fornication, adultery, obscenity, gossip, murder, scurrility, drunkenness, bitterness, anger, and malice.

He paused and looked around, savoring a moment's suspense. The Roman soldier was drowsing. But everyone else was alertly watching Paul. From the corner where the three women sat he seemed to hear the floorboards creaking with expectancy.

Let women be subject to their husbands as to the Lord. Because the husband is the head of the wife, as Christ is the head of the Church. He is the Saviour of His body. Therefore, as the Church is subject to Christ, so also let the wives be to their husbands in all things.

Husbands—love your wives, as Christ loved the Church, and delivered Himself up for it, that He might sanctify it, cleansing it by the laver of water in the word of life. That He might present it to Himself a glorious Church, not having spot or wrinkle, or any such thing, but that it should be holy and without blemish.

So also ought men to love their wives as their own bodies. He that loveth his wife, loveth himself. For no man ever hateth his own flesh, but nourishes and cherishes it, as also Christ does the Church. Because we are members of His body, of His flesh, and of His bones.

For this cause shall a man leave his father and mother, and shall cleave to his wife, and they shall be two in one flesh. This is a great sacrament.

Priscilla and her friends looked at each other in wonder. A wife and a husband—the Church and the Christ! The comparison was almost unbearable in its majesty. The words of Jesus, quoted by the apostles, surged through their minds . . . "the bridegroom cometh!"

Before Christ, marriage had been a holy union; now it was also a great sacrament, symbol of the mystery of the love of Christ for the

Church. The women looked up at Paul with wonder, and humility in their eyes, too stunned to speak.

But Paul was already passing on to other things, to the duties of children and parents, and, with an eye on Onesimus, the duties of servants and masters. He was nearly through the letter when he was interrupted by a rasping, snuffling snore.

The pride of the Praetorian Guard was asleep.

Paul smiled. He studied the full-bellied man sprawled on the cot, saw the armor, the breastplate, the boots, saw the shield and sword and helmet lying discarded on the floor. He gestured to Timothy to write as he dictated:

Finally, brethren, be strengthened in the Lord, and in the might of His power.

Put you on the armor of God, that you may be able to . . . resist in the evil day, and to stand in all things perfect. . . .

Stand therefore having your loins girt about with truth, and having on the breastplate of justice, and your feet shod with the preparation of the gospel of peace—in all things taking the shield of faith, wherewith you may be able to extinguish all the fiery darts of the most wicked one. And take unto you the helmet of salvation, and the sword of the Spirit (which is the word of God).

A fly buzzed over the sleeping man.

He stirred and rippled his lips as Paul finished up the letter. Gasping and snorting, he flung himself sideways to escape the attentions of the fly.

An instant later he was fully awake, sitting on the floor nursing a bruised head. His helmet wobbled in protest beside him.

No one laughed. Aristarchus helped him to his feet. Luke went over to examine his skull.

And Paul said, and Timothy wrote:

Grace be with all them that love our Lord Jesus Christ in incorruption.
Amen.

Chapter 94. A LETTER HOME

WINTER lodged in the very walls of the house. A brazier of coal glowed orange and gray in the center of the room. Below the window men sludged through muddy streets, cloaks wrapped high against the sepulchral air. That new year in Rome, A.D. 62, brought dark ice to the River Tiber where worshipers of the Egyptian goddess Isis walked with bleeding bare feet, and a chill to the hearts of sober citizens concerned for the Empire.

Nero was on a rampage.

As a boy he had been content for his two guardians, Seneca and Burrus, to tend the affairs of state, while he toyed with his lute and his harp and strutted through his days of luxury. But with Poppaea reclining at his side, Nero had begun to grow in his own esteem. He had come to believe Poppaea's insinuations that Seneca and Burrus were deliberately keeping power in their own hands because they feared to let the world know the full magnificence of his genius. Nero was certain that no more perfect emperor ever lived.

For a while, with petulant shrugs and winks at the full-lipped Poppaea, he had simply ignored his guardians' advice. He made decisions without consulting them. Still, men of Rome had felt safe, knowing that Seneca and Burrus stood by, ready to check any rash errors.

But suddenly—where was Burrus? The burly chief of the Praetorian Guard had vanished without a trace save for the rumors rippling ominously through the city: Burrus was murdered by order of Nero!

Paul's room, crowded always with students and disciples, opened now to men with despair on their faces, who foresaw the destruction of an empire. Rome the Magnificent had fallen into the hands of an overweening idiot.

"His poetry is conceited. His songs are abominable. He threatened to execute the musician who dared criticize his voice. He murdered Burrus—and his own mother. He is insane, possessed of a devil, ridden with every vice. His mistress is satanic. What will happen to Rome now?"

"What can a man hold on to in a world like this?" they asked Paul. And many of these men found their answer in baptism and Christ.

The daily shift of soldiers in Paul's lodgings muttered and grumbled fearfully about their chief's disappearance. Already word had come that he would be replaced by two men. Nero was splitting the command, whittling the power of his subordinates. Tigellinus, brute-jawed court favorite, and Fennius Rufus, a well-meaning weakling, were to run the Praetorian Guard.

"If Tigellinus takes your case, have a care, Paul of Tarsus. He'd have you in the cells of the Mamertine inside an hour, laws or no laws. He kills first, and asks later!"

Paul thanked his guard for the warning, but he betrayed no fear of Tigellinus. His eyes rested on Luke, busy now with a new book written from the daily notes he had kept throughout the years. That history of the Church since the Resurrection, is today called The Acts of the Apostles. The Gospel According to Luke was finished. Already dedicated men were making copies for church libraries across the Empire.

In the far corner was Timothy, his brown head bent earnestly as he talked to two freedmen from the palace who came seeking word of the King of Kings.

At Paul's feet squatted Aristarchus, rubbing his hands above the brazier, and talking in eager anger.

"You would think there were two kinds of Christians—Jewish ones and Gentile ones! Just because you have baptized so many in Rome, and really accomplished something, the Jewish preachers are scrambling head over heels to make more Christians than you do. You'd think this was an arena contest between Jewish Christians—and you!"

Paul rubbed his own Jewish nose wryly.

"Am I no longer a Jew then? What does it matter so long as souls are brought to Christ? When Peter comes back he will tell them again that we are all one in Christ, for God is no respecter of persons. And Peter will rejoice to see such an army of Christians, both those I have taught and those the others have taught."

The others! Paul looked down into the charcoal flames, and past the flames to the days when he was a Jew among Jews. Nostalgia throbbed through him, a bleak need for old friends and ways, for the simple comfort of speaking his native tongue. Twenty odd years now he had spoken Greek and Latin; filled with the Holy Ghost he had on occasion spoken in "the tongues of many men," but seldom in Hebrew. For what Jew would listen to him? Always he had taken his burning message of faith "to the Jews first"—and always as a group they had rejected him. Though he was surrounded by friends—faithful, true, beloved—most of them were Gentiles.

He was a man without a people, refused by the Jews, but neither was he a Gentile—an exile, an apostle. For the sake of Christ he had given up mother tongue and brotherly ties, left his old home, abandoned his old self. All this he had done gladly, proudly. Yet memories plagued him. He hungered for the loving smile on a Jewish face, for the taste of welcome in familiar surroundings.

Perhaps, if he tried once more, he could break down the barrier between himself and the race he loved?

The news from Jerusalem was disturbing. James and the Church were meeting with little success. There were few Jewish converts, and those few were under constant pressure and boycott from their fellows. Paul knew that treatment well, and he sorrowed for them.

Travelers stopping to see Paul told of growing currents of revolution in Judaea, a movement to challenge the power of Rome. Paul needed no gift of prophecy to foresee the outcome of that revolution. Jerusalem would soon lie desolate, and the Temple in ruins, even as Jesus had said!

Why was James having such a hard time persuading the Jews that Jesus was the Messiah? James, after all, was a cousin of His, a blood relation. He was a good talker, an able mind, a ritualist who adhered to the beloved old customs of his own people, as Jesus had, and an ardent Christian. Surely if anyone could convince the Jews it would be James, unless something, or someone, was working against him.

Paul leaped to his feet. Could he himself be the stumbling block for James? Paul's words were so often misquoted, misunderstood. Perhaps the men of Judaea had heard deliberately garbled stories of what Paul was saying; perhaps they thought he meant there was no room for them in a Gentile religion.

Converts in Jerusalem were being called "traitors," disloyal to the cause of their own nation. Paul knew all too keenly the sharp stab of that charge, and the difficulty of explaining that loyalty to Christ meant no disloyalty to country, or race, or family, or friends. Thunder clouds gathered over Jerusalem. Could the little band of converts stand firm?

His body trembled with the earnestness of his prayer. He fell to his knees before the cross. *Oh God, help me to help the men of my own blood. Let them hear me when I speak Your truth. I love them. I want to bring them to You.*

The light of the brazier flickered on his head as he knelt, oblivious of the tears standing in the eyes of his friends.

Timothy sharpened his quill with pumice stone, smoothed a sheet of papyrus, and waited. Paul was usually slow at dictation, taking minutes to choose the precise words to clothe his thoughts, stopping for hours to condense the statement of the doctrine. Timothy was ready for a leisurely bit of dictation, in Greek, of course.

Paul settled on a stool, wrapped his arms around his knees, and began to speak—in Hebrew.

A smile softened the little, wrinkled face of the apostle as his tongue fell gratefully into the idiom of his childhood. He spoke as a rabbi, a teacher in love with a familiar topic. No need to weigh his words. No need to plot the structure of this letter. Paul was writing to the men of his homeland, telling them all that was in his heart.

God, who at sundry times and in divers manners, spoke in times past to the fathers by the prophets, last of all in these days has spoken to us by His Son—whom He appointed heir of all things, by Whom also He made the world.

So Paul plunged into his Epistle to the Hebrews. And Timothy, son of a Jewish mother and a pagan father, happily scribbling in his boyhood tongue, had hard work keeping up with the flow of words.

Paul began by stating his premise: the Son of God had been here on earth and had spoken to men.

He knew his Hebrew readers' every reaction. In his mind he kept a running dialogue with the long gray beards of the Sanhedrin, the expert theologians. He answered each argument he knew they would raise.

They would say: this Man from Nazareth was just another prophet. Why honor Him?

And Paul would remind them that they already honored the angels, and yet—

. . . to which of the angels has He said at any time, "Thou art My Son, and this day have I begotten Thee"? . . . To which of the angels said He at any time, "Sit on My right hand, until I make Thy enemies Thy footstool"?

The Roman guard blinked and scratched his head. His prisoner had spoken Greek and Latin with the polish of a world traveler. Yet this same man, hunched on the stool, was talking the language of the rich Jewish merchants of the city. The soldier understood little Hebrew, but he knew well the familiar gestures Paul was using—the shrug of the shoulders, the upturned palms, the raised eyebrows, as question followed question.

Paul threw back his head and laughed in sheer exhilaration at finding himself using phrases half forgotten, echoes of the days when he studied under Rabbi Gamaliel. And Luke, who had mastered the Jewish language in his youth, put away all thought of medicines and herb brews for his patient, and listened.

The apostle hugged his knees under his chin, and went on:

Therefore ought we more diligently to observe the things which we have heard, lest perhaps we should let them slip. For if the word spoken by angels became steadfast, and every transgression and disobedience received a just recompense of reward—how shall we escape, if we neglect so great salvation? . . .

Take heed, brethren, lest perhaps there be in any of you an evil heart of unbelief, to depart from the living God.

Do you balk at throwing over the old Law of Moses to embrace Christ? (So ran Paul's argument.) But Christ is come not to destroy the Law but to fulfill it. The Ten Commandments still stand. But you are freed from the burden of the thousand tiny Laws of Moses. They were designed to help lead man to God, and now they are replaced by the love of Christ, and the greatest spiritual bulwark of all time—the all-powerful, all-saving Holy Eucharist. The old covenant, the clutter of the old rituals are gone—replaced by the life and freedom of the New Testament. Did you expect a Messiah would not bring some changes into the world?

Consider the texts of Scripture and the Prophets on which you and I were raised, said Paul. See where David sings of a new kind of priesthood to come, according to the order of Melchisedech. Search the texts! You will see that Christ Jesus is the high priest of a New Testament, a new covenant between God and man.

Paul reminded them of the words of Jeremiah the prophet who said:

"Behold the days shall come, saith the Lord, and I will perfect unto the house of Israel and unto the house of Juda a New Testament."

He paused until Timothy finished the quotation he had rattled off so familiarly, then went on in his own words:

Now, in saying a "new," He has made the former "old." And that which decays and grows old is near its end. The former indeed had also justifications of divine service, and a worldly sanctuary. For there was a tabernacle made the first, wherein were the candlesticks, and the table, and . . .

Paul's voice softened as in his mind he saw again the tabernacle where he had worshiped in his youth, with the shewbread, the golden censer, the ark of the covenant, the rod of Aaron—and beyond that the Holy of Holies, where only the high priest might go once a year—and the sacrifices, the cleansing rituals.

But Christ, being come an high priest of the good things to come, by a greater and more perfect tabernacle not made by hand . . . neither by the blood of goats or of calves, but by His own blood, entered once into the holies, having obtained eternal redemption. . . . For Jesus is not entered into the holies made with hands, . . . but into heaven itself! That He may appear now in the presence of God for us. . . .

A man making void the Law of Moses dies without mercy under two or three witnesses. How much more do you think he deserves worse punishments who has trodden under foot the Son of God?

Paul closed his eyes. Logic never yet saved a soul, and Paul knew it. Logic and reason were bulwarks to faith, but they could not spark the soul to belief. But how does a man tell another man about faith?

How does a man tell of the love that is in his heart, or the faith in his soul, without crushing it in words? *Holy Spirit, tell me how to say it!*

Now, faith is the substance of things hoped for, the evidence of things not seen.

He suddenly stood and began to pace the room, face shining.

Through faith we understand that the worlds were framed by the word of God, so that things which are seen were not made of things which do appear.

By faith Abel offered unto God a more excellent sacrifice than Cain, by which he obtained witness that he was righteous, God testifying of his gifts: and by it he being dead yet speaketh. . . . But without faith it is impossible to please Him; for he that cometh to God must believe that He is, and that He is a rewarder of them that diligently seek Him. . . .

By faith Abraham, when he was called to go out into a place which he should after receive for an inheritance, obeyed; and he went out, not knowing whither he went. . . . Through faith also Sarah herself received strength to conceive seed, and was delivered of a child when she was past age, because she judged Him faithful who had promised. . . .

These all died in faith, not having received the promises, but having seen them afar off, and were persuaded of them, and embraced them, and confessed that they were strangers and pilgrims on the earth. . . .

By faith Moses, when he was born, was hid three months of his parents, because they saw he was a proper child; and they were not afraid of the king's commandment. By faith Moses, when he was come to years, refused to be called the son of Pharaoh's daughter; choosing rather to suffer affliction with the people of God, than to enjoy the pleasures of sin for a season; esteeming the reproach of Christ greater riches than the treasures in Egypt: for he had respect unto the recompense of the reward. . . . By faith they passed through the Red Sea as by dry land; which the Egyptians assaying to do were drowned. . . .

And what shall I more say? for the time would fail me to tell of Gideon, and of Barak, and of Samson, and of Jephthah; of David also, and Samuel, and of the prophets, who through faith subdued kingdoms, wrought righteousness, obtained promises, stopped the mouths of lions, quenched the violence of fire, escaped the edge of the sword, out of weakness were made strong, waxed valiant in fight, turned to flight the armies of the aliens. Women received their dead raised to life again; and others were tortured, not accepting deliverance, that they might obtain a better resurrection; and others had trial of cruel mockings and scourgings, yea, moreover of bonds and imprisonment: they were stoned, they were sawn asunder, were tempted, were slain with the sword; they wandered about in sheepskins and goatskins, being destitute, afflicted, tormented (of whom the world was not worthy); they wandered in deserts, and in mountains, and in dens and caves of the earth.

And these all, having obtained a good report through faith, received not the promise; God having provided some better thing for us, that they without us should not be made perfect.

Wherefore seeing we also are compassed about with so great a cloud of witnesses, let us lay aside every weight, and the sin which doth so easily beset us, and let us run with patience the race that is set before us, looking unto Jesus the Author and Finisher of our faith; who for the joy that was set before Him endured the cross, despising the shame, and is set down at the right hand of the throne of God.

Paul sank down to the stool and drew a deep breath. His face was flushed; strands of white hair floated at angles to his forehead. Timothy put out a hand to steady him, but Paul waved him back to the desk. Timothy tested his pen and methodically picked up the pumice, with one eye cocked to see if Paul would rest, even to catch his breath.

But the old man drummed his fingers on his knee while his secretary so purposefully dawdled. Paul's mind had leaped to the painful thought of the persecution which the new Jewish converts were forced to share with him. Somehow, he must convince them that whatever we suffer on earth is a kind of discipline for the soul. Whom the Lord loveth, He chastiseth, and He scourgeth every son whom He receiveth!

God deals with you as with His sons—for what son is there, whom the father does not correct? If you be without chastisement, whereof all are made partakers, then are you bastards and not sons.

Paul's hands, weighed down by the punishing chains, lay at peace on his lap. He stared into the golden depths of the fire.

For ye are not come unto the mount that might be touched, and that burned with fire, nor unto blackness, and darkness, and tempest, and the sound of a trumpet, and the Voice of words; which Voice they that heard entreated that the word should not be spoken to them any more (for they could not endure that which was commanded). . . .

But ye are come unto mount Zion, and unto the city of the living God, the heavenly Jerusalem, and to an innumerable company of angels, to the general assembly and church of the firstborn, which are written in heaven, and to God the Judge of all, and to the spirits of just men made perfect, and to Jesus the Mediator of the new covenant, and to the blood of sprinkling, that speaketh better things than that of Abel.

See that ye refuse not Him that speaketh. For if they escaped not who refused Him that spake on earth, much more shall not we escape, if we turn away from Him that speaketh from heaven. . . . He hath promised, saying: "Yet once more I shake not the earth only, but also heaven." And this word, "Yet once more," signifieth the removing of those things that are shaken, as of things that are made, that those things which cannot be shaken may remain.

Wherefore we receiving a kingdom which cannot be moved, let us have grace, whereby we may serve God acceptably with reverence and godly fear:

For our God is a consuming fire.

Only the bitter rain and wind were heard in the room, and the faroff voices of men cursing mud and horses and a broken chariot wheel.

Paul's spirit was in Jerusalem, his heart with James and with the men to whom he felt flesh kinship. He remembered the words of Jesus as he had learned them, the desolate prophecy of ruin for the holy city. In that silent moment Paul longed to avert the destruction, to clench friends and enemies to his heart, and in love erase all misunderstanding.

Grace be with you all.

Amen.

Paul clasped his hands. He was suddenly tired—more bone-weary than he had been since the day he stood on the steps of the prison castle in Jerusalem to speak in the Hebrew tongue to the mob that clamored for his death.

Chapter 95.   GO IN PEACE!

THE only way Paul's letter could travel was in the fold of a traveler's cloak or in a donkey's saddle bag. The Epistle to the Hebrews went off in January, to travel the circuitous overland route to Jerusalem. Months would pass before it could end in the hands of James the Less; more than half a year before an answer might come.

But for the Emperor, mail sped in non-stop relays of man and horse and chariot. Across Asia Minor, through Greece to Rome, daily dispatches hastened from the governors in Palestine.

In the warm, leaping days of May in that same year came a courier from Judaea to the Palatine Hill, with a report to be scanned by Nero's officers. One of the Praetorian Guards, a clandestine Christian, read that bulletin. Inside an hour he was at Paul's side.

"James the Less is dead! He was tried by the high priest before the Sanhedrin, found guilty of blasphemy, and stoned to death."

Paul shrank back; his eyes clamped shut in horror. James stoned . . . as Stephen had been stoned, before Paul's never-forgetting eyes. Stoned to death.

He saw James clearly in his memory, that tall, spare cousin of Our Lord, austere, barefoot, the black hair never touched by shears hanging below his shoulders; in linen tunic and mantle, traditional garb

of the Jewish priesthood, the gold plate dangling round his neck
emblazoned with the "Holiness of Jehovah." James, whose aunt was
Mary the mother of Christ, whose whole life was bound in Him—
was slain.

"The dispatch referred to his death only in passing. But it added
one detail—a curiosity that made Tigellinus laugh loud." The guard
lowered his voice to a whisper. "When they examined James after
his death, they found his knees were as callused as a camel's. That's
the exact phrase they used. From praying, I suppose."

A shiver ran through Paul. Luke came to lay a practiced hand on
his brow, but Timothy motioned the physician away. The young
man's face was pale as he leaned over Paul. Instinctively Timothy
knew the horror that underlay the apostle's grief, and tenderly he
tried to push it away.

"Paul—you do not even know that your letter has yet reached
Jerusalem—"

The old prisoner's eyes flew open. Timothy went on:

"Christians do not ride in chariots, and it is a long walk from these
rooms to the Temple. It is probably still not there. You cannot
blame his death on your letter. Paul, listen to me! You had nothing
to do with it."

But Paul heard only the voice inside him.

*I held the cloaks when Stephen was stoned, and he prayed for me.
Who held the cloaks when James was murdered?*

*He was loved by the Jews in Jerusalem, admired and welcomed
even by those who thought him deluded about his Cousin. What
could make the high priest turn on him? What else but my letter?*

Paul went on his knees, and wept.

Six weeks later Christian Jews from Judaea dined with Paul. They
brought a letter to all the churches, written by James a few days
before his death.

These men had seen him die—stoned, then beaten with a club.
They who in the past had seen him kneel by the hour in the Temple
while other Jews stood, as always, to pray, had seen him kneel again
under the shower of stones and pray God to forgive his murderers,
as Stephen had done.

And Paul's epistle—had it reached Jerusalem? Paul spoke the question with difficulty.

His guests shook their heads. "We would not know. We only arrived there the day of the trial itself. This letter, from James, was smuggled out to us. We left hastily after the execution."

A wry grimace stole over Paul's face.

He held James's last letter and kissed it, and handed it to Timothy to read aloud.

James, a servant of God, and of our Lord Jesus Christ, to the twelve tribes which are scattered abroad, greeting!

My brethren, count it all joy when you shall fall into divers temptations, knowing that the trying of your faith worketh patience. And patience hath a perfect work, that you may be perfect and entire, failing in nothing.

But if any of you want wisdom, let him ask of God, who giveth to all men abundantly and upbraideth not. And it shall be given him.

Paul listened as to a voice from the grave, a voice he had not heard in person since his last visit to Jerusalem, five years before. Slowly Timothy read James's one written testament to the world, the words of a man who had been the Lord's own flesh and blood, building to a crescendo the theme:

"Faith without works is dead!"

No need to ask whether Paul's letter had reached him. Here was James's answer, not to Paul, but to thousands of men in churches everywhere who would hear the Epistle to the Hebrews read aloud before the altar—and perhaps misunderstand Paul.

Paul had glorified the wonders of faith, yearning, aching to pass its burning brand to cold and empty hearts.

James, a man of supreme faith, had seen that men might someday rationalize Paul's glowing words, might one day claim him as good authority for the total sufficiency of belief.

As the body without the spirit is dead, so faith without works is dead also!

wrote James in an hour stolen from prayer. Taking Paul's own examples, from the Epistle, James pointed to the fact that all the men of faith were also men of deeds. Paul had figured Abraham as a man of heroic faith, and James rounded out the picture:

Was not Abraham our father justified by works, offering up Isaac his son upon the altar? Seest thou, that faith did co-operate with his works, and by works faith was made perfect?

And what works does an ordinary man need to perfect his faith?

Religion clean and undefiled before God and the Father is this: to visit the fatherless and widows in their tribulation, and to keep one's self unspotted from this world . . .

If any man offend not in word, the same is a perfect man. He is able also with a bridle to lead about the whole body. . . . Every nature of beasts and of birds and of serpents has been tamed by the nature of man: but the tongue no man can tame, an inquiet evil, full of deadly poison. By it we bless God and the Father, and by it we curse men, who are made after the likeness of God.

Out of the same mouth proceedeth blessing and cursing. My brethren, these things ought not to be so.

Visit the sorrowful, the sick, the poor, bridle your tongue and your passions, and pray:

Confess therefore your sins one to another, and pray one for another, that you may be saved. For the continual prayer of a just man availeth much. Elias was a man, possible like unto us, and with prayer he prayed that it might not rain upon the earth, and it rained not for three years and six months! And he prayed again, and the heaven gave rain, and the earth brought forth her fruit.

One of the travelers raised his head. "When we were in Jerusalem men told us how James ended a drought, months of no rain, by raising his hands to heaven, and praying for water."

His companion nodded. "And they said that even the hem of his tunic could heal the sick. Every time he went out a small crowd followed, just to touch him."

Timothy had only one more sentence to read. James had written:

My brethren, if any of you err from the truth, and one convert him, he must know that he who causes a sinner to be converted from the error of his way shall save his soul from death—and shall cover a multitude of sins.

Paul watched Timothy reroll the papyrus and tie it again with cord.

A chapter of his own life was closed within that scroll, the story that began in conflict, when James first challenged him on his exuberant teaching of the uncircumcised, and ended in harmony, in actual co-operation.

James was pre-eminently a man of faith, of monklike austerity, of prayer and contemplation. Paul shone as a man of action. Yet it was Paul, his wrists chain-marked, who wrote the epic of pure faith, and James, of the camel-callused knees, who penned a hymn of praise to practical Christianity. For both men were whole-souled.

In the face of arrest and death, without bitterness, in holy haste, James had written to the world an explanation of the Epistle to the Hebrews—and a eulogy of Paul.

Paul pushed back his bench. Neither he nor the world would ever know the precise role his epistle had played. But Paul was too truly humble to allow himself the luxury of taking the blame for James's death.

He dared not arrogate unproven guilt to his soul. It is sometimes easier to judge yourself harshly and feed your pride with prolonged breast-beating and tears, than to own the fact that your actions can neither make nor break God's schemes. But Paul could not take the easy way. He knelt on the bare wood floor to pray the fervent prayer of a man who tries to be just. The others knelt with him. They prayed for the soul of James, for those who condemned him and stoned him. And Paul, remembering the last words of the letter from Jerusalem, prayed to be able to save more men from the error of their ways, to save his own soul from death, and cover a multitude of sins.

Everyone, including the guard, was still on his knees when the news came.

A clanking and stomping on the stairs heralded the arrival of two major officers of the Praetorian Guard. Paul's jailer leaped to his feet and saluted.

The other Christians finished their prayers, unhurried by the audible impatience of the imperial visitors. Paul rose to greet them after the final Amen.

"Are you Paul of Tarsus?"

"I am."

"According to the law of Rome, the accuser has two years to bring his case to trial; if he fails to do so he loses by default. No one has appeared to press a complaint against you. None of the witnesses is here. Therefore by the power vested in him, Tigellinus has declared that you are free of all charges against you, and all restraint on your person."

His boots dug v-shaped scratches into the floor as he strode forward to unlock Paul's chains.

The manacles fell from Paul's wrists, uncovering pale bracelets of flesh, callused and chafed and wrinkled. For the first time in two years his hands were free. He felt out of balance, giddy from the loss of the five-pound weight on his arms.

He saw that the two officials were leaving and forced himself to speak. "I thank you!" he called, but they were already halfway down the stairs. "Go in peace," he whispered.

"You go in peace, indeed!" cried Timothy. "Paul, you can go wherever you want to go! You used to dream of Gaul, and Hispania—"

"And I *will* go there," Paul laughed. "To the furthermost parts of the Empire. To Hispania, and then—back to my old friends. And Timothy, we must get to Crete, too."

"But Hispania first!"

And the dauntless little old man with the whitened wrists ran to the wall where hung the cross, and clasped his hands together in thanksgiving.

BOOK NINE

Nero Ends Christianity

Chapter 96. THE DEVIL DANCE OF FIRE

THE hired lodgings of Paul near the camp of the Praetorian Guard were empty of the cross.

Luke had gone home to Antioch to finish his history of the apostles, and to help in the local church. Paul and Timothy were a-voyaging again. They sailed to Gaul and the port we now call Marseilles, where, so men said, Lazarus and his sisters Mary and Martha were telling of the Christ. And on from Gaul to Spain, where rose the pillars of Hercules and where that self-effacing member of the original twelve apostles, Simon the Zealot, was preaching.

Back in Rome two men and a woman began to sketch out the ruin of a city, and the death of an army of Christians.

Staff in his still powerful hands, with Mark by his side, Peter came back to Rome. He brought news of the other apostles, the old friends whom he missed so sharply. Three years they had all traveled together with the Master; eleven more they spent together in Jerusalem; since then close to twenty years of apostolic labors had cut them off from each other almost completely.

From turbaned caravans out of the east Peter had heard good news about Bartholomew Nathaniel, working on the Arabian shores of the Red Sea; and of Jude, sorrowing brother of James the Less, still preaching in Asia Minor, his children and their in-laws trooping along to help feed the poor and tend the sick.

Dark-skinned men in the slave markets told tales of Matthew, the Gospel-writing tax expert, who had gone down to the steaming slopes of Ethiopia, living on fruits and herbs, to preach Christ. Philip was busy in the churches of Phrygia. Matthias, elected to replace Judas in the original band of twelve, was covering the northern boundaries of the Empire. And Thomas, so men said, had ventured beyond the flags of Rome, to India, land of spices and silks and strange gods of destruction. These same reporters said Thomas had found the three Wise Men there, and baptized them at last.

Peter had been in Ephesus to visit with John the Beloved, and reminisce. But his own brother Peter had not seen. Andrew was somewhere along the banks of the Danube, opening fresh territory for Christ, penetrating as far as Scythia and the Black Sea. Peter did not try to reach him. Apostles had no time for family reunions.

Peter could not look calmly on the troubling tensions outside his flock. Men did not walk so freely in the streets these days. They whispered when they spoke the name Nero. They bowed before his statue in public silence, and muttered in the back alleys.

And Nero, hearing echoes of those mutters even in his fountain-cooled dining hall, ordered more public entertainment to quell the rumbles of distrust. In the arena at Circus Maximus men with strong shields fought unarmed slaves and wild boars and imported lions till blood splattered the bleachers and drunken women cheered. In the theaters on the Field of Mars playwrights vied in realism, portraying the stories of the Roman gods in all their bestial glory.

Rape and adultery on the stage, sadism and murder in the arena. And in the taverns and the shops, in the slave quarters of rich households, in the crowded *insulae*, in the palace itself, fear grew heavier in the sultry air.

July 19 in the year 64. A day when the sun singed the eyeballs of slave farmers, and shopkeepers folded their doors closed, and peddlers sat silent by fountains in public squares. Nero and his pout-lipped beauty were out of town. Poppaea had passed through the streets of Rome in her perfumed litter, preceded by no less than five hundred she-asses and a bedizened retinue of slaves. The imperial pair had gone to enjoy the cool of their summer villa. And Rome sweltered.

Peter had spent the afternoon in the cemetery at Goat's Marsh, baptizing new converts, confirming older ones, and telling again the story of the God who chose him to fish for men. In the evening,

while Priscilla moved with quiet quickness in the kitchen with her pots
and kettles before the main meal, Peter went to the roof to be alone.

Even at sunset the air around him was hotter than in the thick-
walled, high-ceilinged rooms below. Peter ran his hands through his
long beard and his thick white hair. His blue eyes held the memory
of the Lake of Galilee, where a man could fill his lungs with clean,
cool air. His giant frame ached to stretch out on green grass again, to
feel the crunch of shell-strewn beach beneath his sandals, and the
sway of a boat. He looked at the box houses around him, as close as
seats in an arena, piled one on top of another with never a place to
see the sky, save in the brown dust and ashes on the roof.

With a grunt and a sigh he eased himself down on his knees.
Only these moments of aloneness, at-oneness with his God, refreshed
him. How could men stand it never to hear their own thoughts, never
to set their souls free, naked before their Creator? Peter raised his
eyes in love to the new-flung stars.

He never said the prayer he had in mind.

The sky was no longer blue. It glared orange and yellow, black, and
somber gray. Peter's weather-trained eyes knew no storm could paint
clouds like those. Even before the shrieks and pounding heels of
thousands of men swelled in the distance, Peter was praying with
new urgency.

"Oh God, protect these people from the flames. Save them! In the
Name of Jesus Christ I ask it!"

Rome was afire.

For six days and six nights Rome burned. The fire, coming to life
in the flimsy trade stalls huddled next to the Circus Maximus,
skimmed over brick and cobblestone, hurdled clay and marble to
snatch at the overcrowded tenements.

Men stumbled through bodiless flames, seeking escape. Women,
with hair burning on their heads, fled with their babies to the fountains, to the public baths, then fled again as the fire raced on.

Mysteriously, the orange wraiths of flame sprang up, now here, now
there, springing in a devil-worship dance to seize their victims from
temple and cellar, from parched back-yard gardens and sculptured
parks.

Six days and six nights. No man could name the heroes or the
dead in that nightmare race for safety. The River Tiber was clogged

with corpses, some sinking under the steady torrent of wind-tossed wreckage, never to be found. The hilltops were littered with men felled by new sheets of flame shooting suddenly to life.

In the fields outside the city, in the elegant cemeteries along the Appian Way, survivors searched sleeplessly for each other. Chairs, and water jugs, money coffers, bedding stood propped against carven monuments. Men with precious rolls of parchment clutched in their armpits, men with ceremonial swords or wooden crosses ripped from the wall in flight, women with bundled tapestries, a mirror, a Syrian table of fruitwood, one with an empty reed cradle slung on her back —all staring across the river at the fire. Their silence was broken only by a dry sob, an infant's wail, an occasional shout of welcome.

Then, as fast as the flames on the hills of Rome, a strange message sped across that crowd in a whisper, in a mutter, a gasp, a roar of indignation.

"Nero stands on the aqueduct. Look! He is singing, and playing the lute while Rome burns!"

On the lofty arch of the waterway the round-bellied emperor in purple-and-white tunic postured and posed in classic style. His face, short-browed, shadowed by bushy black hair and laurel wreath, glowed orange in the light of the flames.

Beside him stood Poppaea; behind them Seneca, his face turned away from the pyre of Rome, and Tigellinus, and a cluster of the emperor's favorites, flushed and disheveled after the long ride from the summer palace.

No one in the flames, no one in the Tiber, none huddled in the shadow of mausoleums and promenades could hear the words Nero sang. They heard instead whispers passed from smoke-blackened lips:

"Nero set the fire."

"I saw his men with torches in the Circus Maximus . . ."

"Nero planned to raze Rome. He ordered it. They say he has worked for months on a song about the burning of Troy, and sings it now in a setting he staged himself. He loathed our city, and he burned it."

"A madman!"

Across the river the devils of fire wearied and sank at dawn. Ruins smoldered in dying gasps of flame. Smoke hung nearly motionless over all save the tops of the seven hills.

The men and women of Rome straggled back across the Tiber, through death-strewn rubble and stench, to climb the Palatine Hill. They stood in the statued plaza before Nero's palace and screamed for him to appear.

His purple-and-silver toga was tarnished. His fat knees shook as Poppaea nudged him on to the balcony.

"You burned our homes! Murderer!"

"Murderer! Mother-killer! Adulterer!"

"Death to Nero!"

Nero ran back into the palace, slamming the balcony door behind him. The mob moved toward the massive entrance gates, advancing on the uncertain sentries.

In a corner of the palace park on the fringe of the crowd Peter towered in the tree shadows, watching, and praying that no violence be done.

The men of Rome did not kill Nero. Tigellinus and Poppaea were clever and quick-acting.

The Praetorian Guard, carrying bushel baskets of bread and the keys to imperial storehouses, marched to meet the rioters. Every family should eat its full at Nero's expense, and take enough grain to stave off hunger in the weeks of rebuilding ahead. And while angry mouths were silenced for the moment by food, Poppaea and Tigellinus conferred with the shivering emperor.

The people wanted blood. Somehow, blame for the fire must be shifted from Nero's flabby shoulders. Let the mob take vengeance on anyone, except Nero. But on whom?

Tigellinus ran a finger over the edge of his short sword.

"The Christians burned Rome," he suggested.

"Hmmm . . . Who? Christians? Who are they?"

"Superstitious weaklings, Excellency. Traitors who refuse to worship you or bow before your statue." Tigellinus fixed Nero's twitching face with a hard stare. "The Christians burned Rome."

Before half an hour had passed, these three had concocted complete proof of Christian guilt.

Christians were seditionists, disloyal to the emperor. Christians were foes of the state religion, enemies of Jupiter, and therefore servants of the devil. Worse yet, Christians were cannibals—men who boasted of eating the body and drinking the blood of one named

Jesus. Of what crime, asked Tigellinus, would such perverts not be capable?

Besides, everyone had heard Christian street preachers foretell that Rome would be erased by heavenly fire.

Nero smiled in relief. "Tigellinus, if I were not myself divine, I might believe your brain to be inspired. Go tell the people what the Christians have done. Build a new arena, a big one, across the river. They must die for their crime. And we shall meditate on some new forms of torture of a grandeur to match the crime."

Peter sat on a ledge underground, a small balustrade beside smooth steps of stone in a city of the dead.

On the steps, in every passageway, in niches built for marble statues, atop jugs of oil and incense and water, Christians sat and whispered or lay in crumpled sleep. Candles glittered in their own curled valleys of wax, smoking in the damp draft.

At Peter's feet sat Sylvanus, that old friend whom the apostles called Silas for short, and Mark, his curly brown hair plastered on his skull with caked sweat and soot. Peter's beard was gray with dust, and his once white cloak was ripped down the armpit. But peace dwelt in his eyes.

Overhead the spurred boots of the Praetorian Guard strode the city streets. A woman screamed. She could hardly be heard under the roar of a vengeance-crazed crowd.

Peter looked around at his fellow refugees—slaves and freedmen, Roman, Greek, and Jew, dark-skinned and light. The Holy Communion had been celebrated only an hour before in this underground labyrinth of tombs. The shadowed faces around him showed no fear. In a corner a few still sang the refrain of a hymn to the love of God.

"Silas, my son, you must write a letter for me. See, Mark's eyes droop. He has run the length of the city today searching for our friends, to tell them where we are.

"But the letter must be written. You know I have no skill with words. I am no writer. Our Lord Jesus Christ chose me, He strengthened me. He showed me my weaknesses, and then He showed me that in spite of my own wretched self, and with His help, and the guidance of the Spirit, I could serve Him as He wished.

"He told me to feed His lambs, and shepherd His flock, to tell the Gospel to all men. But never did He say to me: Write! His Church was not to rest on the written Scripture, but on the living tradition of the Word we preach, and the Way we preach." Peter's voice trailed off into revery; his eyes seemed to rest on the grassy hills of Palestine, where so often he had heard the Master speak. Then, as with an effort, he dragged himself back to the fetid dampness of the present in the hidden catacomb.

"Paul—there is the man who knows how to wield a pen. His epistles may be difficult at times, but he writes with fire and love. Still Paul is not here. And someone must speak now in this terrible time of persecution. A letter must be written, Silas—may God help me!"

Silas, who had traveled with Paul and transcribed so many of the tentmaker's letters, smiled confidently as he laid out his writing materials on the smooth-hewn stone steps. He had no doubt that Peter's first pastoral letter would not fall short of its mark.

Peter . . . to the strangers dispersed throughout Pontus, Galatia, Cappadocia, Asia, and Bithynia . . .

Strangers! Silas savored the word in his mind, even as his stylus scratched busily forward across the scroll. The word reminded him of Paul's own phraseology, and of the beautiful idea that a true Christian, born again of Jesus Christ, is a citizen, not of earth, but of heaven. *Strangers!* A hundred questions pressed to Silas' tongue, but he wrote in silence, as Peter dictated.

From the shadows men had crept to the stairs to catch Peter's slow-falling words. Slaves, collars around their necks, pressed against men in noble purple-striped tunics, listening.

Dearly beloved, I beseech you as strangers and pilgrims, abstain from fleshly lusts, which war against the soul.

Peter paused and stared deep into the eyes of these men hiding from Nero, the tyrant king, that insanely conceited ass with a crown on his head and lust in his heart.

Be ye subject therefore to every human creature for God's sake: whether it be to the king as excelling, or to governors . . . for so is the will of God, that by doing well you may put to silence the ignorance of foolish men. . . .

For what glory is it, if committing sin, and being buffeted for it, you endure? But if doing well you suffer patiently; this is thankworthy before God.

For unto this are you called: because Christ also suffered for us, leaving you an example that you should follow his steps. "Who did no sin, neither was guile found in his mouth." Who, when He was reviled, did not revile: when He suffered, He threatened not: but delivered Himself to him that judged Him unjustly. . . .

Dearly beloved, think not strange the burning heat which is to try you, as if some new thing happened to you; but if you partake of the sufferings of Christ, rejoice that when His glory shall be revealed, you may also be glad with exceeding joy. . . .

But let none of you suffer as a murderer, or a thief, or a railer, or a coveter of other men's things. But if as a Christian, let him not be ashamed, but let him glorify God in that name. . . .

Be sober and watch: because your adversary the devil, as a roaring lion, goeth about seeking whom he may devour. . . . But the God of all grace, who hath called us unto His eternal glory in Christ Jesus, after you have suffered a little, will Himself perfect you, and confirm you, and establish you. To Him be glory and empire for ever and ever.

Amen.

Peter let his head sink in his hands.

Somehow he must tell the rest of his church of his whereabouts, for he was still their supreme leader and head. It would be imprudent to say in so many words that the letter was written from Rome. If it should fall into the hands of the Emperor's spies, Peter knew they would ransack the whole city for him, prize captive of all. Such a search would endanger thousands like the men clustered in these catacombs.

A code name was needed, a name that to men grounded in the Old Testament could signify only one place.

The church that is at *Babylon* saluteth you!

Babylon. Harlot-queen of cities, historical capital of sin, blood sister to the Rome of Nero!

In the silence of the graves that hid the men who might win everlasting life, Peter finished his first epistle.

Overhead the voices of Babylon grew dimmer: "Death to the Christians!"

In the catacombs the prayer sounded as an antiphon:
"Thy will be done."

Chapter 97. THE MAN WHO COULD NOT REST

THE tan of Spain's gentle sun was fading from Paul's brow. His back was yielding a bit to the weight of his years. But he would not rest.

As a late-comer to the feast table of truth, he lashed himself to zeal. Since the day on the road to Damascus when the beauty of Christ first blinded him, Paul had not spent one moment on himself. He had more calluses on his feet than a traveling peddler. He had endured stoning, chains, prison, shipwreck, exile.

For Paul no suffering, no labor was enough to pay his debt to God. The fruitful years of his apostolate dwindled to nothingness in his mind. The early years when he persecuted Christ, the years of his soul's blindness, loomed large.

To Timothy, who begged him to rest, Paul had one answer: "I have so much to make up for—so many years lost!"

From Rome to Gaul to Spain, and back by ship across the Mediterranean went the wanderfoot apostle. On the return from Spain he and Timothy sailed to the land we call Turkey, which they knew as the province of Asia. They made straight for Colossae, home of Philemon and Onesimus, the runaway slave. In his letter to Philemon, Paul had promised to visit him again. He arrived in the summer of 65.

Philemon greeted him with the kiss of peace. Onesimus, now in the linen cloth of a freedman, knelt for the apostle's blessing. Behind him a whole household of emancipated slaves crowded the courtyard on their knees. A welcome feast was ready for the travelers, and for an hour Paul relaxed. But when the last of the prize melons from Syria was cut, Paul drew Philemon aside.

"Delay no longer. Tell me of Peter. Is he still alive? Word of the fire and of Nero's edicts against Christians was on every man's tongue in Gaul. But no one could give us any facts."

Philemon's face was grave.

"Peter lives. Rome was destroyed, and Nero has nearly built it up again all new. He set up tent camps for the homeless outside the Trastevere. The plans for the new city were already drawn before the fire. First to be built was the new arena. Paul, the slaughter is only beginning!"

Philemon paced the darkening porch, his fists clenching the gold tassels of his sash. "They say the arena will seat 350,000 at a time. The underground pens for lions are twice the size of those anywhere else." He gripped Paul's age-dried hands. "Today it is a crime to believe in God! Treason to be baptized! We are blamed for everything —not only the great fire, but for every trouble that has hit Rome in the last fifty years."

Paul nodded, and withdrew his wrists from Philemon's manacle-like grip.

"Philemon, where is Peter? I must see him."

"He lives, so they say, with his flock in the darkness of the catacombs. The church has gone under the ground, into the lower levels of the cemeteries owned by certain rich Christians. They have even tunneled new passages into the earth in which to hide—men, women, and children, behaving like moles. You must stay away from Rome. You are too valuable to us all. Besides, if you are caught seeking him, you'll both die!"

Paul thought for a moment. "I must die sometime. I would not fear to go to Rome. But I dare not endanger Peter. Tomorrow I go to Ephesus. There is much to do before Nero finds there are many Christians outside Rome, too."

"Stay here, Paul. With us you are safe. . . ."

Paul raised a hand. "What do you know about Crete, Philemon?"

"Crete? Oh, no, Paul. No more travels! You are too old, now. You are too important to us. And no one can do anything in Crete anyway. You know the old saying: 'The Cretans are always liars, evil beasts, and slothful bellies.'"

"They have souls."

"Crete is hundreds of miles out in the Great Sea. . . ."

"I know. We sailed there just before the shipwreck on my way to Rome. We stayed at Fair Havens a while. We should have stayed longer, in fact, but . . ." His voice trailed off into memory of those tempest-tossed days. Then, "Philemon, I must go to Crete! I shall visit the churches near here, Ephesus, Hierapolis—perhaps even those in Macedonia. But I will go to Crete. The faces of the men I talked to there will not let me sleep."

The men of Ephesus, who had been baptized by Paul, who loved him as the father of their new lives, clung to him, begging him to stay with them in the days of crisis. Fear had crept into their church, lurking in the shadows of the candles, chilling the fervor of faith. From Rome came tales to send the weak skittering to the nearest temple to burn sacrifice before idols, and deny Christ.

Nero was a frustrated playwright. His perverted sense of drama demanded epic tortures to baptize the new arena in blood. Crosses stood in the sand of the stadium, and blazing fagots were bound to the ankles of Christians hanging by their wrists. So died the old men of the Trastevere, the cobblers, the tinkers, the scribes whom Peter had brought to belief in the Crucified One. On another evening, Nero's own new public parks on Vatican Hill, completed long before the homes for the public were begun, were illuminated with special torches, the flaming bodies of Christian families coated with pitch.

But Nero had more spectacular plans. The Roman religion, with its seven thousand lesser deities and some fifty major gods, boasted hundreds of gory legends. What more fitting, laughed Nero, than to force these Christians who mocked the gods to enact the myths in the arena?

A Christian playing the role of Orpheus, son of Apollo, was torn to pieces by wild bears before the applauding Romans. A Hercules, clothed in blood-soaked white cloak, was forced at spear's point to build his own funeral pile of trees, climb it, and lie down under a lion skin to die in flames.

The arched back of a young Christian, dressed as Ixion, legendary king of Thessaly, was tied with stage-prop serpents to a wheel and rolled through gravel and red-stained sand until he perished. And a Christian maiden with long blond curls playing Leda, the Spartan queen, was ravished before the greedy eyes of thousands by a man dressed as the Swan of mythology—and many said Nero himself was the rapist!

These were the main events, recorded in court letters and official histories of the day. No one bothered to try to chronicle all of the grand total of daily deaths.

But Seneca, Nero's outcast friend, was recording, not only the utter savagery of the emperor's world, but the miracle of Christianity— the eagerness to suffer. In one of his own epistles he says:

Tyranny has at its disposal steel and fire, chains and wild animals, to set upon the bodies of men. I can recall these persons, the tortures of the cross, the iron hooks, and that pale driven into a man's midriff and forced out of his mouth. I can still see how limbs were torn from bodies attached to wagons driven in opposite directions, that tunic lined with inflammable stuff, and all the rest of the inventions of diabolical fury. . . . In the midst of all these tortures there was one who did not moan; no, he did not beg for his life; no, I saw more, he smiled as though there was happiness in his heart.

And that one letter told only an infinitesimal part of the epic of Christian heroism—and devil-driven torture.

Paul heard those reports. He stood, an old man in a weather-beaten cloak, with his hand on Timothy's arm. Around him pressed the faces of his friends in Ephesus.

"Stay with us, Paul!"

"You know the danger. You are asking for death, going out to preach now."

"We are your friends, Paul. Stay and rest."

The face of Titus, veteran of the long early missionary journeys, pleading with Paul to rest. Of Tychicus, who had stayed at Paul's side for half the Roman imprisonment before taking the Epistle to the Ephesians. Of Trophimus, who had unwittingly caused Paul's arrest in the first place by his ill-fated visit to the Temple in Jerusalem so many years before.

For an hour the men in the shuttered room of Titus' house tried to talk Paul out of going anywhere. They pointed to new heresies that must be fought right here in Ephesus. They said only Paul could help them. Paul shook his head. They warned of persecution, of his own health.

The old man leaned on Timothy and smiled.

"I leave for Crete tomorrow. Who dares come with me?"

In the morning he bought passage on a ship bound for the island. With him went Titus, Tychicus, Trophimus, and three newcomers: Artemas and Apollos and a lawyer turned evangelist whose name was Zenas.

But Timothy did not board the ship.

He stayed in Ephesus, on Paul's command, to battle the new crop of doctrinal misunderstandings and govern the local church. Paul was giving the Ephesians the one he loved most in the world, Timothy, whom he thought of as his son. In words, Paul promised to come back to Ephesus as soon as he could. In his heart he wondered if he would ever see Timothy again.

When the ship weighed anchor Paul's fading eyes searched the wharf for a last glimpse of that fine-chiseled face.

Chapter 98. THE LAST MISSION

IN CRETE, the land where once the god Jupiter raged at birth, where the monster Minotaur in his labyrinth devoured hostage virgins from conquered Athens, Paul found only the flotsam of a wrecked civilization.

Porters and tradesmen ambled down to the dock dressed in rainbow tunics. A bit apart Paul could see a group of four men and eleven women and a blur of children of all ages. The men, in silk cloaks, sat on kegs and piles of rope, plying small glittering bottles of wine. Every now and then between dainty gulps they would aim the back of their hands at the nearest shouting boy.

Titus tried to steer Paul past this group, but the four men strode toward the apostle in full-bellied amiability.

"Paul of Tarsus, welcome! We are the elders of the church of Crete."

Seven years ago Paul had seized the chance at Fair Havens to speak of Christ to some of the villagers, to an innkeeper, a sea captain, a fur trader. Since then a few missionaries had ventured over the sea to Crete. Mostly the island Christians had remained isolated; the faith, untended, undisciplined, had run wild.

To the single vine of truth the Cretans had grafted some Jewish rituals plus the most enjoyable pagan practices. The result was a monstrosity. In their version of Christianity a man could commit adultery, but not eat pork. A priest could have a harem, and get drunk; having purchased his ecclesiastical powers, he could do no wrong. Not one of the seven sacraments was properly observed, yet their homemade code of church laws would have filled two scrolls of papyrus.

The wise old disciplinarian Paul pulled his belt tighter and straightened his shoulders. To preach faith to pagans is clean work, adventure to sharpen the spirit. But to reclaim the faith from a refuse dump of self-will and ignorance is a depressing task.

Paul had planned to stay one month. He stayed two. Deploying his helpers like a guerrilla band across the hundred ornate cities of Crete, he ordained new priests and uncompromisingly retired the old self-made frauds. He baptized and forgave sins, witnessed marriages, and anointed the sick. Regularly he celebrated the sacrament of the Last Supper. Daily, from the time dawn struck the mysterious snows of Mt. Ida till moonlight spilled over the statues of the Minotaur, Paul preached.

Finally, he could not stay longer. He knew too well the dangers of sea travel in winter. To delay another week meant staying six more months cut off from the congregations of the mainland to whom he had promised help.

Of his crew of helpers he chose Titus as the most competent and zealous, consecrating him first bishop of Crete. Then, with the rest Paul sailed for Europe. He carried no illusions about the job he left for Titus. Soon a letter to that new bishop, preserved for posterity, would declare:

One of themselves, a prophet of their own, said: "The Cretans are always liars, evil beasts, slow bellies." This witness is true.

Paul spent the winter of 66 in Nicopolis, City of Victory, built by the Romans in the region today known as northwest Greece. Across the Adrian Sea lay the toe of the Italian boot, and Rome.

When was Paul busier, or more lonely, than that winter? He would stare at the sun setting over the sea and think of Peter, of those who were dead, and those who would soon die. No man on earth would Paul have rather had as a friend than Peter. He yearned to talk his fill, hour on hour, with the giant Galilean. Their meetings had been few, shortened by the urgency of their callings.

In the nomad life of an apostle there are few hours for friendship to mellow, no time for long visits or the quiet sitting together that says more than words. Friends must brush past each other with a fleeting hail, hurrying on to their God-given tasks. Luke to his writing, Barnabas, Aristarchus, Philemon, and the host of others to their own bishoprics and problems.

"Leave all things and follow me."

Paul followed gladly. But in the recesses of his heart were protests that he could not still.

Using Nicopolis as a base, Paul toured Macedonia all winter. Along frost-silvered trails, away from the main roads, he led his band to Philippi, the city of old soldiers, to Thessalonica, Beroea, Apollonia. Along the road of memory he strode, revisiting scenes of earlier triumphs. At each stop he found faith pockmarked by fear, and he bolstered it with love and truth.

Work leapt to his hand, heresy and misunderstanding, apostasy and terror, to be put down with the sword of truth, and the warm shield of faith. He had hoped to get back to Ephesus before spring to see Timothy, but his duty lay in Macedonia. November's leaden clouds passed into the snows of December, and Paul grew lonely for Timothy.

He had watched the weeping small lad of Derbe grow into a strong-browed soldier of the spirit. He had baptized and circumcised Timothy, ordained him, guided him. In the two years' captivity and on the long trip to Spain and back, he had come to know Timothy better than any other living soul. The warring emotions of a father: the masked tenderness, the stern concern, the unspoken longing for companionship, all these Paul felt for Timothy. He had come to rely on that quiet voice, the blue eyes of that fine-chiseled face.

Paul himself had assigned Timothy to Ephesus. He could replace him. One word could bring Timothy to his side, and ease an old age under a forlorn winter sky.

Paul sat down to write a letter in his own hand. No secretary now should get between him and the words of his heart:

"Paul . . . to Timothy, his beloved son in faith . . ."

He paused, pen between his teeth, then began to write, not a command to return, but instead shining words of counsel for a young bishop, a guide for clergy and laymen on matters of faith and on the niggling problems of every day.

These things I write to thee, hoping that I shall come to thee shortly, but if I tarry long, that thou mayest know how thou oughtest to behave thyself in the house of God, which is the church of the living God, the pillar and ground of the truth. . . .

Oh Timothy, keep that which is committed to thy trust, avoiding the profane novelties of words, and oppositions of knowledge falsely so called, which some promising have erred concerning the faith.

Grace be with thee.

Amen.

The profane novelties of words. The babblings of men who pretended to knowledge, who thought they could formulate their own church and still call it Christ's Church. Earnest men, who believed themselves true Christians, were already trying to redesign the mystical house that God built.

Paul plodded on through the chain of churches with his helpers, fighting down the mistakes, clearing away the litter of homemade theology, keeping God's house in order. With Peter incommunicado in the catacombs, only Paul was left to speak in the name of truth. And he could not rest. Always the thought returned to chill him, that one day men might wander from the pillar and rock of the truth and build new houses on the sands of error.

He shivered and drew his cloak closer. He woke Tychicus and Trophimus and the others from their sleep, and urged them on the twisting midnight road.

In January's sleet in the year 67 Paul slept in the house of Carpus, in the town called Troas.

Paul was no stranger to that three-storied house. In its giant attic hall, with Trophimus and Tychicus witnesses, Paul had preached—and raised to life a young man named Eutychus, who had gone to sleep during that sermon, and tumbled out of the window seat.

On this freezing January night ten years later Eutychus was not so sleepy. With Carpus he kept Paul talking past the first cockcrow, till the wick died in the pewter bowl. They pulled their cots then close to the fire, and slept, exhausted.

A slashing gust of air woke them. The room was filled with soldiers in burnished helmets, and long, gray winter cloaks!

Rough hands dragged Paul from his pallet, and grasped his sinewy shoulders, pushing him toward the open door. In his tunic, without cloak or shoes, they propelled him out into the clouded dawn.

Tychicus scrambled up, snatched Paul's shoes, and ran after him.

Trophimus stared wildly, picked up a loaf of bread, and dashed down the road, too.

Three soldiers remained. They grunted at Carpus and Eutychus, kicked at the mattresses, and, finding no money, slammed the door and left.

For the final time Paul had been arrested.

Chapter 99. "MY CLOAK AND MY BOOKS!"

From Troas Paul was carted to Ephesus, capital of the province of Asia, for trial.

The pillared courtroom was crowded with familiar faces. Luke, who had ridden three days and nights to get there from Philippi, kept his anxious eyes on the brave figure standing before the judge. Aquila and Priscilla. Onesiphorus, who met the prison caravan on the road outside Ephesus and bribed guards to give Paul a cup of hot soup he had brought. Trophimus and Tychicus, who tagged along all the way from Carpus' home.

In a corner by a pillar stood Timothy, tears rolling unashamed down his cheeks. He had waited so long for Paul to return to Ephesus —to see him brought there as a prisoner! Paul looked over the heads of the crowd, saw Timothy, and smiled.

The huggermugger trial went according to plan, a police-state trial with verdict already written. Paul is a leader of the Christians and Nero wants him killed, so be quick with this mockery, and pack him off to Rome.

"Call the main witness!"

Alexander, the coppersmith, stepped forward. His hands were yellowed with acid. His face was eaten away with bitterness. A year ago Paul had rebuked this craftsman publicly for uttering blasphemy, for saying that Jesus was nothing more than a very good man. Now see, Paul, whether the dead man you call God can help you!

"He preaches a new God, and blasphemes against the gods of Rome!"

One by one the accusing witnesses testified. No one was allowed to speak in Paul's defense. In an hour the trial was ended. Paul was hustled and shoved out to the street and into a cart, heading for the docks and a Rome-bound ship.

Luke swept up the edges of his cloak in his arms and broke into a dog trot beside the cart. At his heels ran Trophimus, Priscilla and Aquila, Timothy, and a panting new arrival, Erastus, treasurer of Corinth. At the docks all six bought passage to Rome. Paul peered under the arm of a soldier, saw Timothy, and shook his head violently.

"Stay in Ephesus. Stay with your trust!"

Timothy bowed his head. He climbed down off the ship. From the land he gazed up for a last look at Paul, and smiled through his tears as he waved.

Five friends sailed with Paul from Ephesus. Two he sent back at the next port, Priscilla and Aquila, to stay with Timothy in Ephesus. Trophimus found his stomach weak on shipboard; he went ashore at Miletus. And when Paul's party changed ships at Corinth, Erastus pleaded duties in his home town, and stayed there. Only the man he had long called his "beloved yokefellow," Luke the physician, his long slender face creased with age, stayed with Paul.

The first time Paul went to Rome, friends came to greet him, swelling his procession to regal size. Now he came almost alone. No one waited for him at Appii Forum, no one sat in the shadowed courtyard of Three Taverns. The Christians of Rome were afraid.

At the Capena Gate, even Luke was shouldered aside by a contingent of the Praetorian Guard.

Paul went alone to prison.

He was led from the castle of the Guard to the Mamertine Prison, down to the dungeons where enemies of the state were held for trial. Water oozed on the curving rock steps, and the tainted odor of dead damp made his eyes swim. At the lowest level the guards halted, then flung open a barred door.

A sword-callused hand pushed Paul into the darkness. He hurtled across the six-foot cell, his feet skidding in the slime. His chains clattered against a wet stone wall. The door closed.

He was alone.

Tigellinus spread his legs and leaned back in his cushioned seat. An African slave in slit skirt and glittering veil waved a dried palm leaf over his head. A captain of the Guard stood at attention before him.

"The man Paul is in prison, as you ordered."

Tigellinus grunted. "He must have a trial because he is a Roman citizen. We can manage that quickly." He brushed away the girl's fan and stood up. "But not too quickly. We must have Peter too. This Paul makes a lot of noise and goes around stirring up the people—

but he is not the ringleader of this mess. He works under Peter—that I know from those who have deserted their movement."

He looked into the captain's eyes and said:

"Find Peter. If you have to rip up every grave in the city, find that man!"

The cell stank. Never had the sun seen it, never had a breeze found entrance. The air rested on him, cold and damp as a fish's belly skin. Paul's old fever came back, and he trembled with chill. He could not eat the slops in his bowl. He stayed on his knees, till at last he fell asleep.

To a tiny room behind a jewelry bazaar in the Trastevere came a strangely assorted crew. A man with a dark cloak tightly covering his purple-striped toga came on foot from his villa on the Aventine; he was Senator Pudens, Peter's first highly positioned convert and friend. He was joined by the ex-slave named Linus, a veiled woman called Claudia, an unidentified man called Eubulus, and Luke the physician.

Though they were alone, they whispered, plotting a conspiracy for which each one might die on a cross or a headsman's block.

The senator handed Eubulus a purse.

"Give three coins to the scar-cheeked man at the side gate of the prison. One to each of the others you will meet. Go only at night, for the day guards scorn such small sums. What coins are left save for other visits. We will all need the same tokens to get in."

Claudia spread a moth-colored cloth on the table and began folding into it candles and flint, soap, bread, and cheese. From the wide sleeves of her robe she drew pen, ink, pumice, and papyrus to add to the bundle. Luke filled a small leather bag with herbs and powders, and a note of instructions for his patient.

Eubulus stowed the two bundles beneath his cloak, the purse in his sleeve, and vanished out the door into the night.

Linus peered after him, then seeing no signs of danger, closed the door and went to the table against the wall where stood the Bread and the Wine.

The others knelt on the floor facing the homemade altar.

Night by night friends filtered through the bribed guards to the depths of the prison.

Linus came to whisper news of Peter. For months the man of rock had stayed in the catacombs carrying on his ministry, strengthening and encouraging every Christian, setting up a full church at death's level in the earth. But for a long time now Linus and Clement and Mark and all the others had been urging Peter to quit the city. He had refused, swearing he would never desert his post. They in turn had tried to make him see that the Church would suffer a mortal blow if he were killed, that he could do more good outside of Rome. And finally, Peter had agreed. He was leaving for the country in a day or so, said Linus. And Paul smiled in the darkness.

Pudens came, his face masked even from the guards he bribed. As one of Peter's first converts and dear friends, he brought him Peter's own messages of loving farewell and blessing. Luke came every night to check on Paul's health, to force him to drink bitter herb brews and rub ointment on his chilblained legs.

Paul had made a friend of his immediate night guard, without benefit of gold. The jailer looked the other way, as every evening Paul lit one of Claudia's candles and took up his pen. He was writing a letter to Timothy. Only a few lines could be done at a time; when other guards wandered through, Paul's cramped hands must pinch out the light and hide his things from the military lanterns.

There seemed no way to get the letter to Timothy. Paul would not ask any of his friends in Rome to undertake such a dangerous journey. But there was comfort simply in writing the letter, in pouring out his heart to the man he thought of as son. So, in the tense silence of candlelight he would write:

To Timothy, my dearly beloved son . . . I thank God . . . that without ceasing I have remembrance of thee in my prayers night and day. Greatly desiring to see thee, being mindful of thy tears, that I may be filled with joy . . .

As Paul wrote one evening, the jailer suddenly signaled him to hide his candle.

Down the damp corridor came the shuffle of hesitant footsteps, the clink of a well-filled purse. The guard grinned, and put out his palm. A moment later Paul had a guest, Onesiphorus from Ephesus.

The genial face of his old friend brought a smile to Paul's pain-pinched face. Onesiphorus, who had fed him soup at Ephesus, had crossed Greece to find him again. He brought rare fruits from the

East—sweet lemons and oranges big as melons—and cold meats, ready-sliced in his sack. While Paul and the guard sat on opposite sides of the bars, sharing this feast, Onesiphorus offered:

"Whatever I can do for you, name it. I will stay in Rome as long as you need me."

"Onesiphorus, the greatest favor you could do me would be to go home to Ephesus—and carry a letter to Timothy for me!"

Pushing aside the food, Paul picked up his pen and began to scribble by the candlelight. He told Timothy of his latest visitor, blessing the name of Onesiphorus. Briefly he mentioned how his other friends had deserted him. But no self-pity tainted his words:

Wherein I labour even unto bands, as an evildoer; but the word of God is not bound. . . . If we suffer, we shall also reign with Him. If we deny Him, He will also deny us.

The pen scratched on, nearly blotting in his haste, as Paul veered from his own troubles to those Timothy and the whole Church must face.

I charge thee, before God and Jesus Christ, who shall judge the living and the dead, by His coming, and His kingdom: preach the word: be instant in season, out of season reprove, entreat, rebuke in all patience and doctrine. For there shall be a time, when they will not endure sound doctrine; but, according to their own desires, they will heap to themselves teachers, having itching ears: and will indeed turn away their hearing from the truth, but will be turned unto fables. But be thou vigilant, labour in all things, do the work of an evangelist, fulfil thy ministry. Be sober. For I am even now ready to be sacrificed: and the time of my dissolution is at hand.

I have fought a good fight, I have finished my course, I have kept the faith.

As to the rest, there is laid up for me a crown of justice, which the Lord the just judge will render to me in that day: and not only to me, but to them also that love His coming.

Paul sighed, and whispered a prayer, as he wrote at last the summons he had so longed to give many months before:

Make haste to come to me quickly. For Demas hath left me, loving this world, and is gone to Thessalonica: Crescens into Galatia, Titus into Dalmatia. Only Luke is with me. Take Mark, and bring him with thee: for he is profitable to me for the ministry. But Tychicus I have sent to

Ephesus. The cloak that I left at Troas, with Carpus, when thou comest, bring with thee, and the books, especially the parchments. . . .
Make haste to come before winter!
The Lord Jesus Christ be with thy spirit. Grace be with you.
                                                        Amen.

The old man stared at his own letter, and wondered if Timothy would arrive in time.
"Do thy diligence to come to me before winter."
Would that be soon enough?

Chapter 100.   "WHERE ART THOU GOING?"

ALONG the sun-filled paths of spring, safely outside Rome, Peter walked slowly, after months under the earth. His mind was not easy, his heart sickened with trouble.

He had not wanted to leave Rome. He yearned to stay with his flock, even, if God were willing, to suffer death for the faith. Almost, he had stayed. Then one argument, spoken by Linus, had struck home.

"You must not let your own wishes stand in the way of the Church, Peter. You can do more good alive. We cannot afford to have you martyred."

And Peter, who spent his life trying to learn humility, had closed his eyes and listened, wondering. He knew that the welfare of the Church did not hinge on his life. He knew the Church was immortal, eternal with the Christ who governed her. The Church would live, no matter who took his place.

No matter what clamors and alarums might shatter the calm of Christianity, no persecutions from without or battling factions and heresies within, not hell itself could prevail against the Church. Of that truth Peter was imperturbably certain. Christ had promised that the Holy Spirit would remain with His Church forever, to comfort and guide the men who must serve as shepherds of the flock. Without that guidance, no human effort could save the Church; with it, no man's weakness or mistake could destroy it.

Peter had no qualms over the future of the Church. He feared only one thing—to offend God, by pride, by insisting on the wisdom of his own opinion. And that was why, in the dawn of an April day, he had taken his friend's advice and left the city in secret, slipping out in the darkness, bound for the churches of Asia.

But his soul was ill at ease.

In silence, Mark strode beside him in the early morning sunlight.

Suddenly, Peter stopped. The path to his sight was filled with a glow of greater radiance than the sun. Then, in the center of the light, he saw the beloved figure of the Master, facing him, walking toward Rome.

Peter fell to his knees in the dust.

"Quo vadis?" . . . "Lord, where art Thou going?"

Mark stared, seeing nothing, but he, too, went on his knees.

And Peter heard again the clear wondrous voice, so soft, so strong: "I go to Rome to be crucified."

"Lord, art Thou being crucified again?"

"Yes, Peter, I am being crucified again." And in that instant He was gone.

Peter rose to his feet and turned his face back to Rome.

"Mark! Come! We are going back, back to Rome. Three times I denied Him. But never again!"

And Peter walked back into Rome like a conqueror, his head high. There was a smile of bliss on his face when he was recognized and arrested.

Paul slumbered lightly in his cell, propped up against the wall to keep his head off the damp floor.

Suddenly the door clanged open.

Ten guards surrounded one tall old man. With sword points they nudged him into the cell. The bolt slammed shut.

"Paul!" said the newcomer calmly. "Paul—greeting!"

Paul rubbed his eyes with the back of his fists, and stumbled to his feet.

"Peter? Peter at last!"

A tall old man of eighty, the untutored son of poor parents in Galilee, trained to hard work in the sea-freshened air—and a wizened scholar of seventy. They met again in a dungeon.

As men, they were alien to each other, strangers from opposite poles of society. But they saw each other not as men but as servants of Christ, soldiers of the faith.

Chapter 101. THE SONG IN THE CITY UNDER
                THE CITY

PETER had no trial.

Paul, because of the dignity of his Roman citizenship, was hauled
off to a court near the Forum, tried without lawyer or witnesses, and
convicted by Tigellinus.

The next morning Peter and Paul left their prison, together for
the last time on earth.

"*Amen, amen I say to thee, when thou wast younger, thou didst
gird thyself, and didst walk where thou wouldst. But when thou shalt
be old, thou shalt stretch forth thy hands, and another shall gird
thee, and lead thee whither thou wouldst not.*"

And this Jesus had said, signifying by what death Peter should
glorify God. And when He had said this, He said to Peter: "Follow
Me."

Peter stretched out his hands. The centurion bound his wrists with
rope and chain. A soldier took the rope as a leash, and led him out
of the Mamertine.

The light of the June morning dazzled Peter's old eyes. Warm
breezes toyed with his unkempt beard, fluttered in his long white
hair.

"*Follow Me!*"

Behind him another group of soldiers led Paul away in the opposite
direction, down the stone street toward the outskirts of the city.

No one stood in the courtyard to watch Peter's procession. Street
crowds thinned as they passed.

In the market place Peter heard a voice saying:

"Who is that old man? Weren't you a friend of his?"

And Peter heard the reply: "I never saw the man in my life."

Across the city they walked, prisoner and executioner squad,
through the new apartment-house district, past splendid shops and
public squares.

A man at a drinking fountain wiped his mouth and nudged another. "I saw you with that man once."

Peter heard the reply: "I don't know what you are saying."

They climbed the Vatican Hill, to Nero's own gardens, thrown open now to the populace. Pillars of wood coated with pitch stood at the corner of every path. Some still waited to be lit. Others bore burned corpses of Christians.

Crosses stood on the hillside among the grass and flowers. The centurion halted before one. By twos and threes a crowd gathered to gawk at death. A woman's voice sounded over the hum of bees and the clank of swords.

"You—weren't you a Christian, too, a friend of this Whitebeard?" And Peter heard the answer plain: "Not I!"

And in a sudden rush of compassion, Peter understood that for his betrayers he could feel only pity—and love—and a longing to comfort them when remorse came later.

With his old brawny stance he stood fearlessly before the centurion. He uttered no farewell, his prayers were silent. He had but one last request of the world:

"I am not worthy to die as our Lord died, on the cross. If I must be crucified, let it be—head downward."

Thirty minutes later he hung on the cross, his travel-crusted feet in the air. His hair blew in the wind. The majestic white beard veiled the bleeding face of *St. Peter.*

They took Paul to a lonesome valley three miles from the walls of Rome. The name of the valley was Three Fountains, the Place of Healing Waters.

Paul, born a Roman citizen, did not walk the sad way alone. As he paced in chains between armed guards through the city, people fell in step with him. Jeering and jibing, weeping and wondering, his enemies and his friends trailed beside him along the Tiber toward Ostia. More joined the crowd, as they turned left amid the fragrant warmth of June foliage, through the countryside to Three Fountains.

A blind hag stood by the roadside. Her name was Petronilla. In her hands she clutched her only veil, a sheer white square with the ends carefully gathered. By ear she found her way among the heavy-booted guards. She ran her fingers over Paul's arms till she touched his chains. Into his hands she pressed the veil.

"Use this to bandage your eyes." And with these words the gentle old crone disappeared from the pages of history.

Two guards shoved her back to the roadside, among the early roses and the tall grass. Paul smiled his thanks and walked on.

In the valley the procession halted. The centurion came to blindfold Paul, and the old lady's veil tightened over his eyes. Two men bound Paul to a stake on a grassy mound, and scourged him, as prescribed, till the blood ran. They untied him and led him to another knoll and made him kneel.

"Our Father, Who art in heaven . . ." said Paul.

The sword glistened and fell. The man of Tarsus had died the honorable death reserved to Roman citizens. Paul's head lay on the grass.

The soldiers left. The jeerers and the curiosity seekers scattered.

Luke ran forward and buried his face in the grass beside the body of his friend.

In silence the Christians who remained carried the body and the head back along the road to Rome as far as the cemetery of the matron Lucina.

And they buried St. Paul.

The gardens on the hill called Vatican were silent that twilight. No one came to admire Nero's living torches, or cheer at the sight of the corpse of the Christian leader.

Tigellinus had moved boldly, killing both major enemies of the state at once. He could not understand the silence.

"Sir, we took the body of Peter and buried it in the public part of the graveyard near the gardens. We put no marker there," the centurion reported.

Tigellinus stared out the window at the starlit city. "I have killed them. I have put an end to the foreign superstition. I have saved Rome from those who would destroy her gods."

In the city below the city—in the rooms of cemeteries, in storerooms and counting houses, in spare bedrooms and cellars—men and women were singing that night. They sang praise to God the Father, and God the Son, and God the Holy Ghost.

They had lost Paul, the soldier of Christ, the greatest voice of Truth they knew. Paul is dead. His words live.

They had lost Peter, the head, the rock, the shepherd. Another man already held the keys of heaven, Linus, the ex-slave. Peter is dead, but Peter lives.

Thousands of these men and women would die themselves in the arena, burning on pitch-soaked pyres, crucified, they would die for Jesus Christ, and for the Faith, the Church that Christ founded, built on the Rock, close-hewn and guarded by the voice of truth.

They would die that we might live in the greatest faith ever known.

They sang that night of glory to God, to Jesus Christ, who had conquered death.